LESSONS FROM LIFE AFTER KINDERGARTEN

TERRY TRUDEL, M.D.

BLADENSBURG, MARYLAND

Paperback ISBN 9781957497266

Published in the United States of America

This book is dedicated to people who have pursued truth and found it. Their lives provide examples for us to carefully consider and follow.

Contents

Introduction

We all seek the American Dream. This concept of the American dream has been expanded and exported to countries worldwide. People from all points of the compass desire to immigrate to the United States to make this dream a reality. I was on an errand with a friend who was driving. When he started his engine, a caution message appeared on his GPS screen about distractions causing accidents. Distracted driving can be dangerous and even lethal. Have you seen a caution light anywhere about the dangers of **distracted living?** Distracted living is the subject matter of this book. People distracted at work get fired. Married couples distracted from their relationship file for divorce. People distracted by alcohol and drugs fail to notice distortions in their emotional and relational lives. Distracted living produces confused living, and confused living produces a life filled with chaos. You will not find the American dream in chaos.

What causes all this distraction and confusion? And what is the solution? This book is about the process issues of distraction and confusion and how they destroy individual lives and the American dream. The American dream is a group of ideals and goals that are born from the freedom of living in a republic. "It includes the opportunity for prosperity and success, and upward social mobility achieved through **hard work**."[1] In 1931, historian and author James Truslow Adams published a book, *The Epic of America*, in which he used the term "American Dream." He defined it as follows: "Life should be better and richer and fuller for everyone, with opportunity for each according to ability or achievement" regardless of social class or circumstances of birth. Execution of this idea created a large, prosperous middle class. For these people, the American Dream became reality. It is a unique experiment in world history. It is the envy of every continent.

It sounds a little like a fairy tale. Unlike fairy tales which usually have a happy ending, the American Dream is unravelling, prompting the assertion

1 www.liquisearch.com/american_dream

of some that the dream is turning into a nightmare.[2]

This process is generating fear, anger, and a range of other emotions in the people who constitute the heart of this country… the middle class. The result is discouragement, anxiety, depression, and increasing rates of homicide and suicide.

Lessons from life after kindergarten is a phrase referring to process issues. A process issue is a belief, emotion, or event resulting in a decision. Decisions are being made on individual, community, state, and national levels which are impacting the American dream. Process issues determine the outcomes of those decisions. Process issues fall into five categories: **beliefs, emotions, behaviors, physiology, and spirituality.** These are the five domains of humanity. Everything a person does in life falls into one or more of these five categories: thought life, emotional life, behavior…what you do or don't do, underlying physiology, and spirituality. Each domain has a different set of process issues. Deception is a prominent process issue working right now dismantling the dream you have for your life. The process of deception is noted below:

Distraction>confusion>deception>evil desire>sin>consequences

The origin of this process and its implications will be the focus of the following chapters. Consider the following questions:

1. What does everyone have in common with Thomas Jefferson determining the fate of the middle class in America?
2. What does the Mayflower Compact provide for a solution to the political divide in the U.S. and elsewhere?
3. What topic do philosophers discuss, politicians claim, and people in power define?
4. What is the difference between frustration and anger?
5. Are you acquainted with the affairs of the heart, cognition/thinking, affective/emotion, will/decision making?

These, other questions, and their answers are the subject matter of this book. Each of these questions relates to "Lessons from Life after Kindergarten." People do not entertain these questions because they are distracted by the tasks of earning a living and taking care of their families. Yet, knowledge of these process issues is vital to properly care for the people they love. Ignoring these issues is how deception destroys your dream.

2 www.newsmax.com/charlesmizrahi/american-dream-god

Introduction

This book teaches from stories because process issues determine the outcome of stories, including the story of your life. The stories are taken from the Holy Bible, history, my psychiatric practice, my life, and current events. The examples provided in these stories assist the reader in understanding the role of process in determining outcome.

A large portion of history relates to content rather than process. Content issues provide information but often do not play a big role in decision making. For example, content issues in writing this book are the type of paper used for printing and what days of the week were devoted to writing. This information is important but does not determine the value of the book to you. It is what you learn about process issues in these pages that will produce satisfaction, pleasure, and a better outcome from reading it. Satisfaction, pleasure, and better outcomes are process issues that will stimulate you to finish reading each chapter. They are important process issues in your decision about reading more of the text…or stopping at this point. As you continue through the stories, you will become more proficient at distinguishing process from content. The book alternates between stories and discussion of the process and content issues the stories illustrate. Being able to identify process facilitates creating success from our experiences in life, even from those that are difficult and painful.

Failure to be acquainted with our stories and refusal to learn from them results in making the same mistakes over and over. "Insanity is doing the same thing over and over again and expecting different results."[3] This definition of insanity is not about psychiatric diagnosis. It is about insanity in the decision-making process… making decisions that defy common sense. For example, in the cycle of domestic violence, physically abused women often refuse to leave their mates despite an established pattern of beatings. **If the content of these stories or questions is disturbing, generating anxiety or depression, please stop reading and consult a professional counselor.**

Here is an example of process issues in relationships: a seven-year-old girl who is sexually abused by a male teacher at school may find the school environment threatening and unsafe. However, another seven-year-old girl who is being sexually abused at home by an older brother may find the school environment the safest place she has in her life. The **location** of the **abuse**

---

3 www.quoteinvestigator.com, "insanity is doing the same thing over and over again"…this quote is attributed to a person at an Al-Anon meeting reported in a Knoxville Tennessee newspaper in October 1981.

event becomes a process issue because it leads to a decision point in the mind of each girl about where she is safe. One girl feels safe at home while the other feels safe at school. **Belief** about **safety** becomes a process issue.

There are also **painful emotions** generated by traumatic experiences which contribute to the thought of being unsafe. These emotions are often some combination of confusion, guilt, shame, fear, hurt, disappointment, and sadness. They contribute to various **behavior** changes: sleep disturbance, nightmares, social withdrawal, poor school performance, loss of appetite, and other symptoms. These symptoms are a manifestation of the painful emotions and the thought of being unsafe. The **physiology** of the nervous system is reset; anxiety begins, which is a physiological process. The child begins to **question God**...why did God allow this to happen? She may decide to withdraw from church-related activities, a behavioral response. These process issues work together in the mind of the child. The process of establishing safety becomes a primary focus for the child. The rest of life fades in importance.

These process issue/s shape decision making on how to stay safe. This is very straightforward and makes sense. Ordinarily, the location of the event might be a content issue. But in this example, the **fear** associated with the abuse becomes generalized to the place of the event, a process known as *generalization*, so fear influences her belief about where she is safe and who is safe to be around. **How you handle fear** will influence many of your decisions in life, including what you do or don't do to achieve the American Dream. Process issues shape every person's worldview about relationships, work ethic, family, spirituality, and sexuality.

Process issues in this book are often written in **bold type** to help you identify them. As you progress through the book, you will be given more responsibility for identifying the process issues. A word of caution... understanding process issues is of little value if you do not apply them to what is happening in your life. Sometimes people are aware of process issues and choose to ignore them. Distracted driving and distracted living are examples.

You may be wondering if this book will be helpful to you. In the broad sense, it can be helpful to many because process issues and decision-making affect everyone. From a more narrow perspective, it addresses a variety of issues including **boundaries, trust, abuse, low self-esteem, anxiety, depression, defense mechanisms, talk therapy, communication, politics, science, love, and how spirituality** interacts with each of these issues.

Another way to think about this book is having a discussion about making good choices. Everyone makes choices, so the process issues discussed in this book can be helpful to people who recognize them and use them to their advantage.

If you plan to go through this book in a couple of hours, you will miss the whole point of the book. This book is not for sissies. It is a book for people with open minds who are **willing to examine themselves and the world in which they live**. An examination of this nature can be **hard work**. Hard work can lead to changes in each of the five domains of humanity.

Be diligent in your approach to reading this book. Take time to answer the questions about process issues working in your own life. Do you know what diligence requires? If not, look up the definition of the word diligence in a dictionary and think about how it applies to your life and reading this book.[4]

Stay with the process of reading and **considering** the material before you. This book is an opportunity to examine your life. Remember, process always determines outcome. That includes your approach to this book.

The first chapter examines a process for determining truth, and gives examples from the lives of Isaac Newton, Steven Hawking, and Charles Darwin.

Mark Twain said, tongue in cheek, "Set your facts first, then you can distort them as you please." The first chapter examines the reality of what Twain was talking about.

---

4 All dictionary definitions are taken from an edition of Webster's Dictionary unless otherwise noted.

Newton, Hawking, Darwin, and Truth

Truth is an odd topic. Politicians claim it, philosophers discuss it, and people in power define it by the power they possess. These realities help us understand the nature of politics. It is simply a branch of philosophy with particular rules that govern a country.

The founders of our country were aware knowing truth is necessary to finding the American Dream. This concept has its roots in the Declaration of Independence. Thomas Jefferson wrote in the second paragraph of the Declaration of Independence: "We hold these truths to be self-evident, that all men are created equal, that they are endowed by their Creator with certain inalienable rights, that among these are life, liberty, and the pursuit of happiness." This sentence raises questions which should be of interest to every citizen of the United States:

- Is there a creator?
- Are human rights truly inalienable?
- Are life, liberty, and the pursuit of happiness included in those rights?
- Are these truths as obvious as Jefferson suggested?
- What do we know about Jefferson himself?

This chapter takes a brief look at Jefferson the man, examines the concepts of bias, worldview, and truth, introduces the strategy of discernment, and uses discernment to evaluate the work of Isaac Newton, Stephen Hawking, and Charles Darwin.

Thomas Jefferson

Jefferson was like you and me in three respects: he was a complex person, he was influenced by events in his life, and he was flawed. Jefferson was born in 1743 on a 3000-acre Virginia tobacco plantation owned by his family, eventually inheriting the plantation and the slaves who labored on it.[5] Jefferson's formative years were saturated in a culture in which slavery

5 The Jefferson Monticello, Crops, produce, and livestock

was a dominant feature. These years certainly contributed to his philosophy about slavery, which he opposed.

Jefferson married 23-year-old Martha Wayles Skelton, the young widow of a classmate of his at William and Mary College. Martha is described as especially attractive to Jefferson because of her education and interest in music, both of which captivated Jefferson. During their courtship, she sang while Jefferson accompanied her on piano.

Eighteen months after their marriage in 1772, Martha's father died, leaving his substantial estate and his debts to Jefferson. As he acquired additional land and slaves, it was cheap to have slaves work tobacco, which helped mitigate Jefferson's persistent struggle with debt. His father-in-law's estate included Betty Hemings, the long-term Black mistress to Martha's father, widower John Wayles. John Wayles and Betty Hemings had produced several children from their relationship. These included Sally Hemings, a future mistress to Jefferson himself. This put Jefferson in the awkward position of "possessing a family of slaves who were the unacknowledged half siblings of his spouse." Jefferson had already gone on record with his objections to slavery.[6]

How did Jefferson rationalize these ideologies which were in conflict? We do not know all the goings on in the heart of Thomas Jefferson. It seems probable that he was influenced by the reality of owning thousands of acres of agricultural land, a crop requiring intensive labor, and by the awareness that there would be no lasting union of the colonies if slavery were abolished.

The mutual love of Thomas and Martha produced six children in ten years, four of whom died during infancy. As she was dying after the birth of their last child, Martha extracted a promise from Jefferson to not remarry, apparently to avoid their children being raised by a stepmother. After Martha passed, Jefferson burned their letters to one another and went into seclusion for weeks. He rarely spoke of Martha following her death.

Jefferson was a man who repeatedly faced grief over the loss of those he loved.

Two years after Martha's death, Jefferson left Monticello and accepted a position representing the thirteen colonies to France. He "fell in love" (my quotes) with French culture, French cooking, French architecture, French gardening, and European politics. His acceptance of an appointment to France may have been an escape from the painful memories of loss he experienced

6 www.sparknotes.com.studyguide: marriage 1770-1782, much of Jefferson's personal history comes from this resource.

at Monticello. Many people choose to avoid the pain of grief. These emotions are stored in the mind…often in the unconscious. They often lead to poor relationship decisions in the future, as they did with Jefferson.

Jefferson was in Paris for five years. Sally Hemings was one of the slaves he brought with him. It was during this time he began his sexual relationship with Hemings, which eventually produced several children.[7] She was likely a young teenager when her sexual relationship began with the middle-aged Jefferson. No portrait exists of Sally Hemings and details of their relationship are left to speculation.[8] This fact alone speaks to the disparity between Jefferson's relationship with Hemings and Martha Wayles. The relationship with Ms. Hemings may have provided some form of intimacy for Jefferson without the risk of another huge emotional loss. The master/slave relationship dynamic raises the specter of rape and sexual abuse by Jefferson. Jefferson was not only flawed by owning slaves but also by having a sexual relationship with a slave woman over 20 years his junior.[9, 10]

Thomas Jefferson is a perfect example of someone who recognized evil but was unable to overcome it through his own effort. If you are willing to examine your own lives, or take input from others, many of you will discover an area of weakness, an area where evil is in charge. We are no different than Jefferson. We are complex, influenced by events, and we are flawed. Everyone is flawed! If the lives of George Washington, Benjamin Franklin, Abraham Lincoln, Teddy Roosevelt, Dwight Eisenhower, Martin Luther King Jr., and Barack Obama were examined, each of these men would be found flawed. The content or nature of the flaw would be different for each person, but the process of deception is the same for everyone. **We are all flawed, and like Jefferson, are unable to overcome evil by ourselves.** Personal flaws are content issues. **Deception** is the process leading to these flaws. Consider the people you know. Do you know anyone who is not flawed? **Being flawed does not prevent valuable contributions to society.**

Consider the life of Thomas Jefferson. Jefferson is perhaps best known for his involvement in the movement to disengage from Britain. In his pamphlet titled "A Summary View of the Rights of British America," he stated the

---

7 Monticello.org, Jefferson Monticello, Minister to France

8 youtube.com, a documentary on Sally Hemings

9 www.monticello.org, Monticello affirms Jefferson Fathered Children

10 web.mit.edu/racescience/in-media, DNA Tests Offer Evidence Jefferson Fathered a Child

British parliament had no authority over the American Colonies. Jefferson was selected to be a delegate to the Second Continental Congress. Beginning on May 10,1775, the purpose of the Congress was to determine the response of the colonies to British demands. However, the war had already started with the skirmishes at Lexington and Concord five weeks earlier. The time for negotiation had passed.

Jefferson was one of five committee members tasked with the responsibility of putting into words the reasons for pursuing independence from Britain. From Jefferson's original draft of the declaration, the text was edited to its final form adopted on July 4,1776. Jefferson himself said the credit for the Declaration of Independence "must go to Locke, Montesquieu, the Scottish Enlightenment, and the long struggle for English civil liberties."[11] Jefferson was a slave owner yet he wrote a section staunchly opposed to slavery for the Declaration. This was removed from the Declaration by other delegates.[12] It is apparent Jefferson was acutely aware of the concepts he wrote about regarding the liberties of individuals and the responsibilities of representative government. Tragically, he was unable to live out these responsibilities in his personal life.

During the constitutional convention of 1787, Jefferson was representing the colonies in Paris. Though he was not a delegate to the convention, he was not shy about expressing his opinions. When Jefferson learned the convention meetings were being conducted in secrecy and not available to the public, he wrote a letter to John Adams noting the "ignorance of the value of public discussions" and accused the convention of being "an assembly of demigods."[13] Conflict and dissension were part of the birth of the American Dream.

Jefferson was also the third president of the United States from 1801 to 1809. During his tenure he founded West Point Military Academy, arranged for the Louisiana Purchase from France which doubled the geographical size of the United States, ordered the Corps of Discovery Expedition of Lewis and Clark to explore the new territory, and encouraged Congress to pass the Act Prohibiting the Importation of Slaves by which no new slaves were allowed to be imported into the United States. He signed this into law in 1807. Unfortunately, the slave trade <u>within</u> the United States continued

11 daily.jstor.org, Who wrote the Declaration of Independence

12 www.blackpast.org, the Deleted Passage of the Declaration of Independence

13 Study.com, Thomas Jefferson and the Constitutional convention

until the Civil War of 1860 and the subsequent emancipation proclamation by Abraham Lincoln. At other times, Jefferson served his country as Governor of Virginia, Secretary of State, Vice President of the United States, and founder of the University of Virginia. It has been said, "He enriched whatever he touched." It often goes unnoticed that he wrote somewhere around 20,000 letters during the course of his life. In the year 1820, he received and responded to 1267 letters, all handwritten. He maintained relationships at every level because people were important to him, irrespective of their position in life.[14]

You can discern from these brief biographical notes that Jefferson was a complex person. However, he was no more complex than anyone reading these paragraphs. His complexity simply manifested itself differently. The complexity and flaws of human personality will be seen in the following stories of Newton, Hawking, and Darwin later in this chapter. My own flaws will be noted in later chapters.

The process issues discussed above are the same influencing society today: human beings are complex, influenced by the events they experience, and they are flawed. The people who hold power in each election cycle are flawed. Yet they are the ones who legislate and determine justice. These are the process issues that produced 200 years of plantation slavery. These same process issues will lead to freedom or slavery in society today. There are many faces of slavery. The different faces of slavery are content issues, including the current trends toward economic and political slavery. As the middle class diminishes in size, amount of income, and influence, the American dream is shrinking along with it.[15, 16, 17] This is the problem we face as a nation. If you appreciate the importance of these process issues you will find the rest of this book illuminating and challenging. In each chapter there are suggestions for possible solutions.

Consider the following two important process issues, **bias** and **truth.** The reference here is to moral truth.

Bias and truth both lead to decision points but usually those decisions lead in opposite directions.

---

14 Selections from the Writings of Thomas Jefferson, Selected and Edited by Saul K. Padover

15 www.pewresearch.org, the Diminishing Middle

16 www.pewresearch.org, the American Middle Class is Stable in Size, but Losing Ground Financially

17 finance.yahoo.com, Middle-class Homeowners Will Get Priced Out Permanently

Bias

Bias is a distortion or distraction from the truth. It is a lie to the self, often occurring unconsciously. It is what Mark Twain was talking about, distorting the facts.

There is no one walking the face of the earth without bias. Everyone reading this book has bias, which originates from their worldview. People may insist they have no bias, but they do. It is affecting their decision making unconsciously.

The main bias of this author is the truth of Christian doctrine. The 66 books of the Bible, written by man, but inspired by God, offer truth to all who have a relationship with Jesus. Jesus is the only human without bias. He could not be biased because He embodied truth, He was truth, He spoke truth. He did not speak a word that did not come from His Father, the God of Creation (John 12:48-50).

The question for every person is, did Jesus speak truth? Considering this question in the following paragraphs and chapters will provide helpful information for the reader to consider. It will not stop anyone from making his own decision about what is true. Most people do not investigate this question. They make a decision for or against Jesus based on what they are taught or a life experience where things did not turn out the way they desired. I fell into this trap, which is described a few paragraphs below in the section on discernment.

People who are biased make decisions based on distortions of reality. Since the information is distorted, the resulting decision is often a poor choice leading to a bad outcome. In contrast, a decision based on truth is more likely to lead to a good outcome because it is built on information a person can trust.

Truth

Truth is the antidote for bias. Historically there have been two types of truth: 1) truth based on the laws governing the physical nature of the universe, e.g., the law of gravity, and 2) metaphysical truth. Everyone understands gravity. For people my age, it is why it is hard to get out of a chair. Metaphysical truth is more complex. Metaphysics includes such concepts as morals, ethics, the origin of the universe, karma, and religious beliefs including absolute moral truth. Both types of truth will be reviewed briefly.

The topic of moral truth has been discussed for thousands of years without general agreement on what is true. **Every person decides this for**

himself. Many younger people deny the existence of truth or have given up finding truth. One reason is because society has moved away from the moral truths originating in Judeo-Christian doctrine. The reason for this change is largely because our current educational system no longer teaches these moral truths. Instead, it teaches there is no absolute moral truth, only truth claims. This is a principal tenet of postmodern philosophy where absolute moral truth has been replaced by ideology.[18] Ideas about morality, ethics, and even science are accepted without adequate investigation.

There are two important process issues to consider when searching for moral truth: **worldview** and **religious beliefs**. Most people trust their worldview and religious beliefs to determine the truths that guide their decision making. We'll begin by looking at the concept of worldview. Later, we will turn our attention to religious beliefs and how those beliefs influence worldview. We will examine how these process issues impacted the careers of Newton, Hawking, and Darwin, and then we will put a microscope on science and discover what you cannot see without some magnification.

Discernment

There are different approaches to discover truth, but the approach offered here is discernment. Discernment is partly spiritual, but God does not ask you to suspend your intellect. Discernment is an investigation involving the mind, the emotions, and the will. It goes to the heart of the matter. This will be addressed again in later chapters on "The D Words" and "Affairs of the Heart."

During university, one of my three interdepartmental majors was psychology. I do not recall professors discussing unplanned pregnancies and solutions to that predicament. An unplanned pregnancy is a predicament for the woman because she is distracted by the way it changes her life. She wants to get her life back to the way it was. Of course, that is a natural desire, but is not possible. Whatever her decision, her life will be changed forever. Because her focus is the unexpected pregnancy, she unconsciously ignores the reality of her situation, including the life of the fetus. How quickly your mind can alter perception.

By the time I graduated, I was convinced abortion was an appropriate alternative for those who would not allow adoption. My thoughts: what would it be like for the infant to be raised in an environment where it was not wanted. And then, there are overwhelming economic challenges for

18 www.britannica.com, Postmodernism Philosophy by Brian Duignan

many young single women. These thoughts distracted me from the life of the baby. These thoughts are a testimony to the power and subtlety of the process of deception.

Fast forward five years; I'm on my obstetrics rotation during internship. A 16-year-old white female is admitted to the hospital five months pregnant for an elective abortion by saline injection. Another intern and I are assigned to perform the injection. He asked if I wanted to perform the injection. I declined, offering the excuse I had no experience with the procedure. While he was doing the injection, I was wondering to myself, *what is this girl thinking while two men appeared she did not know to end the life of a baby she did not want?* We knew nothing of her circumstances nor did we ask.

We happened to be unavailable to monitor the delivery when she expelled her baby. It was attended by another doctor she did not know. I thought about visiting her later to give her an opportunity to talk, but I did not go. I did not realize yet that relationship is more important than task. This young woman and her infant paid the price of our ignorance. Her circumstances and our bias conspired to end the life of her baby. Bias often leads to a poor outcome.

It was not until three years after that I realized ending the life of a baby inside the womb was the result of distraction and confusion in the minds of people outside the womb. There is never any communication between the people deciding to end the life of the baby outside the womb and the developing infant inside the womb. When we had our first child, I realized the true nature of conception and birth, miracles of God. Looking at our newborn baby, I realized I had failed that young woman. At this point in my life, I had not even heard the word discernment.

Discernment is a process of investigation to determine the spiritual nature of something. Is it coming from God or Satan? The mind investigates known facts, spiritual perspectives from relevant scriptures, emotions, and the consequences of various options. This is time-consuming, but can you think of anything more important than discovering the truth? When this work is done, the CEO of your heart, which is the will, makes an executive decision about what is true. This leads to a course of action. If you are a non-believer but have a desire for truth, simply ask God to help you discover the truth during your investigation. He offers truth to people who seek it (Matthew 7:7-8).

When I realized conception and birth were contemporary miracles of God, I began to investigate secular opinions instead of accepting them at face value. I wrote to my state medical association and inquired about their position on abortion. The response I received was disappointing. They wrote abortion was so controversial it had been banned from discussion. Wow! A large group of physicians, people trained in the sciences, could not agree on the issue of the beginning of life. The decision to not discuss such an important matter certainly was not made on the basis of science. Were the doctors who made this decision distracted by politics? Are politicians taking the place of doctors in determining medical practice? Is this an example of the process of deception?

This was certainly an early example of what has become so pervasive in our society, currently the suppression of speech about controversial topics. I cancelled my membership in the state medical association and the American Medical Association. I was practicing discernment although still not familiar with the word or its scriptural origin (I Corinthians 2:10-15, see Amplified Bible Translation).[19]

A few years passed. I was in my early 40's coordinating Lutheran Lay Renewals in Western states. Lay Renewal is a program in which a team of lay people go to a church at their invitation to witness how Christ is working in their life. These were fascinating weekends. You could feel the presence of the Holy Spirit. The peace of God during these weekends was exhilarating. It may seem contradictory but you can be energized while experiencing God's peace.

Following a meeting at a church in Arizona, one of the team members sent a letter to me. He thanked me for leading the team and then wrote, "I perceive you have the gift of discernment as well as other spiritual gifts." I showed the letter to my wife. We wondered what he was talking about. So, I got my Bible out. We learned the gift of discernment is one of the gifts of the Holy Spirit (I Corinthians 7:7, 12:1-11).[20] I asked my wife if she thought I was discerning. She said, "Yes." I wondered, is she correct and what are the implications?

People who pursue counseling have all kinds of questions. They often have their own answer to the question but are uncertain about it. They want the opinion of their therapist. Many clients would bring a book for me to review and asked this question: "Does this book represent the Gospel of Christ?" One question always in my mind in answering: does the book point to Jesus

---

19 Quotations/references from scripture unless otherwise noted are encouraged to be examined in the Amplified Bible for clarity of translation. If you find these quotes wordy, I suggest using New King James or New Living Translation.

20 There are also gifts from the Father and gifts from the Son

or point in some other direction? Do you think that question is important to the process of discernment? **The gift of discernment is helpful in sorting these things out.** Notice, this is only a gift. It is a tool God provides to build the body of Christ. The word of God and common sense are equally important in discerning the origins of a spiritual issue.

Spiritual gifts not exercised can slowly dwindle and be smothered by secular teaching (I Timothy 4:14). They wither slowly but can be revived. You can refuse to utilize gifts from God but He does not take back His gifts. He does not force you to use His gifts. He does not force anyone to accept His greatest gift, the atoning blood of Christ on a cross!

You will observe discernment at work in the following paragraphs and chapters of this book. Consider using the process of discernment to evaluate this book. Answer the questions. Meditate on them. Research them. Read the references supporting the opinions offered on various issues. God desires everyone to be discerning. The choice is, be discerning or be deceived. Choose wisely (Deuteronomy 30:19-20).

Worldview

An early reference to worldview appears in Paul's letter to the Roman Church almost 2000 years ago. Romans 12:2, "Do not be conformed to this world (this age) but be transformed by the [entire] renewal of your mind so that you may prove [for yourselves] what is the good and acceptable and perfect will of God, even the thing which is good and acceptable and perfect for you."

Paul is saying the world shapes our thinking and emotions, which influences our behavior. The world offers a superficial life which directs a person away from the deeper, spiritual life which God desires us to experience and enjoy (Matthew 16:24-26, Ephesians 2:10). We need new ideas and a new attitude to discover the will of God in our lives. Paul does not say, but it is implied, that this superficial life comes from Satan, who is the ruler of the world (John 14:30). Paul uses the imperative tense of the verb, commanding all believers to be changed by the renewal of their minds. He is representing Jesus, who is concerned about our being separated from the truth. Paul himself was separated from the truth initially (Acts 9:1-20), and his change of heart provides hope and direction for all of us. Paul wrote the above words out of love and concern for you and me.

Worldview is similar to bias discussed above. Worldview is the origin of bias. The more distorted a worldview is the more bias a person will have. But if a person has a set of life experiences producing little distortion and pursues truth through the process of discernment, he will have little bias and an accurate worldview.

The influence of worldview in daily life is discussed in a later chapter, "How Quickly Your Mind Alters Perception." Worldview is the lens or filter through which our understanding of self, others, and the world is determined. Process is a progression of events that leads to a decision which produces a certain outcome or result, and worldview influences that decision-making process.

Worldview is a very important process issue. It is a filter that changes the perception of everything a person experiences from reality to something else which can be very subjective and misleading. Filters on cameras change a landscape from the way it actually looks to the way a photographer desires it to appear. Each filter has a specific purpose: to reduce glare, accentuate color, create contrast, or achieve some other objective. Each part of a person's worldview reduces, accentuates, magnifies, or eliminates the importance of various ideas, emotions, and behavior. The stronger the filter the more it distorts reality, for a camera or worldview. The filters distorting your worldview result in the world appearing the way Satan wants you to see it.

Worldview can enhance the experience of living when accurate or make life miserable and intolerable when distorted. Worldview is based largely on experience. A person's view of the world comes from his experience of living in the world. Genes contribute to temperament, inheritable diseases, IQ, physical characteristics etc., but genes generally do not determine emotional responses and specific thinking patterns.

Worldview is a compilation of thoughts and emotions which are stimulated by various experiences in a person's life. Your mind adds these thoughts/emotions/events together, and the sum equals your worldview.

Certain experiences are more influential than others. Your parents' worldview, trauma, peer pressure, education, substance abuse, and spirituality are examples of important influences. A worldview can change dramatically when a person leaves home, attends college, joins the workforce, spends time in the Armed Forces, becomes homeless, or experiences any life circumstance that impacts thinking, emotions, behavior, health, or spirituality. These experiences provide new data that may conflict with and modify a prior worldview.

Trauma produces painful thoughts and emotions and causes people to experience the world as intimidating. Fear of re-experiencing these thoughts and emotions produces an avoidance response. Fear is an obstacle that prevents engagement with people, events, and new information which could change an existing worldview. This process of avoidance or being **restricted** is discussed in the chapter "The Beginning of Everything."

Avoidance is protective but produces a worldview resistant to change. The thought of engaging the part of the world that produced the trauma results in anxiety. Refusal to examine these thoughts and process the feelings may lead to unresolved grief, depression, post-traumatic stress disorder, social anxiety, or other psychological maladies. Premature sexual experience through abuse, rape, or promiscuity tends to produce a worldview which is sexualized or, alternatively, avoids sexual pleasure. Generalizing fear from a personal experience to the rest of the world is distracting, confusing, and misleading. It produces deception in many aspects of life.

Peer pressure distracts children and adults from the truth. People of all ages want to be accepted and loved. The pressure to conform and be accepted is enormous and can change worldview quickly.

Education can be a boom or bust experience. It is a boom if it stimulates curiosity, an open mind, debate, and a desire for knowledge. It is a bust when it suppresses diverse opinions, intellectual exploration, and discussion. Teachers and professors may have a huge impact in forming a student's worldview.

People who are unable to process their traumas may resort to alcohol or street drugs to disconnect from their thoughts and emotions. These people develop a worldview in which use of a substance becomes a primary coping strategy. The substance becomes their most trusted friend, but this friend removes them from the pain of life while preventing them from processing traumas. This friend destroys body, mind, and spirit. Life becomes a cycle of sobriety alternating with intoxication, a very limited world devoid of healthy experience.

Spirituality/faith/religion is often a large factor in determining worldview. People usually assume the religion they embrace contains truth they can rely on to guide their decision-making. The existence of large numbers of religious persuasions contradicts this belief. Since they contradict each other, they can't all be true. Atheist and agnostic individuals rely on themselves for truth. This seems extremely risky considering the abundant evidence available regarding the foolishness of humanity (I Corinthians 1:17-25).

What are the primary influences that have determined your worldview?

____

____

____

____

____

The above paragraphs indicate that worldview is somewhat plastic. Religious beliefs are also known to change over time. The question is how a person knows when their worldview or religious beliefs need to change. Answer yes or no to the questions below to unravel the intricacies of your worldview and religious views.

1) Worldview and religious beliefs should assist in helping us understand what we experience in the world regarding ourselves, others, and the ups and downs of life. It should educate about how truth originated, how to discover it, and how to follow it. Do my worldview and religious views have explanatory power? Worldview_____ Religion_____
2) Do they help me experience love, joy, and peace? Worldview_____ Religion_____
3) Do they help me to understand emotional pain/anxiety and how to cope with it? Worldview_____ Religion_____
4) Do they help explain the origin of good and evil? Worldview______Religion_____
5) Do they define guidelines for relationships, relationship boundaries, and how to love and be loved? Worldview______Religion_____
6) Do they help change behavior that is not producing a healthy outcome? Worldview______Religion_____
7) Do they help explain the world itself, how it came into existence? Does it answer corollary questions such as, what is the origin of love? Worldview______Religion_____
8) Do they help you determine the reason for your existence? Worldview______Religion_____
9) Do they provide a strategy for changing your worldview? Worldview______Religion_____
10) Does following its teachings produce success in life, at work, in relationships? Worldview______Religion_____

If you answered no to one or more questions above, your worldview or religious beliefs are not working well for you. Carefully consider what you are willing to do to change your worldview or religious beliefs. This will take time, effort, humility, teachability, and exposure to the truth. Truth is a good place to start any investigation.

People often assume what their religion says about truth is true. But is it? Let's look at several religions to discover a little about the founder and what the founder says about truth. If what a religion says about truth is false, then the rest of its doctrine is likely to be false.

The reader is encouraged to make a thorough study of each religion before incorporating the teachings of a particular one into your worldview. This chapter briefly addresses what each religion says about truth. Only six religious persuasions are provided for review, but the process described above could be utilized to evaluate any religious doctrine.

What Six Religious Expressions Say about Truth

Hinduism: Unlike many other faith disciplines, Hinduism is not founded on the teachings of a single individual or God. It is a collection of many religious concepts which have their origins between 2000 B.C. and A.D. 500. It is a religion which has evolved through different periods of transformation and continues to change in the modern era. The principal deity is Brahman, but other gods and goddesses are also recognized.

In the teachings of Hinduism, truth is an aspect of Brahman, a characteristic of existence, the support of creation, a quality of gods, moral virtue, philosophical concept, spiritual practice, instruction, and the personification of Dharma (Law) and Rita (Order). Truth is divinity itself. Brahman is truth personified. When people are truthful and firmly established in the truth, they become one with Brahman, the true being. They become free from the cycle of births and deaths, and they ascend to the world of truth.[21]

Buddhism: Buddha was born a prince, living a very protected and luxurious life. As a young man, his observations of suffering in the world stimulated a spiritual search through meditation. This resulted in a state of enlightenment including his understanding of truth. Buddhism shares many beliefs of Hinduism, but the ultimate truth in Buddhism is gained only through meditation. It does not originate from divine revelation. Through meditation, the Buddha gained understanding about how to escape the cycle

21 www.hinduwebsite.com, Truth According to Hinduism

of birth and rebirth (reincarnation) that is a prominent feature of Hinduism.

Centuries of cultural and environmental influence have made Burmese, Thai, Chinese, Tibetan, Sri Lankan, and Japanese Buddhism different. But these practices are not in conflict, because the Buddha taught that while the truth remains absolute, the physical manifestation of this truth can differ according to the way of life of those who profess it. Buddha described Four Noble Truths as follows.[22]

"The First Noble truth is the existence of sorrow. Birth is sorrowful, growth is sorrowful, illness is sorrowful, and death is sorrowful. This truth applies to all living things to some degree. Simply put, pain and fear are the unavoidable complementary aspects of pleasure and need. Both are innately necessary emotional responses in life. That is the yin and yang of life, so to speak."

"The Second Noble truth is the cause of suffering, which is lust. The desire to live for the enjoyment of self entangles us in the net of sorrows. Pleasures are the bait, and the result is pain. Attraction and aversion (need and fear) are the driving forces behind life's response to stimuli. For example, both a human sunbather and a sunflower experience a need for sunshine. The difference between the two is the capacity for thought. In humans, primal need mixes with thought and generates desire (expectation, lust, envy, greed)."

"The Third Noble truth is the cessation of sorrow. He who conquers self will be free from lust. He no longer craves, and the flames of desire find no material to feed upon. Thus, it will be extinguished."

"The Fourth Noble truth is the Middle Path that leads to the cessation of suffering. There is salvation for him whose self disappears before truth, whose will is bent on what he ought to do, whose sole desire is the performance of his duty. He who is wise will enter this path and make an end to suffering."

Christianity: Christianity is discussed in detail in the chapter, "The Beginning of Everything." It is noted here the God who created the universe also provided His Teaching/Word/Jesus to guide worship and life. Jesus is the Son of God, the expression of God's love for mankind who was sacrificed on a cross for the sins of the world (John 3:14-18). Salvation is not earned, but rather a gift to those who rely on and trust in Jesus instead of themselves as they go through life on earth.

In this section we will limit our focus to the New Testament and further narrow our search to scriptures spoken by Christ, the Messiah, and to Paul's letters, about truth.

---

22 www.centertao.org, Buddha's Truths Pertain to All Life

The New Testament was originally written in Greek. The Greek word for truth is *alitheia,* which has different meanings in different contexts. Two of these contexts are:

1. The reality of life as opposed to illusion or deception, e.g., the truth of Christian doctrine, and
2. The truth regarding sincerity and integrity of character.[23]

Truth on the reality of life, references from Jesus:

John 8:31-32, A conversation between Jesus and some of His followers. "Then Jesus said to those Jews who believed Him, 'If you abide in my word, you are my disciples indeed. And you shall know the truth and the truth shall make you free.'"

John 14:5-6. A conversation between Thomas, an apostle, and Jesus. Thomas said to Him, "'Lord, we do not know where you are going, and how can we know the way?' Jesus said to him, 'I am the Way, the Truth, and the life. No one comes to the Father except through Me."

References from Paul:

Romans 1:24-25. Paul writing about people who exchanged the truth of God for a lie. "Therefore God also gave them up to uncleanness, in the lust of their hearts, to dishonor their bodies among themselves, who exchanged the truth of God for the lie, and worshiped and served the creature rather than the Creator, who is blessed forever. Amen."

Ephesians 4:20-21. Paul, writing about the new nature of man after accepting Christ as savior. "But you have not so learned Christ, if indeed you have heard Him and have been taught by Him, as the truth is in Jesus."

Truth referring to sincerity and integrity of character, reference from Jesus:

John 8:44. Jesus speaking to the Pharisees who were plotting to kill Him. "You are of your father the devil, and the desires of your father

23 Vine's Complete Expository Dictionary of Old and New Testament Words, 1996, Thomas Nelson

you want to do. He was a murderer from the beginning, and does not stand in the truth, because there is no truth in him. When he speaks a lie, he speaks from his own resources, for he is a liar and the father of all lies."

Islam: The doctrine of Islam was given by divine revelation through the prophet Muhammad approximately 600 years after the ministry, death, and resurrection of Jesus. The teachings of Muhammad were rejected by His own clan as well as by other polytheistic tribes in his hometown of Mecca. He was forced out of Mecca and moved to Medina where he orchestrated a series of battles with Meccans over several years resulting in consolidation of His power, the establishment of Islam, and unification of the Arab nation. Islam not only established a religion but also a political state.[24] Teachings of Islam describes many steps to finding truth.[25] Islam is a religion in which you earn salvation by what you do.

1. Know what Islam means. Islam means submission to the will of the only God and peace. That God (Allah) is our creator, who created us out of nothing and deserves our praise.
2. Know the prophets of religion. The Lord sent a prophet to every nation to teach them right from wrong and warn them of the Day of Judgment.
3. Acknowledge the other scriptures. Five known scriptures were revealed: the Scrolls to Abraham, the Torah to Moses, the Psalms to David, the Gospel to Jesus, and the Quran to Muhammad. Islam views Jesus as a prophet but denies His claim as the Son of God.
4. Don't believe everything you hear. Investigate for yourself. Seek the answer first from Quran, then Sunnah, then Ljma (union of Umma) and then Fiqh (Islamic jurisprudence).

Guidelines for Muslims:

1. Allah is the only God, and Muhammad (Peace Be Upon Him) is his prophet.
2. To pray five times a day, every day, at the correct time.
3. To fast during the holy month of *Ramadan.*
4. To give part of your wealth to charity on a regular basis.

---

24 www.al-islam.org a restatement of the history, The Battles of Islam

25 www.wikihow.com, How to Find Truth according to Islam

5. To visit the Kabba in Mecca, if able to do so.

Baha'i: "A fundamental principle of the Baha'i Revelation is the independent investigation of truth. The central tenet of this principle is for each person to refuse to accept what others say about truth. This is a do-it-yourself project. It is not acceptable for other people to tell us what to believe: … every individual member of humankind is exhorted and committed to set aside superstitious beliefs, traditions, and blind imitation of ancestral forms in religion and investigate reality for himself. Inasmuch as the fundamental reality is one, all religions and nations of the world will become one through the investigation of reality."[26]

New Age Religion "New Age beliefs include the various eastern religions—Buddhism, pantheism, Hinduism, etc. The core teaching of these religions is that people are essentially good and even divine. The other focus is that we are all in harmony or union with each other in nature. New Age beliefs have no formidable right or wrong, and no absolute truths. Moreover, those who practice New Age conspire to have truth, even though truth is relative to how an individual feels or what they think. New Age beliefs hold to no afterlife. They encompass the occult practices of divination, crystals, journaling, astrologers, and visualizing."[27]

What Six Religious Expressions say about Flawed Humanity

In the last paragraph of the article "The Concept of Truth in the Holy Quran," the author Ahiz writes, "Considering the importance attached to truth in the Quran, one would think that Muslims would be famed in this world for the truth telling. Yet the case is unfortunately the opposite. May Allah help us all to abide by the truth." The same could be said about followers of other religions. As difficult as truth is to discover, it is even more difficult to follow.

One truth that many people accept is that humanity is flawed. This assertion is verified by ordinary experience familiar to every person. Deceitfulness and manipulation in relationships, the daily news, and examination of history all support the concept of humanity being flawed.

Hinduism and **Buddhism** do not directly explain the origin of evil and the concept of flawed humanity. Instead, Hindus and Buddhists focus

---

26 www.truebahai.com, the Independent Investigation of Truth is Violated by Authoritarian Leadership

27 www.allaboutspirituality.org, New Age Belief

on *karma*, a Sanskrit word that roughly means action. Each action a person performs, good or bad, has an impact on their future, producing a good or bad outcome as well as determining their station in their next life.

Christianity documents the origin of evil beginning with the rebellion of Satan. This evil desire to rebel is passed to all humanity through the disobedience of Adam in the Garden of Eden. Deception is the process that underlies the formation of evil desire in every human heart. When Christians or nonbelievers fail to discern the presence of evil desire, they make evil choices resulting in poor outcomes for themselves and others. Deception obscures truth.

Islam also views humanity as flawed. "The best among us are those who are aware of their flaws and work to address them."[28] However, the narrative in Islam is very different from the story in the Garden of Eden. "In Islam, the devil, who is sometimes called Lbliss and sometimes Shaytan, rebels against God <u>after</u> the creation of humanity. When God orders all spirits to bow down to Adam, the devil refuses and God rejects him until judgment day. From that beginning, the devil promised to tempt humanity with evil and turn them away from God's path."[29]

According to **Baha'i Scripture**, there are many aspects to the question of suffering and evil. Disciples of Baha'i believe that God created the universe, and since God is the source of all good, there cannot be any evil force in the universe such as Satan, the devil, or evil spirits.[30]

New Age Religion does not have a uniform collection of doctrine. It is a religious movement centered in self—all you need is within—with no defined order of sin, repentance, or salvation. You become your own God. Followers deny the existence of sin and evil.[31]

These summaries of religion are extremely brief excursions into each of these faiths. Do not rely on these summaries. Examine in detail the founders themselves, when possible, along with their writings and their doctrine. Pray for the God who created the universe to guide your process of discernment. Listen for what He wants you to understand. At this point of discernment, humility and teachability are paramount. This is where you must invest time and effort to discover and expose yourself to truth. If you have accepted

28 www.islamicsolutions.com, Flawed Humans

29 https://classroom.synonym.com, The concept of Evil in Islam

30 www.patheos.com, Suffering and the Problem of Evil

31 www.jeremiahproject.com, Seven Major Teachings of the New Age

the premise of this book that process issues always determine outcome, it is vital you discover the nature of the process producing a flawed humanity. This is easy to say but difficult to accomplish. This question will be revisited in later chapters, so be patient with the process of discernment.

Isaac Newton, Steven Hawking, and Charles Darwin

The lives of Newton, Hawking and Darwin provide an opportunity for discernment, investigation, and inquiry.

Isaac Newton: Isaac Newton was certainly the greatest scientist of his day and perhaps all time. An uncle who was a graduate of the University of Cambridge's Trinity College persuaded his mother to enroll him at Trinity in a work study program in 1661. He became fascinated with philosophy and science and graduated with four years of financial support for further education.

Two thousand years had passed between the historical period dominated by the thinking of Plato and Aristotle and the birth of Newton. Aristotle maintained the motion of the sun, moon, stars, and planets was circular. Astronomer mathematician Johannes Keplar determined they were elliptical. Newton showed that these elliptical orbits were the result of the gravitational force of the sun that could accurately be calculated using his theory describing the law of gravity: every point mass attracts every other point mass by a force pointing along the line intersecting both points.

Newton is also acclaimed for describing the three laws of motion which bear his name. He is known for his studies in light, optics, and formulating the mathematical discipline known as calculus. Newton also deserves credit for developing the scientific method which has served humanity well for about 350 years. He determined the truth of science requires an analysis based on experiments and observational evidence and not based on popular opinion or by assertion of authority figures.

Newton was also a religious man pursuing the study of Christianity, utilizing similar strategies he relied on in his research of science. He wrote, "Let me therefore beg of thee not to trust the opinion of any man concerning these things, for so it is great odds but thou shalt certainly be deceived. Much less oughtest thou to rely upon the judgment of the multitude, for so thou shalt certainly be deceived. But search the Scriptures thyself and that by frequent reading and constant meditation upon what thou readest, and earnest prayer to God to enlighten thine understanding if thou desires to find the truth.

Which if thou shalt at length obtain thou wilt value above all other treasures in the world by reason of the assurance and vigor it will add to thy faith, and steady satisfaction to thy mind which he only can know how to estimate who shall experience it."[32] This author's translation: Do not rely on the opinion of any single person or group for the truth of God because you will be deceived. Instead meditate on the scriptures and pray for understanding which leads to spiritual treasures including increased faith and contentment, only known by those who experience it.

Some quotes from Newton to help understand the nature of his spirituality and his worldview.[33]

- "All my discoveries have been made in answer to prayer."
- "Plato is my friend, Aristotle is my friend, but my greatest friend is truth."
- "Gravity explains the motions of the planets, but it cannot explain who sets the planets in motion."
- "As a blind man has no idea of colors, so we have no idea of the manner by which the all-wise God perceives and understands all things."
- "I can calculate the motion of heavenly bodies, but not the madness of people."

Steven Hawking: Stephen Hawking was born in Oxford, England in 1942, 300 years after the birth of Newton. From his early years at school, Hawking is described as having prodigious talent and unorthodox study methods. At Cambridge, he studied physics, leading to a B.A. degree with honors. It was during his time at Cambridge he began to develop symptoms of amyotrophic lateral sclerosis (Lou Gehrig Disease), an unrelenting progressive neuromuscular disease resulting in nearly complete paralysis. At the time of his diagnosis, his medical doctors gave him two or three years to live. He surprised them, and everyone else, by living another 55 years.

In some ways, Hawking imitated the steps of Newton. Both started their studies at Cambridge University and held the Lucasian Professorship of Mathematics at Trinity College in the Cambridge University system. Newton's

---

32 rsc.byu.edu/converging-paths-truth/a Brief Survey of Isaac Newton's Views on Religion

33 www.everydaypower.com, Fifty Isaac Newton Quotes

career was hampered by psychological issues while Hawking was challenged by physical disability for much of his adult life. Despite their respective obstacles, they both prospered in their chosen field of study. Hawking focused his research on theoretical cosmology and quantum gravity using the mathematical system of quantum mechanics.[34] He is best known for his theories regarding the origin of the universe (the big bang theory) and the existence of black holes. However, he was not the first to conceptualize either of these theories.[35]

The big bang theory in brief: an extremely small, extremely dense, extremely hot bit of matter of unknown origin (referred to as a singularity) suddenly expanded and later cooled for reasons unknown, creating the universe as we know it. Hawking's primary contribution was to use the theory of quantum mechanics to integrate the big bang theory with the theory of black holes.

Some quotes from Steven Hawking which reveal his worldview:[36]

- "My goal is simple. It is a complete understanding of the universe, why it is as it is and why it exists at all."
- "The whole history of science has been the gradual realization that events do not happen in an arbitrary matter, but that they reflect a certain underlying order, which may or may not be divinely inspired."
- "It is a waste of time to be angry about my disability. One has to get on with life and I haven't done badly. People won't have time for you if you are always angry or complaining."
- "Things can get out of a black hole both on the outside and possibly to another universe. So if you feel you are in a black hole, don't give up—there's a way out."
- "Quiet people have the loudest minds."

These quotes suggest the concept of a black hole might be a metaphor for Steven Hawking's life after the onset of his paralysis. Amyotrophic lateral sclerosis sucked the physical life out of Steven Hawking. He could not do much in the physical universe, so he escaped to the universe of his mind. He was blessed in that he had a mind that allowed unfettered exploration. Hawking deserved a Nobel Prize for courage, if one were given.

---

34 www.biographyonline, Steven Hawking Biography

35 www.bbc.com, earth/story/20160107-These are the Discoveries that made Steven Hawking Famous

36 www.biographyonline, Steven Hawking Biography

Evaluating Newton and Hawking's Work

Hawking's writing about the Big Bang and black holes is all theory. It reminds one of the old saying, "If you can't dazzle them with brilliance, baffle them with b---s--t." Theorizing can be a process issue leading to deception. It often plays a major role in determining outcome.

When a theory is stated over and over by someone who appears to know what they are talking about, people are prone to accept it whether it is true or not. Then the theory becomes fact and is incorporated into their worldview. In the seventeenth century, Newton's research findings struggled against the teaching of Aristotle, who said the motion of the sun, moon, stars, and planets was circular. People believed what Aristotle said for two thousand years because Aristotle said it. This process is magnified when people don't understand the dialog describing the phenomenon, i.e., quantum mechanics.

A more detailed examination of Hawking's work reveals that he is mostly known for his work and writing in the discipline of **theoretical** cosmology, which is defined as the study of the cosmos. The cosmos is "the universe regarded as an orderly harmonious system." This definition of the cosmos means cosmology should be the study of the science that keeps the universe functioning as an orderly harmonious system. However, Hawking mostly wrote about the *origin of the universe* rather than the science that maintains the universe. He was articulating theory. **Hawking changed the meaning of the word cosmos** without informing the reader of his new use of the word. This is a distraction from what he purported to be writing. It leads to confusion in the mind of the reader. Confusion is the second step producing deception.

Since the primary focus of this book is process issues, consider a process issue associated with Hawking's big bang theory, Hawking's "strategy" of changing the meaning of words. Hawking may have done this unconsciously. Today, it is happening consciously with malicious intent.

Changing the meaning of words has become a principal strategy for various groups promoting political agendas. Think of this phenomenon as the politics of word games. Some examples:

- For thousands of years, the word marriage referred to a union between a man and a woman. More recently, the meaning has changed to include a same-sex relationship between two consenting adults who desire to live together.

- At rallies, feminists chant, "my body, my choice" as they march.[37] Is it the life of their own body they are terminating? Of course not! Choices are only good choices when they have a good outcome. Choosing abortion has a fatal outcome for the fetus.

A current issue is the definition of the word *re-imagine* in the context of life in America. The idea of re-imagining is a fascinating concept as used by liberal politicians. It suggests that your belief about something had its origins in your imagination rather than reality. But that is not the case. For most American citizens, their beliefs about life in America are based on their experience of living in America. Asking these people to reimagine distracts them away from the reality of their experience toward something else. It turns out "something else" is usually a political agenda. This is very confusing! *Reimagining economics* means refashioning a capitalist economy to a Marxist economy. *Reimagining policing* means defunding the police. *Reimagining education* means indoctrinating our children. *Reimagining free speech* means agree with us or we will silence and destroy you. *Reimagining gun control* means taking guns away from citizens while surrounding our legislatures with hundreds or thousands of armed troops to protect our lawmakers. *Reimagining the lives of Black people* means stop discriminating against blacks and begin to discriminate against whites. What a bunch of blarney, balderdash, blather, and general nonsense. It produces mischief, misconduct, and malfeasance.

Would it not be wiser to simply provide equal opportunity for all citizens? Would it not be wiser to have debate than lose our first amendment rights? Would it not be wiser to reform policing rather than defunding the police? In the next chapter, the processes of distraction and confusion will be examined in detail. They lead to deception. And that, of course, is the reason politicians are using the term *reimagine* so frequently. Their intent is to distract, confuse, and deceive. Mark Levin discusses the origin of the term reimagine in his book, *American Marxism*. He notes this term has become part of the "Marxist lexicon." That is more than a little scary. Do you want the U.S. to become a large-scale Cuba, Russia, or China?

In each of these examples the new meaning becomes part of the worldview of the person who accepts it. If enough people accept it, it becomes part of the culture. If only half the people accept it, it creates division and conflict in society. **In the absence of discernment, there is an absence of wisdom**

37 www.lifesitenews.com, behind the rhetoric, 'my body my choice'

and unity. The new meaning of the word becomes a god in the life of the person who accepts it. This process is known as idol worship. It is religion without truth. It is politics. Politics becomes religion in the minds of these people. Sex, abortion, greed, power, social justice, or something else replaces the God of the universe in their lives.

Theories about the origin of the universe do not fall in the realm of physics but rather in the realm of metaphysics. The big bang theory is simply Hawking's philosophy about how the universe came into existence. It's philosophy, not science. It's an idea, an ideology. It's not fact; it's opinion. Embedding his opinion in Einstein's general theory of relativity and quantum mechanics is confusing and deceptive and makes it sound like science, but it is not science. A definition of science: the observation and explanation of natural phenomena. The observation part is missing. Therefore, it is not science. This is what Nobel Prize winner Dr. Peebles meant when he said, "We don't have a strong test for what happened earlier in time."[38] The scientist who deserves the most credit for research into the study of the universe as an orderly harmonious system is Isaac Newton.

Another problem with the big bang theory is that it is counterintuitive. It doesn't make sense because it does not answer the following questions: Where did this bit of matter known as a singularity originate? Why did it appear when it did? What caused it to appear? What caused it to explode? Do explosions create the kind of order described by Newton that we see in the universe? Of course not. Explosions produce random destruction. A die-hard evolutionist might respond, if you have billions and billions of explosions one of them will produce an orderly harmonious universe. My response to that nonsense...show me!

No one has been able to answer any of these questions. Of particular importance is the issue of cause. Every event has a prior cause. This is sometimes referred to as the prime law of the universe, or the law of cause-and-effect. The big bang theory violates the prime law. An infinite being is the only thing that can exist without a prior cause, and that would be the creator of the universe, i.e., God.

Another criticism comes from the discipline of logic. Consider the following:

> If **A** caused the creation of the universe, and **B** is the universe itself, **B** cannot be the cause of **A**, which means that science, which is

38 pays.org/news, Top Cosmologist's Lonely Battle Against Big Bang Theory

part of **B**, cannot be the cause of **A** or **B**. The only thing Science can tell us about **A** is that **A** created science, which is part of **B**.

For example, if Telephone Company **A** manufactures cell phone **B,** you could examine the cell phone and determine how it works (science) but the science of how the phone works tells you nothing about the origin of the phone. The science of cell phone **B** cannot be the cause of telephone company **A** or cell phone **B**. The science of how the phone works does not explain the existence of the telephone company **A**. The only thing science can tell you about its creation is that something created science which is part of cell phone **B**. It would be necessary to speculate or develop a theory about the origin of cell phone **B**, how it came into existence, when, where, and who is responsible for its appearance. Similarly, the science of the universe tells us nothing about how it was created.[39]

This progression of logic supports the theory of intelligent design, not the big bang theory. "The theory of intelligent design holds that complex features of the universe and of living things are best explained by an intelligent cause, not an undirected process such as an explosion."[40]

The same idea as above, but perhaps more clearly and simply stated, is the "Nothing Hypothesis," which is a name applied to it by this author. The nothing hypothesis was found in Dake's Annotated Reference Bible under a category titled, *True Science Rejects*. Dake wrote, "Nothing working on nothing by nothing, through nothing, for nothing begat (created) everything". This is the belief of the followers of Hawking and Darwin. Dake rejects it because the nothing hypothesis does not hold water, which means it is contrary to both science and common sense. Anyone can test this hypothesis by filling a cup with water and pouring the water into space. The water will splash onto whatever surface is under the cup as predicted by Newton's law of gravity. You can't hold water with nothing. Cups and thermos containers hold water, swimming pools hold water, dams hold water, riverbanks hold water. These are scientific observations. That is science...the observation and explanation of natural phenomena. We all know this but fail to apply it to creation because we are distracted and confused by the pronouncements of the disciples of

39 This progression of logic was found on the Internet. When I searched for the reference, I was unable to locate it.

40 intelligentdesign.org, The Definition of Intelligent Design

Hawking and Darwin. The big bang and evolution remain unproven theories with no science to support either.

The science of mathematics also rejects the nothing hypothesis, 0 x 0 x 0 x 0 = 0. It does not equal everything you observe in the universe or even what you see outside your living room window. If you don't like the operation of multiplication add 0 + 0 + 0 + 0. You always get 0 on the other side of the = sign. Refuting the nothing hypothesis is easy yet millions of people continue to believe it.

Is the process of discernment interesting to you? Are you willing to use it to discover religious and moral truth? Do you believe truth exists? Are you beginning to appreciate the complexity of the human personality? Do you think events influence your worldview? Do you think humanity is flawed? Do you believe there is a creator of the universe? Do you believe we have inalienable rights? Answer these questions in the space below.

____

____

____

____

____

Darwin's Theory of Evolution

In Western culture today, science is an official doctrine of society. Most of the comforts we enjoy are a result of applied science. Little thought is given to the struggle Newton experienced debunking the teaching of Aristotle about the orbits of the planets. Darwin has taken the place of Aristotle in our culture today. His theory of evolution is no longer taught as theory. His teaching on the origin of the species is accepted as fact. It is taught in grade school, high school, and college classrooms as absolute truth. It is "gospel." Or is it?

Charles Darwin was a contemporary of Abraham Lincoln, sharing the same birth year of 1809. Darwin was interested in biology from childhood. A mentor at Christ's College apparently was impressed with Darwin and recommended him for the position of naturalist at age 22 on an extended voyage by the Royal Navy to chart waters in the southern hemisphere. His ship, the *HMS Beagle,* left England on 12/27/1831 for a voyage that lasted almost five years.

Darwin spent 19 days on land in the Galapagos Archipelago, where he collected several birds with slight differences in the shape of their beaks.[41] These became known as Darwin's finches, although it is thought they were actually a species of blackbird or mockingbird. Darwin carefully preserved these specimens for further study after his return to England where he consulted with an ornithologist, John Gould, who claimed 12 of the 14 specimens were new species unique to the Galapagos Islands.[42] Darwin came to believe the differences in the beaks were secondary to the different types of food the birds ate on the four different islands he visited, and that isolation over long periods of time resulted in speciation.

Historians generally agree Darwin did not formulate his ideas about evolution until some years after his trip. He may have been reluctant to share his thinking, as it represented a stark contrast to the accepted belief at the time, creation according to the Holy Bible. His wife, Emma, was Christian, which may have increased his reticence to share his ideas with the public. Quotations from Darwin reflect his struggle with the theory of intelligent design and evolution:[43]

- "The impossibility of conceiving that this grand and wondrous universe, with our conscious selves, arose through chance, seems to me the chief argument for the existence of God."
- "I cannot persuade myself that a beneficent and omnipotent God would have designedly created parasitic wasps with the express intention of their feeding within the living bodies of caterpillars."
- "Another source of conviction in the existence of God, connected with reason and not with feelings, impresses me as having much more weight. This follows from the extreme difficulty or rather impossibility of conceiving this immense and wonderful universe, including man with his capacity of looking far backwards and far into futurity, as the result of blind chance or necessity. When thus reflecting I feel compelled to look to a First Cause having an intelligent mind in some degree analogous to that of man; and I deserve to be called a theist."
- "The question of whether there exists a Creator and Ruler of the universe has been answered in the affirmative by some of the highest intellects that have ever existed."

---

41 www.voyagers.travel, Charles Darwin and His Trip to the Galapagos Islands, www.smithsonianmag.com/ science-nature, The Evolution of Charles Darwin

42 www.thoughtco.com, Charles Darwin's Finches

43 www.azquotes.com, Charles Darwin Quotes About Atheism

- "As for a future life, every man must judge for himself between conflicting vague probabilities."

In various letters, Darwin expressed the thought that Christianity and evolution were compatible philosophies. He also wrote that opinions were "of no consequence" and that the subject of God was "too profound for the human intellect."[44] He chose agnosticism. The above quotations suggest a quality in Darwin not seen in many scientists of the modern age: the trait of humility.

An abbreviated summary of Darwin's theory of evolution:[45]

- Living organisms have modifications from species that lived before them.
- Natural selection explains how these modifications have occurred. Organisms require resources for survival.
  - There is competition for resources.
  - Genetic mutations create modifications which are passed to offspring.
  - Organisms with modifications which are adaptive to existing conditions are more likely to survive while others become extinct.

Very little of Darwin's theory has been proved to this point in time.[46] Although Darwin is described as a naturalist by his biographers, he does not appear to understand a fundamental law of nature. Nature provides for nature. Specifically, he abhorred the concept of parasitic wasps feeding within the living bodies of caterpillars and cats playing with mice before devouring them. A significant focus in his life was "too much misery in the world." This abhorrence of the cruelty of nature may relate to the premature death of three of his children without a diagnosis and modern treatment based on science.

His theory of evolution really rests on his theory of natural selection. Natural selection relies on genetic evidence which has not been provided to this point in time.[47] Moreover the same criticism of Hawking can be applied to Darwin. There is no explanation regarding the origin of living organisms, which is a violation of the prime law of the universe, for every event there must be a prior cause. Scientists who followed Darwin inflated his theory

44 www.christiantoday.com. Charles Darwin, Atheist, Christian, Agnostic?

45 www.pbs.org, Summary of Darwin's theory of Evolution

46 science-of-involution.org, Criticism of Darwinism

47 www.allaboutcreation.org, All About Creation, click on DNA Code - Computer Language and Memory, Evolution and Gradual Changes, Page 2

beyond Darwin's original parameters and then worshipped it. It became an idol which is worshipped in most universities today. Secular universities were initially established as places of learning. They routinely ridicule Christianity yet are unaware they have become houses of worship. This is a perfect example of the subtlety of deception.

Many of these worshippers are unwilling to engage in debate about evolution. They mock those who disagree. They are destroying the scientific method established by Newton, which has served civilization well for over three centuries.

With Hawking and Darwin, we observe their "disciples" (my quotes), presenting theories as truth which they say "no reasonable person" would contradict.[48] We cannot fault Hawking and Darwin for the deceptions of their followers.

There are other abuses of science including faking data, distorting data, suppressing or withholding data, loss of objectivity (research bias), and adding politics to science to advance a political agenda.[49] True science reveals truth. Distortion of science reveals an evil desire lurking behind the "science." Some examples:

Faking and distorting data: The branch of science known as archaeology may be the most notorious for this moral trespass. Archaeology is the study of fossils and artifacts of past human cultures. It is supposed to be a branch of science, that is, a scientific study of fossils and ancient artifacts.

Science is defined as the observation and explanation of natural phenomena. This presents an obvious problem with archaeology, which is, no one was there to observe bones being deposited in the soil that create the fossil record. Anyone can put bones in the soil and claim they are 500,000 to several million years old.

In 1912 Charles Dawson, an amateur archaeologist, claimed to have discovered bone fragments to the missing link near Piltdown, Sussex, England. This "find" was known as Piltdown Man, Eoanthropus Dawson.[50] A couple years later he found a second set of bones, including a canine tooth and a bone which had been carved to resemble a cricket bat. This later bone

48 science-of-involution.org, Criticisms of Darwinism, Preface

49 www.scientificamerican.com, Yes, Science is Political

50 https://www.livescience.com, Piltdown Man: Infamous Fossil; www.textbookhistory.com, Henry Fairfield Osborn and the Tragic Legacy of Piltdown Man

resulted in a theory that Piltdown Man had played a rudimentary form of cricket. Cricket? Really? Weren't prehistoric men kept busy finding food and firewood? These findings misled most of the archaeological community for approximately 40 years. Eventually, it was discovered that Dawson or perhaps an accomplice had stained the bones with iron and potassium dichromate to make them appear ancient. It was also determined that the jaw and canine tooth came from an orangutan.

The chicanery behind Piltdown man is hardly unique. In 1856, a collection of bones was discovered in Germany's Neander Valley. This discovery was soon known as Neanderthal man (Homo neanderthalensis).[51] This find also became a suspected "missing link." Four decades passed before a repeat examination of the original work revealed "extreme evolutionary bias in the reconstruction of Neandertal Man." Other "discoveries" casting doubt on "the fossil record" include the discovery of Nebraska Man, Lucy, and Zinjanthropus.[52, 53, 54]

One theory that explains all this trickery is this: The missing link is missing because there is none.

Scripture records that pride overcame knowledge, resulting in Satan desiring to be like God. Scripture notes that Eve wanted to be like God (pride). Scripture suggests Adam's disobedience was related to the fear of losing Eve.

Archeologists and anthropologists desire to be respected and admired by their peers and the public (pride). This results in faked data, distorted data, or loss of objectivity supporting their finds. This process is reinforced by fear that if they do not find something, they will lose funding for their archaeological explorations. It was King Solomon who wrote, "The thing that has been--it is what will be again, and that which has been done is that which will be done again; and there is nothing new under the sun" (Ecclesiastes 1:9, AMPC).

Pride and **fear** are not new. Pride was the cornerstone of Satan's rebellion while pride and fear produced the fall of Adam and Eve. They are process issues that keep the merry-go-round of the world spinning twenty-four hours a day. The maxim in academic circles is "publish or perish." Instead

---

51 https://answersingenesis.org, Neanderthal Man-The Changing Picture

52 https://answersingenesis.org, "Nebraska Man" revisited

53 https://answersingenesis.org /human-evidence/ape/, Human Beings-the Fossil Evidence

54 www.dailymail.co.uk/sciencetech, Ancient Ancestor 'Lucy" was less intelligent; www:// answersingenesis.org, Farewell to 'Lucy'

of publish or perish, it might be "pride and fear." It would show wisdom to get off the academic merry-go-round, which provides a few minutes of notoriety, but prevents serious progress in mastering the lessons from life after kindergarten.

Suppressing or withholding data: An egregious example of this is the pharmaceutical industry. When conducting clinical trials, it is customary to not publish results when they are not favorable for a drug being approved by the Food and Drug Administration.

Adding politics to science to advance a political agenda: Examples include climate change, denying the X and Y chromosome combinations determine biological sex and gender at birth, and politicizing the coronavirus pandemic.[55, 56, 57, 58]

Adding distorted science to politics to Advance a Political Agenda: At first glance, this sounds like the same as above. But actually, it is quite different. Distorting science or falsifying science to support a political agenda introduces a second layer of lies since politics is already distorts truth much of the time. It doubles the amount of distraction and confusion a person has to wade through to discover truth.

A particularly egregious example of this is the current use of social media to distract people of all ages from experiencing intimacy in relationships. Facebook, Twitter, Tik Tok, e-mail, and chat rooms all contribute to this problem. These media are made possible by the research of physicists, mathematicians, and electrical engineers collaborating to create the modern computer. This is a good example of genuine science at work for the benefit of mankind. Like many technologies its has a positive side and a negative side. The computer has become an essential tool to manage information and connect people. It facilitates sharing information, events, and the writing of books such as this. It also has many negative effects.

Computers are promoted as conveniences to initiate and maintain relationships. But that is the problem. The resulting relationships are mostly

---

55 https//:www.acpeds.org, Gender Ideology Harms Children, American College of Pediatrics

56 https//oxforde.com, The Politics of Scientific Knowledge; The politically incorrect guide to climate change by Mark Morano

57 www.brookings.edu, Politics is Wrecking America's Pandemic Response

58 https://imprimis.hillsdale.edu/the-economic-disaster-of-the-pandemic-response, The Economic Disaster of the Pandemic

relationships of convenience. Some of these relationships do not even rise to the level of an acquaintance. They lack intimacy because they lack trust, commitment, and the kind of love that helps you become a better person (agape love). They do not teach conflict resolution which is necessary for serious relationships. Instead you end the relationship with the click of your delete button. Social media invade your boundaries relating to time management. They steal meaningful hours from your day without producing genuine relationship.

But the biggest problem is their addictive nature. They appeal to the innate desire every person has deep within their soul for relationship. This is a Godly desire but it can only be satisfied completely with face to face experience. This is the deceptive nature of social media in a nutshell. This is the reason people who develop romantic ties using social media eventually arrange for a "real face to face meeting" (my quotes). Marketing analysts know they are selling addiction along with computers. The elite class, who is orchestrating many of the social changes we are experiencing, know, when people stop achieving their dreams, they will be prone to relying more and more on government. These issues will be reviewed more thoroughly in later chapters.

There are many other problems associated with the use of social media. These include distracting you from your life goals, exposure to cyberbullies and sexual perpetrators, and contributing to the development of mental health problems. These and other issues are reviewed in a brief Internet article , "10 Negative Effects of Social Media That Can Harm Your Life."

The above events occurring in the modern era were prophesied 2700 years ago by the prophet Isaiah, "Woe to those who call evil good, and good evil, who put darkness for light, and light for darkness, who put bitter for sweet and sweet for bitter! Woe to those who are wise in their own eyes and prudent and shrewd in their own sight" (Isaiah 5:20-21).

Conclusion: Science is only as good as the integrity and expertise of the people who are conducting the studies. Expertise has increased exponentially while integrity has declined at the same rate. Integrity is disappearing from our scientific community more rapidly than the rate of the South China tiger is disappearing from its ecosystem. **The problem with integrity is the same as the problem for the tiger. The ecosystem no longer supports it. We, the people, are that ecosystem.** If that is true, and it is true, the solution will not be found by hiring more social workers or police. The solution will not be found in any new "free" (my quotes) government program. Nor will it be found in in any government program costing our freedom. We, the people, are the problem and ultimately, we must be the solution. There is only one solution: individual and national repentance. This seems very unlikely at this point. There are too many hard hearts, too many people who hate Christ and those who represent Him.

In chapter six, you will **briefly** examine the politics of the first permanent settlement, Jamestown, that eventually lead to 50 states, and… our current problem with integrity. You will discover the process issues in politics never change. They are mostly about power and greed. There is always a group of people who resist the temptations of power and greed. This creates conflict between those who succumb to power and greed and those who resist it. That was the struggle in Jamestown, Plymouth Colony, the American Revolution, our Civil War, and the conflict in our country today.

Politics have not changed. It is the soul of the body politic which has changed. It is the people who live under the authority of the federal government known as the United States of America who have changed. Much of our citizenry are no longer able to discern the evil nature of the people they are electing.

Each chapter of this book adds understanding to how various process issues lead to deception. The process of deception is in conflict with the truth.

Truth Commission

At the time of this writing, there is buzz in Washington DC about establishing a truth commission. Since this is an idea coming from the political establishment and many politicians avoid truth at every opportunity, I vote no for a truth commission. Each person chooses what he thinks, feels, and what he will do. This chapter has focused on the process of discernment. I encourage each person to begin to practice discernment about your own worldview, religion, flawed humanity, the big bang, evolution, and science. Your investigation into these subjects will influence your decision making in many different ways.

Did you witness the process of discernment at work in this chapter? Look for this process in the following chapters. Each person chooses whether he will be discerning about truth or be deceived. Discernment influences what you think, feel, and do. Choose wisely (Deuteronomy 30:19-20).

The focus of the next chapter is a more detailed examination of the processes of distraction and confusion producing deception in daily life.

Deception is the process leading to the demise of the American dream. Please pardon use of the following phrase, but deception should be considered an "existential crisis", a real one!

How Quickly Your Mind Alters Perception

This chapter considers the intricacies of deception in everyday life. Many people would become irritated if you asserted they should not trust their senses to report events around them. They might quote an old saying, "I know what I saw." But worldview and emotions can alter the perception of an experience quickly! This discussion will include fishing, psychotherapy, and life, especially my life, three areas in which I have experience and expertise.

Relationship events are particularly subject to altered perceptions through the process of distortion. It is a natural response of the mind to relational stress and a psychological defense mechanism that maintains a state of well-being. It defends against emotional pain. When stress is extreme, defense mechanisms may contribute to depression and anxiety disorders, including post-traumatic stress disorder. The mind may expunge the initial perception from the consciousness to protect from the stressor. This defense mechanism is known as repression. The mind more often distorts the perception in order to cope.

What Are You Fishing For?

A series of process issues may lead to a final decision point. Sometimes, content issues can morph into process issues when they play a significant role in determining outcomes. Look for how content issues become process issues in the following stories. Make notes on your observations.

I have a T-shirt that says, "I fish, therefore I is," suggesting that fishing is important in my life. What single process issue determines a good outcome for fishermen? Think about this question before reading further, then write your response below.

____

____

____

____

Some people go fishing to catch big fish, while others go fishing for lots of small fish. Some people go fishing to bring fish home to eat, and a few people don't care if they catch any fish at all because they go to relax and get away from work. Others go because they enjoy being in nature and hearing the sound of the stream or being on the water in a boat. These are content issues. What process do all fishing experiences have in common? Satisfaction. Satisfaction and pleasure are process issues that lead to the possibility of future fishing trips. A good outcome for a fisherman is an enjoyable experience. Enjoyment produces the desire to fish again. The decision point is, "Did I get enough pleasure to do this again? There is a decision point with many process issues.

Personally, I enjoy catching a fish or two on artificial flies I have tied, preferably large fish that put up a good fight. I especially enjoy the language of the stream and the beauty of its surroundings. And I like to do it on a day when I feel the sun penetrating my clothing and warming my body. I look for the challenge of catching fish in new places. My love of fishing has taken me to some of the most interesting and enchanting places on earth: Alaska, Montana, Idaho, Oregon, Washington, New Zealand, British Columbia, Quebec, Ontario, Baja California, and Costa Rica. I like to do it in the company of my favorite fishing buddy, my wife. These are all content issues. Each time these content issues work together, I have an adventure, which leads to a satisfying outcome. This is more important than catching fish. These content issues become a process issue because they lead to enjoyment resulting in another fishing trip.

The process issue for my wife is her preference for fishing when the fish are biting, so we do not spend a lot of time fishing together as the "bite" is difficult to predict. There are other content issues to consider for catching fish. With stream fishing for trout, these include river current, food supply, water temperature, protection from predators, location of fish in the water column, and presentation of bait, lure, or fly in a way that stimulates the fish to take it. These content issues inform your decision about where in the stream you will present your bait or fly to the fish. They work together to become a process issue that improves fishing success. These various content issues help determine general satisfaction if catching fish is important. Satisfaction leads to a subsequent fishing trip, and dissatisfaction leads to spending time doing something else. There are other content issues related to fishing that are not as important in determining satisfying outcomes. These include the brand of fishing equipment, the type of vehicle used for transportation, and the day chosen for the trip.

Fish and people have one process issue in common: for fish, it is safety from predators. For people, it is mostly **safety** in relationships. Predators of fish are other fish, otters, birds of prey, people, chemical pollution, etc. When fish perceive a threat, they change their location, usually to deeper water.

The threats creating unsafe environments for people are highly variable. People lack the instinct for self- preservation that fish have. But people have something fish do not: psychological defense mechanisms. These are not instincts; they are mind strategies formed during childhood in response to stress or trauma. They protect but at the cost of being disconnected from reality. Sometimes the disconnect is minimal, with no evidence of impairment; at other times, the disconnect can be disabling. Responding to anxiety by changing location does not help because people take the anxiety with them. Instead, they may stay in one location all the time, usually at home, a condition known as agoraphobia, a fear of being in open places. Safety/being unsafe are process issues the reader will encounter throughout this book. Much psychological illness is related in some way to being stressed and feeling unsafe.

Hells Canyon Fishing

In 1955, the Federal Power Commission issued a license to the Idaho Power Company to build three dams on the Snake River. The Hells Canyon Dam was the lowest of the three dams and the last to be completed in 1967. No provision was made for fish passage, so the salmon and steelhead that had migrated hundreds of miles into Idaho from the mouth of the Columbia River in Oregon were stopped at the base of the dam. The river below Hells Canyon Dam is a tremendous fishery for large populations of rainbow trout, sturgeon, and smallmouth bass.

In the 1990s, I worked for two mental health organizations in northeastern Oregon. Periodically, the directors of all the mental health clinics in eastern Oregon would get together for team building and to discuss issues of common interest. Several of the directors like to fish, so it was suggested they have a campout on the Snake River below Hells Canyon Dam. This required a jet boat trip from below the dam several miles downstream to a small meadow just above a dangerous Class VI rapid known as Wild Sheep.

Since I knew most of the mental health directors and liked to fish, I was invited to join them. After the date had been set, I realized we had invited David and his family to visit us the same weekend. David is a very serious fisherman who can be creative in the way he catches large fish. I got permission from the directors and invited David to go on the campout. David and his brother Jonathan joined us for what proved to be an unsuccessful trip. Due to large releases of water from Hells Canyon Dam, fishing conditions were the worst I had ever seen on the river. Only one rainbow trout was caught the entire weekend.

Saturday afternoon, David asked if fishing one of the creeks coming off the canyon wall was legal. I thought it was okay to fish for trout but not legal to take a steelhead. David and Jonathan went off to see what they could catch.

The following morning, David led me to his cooler. Putting his finger to his lips, he opened the cooler. The head and chest of the fish inside pointed up one side of the cooler toward the sky. The main body of the fish was in the bottom of the cooler, and the tail went up the other side. This was not a pan-sized rainbow trout; it was a huge steelhead… a huge illegal steelhead.

Have you heard the phrase unhappy camper? Instantly, I fell into that category. My change of mood was triggered by the thought of a ranger checking our camp, discovering the fish, confiscating our camping and fishing gear, and writing a nasty ticket. Now that I knew about the fish, I thought, "I am forced to be part of the conspiracy of silence." David quickly whispered, "Don't say anything!" At that moment, I became culpable.

For David, a successful trip meant catching a lot of fish or a big fish, and he got his big fish. For me, most of my process issues for a good trip had been met, even though I did not catch a single fish. However, two other process issues which I had not anticipated played a role in this being a good trip for me:

1. No ranger discovered the fish, so we were not cited.
2. I got a fish story which I have told on many occasions over the last 25 years. A big fish story can be better than a big fish…sometimes.

Commentary on Hells Canyon Fishing

This trip illustrates thoughts and emotions functioning as process issues. I was disappointed with the fishing but still enjoying myself until I discovered there was an illegal fish in the cooler, which instantly changed my perception of the trip. Immediately I experienced disappointment, **fear** of discovery, embarrassment, and irritation. **Fear prompted me to be part of a conspiracy of silence.** Are you experiencing anything similar in our present culture?

How quickly your mind alters perception. Your mind resides in the part of your physical body called the brain.

Our five senses record events and our mind gives us an interpretation of experiences based on our worldview rather than the experience itself. The Snake River story is a perfect example of this. Often, a person is not aware of how their perception differs from reality. When a person has a distorted perception of an event and lacks conscious awareness of the distortion, it often leads to decisions that have a poor outcome. It was a long time after the weekend before I could tell this story. Telling the story gave me pleasure only because we were not caught. If a citation had been issued and our fishing equipment confiscated, my emotional reactions would have been much more intense and very different. My perception of the trip would've changed again. Have you made a decision based on fear or other emotions? Was it a good outcome? Write a brief description of your story, identify the emotions, and the outcome in the space below.

____

____

____

____

____

Process Issues in Psychotherapy

Let's take a brief look at the subject of psychotherapy and the process issues that are important for a good outcome. There are two ways to look at this:

1. What are the process issues for the client?
2. What are they for the therapist?

Ideally, both the client and therapist should have a good outcome.

The client needs to find a good match in a therapist. This is the most important of several process issues for the client. Process issues that produce a good match include a therapist who is relational, patient, gentle, protective, available, maintains confidentiality, listens well, assigns homework, provides a safe environment, understands boundaries, has positive regard for the client, understands the problem, and knows how to facilitate change. When these process issues are in place, most clients learn to **trust** their therapist. This greatly increases the chances of a good outcome.

Many clients seek therapy without knowing what to look for in a therapist. Clients sometimes fail to realize that shopping for a therapist is like getting engaged to be married. You should know who your therapist is before committing to the relationship. This can usually be accomplished in one or two hours of evaluation. While the therapist takes a history of the presenting problem, the client should be evaluating the therapist. The client should ask at least two questions:

1. What is your experience helping people with this problem?
2. What is the process you rely on to bring about change?

A therapist is like the wagon masters who guided wagon trains from St. Louis, Missouri, to Oregon. The wagon master provided the route, specific instructions on where to go and where not to go, knowledge of dangers to avoid, and what was needed for the trip. The people in the wagon train depended on the wagon master to dispense this knowledge. Knowledge is what they paid for. Of the 300,000 people who took the Oregon trail between 1850 and 1860, approximately 30,000 people perished, or about ten percent. My suspicion is a much higher percentage of clients perish in therapy by not having a good match. Prior to therapy, many clients have experienced situations where they felt unsafe, threatened, and helpless. It is vitally important that this type of experience not be re-created unintentionally by the therapist. For this reason, the client should always have the right to refuse any homework assignment or any line of inquiry suggested by the therapist. The therapist reserves the right to bring it up at a later point, if necessary. This should be explained by the therapist at the first or second meeting.

Process issues for the therapist include the client paying for services, being respectful and transparent, keeping appointments, providing adequate history, completing homework, tackling difficult issues, and developing new coping mechanisms. These issues are usually discussed during treatment rather than at the first appointment. Many clients would be overwhelmed if these expectations were presented at the first meeting.

When a therapist takes responsibility for the outcome, worries about the outcome, fails to be paid, or endures unnecessary phone calls after hours, therapist burnout may be the outcome. There's an old saying about therapy, "the only way out is through," meaning there are no shortcuts.[59] Good therapy requires the therapist to identify the client's process issues that are preventing change. These process issues always relate to the five domains of humanity. Therapy itself is a process. The client must respect the process and be patient

59 A process issue articulated by therapist Byron Kehler

with it. The most important process for the therapist and the client is client satisfaction in resolving problems. When the problem is resolved, and these other process issues are in place, both client and therapist have a good outcome. Content issues for therapy relate to the nature and duration of the symptoms, length of meeting time, location of meetings, frequency of meetings, etc.

Here is a brief example of a common presenting problem, **not** an actual therapy. Rachel makes an appointment to discuss her relationship with her 26-year-old daughter Mary, who has finished two years of community college and worked briefly following graduation. Mary broke up with her boyfriend shortly after she lost her job. She is on welfare, believing no one will hire her. Mary calls Rachel nearly every day, complaining about her life. During many of these calls, she asks for money "to get by." Rachel reports she cannot say no to Mary's request for money because she loves Mary and fears Mary might become suicidal if she is denied financial support. Mary uses marijuana several times a week to escape "the misery of my life." Rachel has given Mary $5000 over the last several months. She encourages Mary to look for employment. Rachel is experiencing some depression and gets very anxious when Mary calls. Rachel's presenting problem is wanting to know how to help Mary.

Process issues for Mary include dependency on her mother Rachel, not taking responsibility for her own life, her reluctance to adjust to the realities of being on welfare, her use of a substance, and her refusal to pursue employment. Process issues for Rachel are the inability to set emotional and financial boundaries with Mary, recognition that she is not responsible for Mary, realizing she cannot change Mary, and lack of tools to cope with her sadness and disappointment about Mary. A significant process issue for the therapist is the fact that Mary is not in the office wanting to change by addressing any of her own problems. If the therapist focuses on Mary, the expected outcome is more disappointment for Rachel and failed therapy.

A better approach is to validate Rachel's love and concern for Mary while addressing Rachel's process issues, teaching her how to process disappointment and sadness. The content issues in this therapy are the amount of the gift, $5000, Mary being on welfare, the frequency of telephone calls, marijuana being the drug of choice, Mary having two years of community college, and Mary losing her first job, etc. It is important to know the content because the information leads the therapist to understand the process that has to change. Identifying Rachel's process issues and improving her ability to cope with them is where therapy is most helpful.

Process Issues in My Life

I will turn to examining how process issues have impacted my own life. It isn't always pretty.

It did start out on the sunny side…at least there were some sun breaks.

Each of my parents came from small family farms in Northwestern Ohio. Mom was an only child, while Dad had eight brothers and sisters. Both fathers of my parents did all their farming with a team of horses. My maternal grandfather would leave the house before first light, milk the cow, feed horses, gather eggs and then return to the house for breakfast which usually consisted of coffee, six eggs, and a commensurate amount of bacon, ham, or sausage. After breakfast, he would continue farming 44 acres with his team of horses. My paternal grandfather was killed in a farming accident at age 75. He was bringing the horses home from a day's work when he got off the equipment to open a gate. Something startled the horses, which ran over him with the equipment. He died from his injuries a few days later.

Life was hard, and money was scarce for both families. Our last name, Trudel, derives from the personal name Gertrude, derived from the Germanic word *Gertrudeis,* meaning lance and strong. My parents married in 1928, the year the great depression started. Mom was 18, and Dad was six years her senior. Their spartan formative years prompted them to wait to have children while Franklin Roosevelt was working on his social political processes to bring the country out of the great depression. My parents were able to purchase a house for $4000, financed by a loan from my maternal grandparents. It had been repossessed by the bank for default on the mortgage. In March of 1939, my brother Roger was born, and I followed as quickly as I could, in July 1943.

The earliest experience I can recall is playing in front of our house with toy earthmoving equipment, pushing sand and gravel around. Mom came out of the house and said, "You won't be able to play like this next week. They are going to pave this road, and there won't be sand here any longer." I have often wondered why this is the earliest experience I am able to recall. Was it the loss I experienced associated with the change in my play environment? Was I sad connected to that loss? Was it the soft sand being replaced with hard concrete? Little boys like puddles and mud. Was it the helplessness I experienced about this change? No one asked me if I wanted concrete instead of sand and gravel. Little children sometimes think the world rotates around them. Concrete is a reality that is "hard" to deny. It is interesting that I remember my mother's comments but have no memory whatsoever of the paving project. After all, I was playing with earthmoving toys when she told me about the paving. Would you not think I would be interested in all the equipment necessary to prepare the street for paving?

It is easy for the mind to deny sadness and loss, to park it somewhere in the recesses of the brain where it goes unnoticed for long periods. It can be difficult to know what a child is thinking or feeling, so it is a good idea to ask. Three things come to my mind about this experience:

1. Change can be difficult at any age.
2. Stability promotes security and safety. Change, especially unexpected or unwanted change, promotes uncertainty and anxiety. The anxiety sometimes stems from conscious or unconscious concerns about one's ability to cope with change. It can have a positive or negative influence depending upon the source and nature of the change.
3. Children like it when we interact with them in play or inquire about their experiences in life. It tells them they are important and loved.

When sadness and loss are parked somewhere in the recesses of your mind, it may go unnoticed. Strong emotions often result in impairment of memory. The problem with parking strong emotions is the emotions fade very little with time. They become unconscious process issues influencing future decision-making. Distortions of memory become rules for living which lead to poor outcomes because they do not reflect reality. Poor outcomes produce anxiety. This can be generalized to other situations that, in some ways, are similar to the original experience. At that point, you may have an anxiety disorder but have little understanding of its origin.

Life in Suburban Toledo

I lived in the same house in West Toledo for 21 years with my parents and older brother. Looking back, the house seems small, but it really was not. There were three bedrooms upstairs, all the necessary living areas on the main floor, and a full basement. The people who built it wisely purchased the lot next to it, which gave us extra space, so it never seemed crowded outside. There were several tall red oak trees in the grassy areas, which were remnants of the massive forests that were cleared to make way for our suburb. I grew up awash in oak leaves, acorns, and red squirrels.

One time a squirrel got into our house through the chimney when no one was home. When Mom came home, she attempted to escort Squirrel out of the house. Squirrel apparently misinterpreted her intention as an act of aggression. When she attempted to catch it, Squirrel became agitated and ran up and down the curtains, shredding them and leaving other evidence of its panic. But Mom was determined. The battle was on as she chased the squirrel around the house with a broom. I imagine this was the first time the squirrel had ever seen a broom and certainly the first time with a hysterical woman on one end of it. When she eventually grabbed the squirrel, it bit her index finger. While earlier she had been desperate to catch it, now she was desperate to let it go. She finally got her finger back and declared a temporary truce with Squirrel until Dad came home from work. I suggested we have it for dinner, but Mom said she had been too "attached to Squirrel' to have it for dinner.

I was two to five years younger than all the other boys in the neighborhood except for Dick, who was my age. As soon as we were old enough to walk and play together, Dick and I were inseparable. His father was an accountant; mine was a carpenter. Dick had more expensive toys than I had. There were times when I was jealous of his toys, but I was never jealous of Dick. When we were four or five years old, we made a pledge to get married. Somehow, we realized it was too early to tie the knot. When we started school, Dick went to a private school, and I went to public school. We developed new friends and gradually drifted apart.

Experiencing a love relationship at age 4 or 5 with a person of the same sex has nothing to do with homosexual attraction. During the early years of child development, erotic sexual attraction is not experienced towards the opposite sex or the same sex. When I met a girl named Mary Beth in the second grade, I forgot my promise to marry Dick. I was attracted to Mary Beth because of her softness and beauty. Love relationships exist between young children without eroticism. They should have these experiences free from external pressures forcing them to think about gender issues.

My Relationship with my Dad

A short but unpleasant experience occurred with my father when I was about four. It was early evening, and I was sitting on the bottom steps of our oak stairwell. My dad asked what I was doing, but instead of answering, I blurted out, "I don't like you." He looked at me for a couple of seconds and walked away. This was indicative of the poor communication between us.

We played a lot of pickup baseball games with kids in our neighborhood.

When I was ten or eleven, I asked for a baseball glove for my birthday. When Dad heard about this, he said to Mom, "He doesn't need a baseball glove." He did not realize we did not live on a farm, and my summers were not filled with farm chores. A couple weeks later, Mom spoke to me confidentially, telling me I could have a baseball glove if I paid for it. For a couple of months, I hid it so Dad would not see it.

Eventually, I realized Dad was not connected to the things I was doing. In high school, I played in a church fast-pitch softball league for two years. Dad only went to one game in two years, and then only because I was desperate for transportation. In one game, I hit three home runs and a triple. My pastor was there to see it and congratulate me but not my father. I don't remember being hurt or disappointed by his absence. It was what I grew up with. It was the only world I knew. My father concentrated on working and providing for his family, two traits he learned from his own father. He was very good at both. He earned his living from the carpenter trade. I worked in construction in high school and college, saving money for college. I worked with my father and other carpenters, but I never saw anyone more skillful than my dad. There was no wasted motion, and things were done right the first time. He was diligent at work and at home in managing whatever had to be done.

When I was in junior high, my dad bought two lots in partnership with his brother on Middle Bass Island in Western Lake Erie. My dad and uncle built a summer cottage and planned to build a second one. After other property owners discovered there was a skilled carpenter on the island, he was hounded to build summer places. He always hired a crew of carpenters so he could finish each project as quickly as possible. When he was finishing one of these cottages, he asked me to go next door and put the hardware on the windows so they could open, close, and be locked. I came back after about 15 minutes and informed him the hardware did not fit the windows; it looked like the windows had all been installed upside down. My announcement resulted in a gruff refutation that I was mistaken. However, he investigated, and after inspecting each window, offered the following: "By Golly, they are all set upside down." He then expressed a few choice words for the person who set them.

I am certain I experienced a lot of disappointment in my early years, which prompted the comment, "I don't like you," but I don't remember a lot of specifics. I accommodated to it or simply put it out of my conscious mind. His absence in my emotional and relational life became normal for me, so it never occurred to me to talk with Mom or anyone else about it. My success in sports, peer relationships, and academic work were all confidence builders for me. But I missed having a close relationship with my father. I missed hearing him say I love you or I am proud of you. As an adult, I continued to miss this and eventually developed a strategy to resolve this.

My young family was living in northwestern Oregon, and my parents were planning a visit. I decided when we met that I would give my father a big hug instead of simply shaking his hand. When I hugged him, he returned the hug. Although I did not hear the words I longed to hear, I could feel his love expressed through his hug. He was not able to express his affection verbally, but I was satisfied knowing he loved me. Our relationship remained at a much higher level for his remaining years. Many adults experience depression or low self-esteem secondary to one or both parents failing to express love through words. I encourage them to consider other "routine" things done for them that demonstrate a profound love, such as being employed and providing for the family.

When a person experiences abuse or neglect from an early age, they often rely on the same defense mechanisms that I relied on: accommodation, minimization, disconnection from emotions, and repression. Accommodation is getting used to whatever constitutes the abuse pattern because it is normal for you. This makes it difficult to realize the connection between the abuse and the various problems you are having in life. Or, the person may hate the abuse, hate the perpetrator, and develop a root of bitterness which makes it difficult to establish and maintain other relationships. There are as many patterns of defense as there are people who have been abused or neglected. **Dysfunction** as an adult **can result** from many **different pathways of injury when you are a child.**

Are you able to identify one pattern of behavior that produced problems for you as an adolescent or adult that you can trace to experiences during childhood? Have you been able to overcome that pattern of behavior? Have you been successful at resolving hurt experienced in relationships with your parents? Write your responses in the space below.

____

____

____

____

____

Romance in the "Ancient Past"

My adventures with girls began in the second grade when I got bored with learning to spell a list of 20 words every week. In the first quarter I got a big fat F in spelling. My parents and teacher were unhappy about this. Through some type of extra sensory perception, my teacher suspected I could do better. She announced that she would assign a tutor to help bring up my grade. There happened to be a girl in my class named Mary Beth. Every few days, Mary Beth would wear a white lambswool sweater. When she wore this sweater, she looked like an angel sent from heaven with the express purpose of attracting my attention. This was not sexual excitement, but it was a strong attraction to the opposite sex.

There was no sunset or flower that compared to the beauty she brought into my life. I had a 1 in 30 chance of Mary Beth being assigned to be my tutor—not very good odds. Perhaps my teacher realized my attraction to Mary Beth or noticed my sneaking looks at her. Whatever the reason, Mary Beth was appointed my official spelling tutor in the second grade.

Although I was not concerned with pleasing my teacher, I would do anything to please Mary Beth. I was delighted when I learned I would be spending extra time with her. I wanted her to tutor me forever. However, having her as my tutor posed a dilemma. If my grade improved, I would lose my tutor. But if I continued to do poorly, what would Mary Beth think of me? Relationships are prone to being complicated. I opted to attempt to please Mary Beth. The next quarter my grade catapulted to an A. Unfortunately, the A seemed to stand for alas, because alas, I lost Mary Beth as my tutor. In subsequent quarters, the best grade I could muster was a B. I never expressed my affection to Mary Beth. Communication, especially about feelings, seems fraught with all kinds of risk, even in the second grade.

Barbara was a year older and lived just a few houses down the street. We grew up together, and I really liked her as a friend. When I was about six years old, we were taking turns on the swing behind our house when the topic of conversation turned to the differences between boys and girls. Specifically, the conversation related to girls not having a penis and what did they do when they had to take a pee? Barbara patiently explained that sometimes when she was on the toilet, she could take a straight shot, and other times it kind of dribbled out. There was no embarrassment or awkwardness to this conversation.

About three or four years later, an opportunity came up for me to see

Barbara naked. My brother Roger, who was unable to keep anything to himself, informed me that he, Richard (Barbara's older brother), and Barbara were going to play strip poker. It was really spin the bottle, not poker. Each person took a turn spinning a Coke bottle, and whoever the bottle pointed at when it stopped spinning was required to remove an article of clothing. When I heard about this, I pleaded to be let in on the game, and reluctantly Roger and Richard agreed. Roger and Richard were both going through puberty at that time, but Barbara and I were not there yet. This game of spin the bottle was conducted in a nearby wooded area where we thought we would not be discovered.

As the game progressed, all Barbara had left covering her body were her panties. She was not wearing a bra yet. When the bottle was spun and pointed at her, I thought, "Finally, I'm going to see what a girl looks like." Oops! Not so fast! Barbara refused to pull down her underwear. We pleaded with her and reminded her of the rules. Rules Roger and Richard had established. We complained she was being unfair. She did not seem concerned about the rules. Finally, Barbara pulled down her underwear, but she pulled them up so fast we could not see anything. She did this twice. She believed she had fulfilled her "contractual obligation" because the game had ended. No one made any attempt to force her to remove her underwear. I believe Barbara continued to feel safe around all three of us. I did not know any more about what a girl looked like than before. Shortly after, her father somehow heard about our "poker game" and indicated it would be wise for us to find other things to do.

I moved on to grade six. My friend Jeff called, wanting to know if I would go with him to meet some girls. It turned out well for the plan of an 11-year-old boy. My very first kiss was with Betty, who was very cute. The kisses I had with Betty were exploratory, to discover the experience of kissing a girl. The kiss was on the lips and not in the mouth. There were no sexual thoughts or sexual arousal. She moved out of the school district, and I did not see her again until years later.

When I finally arrived in junior high, my interest in Barbara changed from anatomical curiosity to admiration for her feminine charms. She was very attractive. Our history of playing strip poker had not put any distance or awkwardness in our relationship. Another opportunity came up to play spin the bottle, but this time the rules were different. Instead of removing an article of clothing, the player was required to kiss the person to whom the bottle pointed. Although other girls were present, Barbara was the only girl I desired to kiss. Despite being attracted to Barbara, I never dated her in junior high. In fact, I didn't date anyone in junior high, being a little on the shy side.

Our age difference also separated us. She started high school while I was "stuck" in the eighth grade. The following year we went to the same high school, but I rarely saw her. There were 700 hundred students in my class alone. I didn't hear from Barbara until I got a wedding invitation when I was a sophomore in college. Darn, too late! Barbara was a beautiful bride. I continued to be attracted to her and danced with her during the reception. I chided her for not being willing to wait for me to finish college before getting married. We both laughed… and that was the last time I saw Barbara.

Linda was a year older when I met her at the sophomore dance in the spring of my sophomore year. The sophomore dance was the spring fling at our high school, the last major dance before senior prom. We started dating after the dance when I asked her to go with me on a hayride. It was early spring, and the Saturday chosen for the hayride was bitterly cold, too cold for any romance except holding hands with gloves on. On our next date, someone else was driving, and Linda and I were in the backseat. On the way home, she put her legs on my knees, and I leaned over and kissed her. This was very stimulating, so we continued kissing. I liked Linda, and I liked her kisses.

We dated the following summer. By the time I started my junior year, we had exchanged high school rings which meant we were "going steady," not dating anyone else. I was in the early stages of learning how to relate to the opposite sex. Now, 60 years later, with 50 years of marriage, I am still learning how to relate to the opposite sex. Some processes are slower than others!

Instead of calling Linda by name, I referred to her as "Dear," which irritated her parents to no end. One evening, she said there was something she needed to talk with me about. There was a serious tone to her voice which put me a little on edge, but I asked, "What is it?" She asked me not to refer to her as "Dear" in front of her parents. I could not hide my amusement. I could see their perspective, but not using that particular term of endearment would not change our relationship in any way. Her parents were apparently concerned about how much time we were spending together, or perhaps thought "Dear" should only be used by married couples. They were friendly and welcoming, but I was not around them very much. I saw them mostly at their apartment when I picked Linda up for a date. They never invited me for dinner or any other family activity.

Linda and I talked on the phone incessantly when we could not be together. There was nothing we couldn't talk about. The only phone in our house, an ancient black dial apparatus, sat on a desk in our dining room. There was just enough space under the desk for me to roll into a ball where I could talk and have a little privacy, i.e., my parents could not listen to the conversation. There was something about my saying "I love you" at the end of the call that seemed appropriate for Linda's ears only. One night after Linda and I had talked for nearly an hour, my dad said, "You don't need to talk that long on the phone." I wondered how he could be so certain about how long I needed to talk with Linda. At times, our conversations were about our future together. We were both planning for college…which meant I would be a high school senior while she would be a first-year college student. I occasionally wondered if that would threaten our relationship. However, neither of us brought that possibility up for discussion.

Linda had a girlfriend who was engaged. Linda confided that her girlfriend was having sex with her fiancé. This prompted a discussion about our having a sexual relationship. Neither of us was ready to be a parent. The pleasure of a sexual relationship was tempting… and scary. One thing we did not talk about was religion and spirituality. A small voice in my mind said a sexual relationship was not a good idea. I listened to this voice. Much later, I learned this was the voice of the Holy Spirit. I had attended church for 16 years when I met Linda. I had accepted Christ and committed to follow Him at a summer camp for Hi-Y club members before my sophomore year. Because I listened to this voice, I never pressured her to have sex. We never had a single argument about it. We could both see it was not the proper time, and I never wanted to do anything to hurt Linda or our relationship.

This was the most important conversation we had during our entire relationship. It was a conversation about boundaries, although I did not realize it then. The boundary established was **no sex.** We both took responsibility for maintaining this boundary. Sharing responsibility for maintaining boundaries is highly desirable. If one person has a moment of weakness, the other can protect the relationship. The most common cause of relationship failure is the violation of boundaries. Every relationship has boundaries. A boundary is a barrier that separates one person from another. Its primary function is protection. It separates your needs and desires from those of the other person.

Three types of boundaries can be violated: physical, emotional, and spiritual. Physical boundaries relate to physical closeness, including sexual intimacy.

Emotional boundaries prevent speech or behavior that stimulates emotions of guilt, shame, fear, hurt, sadness, or disappointment. Spiritual boundaries are guidelines for relationships originating in Judeo-Christian ethics and morality.

There are many kinds of boundaries. Boundaries around a city or state exist for the purpose of levying taxes and implementation of other laws. Boundaries around countries protect the needs of the citizens of a country from outside people who would violate those needs. All boundaries require a strategy of enforcement, or inevitably, they will be violated.

Many teenagers allow boundaries to be violated as a relationship progresses. There is often talk justifying these violations in order to "take the relationship to the next level." They fail to recognize that boundary violations always take the relationship to a *lower* level. The lower level is risky as young women are prone to be abused by the young men they are dating. Less often, it can be the other way around.

During the 18 months we dated, we never argued about anything. We simply enjoyed being together and sharing our experience at the time. I don't remember much of what was said, but it was important at the time because we were learning about each other every time we were together.

One weekend, I invited Linda to go with us to our island cottage. Ordinarily, I would spend a lot of time fishing on weekends, but not this weekend. I had bigger fish to fry, or perhaps to catch. On Saturday evening, after dinner, we went out on the dock to watch the sunset. There was no wind. Lake Erie had nothing to say, except perhaps instructing us on how to be calm. The lake stretched before us all the way to Canada. Something about being in the middle of a large body of water gives perspective to the vastness of creation and how small and insignificant we are. We stayed on the dock as the red sky gradually faded to darkness and starlight.

There was a light at the end of the dock which could be switched on and off from the house. Linda and I were enjoying a kiss when, with no warning, the dock light was switched on. Linda was startled. I wondered if we were going to have an emissary visit us from the cottage to tell us we had spent enough time on the dock. Turning on the light turned off the kissing. I was slightly irritated, but we both laughed about it. Then, just as unexpectedly as the light went on, it went off. Were we being given permission to resume making out? Well… that was my interpretation. However, a few minutes later, the light came on again, suggesting a different message. We reluctantly left the dock and made our way to the cottage.

Linda's being a year older had not presented any obstacles to our relationship. However, after she finished her senior year and started to think about attending university in the fall, I noticed some subtle changes when we were together, a little less eye contact, and her hands communicated less warmth when holding mine. It is difficult to pinpoint everything, but I was left with the impression she was withdrawing from our relationship. As the summer progressed, this impression grew stronger. I thought I had to do something, but what? It never occurred to me to talk with her about it.

It was the summer of 1960. I had my 17th birthday on July 10. I was a hard worker and generally responsible but was immature about how to cope with relationship stress. The thought kept coming to my mind it was time to break up with Linda. I thought, "If I break up with her, it will be less painful than if she breaks up with me." I did not realize I had shifted from protecting Linda to protecting myself. How can you be so wrong about something so simple? I now refer to this type of thinking as a thinking error. How quickly your mind alters perception. Thinking errors are process issues that lead to poor decisions. Poor decisions produce bad outcomes. I had a passing thought about talking to Linda, but frankly, I was afraid to bring it up. "The fear of man brings a snare" (Proverbs 25:29). The snare for me was making a serious mistake in our relationship by not sharing my thoughts.

Toward the end of summer, I asked my brother if I could borrow his car. I drove to Linda's apartment without telling her I was coming. When I rang the doorbell, she was very surprised to see me but greeted me with a warm smile. Without explanation, I promptly asked her to return my high school ring. Her look of surprise turned to shock as she sputtered, "I don't have it." Suddenly there was an epidemic of shock at her doorway. I could not believe what I was hearing. How quickly the mind alters perception. My defense of denial was working perfectly. She explained that she had loaned it to her girlfriend, Carol. After three years of attending high school, I had never heard of a girl loaning a high school ring, given as a symbol of commitment, to a girlfriend. Carol was dating a good friend of mine, and I was extremely curious about why Carol would want my ring. I returned Linda's ring to her quickly and left her standing at the door. On my way to the car, I reminded myself that her giving my ring to another girl proved I was right about her withdrawing from the relationship.

I immediately drove to Carol's house, where she lived with her grandmother. Carol was not at home. When her grandmother answered the door, I had to think fast. I did not want to upset Carol's grandmother, yet I wanted my ring back. How would she know I had a legitimate right to the ring? I said, "This is a long story, but to make it short, Carol has my high school ring. I would like to have it. Would you please check her jewelry box to see if there is a De Vilbiss ring there with my initials on the inside (TAT)?" Grandmother disappeared and returned a few minutes later with my ring. After checking to make sure my initials were on the inside, I thanked her and left without further explanation. Driving home, I kept saying to myself, "I did the right thing; I was right. She would not have given my ring to Carol if she really cared about me." When something is thought or said many times, it may seem true despite being a distortion of reality. How quickly your mind alters perception. I might have been right that she cared less, but I was totally wrong about experiencing less pain if I initiated the breakup. I never saw Linda again after that day. I had the pain of loss to remind me of Linda.

Have you noticed I coped with Linda the same way my dad coped with me when I told him I did not like him? This is one-way communication. Children often imitate their parents, and I was imitating my dad with no awareness of doing so. How often do we get into situations where we don't know what we are doing, but we plow ahead as if we do? I never asked Carol why she wanted my ring. Again, no communication! The way we imitate our parents can be pervasive!

At Christmas that year, I sent Linda a Christmas card and signed it "Love, Terry." There was no card from Linda, even though Carol told me that Linda had received mine. At that precise moment, I realized there was no hope for renewal of our relationship. My poor communication played a role in destroying a relationship that was very important to me.

The grieving process lasted several months, during which my mom noticed I was "different" and commented about it. The grieving process did not affect my schoolwork, other relationships, or activities. I was not depressed; simply sad about losing Linda. I had a lot of fun my senior year, but it was not the same without her. The sadness would come and go when I thought about her or the good times we had together. I found myself comparing her to other girls. I did not date anyone during my senior year except for the obligatory dances or club activities. After my first semester of college, I got together with some of my friends from high school to catch up and compare notes on life. Rick mentioned that he was dating Linda and that she was a lot of fun. I felt a twinge of pain in my chest while listening to Rick talk about Linda. I did not want any details. It was a couple of years before I was seriously attracted to another woman. I simply had not found anyone.

At the University of Toledo, I enrolled in pre-medical studies with an inter-departmental major of biology, psychology, and chemistry. After my first year, I was awarded an academic scholarship that paid tuition for the next 3 1/2 years. I performed 50 hours of service for the university each semester to continue receiving the scholarship. My first job was to clean and sterilize the petri dishes that were used in bacteriology studies. These were 5 to 6 inches in diameter, about a half-inch tall, and filled with culture medium to grow bacteria or fungi. My job was to take off the lid and place the dish in an autoclave which would sterilize it so it could be used again. The stench was strong as a skunk but more nauseating. After a couple of semesters, the chairman of the biology department rescued me, and I became an assistant to a professor in the comparative anatomy lab.

In the anatomy lab, I met Sheila, a good student, attractive, and pleasant to work with. I asked if she would like to go to a movie. *Goldfinger*, starring Sean Connery as James Bond, had just opened. The female lead was Pussy Galore. I felt some embarrassment regarding the sexualization, a dominant theme in the James Bond films. I did not know Sheila well enough to know what that would be like for her, and I decided to avoid asking. The great communicator I was not. Instead, I simply asked if she would like to go, and after, if she enjoyed it. She answered yes to both questions.

Our next date was an adventure with a toboggan during Christmas break. I knew of a great hill for sledding at the Sylvania Country Club. There was a small cliff on a hill with a drop of about 12 to 15 feet where the toboggan would be airborne. I did not know if we could even get into the parking lot at the golf club because it was late at night in the middle of winter. The gate was open, the parking lot was empty, and there was no one there to enforce any boundaries. This was not a sanctioned club activity.

There was barely enough room for six people on the sled. As the last person on the sled, I slightly pushed and jumped on. We went off the cliff as planned, but the air time was short. The landing was hard, and the sled turned over, dumping everyone in the snow. Everyone was laughing and talking about the airtime except Sheila, who was in tears. I did not know why she was crying until she explained that she had a chronic problem with her back. I apologized for planning an experience that caused her so much pain. While apologizing, I wondered why she didn't tell me about her back problem.

I could see her forcing back tears as we made our way up the hill and back to the car. I took her home and apologized again before saying good night.

I thought that would probably be the last time she would go out with me. However, when I called a few days later to see how she was doing and asked her, she said yes. I do not recall where we went for our last date. When I took her home, I asked for a good night's kiss. Instead of answering, she stated she could not go out with me again, explaining that her mother would not allow her to date a person who was not a member of her church. I did not know what to say. There was no defense, no response, so I said good night. Her mother had her way. We never went out again.

A few weeks later, a new group of students appeared in the anatomy lab, including Carol, who was also taking premed studies. I was taking advanced courses for my degree in ogling girls then. Carol flashed a smile that would melt the glaciers of Mount Everest. I started dating Carol. One of my closest friends, David, was dating Carol simultaneously. This drama was complicated further by Carol having a verbal engagement to be married to Chuck, who was in his first year of medical school at Columbia University. Carol apparently was serious about marrying Chuck but wanted some casual dates in the meantime. Looking back, there was no way this relationship could turn out well for me. Another detail I should mention is that David, Chuck, and I had spent six weeks together the summer before, driving 13,000 miles through the Western states. Chuck had a disagreement with David and me during this trip, resulting in his leaving for a couple of weeks and then re-joining us to drive back to Toledo. In my mind, I did not think Chuck and Carol were a good match. Naturally, I hoped Carol and I were a better match. Well, hope is a good thing but not always the same as reality.

David was also dating another girl named Jan, and he decided to concentrate on his relationship with her. One afternoon David called and told me he had canceled his date with Carol that night, so all I had to do was call, which I did. Now, all I had to worry about was Chuck. Carol and I had only a few dates, but she was a lot of fun. One night after taking her home, she took me to the side entrance to her house. We stood there kissing. It seemed like an eternity…yet ending after only a few kisses. Time was totally distorted in my mind because I desired those kisses to continue forever. How quick your mind can alter perception.

She would not go out with me after those kisses. What was it about kissing that seemed to jinx all the relationships I cared about? Was there something wrong with my kisser? I thought Carol was attracted to me and refused to go out because she promised to marry Chuck. I pleaded with Carol not to marry Chuck. I said I did not think it would work. My relationship with Carol was strong enough to allow this type of intimate conversation. Carol trusted me, and she listened, but she did not break her promise to Chuck. This was my first attempt at counseling, and it had a poor outcome for Carol and me.

Carol was accepted to medical school at Columbia University and married Chuck a year later. They divorced after a short marriage. I heard Carol dropped out of medical school. What a terrible outcome! I was David's best man when he married Jan. When I finished college, I was still looking for someone like Linda, Sheila, or Carol. In Montreal, while attending medical school at McGill University, I met a young woman who was like Linda, Sheila, and Carol in some ways, and yet different, a French-Canadian woman named Charney, my future wife.

Commentary on Ancient Romance

My relationships with Mary Beth, Betty, and Barbara were all notable for my failure to tell them I liked them and what it was about them that I found attractive. Affection and positive regard that is not expressed is often wasted. Every girl wants to think she is pretty and to hear those words from men she respects and admires.

During my relationship with Linda, we talked about everything except our thoughts on how our relationship was changing. My lack of experience in discussing difficult interpersonal issues and reluctance to bring up my disappointment resulted in massive hurt for me. The abrupt fashion in which I broke up with her may have produced hurt for her also. If we had been able to talk about what was happening, perhaps we could have continued a platonic relationship. I always wanted what was best for her, except when I went to her house to ask for my ring. At that point, I was thinking about myself, protecting myself. I was attempting to control the relationship. When we shift from thinking about others to focusing on protecting self, we find ourselves pushing the control button. The control button could be labeled the "I made a mess out of that relationship" button if there were enough room on the button to put all those words.

My perception of my relationship with Linda changed instantly when I learned she loaned my high school ring to a girlfriend. I was irritated, but it did not change my caring for her. My relationship with Linda had mixed outcomes. We had a wonderful relationship for 18 months. I learned how to grieve after we broke up. I learned how to be intimate with a woman without having sex. That is a huge process issue that prevents emotional and spiritual injury during dating and courtship relationships. It provides a foundation for married men to relate in a healthy way to their wives as well as other women. I could have learned this without experiencing such a huge hurt if my parents had provided more structure and practice communicating. Communication is the oil that helps all relationships run smoothly.

My relationship with Sheila was doomed from the start by her mother. My perception of her changed quickly when I realized her mother controlled our relationship. Sheila was not concerned regarding my emotional boundaries. She should have informed me the first time I asked her for a date that her mother had imposed limitations on our relationship. I would not have dated a woman under those circumstances because it complicates the relationship exponentially. If a mother is going to control the relationship during courtship, what would it be like after marriage? Sheila hurt me, and I was thankful she ended the relationship early.

Carol had excellent boundaries. I knew she was committed to her relationship with Chuck, but my relationship with Carol was doomed by my own pride. I thought she might forget Chuck if we had good times and emotional intimacy. Thinking like that is a good example of poor communication and lack of discernment leading to deception. I was distracted from reality by pride, which often distorts the thinking process outside a person's awareness. Instead of forgetting Chuck, she simply stopped dating me. Although it was very disappointing for me, I admired her commitment to Chuck. I wanted that kind of commitment from a woman I dated. I was saddened when I learned her marriage ended in divorce. Carol deserved a better outcome.

Lack of awareness about boundaries causes all kinds of relationship problems. It is very helpful to have a plan. Here are some suggestions:

- If you want to be effective at maintaining boundaries, you need to know what your boundaries are before starting a relationship. Have a conversation with your parents, pastor, or youth leader about appropriate physical, emotional, and spiritual boundaries for dating. Healthy boundaries should be modeled for you in these relationships.
- Do not rely on input from peers for appropriate boundaries. Most teens have a lot of confusion about boundaries.
- Have your boundaries firmly fixed in your mind before dating.

- Early in a relationship, have a conversation with your partner about appropriate boundaries. If your date is unwilling to discuss boundaries or you are unable to reach an agreement, stop the relationship.
- Double dating or group social events provide more safety than a couple alone. Learn about your partner in a safe environment.[60]

A boundary is violated when someone wants something from you and meets his/her own need without asking your permission or considering how meeting his need will affect you. Asking for permission honors you as an individual with your own set of wants, needs, and values. It communicates respect, which often determines the outcome in relationships. Asking for permission should occur before holding hands, kissing, or close physical contact of any kind. This also includes destinations for dates, driving habits, drinking habits, use of street drugs, etc. A lack of respect is a red flag to stop the relationship. The **initial outcome** you seek when dating is safety in your relationship. You cannot have a healthy relationship without being safe. The first thing to learn about your date is whether or not he/she respects you. Romance can come later. Most teen relationships start with romance and end with shattered boundaries.

Practice boundary setting in non-romantic relationships. Be aware of and respect the boundaries of others. Ask for their permission before meeting your own needs or desires; for example, asking for a hug, helping with homework, or getting a ride home. Work at understanding their perspectives, needs, and desires. Know yourself! This may be the hardest part of establishing boundaries. If you have had serious boundary violations in the past, you may not have any concept about what is appropriate. Explore what is healthy, as noted above. Learn how to spot people primarily concerned about themselves and not others. Avoid those people. If your date is a Christian, check with his/her pastor for a reference. Learn the signs of unhealthy boundaries. Here are some examples:

- Not being honest with others when you feel you're not being treated right.
- Letting other people define you or give your life meaning.
- Saying no to someone makes you feel guilty or like you are letting people down.
- Trying to please everyone around you.

60 www.psychologytoday.com, The Power of Boundaries

- Accepting gifts or circumstances, even when you are uncomfortable accepting them.
- Pretending you cannot handle something just so someone can take care of it for you.
- Falling quickly for someone you don't know well or who has reconnected with you.
- Letting someone touch you or have other forms of physical or emotional intimacy when you don't want to.
- Doing what someone else wants, even if it's against your ethics or moral compass.

In my relationships with Linda, Sheila, and Carol, I experienced hurt and disappointment. Some counselors suggest little or no dating prior to being old enough to look for a marriage partner because most teen relationships end like mine, with hurt and disappointment. Although there is a lot of merit to this suggestion, it may not be realistic for many teens in our present culture. Learning how to cope with hurts and disappointments is part of life. A reasonable approach might be for parents to provide sufficient structure to prevent major adverse events such as physical, sexual, or emotional abuse, and of course, pregnancy. I would have objected to that kind of supervision, but it would have been better for me. In order for teens to accept that amount of structure, they have to have a rock-solid relationship with both parents. Because my relationship with my father was already on rocky ground, I probably would have rebelled against that much authority.

Much rebellion during adolescence is secondary to poor parent/teen relationships. An approach provided in the book *The Difference a Father Makes* by Ed Tandy Mc Glasson is interesting. He spends quality time with his daughters teaching them about a healthy love relationship by modeling one and encouraging them to be virgins on their wedding day by giving them purity rings when they start adolescence. He has somewhat similar yet different strategies with his sons. It would be a challenge for every father to follow his example. We live in a culture dominated by Hollywood, which teaches throwaway romance. The type of romance practiced in the distant past is more healthy for people of any age. Marriage relationships are discussed in the chapter, "Love Stories."

Can you trust your perceptions about boundaries? Or are your perceptions blurred, confusing, or poorly defined in choosing a date, a mate, or a vocation? If you have made mistakes in any of these decisions, are they secondary to your mind altering perceptions in your decision making? Here are some questions for you to consider:

- Can you identify at least one relationship where your perception about it changed?
- Were you accurate regarding your new perception?
- Have you made good relationship decisions based on your perceptions?
- Are you able now to identify emotions or other process issues that determined the choice you made? Take time to meditate on this question.
- Has pride been a problem in relationships?
- Did you have a serious opposite-sex relationship during your teen years? How did it end?
- Did you marry that person?
- If your marriage relationship ended, what process issues contributed to its failure?
- Have you learned from your experiences and avoided repeating the process?

You cannot change the past. The hurts and disappointments experienced as a teen or young adult will remain in your mind until you experience the emotions, forgive, and release the people who hurt you. Strategies to accomplish these objectives are discussed in the chapter "Talk Therapy."

Many of the process issues that impact our life originate in our hearts. The heart is deceitful above all things (Jeremiah 17:7-10). Deception takes place in the heart, rendering the heart deceitful. This will be discussed more in the chapters, *Affairs of the Heart*, and *Intimacy with Evil.* The next chapter examines the process of deception in more detail.

The D Words

There are four D words pertaining to the loss of the American Dream in chapter three, **distraction, confusion, deception, desire, and defenses.** Oh, there is also a C word. It will soon be apparent why it is included.

Distraction is the act of changing the focus of attention. The verb *distract* is a transitive verb derived from a Latin word meaning *movement* or *change from one position, subject, or concept to another*. Distraction is a drawing of the mind, taking attention from one thing to another.[61] The definition of distraction in our discussion is drawing the mind away from the purposes of God to the purposes of Satan.

Confusion is the result of being distracted from the purposes of God. In this spiritual context, confusion refers to uncertainty in the mind about what to think, what to believe, what to feel, and how to act. The result is indecision or decisions with poor outcomes. Confusion often leads to deception.

Deception is simply the spiritual process of being deceived, cheated, or fooled. It often results in the loss of something God desires us to have. It is a process of taking things away. When we have been deceived, we were the victims of fraud. When people have their cars or other personal possessions stolen, they want them back. When their relationship with God is pilfered, it often goes unnoticed. Satan is the source of all deception.

Desire can be a noun or verb and is translated into several different words in the Old and New Testaments. These words convey a sense of longing, craving, or the action of reaching for something, stretching to get it. Desire often relates to wanting something you think will make your life more satisfying. It is often about gratifying the self. But there is also Godly desire, a craving to do what pleases God for those in whom dwell the Holy Spirit.

Defenses is a secular term from the field of psychology referring to strategies of the mind, often unconscious, which protect a person from unacceptable thoughts or feelings.

61 Word definitions are taken from an edition of Webster's dictionary unless otherwise noted.

Discernment is the process of determining the source of something, the spiritual life of an issue: Spiritual discernment answers the question of whether it originates in the Kingdom of God or the Kingdom of Satan. Have you been asking this question in your life?

If you think of these six words as separate process issues, each one demands a careful examination of what is happening. Failure to understand these processes may result in a repetition of what happened in the Garden of Eden, where Adam and Eve were deceived. There was no need for discernment until the snake made its appearance. There is no need to be discerning until one of Satan's demons shows up in your life.

The Origin of Deception

Deception is examined first since, without deception, there would be no evil desire, no defenses, and no need for discernment. The idea that we are all deceived is a new concept for many people. It is contrary to the immense body of knowledge and array of technology we have in Western culture. It seems we live in a very sophisticated culture. We appear to be very sophisticated human beings. Could that be a deception? Do we make being sophisticated the center of our lives at the expense of truth and wisdom? The following paragraphs will examine process issues that govern the relationship between knowledge, spiritual wisdom, and deception.

The narrative regarding the fall of Lucifer is the first recorded deception. It is not clear when Lucifer and the other angels were created by God and later rebelled (Ezekiel 28:11-19). There is no mention of this in the creation story ending with Adam and Eve. What seems certain is that the rebellion of Lucifer and the other angels preceded the disobedience of Adam and Eve. Prior to his disobedience, Satan had the name of Lucifer, a Hebrew word that translates as the shining one, light bearer, son of the morning, or morning star.[62] He is described in the above verses in Ezekiel as being "full of wisdom and perfect in beauty" at the time of his creation. After his rebellion, both his name and character changed completely. He became known by the Hebrew word Satan, meaning *adversary* or *accuser*. His outward appearance became distorted and ugly. Similarly, his inward being, his heart, became evil and foolish, "the father of all **lies**" (John 8:31-44).

The apostle Paul described Satan as **masquerading** like an angel of light (II Corinthians 11:14). Remember, in the garden, Satan masqueraded as a

62 The New Ungers Bible Dictionary

snake to deceive Eve and Adam. Satan uses a mask to disguise his ugliness and corrupt nature. He wears a different mask for each person to be most effective in the process of deception. If we saw his distorted appearance and evil desire to destroy our souls, we would panic and run, so he appears in a different disguise for each person and situation.

The Pretense of Pride is the Origin of Deception

Pretense is an attempt to make something that does not exist appear to be true, an ambitious or false claim that is not true. Pretense is a process issue because if the false claim is accepted, it leads to a decision point that produces a poor outcome. Much of the rest of this book is about separating reality from false claims.

How did rebellion enter the heart of Lucifer? Lucifer was an angel, a created being, with a heart, implying the existence of cognition, affections, and will. Lucifer was created with a disposition to please and serve God. He began to compare himself with other angels and with God. In comparing himself with other angels, he looked pretty good. He became full of himself and concluded he deserved a higher office. He desired to be like God, who created him. He said in his heart, "I will ascend to heaven; I will exalt my throne above the stars of God; I will sit upon the mount of assembly in the utmost north. I will ascend above the heights of the clouds; I will make myself like the most High" (Isaiah 14:12-17). Satan claimed he would be like God. It is the ultimate pretense, but it had a very poor outcome for Satan. He was thrown out of heaven. At some future point, he will be condemned to hell for eternity (Jude 1:1-10, Revelation 20:10).

Logic suggests any created being will be less than the being who created it. But because of remarkable beauty, pride entered Satan's heart. Pride overpowered knowledge, logic, and wisdom (Isaiah 14:11-15, Ezekiel 28:11-18). Pride distracted Satan from serving God and focused all his attention on serving self. At that point, "iniquity and guilt were found in you" (Ezekiel 28:15-18). Satan had a relationship with God, but pride overpowered his relationship. Pride renders knowledge and wisdom ineffective. Pride resists instruction. Pride desires power! This is an example of evil desire discussed in the next chapter. Power may be used to benefit mankind, but it has been used many times to enslave mankind. Power must be used in conjunction with grace, mercy, love, and truth to benefit mankind. Only the God of the universe, the God of the Holy Bible, possesses all these qualities all the time.

People easily become drunk with power. Most of us have observed someone intoxicated. We refer to them as being "under the influence of alcohol." A person "under the influence" is no longer in charge of his thoughts, speech, or behavior. Alcohol is in charge. In this context, alcohol is simply a tool of Satan, a tool that alters decision-making. Pride functions in a similar fashion. When someone is full of pride and drunk with power, they function similarly to someone under the influence of alcohol. Pride and power are in charge. The person is no longer in charge of his thoughts, speech, or behavior. His sin nature has taken charge. Paul writes about sin taking charge in the book of Romans (7:15-17). Paul states he is confused by his own thinking and behavior because instead of doing what his mind desires, he does what his sin nature/flesh dictates. This defies common sense, but unfortunately, it is true. Paul is saying that his disposition to be disobedient is stronger than his mind or his will to accomplish what he desires to do. This is the process issue that prompted Thomas Jefferson to have a sexual relationship with a slave girl. My speculation is that Jefferson knew he was behaving poorly but was unable to stop himself. This is known as the law of sin, the part of human nature that yields to temptation and resists God.

Pride is a complex and insidious tool of Satan. Pride is one of the seven deadly sins. Pride overcoming wisdom suggests that Lucifer had the capacity to choose between serving God and serving himself. This is similar to Eve and Adam having the capacity to choose in the garden. Satan was deceived! Now his evil desire is to deceive the rest of us. He hates God and anyone who follows and serves God.

How did pride originate? The narrative suggests it was taking his focus from serving God, focusing on his wisdom and beauty, and having thoughts like "how wonderful I am." This process spawned an evil desire to be like God. Lucifer's plan to be like God was not a solo mission. One-third of the other angels supported his plan by agreeing with Lucifer. The whole bunch was thrown out of heaven (Revelation 12:4, 9). It seems these angels became the demons that serve Satan by oppressing and deceiving man (Acts 10:38, I Timothy 4:1). These events set a precedent for the rest of creation, for you, and for me. Everyone who agrees with Lucifer/ Satan serves Satan in the matter upon which there is agreement.

In summary, we have a story about God, angels, Satan, and demons having conflict about who was going to be in charge of things. Who is going to oversee things is often what conflict is all about. It is about power. Pride and power are the process issues that underlie playground disputes, marital conflict, political divides, cancel culture, wars, and other misfortunes of life. Pride is the process issue that fuels much of these conflicts (Colossians 2:6-8).

Pride has an infinite number of manifestations. There are as many examples of pride as people with different fingerprints. Here are a few examples that draw people into the abyss of pride: clothing, personal appearance, houses, cars, boats, motorcycles, horses, dogs, cats, property, knowledge, college degrees, money, power, and anything a human being can accumulate to prove he is wiser, smarter, richer, or more powerful than his neighbor. Pride demands we compare ourselves with others. Pride can be a defense against shame for people living in poverty. It can be a stimulus for anger about life being unfair. It can separate a person from God by having too much or too little. Pride is never satisfied because Satan is driving the desire. His desire is for you and me to become full of pride because he knows pride moves us away from being dependent on God.

The whole concept of pride is a deception. "We came into this world hungry and naked. We brought nothing with us. The material things we acquire are all blessings received through the grace of God. We deserved none of it. We leave the world with nothing. The only thing we inherit and own as a possession during our life is our sin."[63]

Pride has serious limitations. Pride will not extend your life. It will not produce love, joy, and peace. It will not produce satisfaction or contentment. It will not help you discover your purpose in life. Pride will not result in following Jesus. It will not get you to heaven. The 49th Psalm addresses pride associated with the accumulation of wealth. A prideful man is compared to the beast that perishes. "He lives a brutish life and dies a brutish death."[64] Pride is foolishness. It is described as follows: "How foolish is it to account yourself a better man than another, only because your dunghill is a little bigger than his?"[65] Dunghills? Really? Do you know what a dunghill is? Can anything be more foolish? Well.... yes. What makes pride so foolish is the process of taking one's focus off Christ and putting it on self, thinking you are God or do not need God because of all the money or stuff you have accumulated.

There is a choice for each person. Accept the gift of salvation through

63 The Treasury of David, Volume I, pg. 411, a paraphrase of commentary on Psalm 51:3 by Samuel Page

64 ibid, pg. 372, commentary on Psalm 49:12 by Charles Spurgeon

65 ibid, pg. 382, commentary on Psalm 49:18 by Ezekial Hopkins

Christ, have your sin transferred to Christ, leave this life debt free, and spend eternity with Jesus. Or cling to your sin, take your sin with you, remember your sin forever, and experience separation from God for eternity in hell. It would seem to be an easy choice. But it is not easy. The process of deception makes it the most difficult decision of your life!

Below is a list of indicators that pride may be an issue in your life. Check each one that applies to you.

____Pride seeks power to control.
____Pride is reluctant to accept help.
____Pride cannot admit a mistake.
____Pride never asks forgiveness.
____Pride talks down to others.
____Pride has to win.
____Pride always justifies its own position.
____Pride must be heard.
____Pride keeps a record of wrongs.
____Pride is critical and condemning.
____Pride has to have the last word.
____Pride does not acknowledge another perspective.

If you checked only one of the above, chances are good you are denying the reality that other statements apply to you. If you do not check any of the above, you are in denial. How is pride working in your life? If you are unable to discern an example of pride, ask your spouse or closest friend to assist you. It's there somewhere, but because deception is so effective, you may need impartial collaboration to find it.

Can you think of examples of pride having a positive impact on your interpersonal relationships? Can you think of examples of pride having a negative influence? Use a comprehensive concordance to examine the scriptures that have the word pride. Does your work on discerning the nature of pride change your thoughts about this important process issue? Write your responses in the space below.

____

____

____

____

____

If you are a Christian, are you able to keep your focus on Jesus as you cope with the stress of life, or do you become distracted? If you are not Christian, what are your thoughts about the narrative that describes the fall of Lucifer? Have you been caught in the trap of comparing yourself to others (II Corinthians 10:12)? What thoughts fill your mind when you think you are better than others? What thoughts fill your mind when you see yourself as less attractive, less intelligent, or less successful than others? Is either comparison helpful? Where did these thoughts originate? Are they related to pride? Write your answers below.

____

____

____

____

____

The account of Adam and Eve in the Garden of Eden is the second recorded deception. Adam was created upright (Ecclesiastes 7:29). Prior to eating the fruit, Adam and Eve were focused on their relationship to each other, to God, and tending the garden. This pleased God, as it fulfilled His plan for creation. Eve turned her attention from God to herself; pride overcame knowledge; she had thoughts and fantasies of being like God. Thoughts produced desire, and evil desire produced disobedience. Adam took his attention from God and put it on himself, thinking he would lose Eve. These thoughts produced evil desire to remain with her, and again, evil desire produced disobedience. He ate the fruit given to him by Eve.

The following pattern: **distraction** leading to **confusion** leading to **deception** producing evil desire leading to disobedience producing consequences, is strikingly similar to what happened to Lucifer. Distraction occurs when a person entertains thoughts, beliefs, mental images/fantasies, that are contrary to God's word. These thoughts or fantasies separate a person from God. Separation results in loss of protection. This process can happen in the blink of an eye or over a prolonged period of time. Disobedience starts in the mind (James 1:13-15). It can be a very subtle process. Read Rachel Scott's description of her experience of deception with tobacco.[66]

66 The journals of Rachel Scott by Beth Nimmo, page 64, a journal entry, Rachel was the first student murdered in the Columbine High School shooting.

"The traces of smoke the cigarette leaves, is a soft string of silk.
It flows through the thin air Creating its unpredictable path.
It seems to be pleasant to the touch But it is only an illusion:
Your hands and thoughts
will never grasp its form.
The cloud of smoke
You exhale from your body Has a solid tone of haze.
It has no appealing form
It creates no beautiful path. It is released from your lungs and with no lacking,
It leaves your presence.
The cigarette has deceived you.
You created this beautiful image in your mind
of the smoke that would dance off your lips.
But you are wrong And like the smoke I will leave you staining your body with blackness and tar…."

What associations/ideas come to your mind from these words:

1. Smoke, a soft string of silk, a symbol for something, what does it represent?
2. The path of smoke is unpredictable.
3. The pleasant nature of smoke is an illusion.
4. Our hands and thoughts will never grasp its form.
5. The cigarette has deceived you.
6. Like the smoke, I will leave you (whom is she referring to?)
7. Blackness and tar (what do they symbolize?) Write your responses below.

____

____

____

____

____

Consider the process of distraction in the Garden of Eden and connect them to Rachel's words. The woman first, and then Adam, was unable to grasp the evil nature of the images formed in their minds. Eve apparently was fantasizing about being like God; Adam, what life would be like without Eve.

These kinds of fantasies are always an illusion, similar to Rachel's thoughts about the smoke of a cigarette. How quickly your mind alters perception and creates illusions to take the place of reality! Satan does not waste time; he seems to know the best point of attack for each of us. His presence always leaves a stain.

The stain on Adam and Eve was pervasive. It started with separation from God. They began to fear God, and He allowed the doors of their minds to be open to the influence of Satan. Their disposition toward pleasing God turned into a disposition toward sin. Under demonic influence, they began to have new thoughts: something is wrong with being naked, we must cover ourselves; new feelings: confusion, guilt, shame, fear, hurt, sadness, disappointment; and new behaviors: hiding from God, blaming God, blaming each other, and hurting each other. During these moments of confusion and conflict, they learned by experience the differences between good and evil, blessing and calamity (Genesis 3:5). Satan had said the fruit would make them like God. What a deception! He said they wouldn't die. They did not die physically but rather experienced a profound change in their nature characterized by separation from God and rebellion against His authority. They died to relationship with God. What happened in the Garden of Eden set a pattern for all subsequent generations. The nature of man turned from being oriented toward God to being oriented to sin.[67] We all continue to experience the consequences of Adam's deception in the garden. Adam had no clue about the consequences of his behavior.

Thinking about the process issue of distraction brings an interesting question to mind. Was Jesus ever distracted? For example, when the Holy Spirit led Jesus into the wilderness for 40 days and 40 nights, during which time He was tempted by Satan, was He ever distracted from his relationship with the Father? Was He ever distracted by Satan's temptations? Scripture only records three temptations by Satan during the forty-day period. The response of Jesus to each of these temptations is immediate and relies on the Word of God (Matthew 4:1-11). Scripture also informs that everything Jesus spoke and did came from the Father (John. 5:19-20, 12:44-50). Jesus was in constant communication with the Father. These scriptures in the books of Matthew and John suggest that Jesus was not distracted from his relationship with the Father.

You and I may not be perfect in our effort to maintain our focus on our relationship with Jesus. But the relationship between Jesus and the Father

67 www.withchrist.org, Free Will vs. Volition by Dan Smedra

provides an example for us to work at following (Matthew 16:24-26). We must guard against distraction. Distraction can be very subtle and yet deadly when it leads to confusion and deception. The way to prevent distraction is to maintain our focus on Jesus while we are at work, at play, and interacting with people God brings into our lives. We focus on what we are doing while being aware of Jesus being there with us…asking for spiritual direction as necessary. Jesus is always with us because He lives in the heart of every believer. We are prone to forget Jesus because of distraction going on around us. When we practice the presence of Christ in day-to-day life, the tasks in life become easier and are accomplished with fewer bumps and bruises (Matthew 11:28-30, Philippians 2:12-13). Having less emotional and spiritual bruising is a blessing we receive when following Jesus. Ask Jesus to remind you of this every morning as you start your day. Ask what He is doing where you are and what you can do to serve Him.

What are the distractions in your life? Write your answers below.

____

____

____

____

____

The Desire of Eve for Her Husband

Desire is the fourth word in sequence describing the process of deception. The word **desire** sounds intriguing. Doesn't that word have something to do with sex? Maybe! The word desire makes its first appearance in scripture in the third chapter of Genesis. It is used to describe the desire of Eve for her husband (Genesis 3:16). Desire refers to an inward craving manifested outwardly by reaching or stretching forth to obtain what is desired. The word desire is one of several words in Scripture that has opposite meanings.

The positive connotation implies a gracious purpose, a good object being in view, with the idea of having the resolve to reach the desired object or goal (Philippians 3:14). This type of desire is established by God. The effort in reaching for and obtaining the "prize" is pleasing to God.

The negative connotation is evil desire. Evil desire "gives birth to sin," and "sin, when fully matured, brings forth death" (James 1:13-15). The word death in this scripture could mean spiritual death or physical death. **Satan will steal and destroy whatever is made available to him.**

The narrative in Genesis 3:16 does not discuss specifically what Eve is craving from Adam. The Hebrew word used to translate desire is *teshuqah.* It is only used three times in the Old Testament. Two other words, lust and covet, convey a similar meaning as desire. When you look up all the scriptures that have the word desire, lust, or covet in a Bible concordance, you will discover the range of circumstances in which these words are used. The evil aspect is a little scary! Here is a brief sample of both:

Desire/the Godly aspect: (Psalm 51:6) "Behold, you desire truth in the inner being; make me therefore to know wisdom in my inmost heart."

Desire/the evil aspect: (Mark 4:19) "Then the cares and anxieties of the world and distractions of the age, and the pleasure and delight and false glamour and deceitfulness of riches, and the craving and passionate desire for other things creep in and choke and suffocate the Word (of God) and it becomes fruitless."

Lust/an evil craving: (I John 2:16) "For all that is in the world—the lust of the flesh [craving for sensual gratification] and the lust of the eyes [greedy longings of the mind] and the pride of life [assurance in one's own resources or in the stability of earthly things] these do not come from the Father but from the world [itself]."

Covet/an evil craving: (Micah 2:2) "They covet fields and seize them, and houses and take them away; they oppress and crush a man and his house, a man and his inheritance."

Eve's desire for Adam was instituted by God, indicating it is positive in nature, a Godly desire (Genesis 3:16). There are different views on how *teshuqah* should be translated in Genesis 3:16. Perhaps she was craving companionship but possibly more (Genesis 2:18). Perhaps she was craving protection, provision, and an intimate loving relationship. Perhaps she experienced desire for an intimate sexual relationship that would birth a man to fulfill the prophecy re: her seed crushing the seed of Satan. Perhaps she desired all those things. It is not known for certain.

The second use of *teshuqah* is to describe the **desire** that sin has for Cain (Genesis 4:7). This desire is qualitatively different. It is what we would think of as evil desire. It also is associated with an inward craving and reaching forth but for something entirely different. Evil desire is reaching for the soul of Cain and for his eternal spirit, wanting to capture both, to bring both into his kingdom! The phrase "sin crouches at your door" suggests a metaphor for Satan crouching and waiting at the door of Cain's mind/heart. Notice: sin must be invited in. Sin patiently waits at the door of our minds/hearts for an invitation to enter.

The third use of *teshuqah* is when Solomon's new bride describes the desire Solomon has for her (Song of Solomon 7:10). In the context of Solomon's description of her physical beauty and her willingness to give him her "love," it suggests a reference to desire for sexual love (S. Of S. 7:6-13). All this to say, there is some controversy about the use of *teshuqah* to describe Eve's desire for her husband.[68, 69]

An interesting Internet article reviews a different interpretation of Eve's desire for her husband. It suggests a better translation than desire is "focused attention, relational devotion, or preoccupation of one lover for another."[70] This interpretation might include her having a preoccupation with emotional connection, protection, provision, sacrificial love, and a mutually satisfying sexual relationship. Those are preoccupations I have heard expressed repeatedly by wives during 40 years of counseling experience. Are the emotional and spiritual needs of wives in the twenty-first century any different from the needs of the first wife?

This interpretation also is consistent with the need women have for their husbands to lay down their lives for their wives as Christ laid down His life for the church (Ephesians 5:25). In other words, wives are preoccupied or have focused attention in the areas of emotional connection, protection, provision, sacrificial love, and sexual fulfillment. When a husband meets her needs in these areas, she develops reverence for her husband and opens herself to him emotionally and sexually. The two become one (Genesis 2:24, Matthew 19:5-9, Ephesians 5:31-33). When this does not happen, the passion fades, and the couple may remain married but often lead parallel lives instead of becoming one. When a married person experiences desire for romance outside the marriage relationship, evil desire has replaced Godly desire.

Do you believe evil exists? Do you relate to the concept of evil desire? Are you a survivor of evil experiences? Have you committed evil acts? If you believe evil exists, what are you doing to combat it? Write your answers in the space below.

____

____

____

____

---

68 biblestudytools.com, Beautiful Lessons in Love from the Song of Solomon

69 findingtruthmatters.org, Is Erotica in the Bible? A Fresh Look at an Old Way of Looking at the Song of Solomon

70 margmowczko.com, Does teshuqah Mean Desire or Devotion in Genesis 3:16

Think of examples of desire in your life that originated in the kingdom of Satan and also the Kingdom of God. Compare the outcomes. Write your responses below.

____

____

____

____

____

The evil aspect of desire is degrading and scary for those who survive it. This will be discussed further in the chapter, *Intimacy with Evil,* and the chapters on Talk therapy.

Satan's Power Grid

Satan's evil desire to be like God sounds very much like the words the snake spoke to Eve in the Garden of Eden, "For God knows in the day that you eat of it (the fruit) your eyes will be opened, and you will be like God, knowing the difference between good and evil and blessing and calamity" (Genesis 3:5).

It is not unusual to want to be powerful like God. Children live out wanting to be powerful through fantasies of superheroes, internet games, sibling rivalry, bullying, and even sexual abuse (children sexually abusing other children). Internet games are particularly seductive for children, giving them a temporary sense of power. The game controller children hold in their hands gives them a temporary rush as they manipulate the screen to destroy things or rack up points to win a game.

For children who are abused in some way, playing the game may be the only part of their life where they can escape a profound sense of helplessness. Some of these children may fail to develop a sense of competence in relationships and life in general. As adults, their perception of life is influenced by fear. They are fearful of trusting God and people. They compensate by accruing power and controlling relationships through pride, anger, politics, greed, the courts, and a host of manipulative, deceptive practices. They are fools in the Biblical sense. King David describes these people in Psalm 53:1, 4: "The [empty-headed] fool has said in his heart, there is no God. Corrupt and evil are they, and doing abominable iniquity; there is none who does good… Have those who work evil no knowledge (no understanding)? They eat up my people as they eat bread; they do not call upon God." Charles Spurgeon has this commentary on these verses: "He who denies God is at bottom a coward, and in his infidelity, he is like the boy in the churchyard who 'whistles to keep his courage up.' When the wicked see the destruction of their fellows they may well quail. Mighty were the hosts which besieged Zion, but they were defeated, and their unburied carcasses proved the prowess of the God whose being they dared to deny."[71]

When I was a child, Superman was my hero, and I often dreamed of being able to fly like him. In the dream, I saw myself taking a small leap and suddenly being airborne, soaring over the countryside and people down below. I did not have other superpowers, only flying. No one else was flying in my dream. It was very puzzling to me in the dream that other people did not want to fly. My dreams about flying may have been an unconscious strategy to be powerful. Flying separated me from the mundane life people were experiencing below. My dream did not work in the real world. I was never able to fly. It was great while dreaming but helped very little during my day job being a child. Fantasies are fun and pleasure-filled but may not promote the development of healthy character. They frequently serve as an escape. Sometimes a temporary escape can be useful, even if it is only in your imagination. It can whisk you away from an experience that is unpleasant or hurtful for a period of respite, but eventually, **you must learn to cope with reality.**

Children develop and refine the skill of being powerful in relationships. The need to be powerful is often observed in sibling rivalry. My brother, four years my senior, established an artificial dividing line in the backseat of our car. If any part of my body went over his "wall' onto his side of the backseat, there was hell to pay. My part of the rivalry was to invade his wall at every opportunity. This gave us something to do on the trip. During adolescence, the desire to be powerful is often acted out through rebellion against authority, especially the authority of parents.

As adults, the craving to be in charge like God is often real but unspoken. If you start to talk about being God in our culture, you're likely to get a referral for a psychiatric evaluation. Although people do not talk much about wanting to be God, many spend much of their lives using various strategies to become as powerful as God. The fact that no one has been successful at becoming God does not deter their efforts to be the first. Perhaps that is

71 The Treasury of David, Psalm 53, commentary by Spurgeon on verse 5

because each of us thinks we have a better strategy than all who have gone before. It may be secondary to multiple episodes of helplessness during our formative years, so controlling others becomes an offensive weapon. Or it could be a combination of many other factors, all of which are **deceptions**. We do everything possible to get friends or family to think and behave the way we want them to think and behave. This does not work, or it works poorly, resulting in the deterioration of relationships. Satan's cash register goes "ka-ching" each time he makes a sale. No one can afford the spiritual price of pursuing power.

Did you have dreams or fantasies as a child that helped you cope with the reality of life? What purpose did they have in your life? Are they continuing to influence you now that you are an adult? Are fantasies of being more powerful influencing your life choices? Write your answers to these questions in the space below.

____

____

____

____

____

The mind wants to avoid every aspect of past traumas, so it develops defenses.

Defenses or defense mechanisms is a term from the field of behavioral science that describes strategies of the mind, many unconscious, that protect from thoughts or emotions we want to avoid. If you think you are a good person without sin, your defenses are working well for you. They are on alert doing their job. However, it is a job that originates from Satan. They result in our relying on ourselves instead of relying on God, Jesus, and the Holy Spirit.

It is a rather strange idea that any person would want to protect himself from his own thoughts or emotions. The explanation for this connects to the paragraph above about evil. If we could see the evil in our own hearts, we would faint from fear, disgust, and revulsion. Then there is the evil that is directed at us from others, which can be overwhelming. The thoughts and emotions we have about evil experiences can be so painful they are rejected by our conscious mind. The mind protects itself from injury with these defense mechanisms. God allows this. He limits our response to evil in this way. God's desire is for us to confess our own evil deeds and rely on Him to process the evil perpetrated by others. This is accomplished through prayer or meditation. Satan is crafty and subtle, but he is always in the hand of God (Romans 11:33-36). And God uses His hand to limit or end the evil deeds of this world.

Some common psychological defenses are **avoidance, repression, denial, rationalization, displacement, and projection.**[72] *Avoidance* is a defense mechanism that is often conscious. The person simply avoids situations that stimulate memories of the original experience. This is helpful to avoid anxiety or other emotions but leads to increasing restriction. *Repression* forces the thoughts or emotions into the unconscious part of the mind and prevents them from becoming conscious. However, bits and pieces of the repressed memory may leak out in the form of dreams and nightmares. Complete repression prevents the person from processing the experience.

Denial is a simple refusal to accept reality as it exists. For example, refusing to accept that chest pain could indicate a heart attack. *Rationalization* changes reality by offering excuses for thinking or behavior not normally acceptable. This may occur consciously or evolve into a lifestyle that is relegated to the unconscious.

Displacement is shifting the direction of an impulse, often aggression, from the desired target onto a helpless person or object which serves as a substitute for the original. *Projection* occurs when unwanted thoughts or feelings are projected onto another person where they are perceived as emanating, often as a threat, from that person.

More than one defense mechanism may operate in order to cope with a particular experience, making it difficult to understand a person's thinking or behavior.

Discernment, as used in this book, refers to **spiritual discernment.** The definition in the amplified translation of First Corinthians 2:15 is perfect for our study: "The spiritual man tries all things, [he examines, investigates, inquires into, questions, and discerns all things]." The purpose of the investigation is to determine the origin and validity of whatever is being considered. In the Garden of Eden, the serpent presented ideas that contradicted the word of God. Had Eve investigated and questioned what was happening to her with her husband or with God, she might have avoided being deceived. She could have avoided the consequences.

Discernment is an investigation that is facilitated by the Holy Spirit. When the Holy Spirit is in charge, we need to put aside all prejudice and

72 www.psychologistworld.com, 31 Psychological Defense Mechanisms Explained

bias. We should be open to the outcome of our investigation. Putting aside bias requires prayer and empowerment by the Spirit. The validity of facts is determined by checking them against the Word of God. Emotions such as fear, guilt, shame, and sadness need to be set aside temporarily, or they will prevent discernment. The ultimate decision should manifest love and bring peace to us in the process.

A decision usually leads to action, often causing confusion to evaporate. The action should glorify Jesus. There are only two possible sources for anything that is spiritual in nature: the Kingdom of God or the Kingdom of Satan. Discernment identifies which kingdom is at work. This is very helpful in decision-making. Discernment may lead to a decision to stay where you are or switch kingdoms. After coming to a decision point, it is wise to check your discernment with other spirit-led Christians.

There is a "catch" in the process of spiritual discernment. This is a fly in the ointment, so to speak, which is explained in First Corinthians. Paul is saying in First Corinthians 2:9-15 that spiritual truths are revealed to individuals through the Holy Spirit.

When a believer accepts Christ, the Holy Spirit dwells in him. Nonbelievers do not have the Holy Spirit. Paul refers to nonbelievers as the "natural non-spiritual man" (I Corinthians 2:14). Paul writes, "But the natural, non-spiritual man does not accept or welcome or admit into his heart the gifts and teachings and revelations of the Spirit of God, for they are folly (meaningless nonsense) to him; and he is incapable (of knowing them of progressively recognizing, understanding, and becoming better acquainted with them) because they are spiritually discerned and estimated and appreciated."

Paul is saying that a person without the Holy Spirit cannot understand or recognize the truths (the process issues that God has created to guide our lives), including the teachings of Christ. Consequently, nonbelievers are not capable of spiritual discernment. Without spiritual discernment, it becomes very difficult for a nonbeliever to identify the process of deception. This has nothing to do with intelligence. Nonbelievers may be brilliant in the areas of art, science, technology, engineering, and math. But they are not capable of determining they are living in the kingdom of Satan. They are not capable of making a spiritual discernment about the origin of a particular issue, whether it comes from Satan or from God.

However, nonbelievers do have a conscience. They do not have all the divine teachings, but their decisions and behavior "show that the essential requirements of the Law are written in their hearts and are operating there" (Romans 2:13-16). This is apparent as early as the story of Cain and Abel from the fourth chapter of Genesis. Cain knew he was disobedient in his offering to God and the murder of his brother Abel (Genesis 4:3-10). Having a conscience is not the same as being indwelt by the Holy Spirit. The Holy Spirit empowers the believer to submit to God and resist the temptations of evil.

This fly in the ointment is a huge process issue that often is not recognized by people in the church or by nonbelievers. This process issue is very difficult for a nonbeliever to accept. But this is the principal reason, the process issue, that divides people on topics of morality, starting with minor things such as driving the speed limit and progressing to major questions, such as voting practices, honesty, divorce, abortion, and sexual morality.

This helps us understand why Jesus said, "Do you suppose that I have come to give peace upon the earth? No, I say to you, but rather division; for from now on in one house there will be five divided [among themselves] three against two and two against three. They will be divided, father against son and son against father, mother against daughter and daughter against mother, mother-in-law against her daughter-in-law, and daughter in law against her mother-in-law" (Luke 12:51-53).

The word of God always divides. This greatly complicates communication between believers and nonbelievers on moral issues. In frustration and anger, Christians will say uncomplimentary, even hateful things, to unbelievers about morals. They use dissonant words and phrases such as "abortion is murder" or "you are going to hell." These words are unloving, judgmental, and unlikely to start a useful conversation.

The result is the creation of greater division and the end of communication. Communication is further complicated because believers sometimes have areas of their life where they have not yet utilized the process of discernment, so they may actually agree with nonbelievers on a particular moral issue. This can be more than confusing. When there is confusion about moral issues, Satan has insinuated himself in the process in some way, because Scripture states that God is not a God of confusion (I Corinthians 14:33).

A nonbeliever can overcome this obstacle by seeking the Lord. There is a condition: "But without faith it is impossible to please and be satisfactory to Him. For whoever would come near to God must necessarily believe that God exists and that He is the rewarder of those who earnestly and diligently seek him [out]" (Hebrews 11:6). If you want to be indwelt by Christ, simply pray the following: "Jesus, I have been disobedient. Forgive me. I want to change. I want a relationship with you. Please come into my heart and lead me in the Christian life." This prayer is not magic. It must reflect a change in your heart, representing disgust with prior sinful patterns of your life (Job 42:1-6, John 10:7-15, Romans 3:23-26). "God prepares all for heaven whom heaven has been prepared for."[73] God desires to prepare you for eternal life in heaven.

Jesus has already prepared a place for every believer in heaven (John 14:1-3).[74]

The process of preparation is exciting and life-changing. For men, it is the only path to complete manhood.[75,76] For women, it is the only approach to producing fulfillment and true femininity (Proverbs 31:10-31, Colossians 2:1-10, I Peter 3:1-6).[77] It results in your being more Christlike as your faith matures. It begins by inviting Jesus into your heart.

Which kingdom are you in most of the time? What are the process issues that lead you to spend time in that kingdom? Do you believe that God exists? Do you believe that God will reward you when you earnestly and diligently seek Him? Do you remember what diligence requires? Answer in the space below.

____

____

____

____

____

This chapter on the D words brings the process of deception out of the darkness and into the light. Distraction can be as subtle as expressways becoming parking lots during rush hour. Or it can come on like the whirlwind when someone you love is diagnosed with terminal cancer. Distraction deceives by producing confusion about choices. The purposes of deception are threefold: to steal, kill, and destroy (John 10:10). That is the triple threat

---

73 Matthew Henry's Commentary, Volume 4, commentary on Ezekiel 11:19-20

74 Crosswalk.com, Did Christ really 'Go to Prepare a Place' for Me?

75 The Quest for Authentic Manhood by Robert M. Lewis

76 King David is an example of an imperfect man yet described as a Man after God's own heart (I Samuel 13:14). Much of David's life is chronicled in the Book of II Samuel and the Book of Psalms.

77 See discussion of the Hebrew word teshuqah/desire in the earlier part of this chapter under "Desire of Eve for her Husband".

that comes from living in the kingdom of Satan. It includes stealing the dreams you have for your life of good health, a family, and satisfying employment. If left unchecked, it will destroy the American Dream.

There are many different roads that lead to evil. There are warning signs on these roads, but people are going so fast they do not see them. In the next chapter, we examine the beginning of deception's influence on humanity. We must learn to be careful, or we will find ourselves deceived. Each deception is like landing on a chute in the board game of Chutes and Ladders. Each deception takes you farther and farther from your goal… of reaching the American Dream.

The Beginning of Everything

The beginning of something is always fascinating, particularly when it becomes something that is unpredictable. The flight experiments of the Wright brothers laid the foundation for space travel. The microscope resulted in a new branch of science, microbiology, and led to the development of antibiotics. A single sperm fertilizing a single egg produces two cells, four, eight, sixteen—the process continues until a small but fully-formed person is created in the womb. Who knew?

This chapter focuses on beginnings. It starts with a brief account of my own spiritual beginning. But more importantly, it gives the reader an opportunity to examine the beginning of everything.

My spiritual beginning is relatively unimportant because if I refuse to walk in the paths God has prepared for me, He will raise up another to accomplish His purposes. I was blessed to be born into a Christian family. I attended Sunday School from kindergarten onward, but in all those years, not one teacher asked me to accept Jesus into my heart.

After my first year of high school, I went to a leadership training camp for members of Hi-Y, a social service club sponsored by the YMCA. On the last evening of the camp, there was a candlelight service where we were asked to dedicate our lives to Christ. I simply accepted the invitation. I felt a sense of peace I had not experienced before. Joining the body of Christ is so simple. Accept the invitation! This invitation from God has many different manifestations. God is so creative! Have you had one or more invitations to accept Jesus into your heart? How did the invitations arrive? What did they look like? Answer these questions in the space below.

____

____

____

____

____

Accepting Jesus does not mean a trouble-free life. It rains on the just and unjust alike (Matthew 5:44-45). I have been deeply hurt by other Christians and unbelievers on more than one occasion. But I did not have to endure these hurts by myself. I have learned that Jesus hurts when I hurt. And He desires I bring my heart to Him for healing. "In all things God works for the good of those who love Him and are called according to his purpose" (Romans 8:28). Examples of this process are provided in the chapters on talk therapy.

Suggesting the first three chapters of Genesis is the beginning of everything may sound a bit like hyperbole, but it is not. Please read the entire book of Genesis and answer the questions before discounting this apparent exaggeration.

I hope you are convinced about the importance of process issues at this point in the book. The origin of many process issues is described in the 50 chapters found in the book of Genesis.

Genesis is a Greek word meaning *origin* or *beginning*. The first chapter describes the creation of the heavens and earth, plants, and animals. Chapter 2 is a short elaboration on creation, including the early lives of Adam and his mate, who was given the name *Woman* (later named Eve). Chapter 3 is the story of the fall of Adam and Eve. Everyone has a story. In these three chapters is the beginning of your story. The other 47 chapters of Genesis detail the rise of early civilization, the generations of humanity from Adam to Christ, the universal flood, and the history of the early Hebrew church founded by Abraham.

If you have not read the first three chapters of Genesis or it has been a long time since reading them, read them now before continuing. Remember that a process issue is a belief, event, emotion, physiological process, or spiritual process that leads to a decision point.

The God of the Holy Bible is complex. Although the first three chapters of Genesis cover the beginning of everything, there is too much in the rest of Genesis to review here. My hope is the text that follows will awaken your interest to read the rest of the book of Genesis. The process issues that relate to God describe His character, who He is, His personality, and how He wants to relate to you. The God who created the universe wants to have a personal relationship with you. That fact alone is amazing.

Before you examine the things God has done, it is helpful to appreciate who He is. The following paragraphs describe the attributes contributing to His character.

The Attributes of God

The first is **grace**. The Hebrew word for the grace of God is *chen*.[78] It has the following meanings: favor, grace, graciousness, kindness, beauty, pleasantness, charm, attractiveness, loveliness, and affectionate regard. The grace of God is often simply defined as merit and favor which we do not deserve. Grace and **love** work together to act (John 3:16). It is out of the grace of God and the love of God that He creates, communicates, and saves His creation. He wants us to know Him personally and intimately. He wants us to know His character, His attributes, His thoughts, His plans, and His blessings for us.

He desires that we know what happened at the beginning so we do not engage in unending speculation about creation (Colossians 2:28). God communicates about the beginning of everything primarily through the process of using words, which are symbols that represent something. These words represent the things God did. They represent the things He spoke into existence. He wants these things for us because when we truly know Him, we will honor Him, desire to know more of Him, and want to be in a relationship with Him. And when we truly know Him, we will fall in love with Him. He wants a love relationship with us, an **agape** love relationship.

God sees us through a worldview of love (John 3:16, I John 4:6-21)). This is the kind of love, affection, goodwill, and benevolence that thinks first of the well-being of others. It edifies and builds and encourages others to grow to maturity (I Corinthians 8:1-3, Ephesians 4:11-16). When we love God, then we will talk about Him and tell others about the many blessings that come through our relationship with Him. We cannot edify or build up God. He is perfect, complete, without blemish. But we can bless God by our thoughts and actions. The Greek word to bless is *eulogeo,* meaning "to speak well of, praise, bless abundantly, invoke a benediction, and give thanks."

When God speaks, He always speaks the **truth**. The word for truth in Hebrew is *emeth*, defined as follows: "certainty, stability, trustworthiness, and truth. *Emeth* conveys a sense of dependability, firmness, and reliability. Truth is, therefore, something upon which a person may confidently stake his life." David prayed that God's truth would continually preserve Him (Psalm 40:11). Scripture speaks of men of truth (Exodus 18:21), the law of truth (Malachi

---

78 Definitions of Hebrew words are taken from Strong's Exhaustive Concordance unless otherwise noted

2:6), the true God or [God of truth] (Jeremiah 10:10), Jesus being the truth (John 14:6). The idea of Jesus being the truth stems from Scripture. "And the Word (Christ) became flesh (human, incarnate) and tabernacled (fixed His tent of flesh, lived a while) among us; and we actually saw His glory (His honor, His majesty), such glory as an only begotten son receives from his father, full of grace (favor, loving kindness) and truth" (John 1:14). The word "tabernacled" is often translated as "dwelt."[79] It is a reference to God dwelling with humanity for a period of approximately 33 years during the life of Jesus. Jesus humbled Himself by taking human form and humbled Himself further by being crucified as a sacrifice for our sins (Philippians 2:5-11).

Interestingly, *emeth* is spelled with the first, middle, and last letters of the Hebrew alphabet. Hebrew rabbis concluded that truth upholds the first and the last of God's creation and everything in between. These elaborations on the word truth perfectly describe the word that God speaks. Do you think words like this are more likely to originate from a divine spiritual being or a random process such as evolution? What would words evolve from? Did words like this evolve from grunts?

Since God talks about things as they really are, we would be wise to listen to what He has to say. His words originate from **wisdom**. The word for wisdom in Hebrew is *chokmah* meaning "wisdom, skillfulness, whether in the artistic sense of craftsmanship or the moral sense skills for living correctly."[80] This noun occurs about 150 times and is found in all sections of the Old Testament. Biblical wisdom unites God, the source of all understanding, with daily life, where the principles of proper living are put into practice. Therefore, one is encouraged to make God the starting point in any quest for wisdom and to seek Godly wisdom above all else to live successfully (Psalm 111:10, Proverbs 4:5-9).

God is **just**. His instructions, decisions, and consequences are always just. They are based on truth, wisdom, and fairness. They are distributed equally among all persons. God shows no partiality (Acts 10:34– 35). Public administration of justice should be equally fair, and public laws consistent with divine law. The Pharisees violated these principles in the treatment of widows in the courts (Matthew 23:14). Do you think we have Pharisees in our culture today? Who are they? What are they doing? Write your answers in the space below.

---

79 Study note on John 1:14 from the Spirit Filled Life Bible

80 The New Ungers Bible Dictionary, revised 1988

____

____

____

____

____

God is a God of **wrath**, which is a term not used much in today's culture. It is often used in discussions concerning God's anger in response to man's sin. In Biblical usage, it includes the idea of punishment for sin. God's wrath/ punishment is tempered by His love, holiness, and mercy. The wrath of man is rarely moderated by either love, holiness, or mercy. Instead, the anger of men is destructive. Review the section on anger in the chapter "Lessons from Jack" for more details about anger.

God is **creative**. The wisdom of God is seen in every act of creation (Romans 1:20).

Consider the things that have been made and examine them. Learn about their workings and interrelationships. The things that have been made tell us about the God who made them. They tell us about His attributes and character. The beautiful things of nature are calling you to experience the attributes of God. God is inviting you to experience Him through His creation. Experiencing nature will lead you to the wisdom of God. Meditating on the things God created will lead you to God. Reflect on the following:

- The maternal instinct of each species reveals the love of God.
- Springtime, renewal reveals the joy of God.
- A wilderness lake at rest reveals the peace of God.
- A hummingbird consuming nectar reveals the patience of God.
- Attentiveness to the needs of creation reveals the kindness of God.
- The beauty of everything reveals the goodness of God.
- The stability of nature reveals the faithfulness of God.
- Falling snow reveals the gentleness of God.
- The natural order of things reveals limits and boundaries God sets to creation, including His creation of mankind.

If you meditate on these nine character traits/fruits of the spirit, you may have entirely different associations to each one. For example, a river finding its way to the ocean demonstrates the patience of God.

The character traits above and their manifestations in nature represent a spiritual approach to recognizing the relationship of God to nature. Many people have a spiritual experience in nature but fail to recognize its true source. When you look at a beautiful flower, you see a reflection of God. What does the flower say to you about the God who created it? Consider the strength of a horse; it is a clue about the strength of its creator. **Nature cannot be silent about the one who created it.** Is there any doubt concerning the creativity of God? There is also a factual, knowledge-based approach leading to the same conclusion above. The book, *A Closer Look at The Evidence*, explores the science of created things. For example, it was noted in the section on Darwin he was unable to reconcile "parasitic wasps…feeding within the living bodies of caterpillars". A study of this phenomenon has revealed the eggs of the wasp injected into the larvae of the pest caterpillar are covered with a virus that prevents the caterpillar from maturing as well as impairing the caterpillar's immune system. These processes prevent the caterpillar larvae from maturing into adults. As a result, they do less damage to crops. When the wasps mature, they kill the larvae. This is a good example of Nature/God providing for nature while setting limits and providing balance to natural processes.[81] If God provides for nature out of His creativity and love, what do you think He is willing to do for you?

The wisdom of God collaborates with the creativity of God to benefit everyone. The glory of God is revealed in the creation. Glory refers to praise and honor given to a person for the things he has accomplished. Who has accomplished more than the God of creation?

In contrast to God, Satan has no creative power. Satan has power but uses it to steal, kill, and destroy the things created by God (John 10:10). God creates to provide an abundant life; Satan perverts everything for his own evil purposes. In social theory, this is somewhat similar to the concept of entropy. Satan masterminds and orchestrates much of the disorder and chaos the world brings. Through deception, Satan is often successful at distracting us and stimulating us to blame God for the calamities of life.

The complex relationships that exist between plants and animals in their natural environments were put in place by God. These relationships are known as an ecosystem. Naturalist Aldo Leopold describes this interaction in his article "Thinking Like a Mountain." This insight came to him after he shot a female wolf with pups. Leopold writes:

---

81 A Closer Look at the Evidence, by Richard and Tina Kleiss, comments on ecology for June 25.

"We reached the old wolf in time to watch a fierce green fire dying in her eyes. I realized then, and I've known ever since, that there was something new to me in those eyes. It was something known only to her and the mountain. I was young then, and full of trigger itch. I thought that because fewer wolves meant more deer, that no wolves would mean hunter's paradise. But after seeing the green fire die, I sensed that neither the wolf nor the mountain agreed with such a view.

"Since then I have lived to see state after state extirpate its wolves. I have watched the face of many a new wolfless mountain and seen the south facing slopes wrinkle with a maze of new deer trails. I have seen every edible bush and seedling browsed first to anemic desuetude, and then to death. I have seen every edible tree defoliated to the height of a saddle horn. Such a mountain looks as if someone had given God a new pruning shears and forbid him all other exercise. In the end the starved bones of the hoped-for deer herd, dead of its own too much, bleach with the bones of the dead sage, or molder under the high lined junipers.

"I now suspect that just as a deer herd lives in mortal fear of its wolves, so does a mountain live in mortal fear of its deer."

Leopold developed wisdom through his observations of nature. He discovered everything is connected. The big question is this, who connected everything? Do you think a person could "die of his own too much?" How would that happen? Write your answers in the space below.

____

____

____

____

Have you seen the fire in the eye of the wolf? Take some time to google "pictures of wolves" and look for the fire that Leopold is describing. Think about the spirit of the wolf. How would you describe it in a single word? Is it a spirit of love, intensity, curiosity, fear, survival, savagery, or something else? Did the spirit of the wolf evolve, or was it put there deep within the wolf by God? Write your answers in the space below.

____

____

____

____

____

The observations of Leopold produced generations of young people concerned about the stewardship of creation. We are prone to forget it was God who created the land, plants, and animals… the ecosystem. It was God who created the wolf, the deer, and the mountain. It was God who created the interdependent relationships that govern the well-being of every created thing. The concept of stewardship was set out for Adam by the Creator in the Garden of Eden (Genesis 1:28, 2:15). Now you and I are the stewards. Are you acting as a steward?

There are also ecosystems in the microscopic realm. Research the mitochondria, the powerhouse of the cell, and discover its complex function in cellular life. Or choose any organ system: the eye, bone marrow, gastrointestinal system, or brain and central nervous system. Study their anatomy and physiology. The brain and spinal cord contain about 86 billion nerve cells and more than 40 different neurotransmitters. There are millions of interconnections. Are you surprised that it is difficult to find an antidepressant agent that targets the specific nerve cells related to depression or anxiety?[82]

Consider the organ systems that comprise your living body for what they are, the miracles of God. Do you think these organ systems and their physiological processes evolved, or were they instituted by a creative, intelligent being? You are a unique ecosystem, with each organ system working in concert with the others.

At this point, you may not understand everything you have read, but you do not have to understand everything in order to realize what is true. Most people do not understand the mathematical equations that maintain the solar system in balance, yet they accept the fact that the Earth and other planets orbit the sun. Learn to use your senses to experience the creation around you. Learn to use your mind to investigate and understand what your senses experience. When you do this, you will discover you are the most important part of the ecosystem. You are the pinnacle of creation. You are capable of reason, have complex emotions, recognize virtue, and have the capacity for a spiritual relationship with the Creator. These qualities separate you from the

82 verywellmmind.com, How Many Neurons Are in the Brain?

rest of creation. You are unique. You are made in the image of God (Genesis 1: 26–27). You are His treasured possession (Psalm 135:4).

God has dominion over everything because of His **power** (Romans 1:20, 11:33-36). There is nothing that compares to the power of God. When God speaks, it is certain to come to pass. God has power over nature (Psalm 48:1-14, Mark 4:35–41), death (Revelation 1:17-18), and nations (Psalm 47:7–8). God has power over everything. The power of God works together with His creativity and wisdom. His purposes cannot be thwarted (Job 42:1-2). In the book of Lamentations, the prophet Jeremiah writes, "Who is he who speaks and it comes to pass, if the Lord has not authorized and commanded it." The power of God charges and saturates His spoken Word (Hebrews 4:12). This has several different manifestations. He speaks with **authority** because He speaks the **truth** (Matthew 7:28–29, John 17:17). His Word is imparted "to give light to those who sit in darkness" (Luke 1:78-79). And the Word gives strength to His people in times of weakness (II Corinthians 12:7–10). It gives protection in times of war (Psalm 91:1–10, Ephesians 6:10-17). It replaces fear and anxiety with peace (John 14:27, Galatians 5:22, Philippians 4:7, I John 4:18).

Do you have peace in your life? Have you ever known anyone to seek counseling because of experiencing too much peace? No, it is anxiety for which people seek counseling. Learning how to stay in touch with the peace of God is one solution for being anxious.

The above blessings all come from being indwelt by Christ and the Holy Spirit. We gain access to the power of the Holy Spirit when we are indwelt by the Spirit of God. Not that we have the same creative power that God displays in the creation of the world, but we have the power to take authority over Satan and build the body of Christ. This power is part of how we prevail in the struggles of life. It is one of the keys of the kingdom of heaven (Matthew 16:18–19). God desires that we have this power because He knows we cannot do well without it (II Corinthians 12:7–10).

Many would be thrilled to spend an hour with the president of the United States because the presidency is a position of honor and power. Being president of the universe is the most fundamental and yet decisive position of power. Are you willing to spend time with the president of the universe in prayer? In study? In worship?

Nonbelievers deny the power of God. They imitate the creativity of God by creating all sorts of philosophical and intellectual theories to explain what they see in the world around them and the universe beyond (Colossians

2:8–9). They demand God explain His actions but refuse to study His Word, which would stimulate understanding and wisdom. Instead of recognizing the kingdom of God, they imitate Him by creating their own individual kingdoms at work, in their homes, in sports, and in politics. In these places, they seek and execute power. Power becomes their God. They become God in their tiny kingdoms while denying the existence of God who created and sustains them (Job 34:14–15). These tiny kingdoms always perish due to the absence of love, truth, and unity. They are like fireworks, flashy for a few moments and then disappearing into the blackness of night. They are known for conflict, division, destruction, and eventual demise (Numbers 16:1–35, Isaiah 40:17–31, Obadiah 1:1–9, 15). You cannot imitate God (Isaiah 14:1–32). It is chasing after the wind (Ecclesiastes 1:1-18). Have you ever been successful at catching the wind?

Perhaps you are wondering what to look for when reading the Bible. Short answer: Ask the Holy Spirit to reveal principles, promises, precautions, and personal application. These are the process issues that will change your life. There is a longer exposition of interpreting Scripture in the appendix.

Genesis 1 reviews some of the process issues important for successful living. There are 65 more books of the Bible that follow Genesis. Are you curious? All these are planted in a story of how God desires to relate to us. I use the word *plant* because as you notice each of these principles, nurture them, and model them, they will grow into a tree of life that produces fruit that satisfies your soul (Psalm 1: 1-3).

Communication is the oil that allows relationships to function smoothly. When we listen to God and talk with Him regularly, our relationship with God grows stronger and more intimate. This is a model for our relationships with our spouse, our children, and others. When we refuse to listen to God, our relationship with Him suffers. This always has a poor outcome. If we choose to stay disconnected, the spiritual part of our soul withers and dies. Does your ability to communicate with God parallel your ability to communicate with your spouse and children? If you communicated well with God, do you think your communication with others might improve? Rate your communication with God on a 1 to 10 scale. Rate communication with family members on a 1 to 10 scale. Are your ratings similar? Do you need to improve your communication skills? Answer these questions in the space below.

God is **relational**. It is difficult to talk about any aspect of God without focusing on His desire to be in a relationship with us. He does His part to maintain the relationship through creation itself, His Word (the Scriptures), the leading of the Holy Spirit, prayer, meditation, and other spiritual disciplines. Nothing can separate us from the love of God which is in Christ Jesus our Lord (Romans 8:38–39). Unlike our human friends/relatives, God continues to love and forgive despite our nonsensical behavior.

There are two process issues that work together and are so intimately related that it is difficult to tease them apart. These are **agape love** and **truth**. Perhaps love is the fountain from which truth springs. Yet it can be misleading to separate truth from love. The relationship between love and truth is this: **love and truth should arrive together!** Take a few moments to imagine water rushing from a spring. Is it possible to separate the water from the spring itself? God's love surges from His being and brings truth along with it. Love attracts, pursues, invites, acts, sustains, heals, and builds people up. People notice love wherever they see it. People desire love above all things. Truth saves! Together they attract, bless, create, communicate, guide, forgive, instruct, nourish, protect, and save. God intended from the beginning that these two processes should work together and arrive together.

There are five exceptional events in the history of the world that changed everything: the birth of Christ, the incarnation of Christ, the crucifixion of Christ, the resurrection of Christ, and Christ indwelling your heart. In each of these events, love and truth worked together and arrived together. Your story is irrevocably connected to these events because your story is a response to these events.

Love accomplishes many things, but it is truth that saves. Love by itself can be soft and lack substance. Truth alone can be harsh and difficult to receive. God loves everyone. He has no desire for any to be lost (Luke 15:1-32, 19:10). Truth builds your house on a rock that will not be swept away by the storms of life (Matthew 7:24-27). Jesus said, "If you abide in my word and hold fast to my teachings and live in accordance with them, you are truly my disciples. And you will know the truth and the truth will set you free" (John 8:31– 32).

If you are new to thinking about these spiritual things, you may not believe you need to be set free from anything. Jesus was speaking about being set free from sin/disobedience to God. If you think you are a good person doing everything in life properly, write the Ten Commandments on a piece of paper and look at them every night to determine your disobedience for the day. Then, ask your spouse to do the same for you and compare the two records. Doing this will demonstrate the truth about your sin nature.

The apostle Paul wrote about this, saying, "Let our lives lovingly express truth in all things, speaking truly, dealing truly, and living truly" (Ephesians 4:12-15). Do you know anyone who speaks and lives truly? Are you attracted to this person? Do you want to be a person with that character? Speaking the truth in love is difficult. It is one of those spiritual challenges that are easy to talk about but difficult to integrate into our interpersonal styles. It takes a lot of practice and the empowerment of the Holy Spirit.

Silence about evil is the opposite of speaking the truth in love. Silence in the face of evil conceals truth, and leads to inaction, decay, decline, and eventual cultural collapse. Silence concerning known truths shows a lack of courage and disrespect for the truth. **Love and truth** are two process issues leading to decision points.

Have you recognized love and truth in the process of making decisions? Write your answers in the space below.

____

____

____

____

____

The above paragraphs describe the attributes and character of God. Now, you are prepared to discover how love and truth worked together at the beginning of everything. This is chronicled in the first three chapters of Genesis.

The Book of Genesis, Chapter One

Genesis 1:3–4: The creation story starts with an amorphous mass. It was "an empty waste shrouded in darkness." The first act of creation was the creation of light. God said, "Let there be Light." How could light evolve from darkness? There had to be an action of some sort to produce light. Action requires someone who performs the action. Can you think of a single example of light being produced that does not require action? The sun, for example, produces heat and light through the process of hydrogen fusion. Fire produces heat and light through the process of combustion, and so on. Without light, all life on planet Earth would cease to exist. It is not a coincidence that Jesus described Himself as "the light of the world." But of course, He was talking about spiritual life. If you do not have Jesus as the light of your spiritual life, then you are in spiritual darkness. You will have trouble finding your way in that darkness. Does the last sentence describe your life to this point in time? Being in spiritual darkness is a state of mind you inflict upon yourself. Come out of the darkness into the light (Luke 1:78–79).

Genesis 1:4: "And God saw the light was good." A principal characteristic of God is His **goodness**. As creation progresses, God sees everything is good. A good God can only produce good things. Take some time to examine creation, and you will see it is good. After it is accepted that God is amazing and you are not, it begins to produce humility about self and a reverent and worshipful fear of the Lord. This is the beginning of spiritual wisdom (Proverbs 1:7). It can also be the beginning of a healthy relationship with God. No one can have a healthy relationship with God while attempting to be God. Have you ever tried to be another person? The other person wonders what is going on with you. Why are you not satisfied with just being yourself? Is it not hard enough to be ourselves without attempting to be God? If you persist in attempting to be God, people around you will begin to complain.

There are a couple of unstated principles involved in the creation process. The first is connected to the process of relationship. Reading the first chapter of Genesis, the reader is left with the impression God is working alone. There is a hint the Holy Spirit is involved since it is mentioned in verse two, "hovering, brooding over the face of the waters." But there is no elaboration on what the Holy Spirit does. Neither is there any mention of Jesus' role in creation. In John 1:3, it is written, "All things were made and came into existence through Him, Jesus, and without Him not even one thing was made that has come into being." This Scripture informs us Jesus is intimately involved with creation but little about His specific role. We can speculate how God, the Holy Spirit, and Jesus worked together to bring about creation, but we do not know. One speculation is this: God spoke, Jesus fashioned, and the Holy Spirit empowered creation. Creation is the first hint we have about the Trinity, the triune nature of God consisting of Father, Son, and Holy Spirit working together. I will assert the Father, Son, and Holy Spirit worked together in complete **harmony** to create. There was no pride, arguing, irritation, jealousy, competition, or discord of any kind in the process of creating the universe. Their harmony is a manifestation of their **unity**. The Trinity models harmony for you and me. It is perfect harmony because it is a perfect unity, without sin. Have you considered what creation might be like if there had not been perfect unity in the Trinity? The Earth might go spinning off into another galaxy to a distant part of the universe.

In view of the fact the Trinity manifests unity, we might expect to find unity in the church. Alas, unity in the Church is often absent. Instead, we often find disunity. This disunity has produced many versions or interpretations of the teachings of Christ. These are known as denominations. For example, there are Lutheran, Presbyterian, Methodist, Baptist, independent, conservative, charismatic, and many other brands of Christianity. Disunity is also observed within single churches. Parishioners are unable to agree on how to administer the business of the church, the theology of Holy Communion, or many other issues that require decision-making. When nonbelievers observe disunity in the body of Christ, they lose interest in learning about Jesus. Christ is not responsible for disunity in the church. It happens because Christians fail to seek the will of God through prayer and fail to understand Scripture by relying on the Holy Spirit (II Peter 1:20–21). Pastors and other leaders in churches are very concerned about unity. They sometimes force unity by controlling the process issues in the church. This does not build the body of Christ. Unity in the church should result from believers responding to the leading of the Holy Spirit. Unity and harmony are difficult to find in the workings of men, but they are goals we should pursue. They are elusive because of events coming up in Chapter 3 of Genesis: a new process issue, the advent of the effects of sin/disobedience.

The harmony of the Trinity points to a second process issue: **relationships** are more important in task completion than the task itself. Relationships are often sacrificed for the apparent benefit of task completion. The tasks in life never end. It seems there is one task after another. Many tasks require working with one or more people to complete the task. Trouble starts when all the energy is focused on getting the job done, but relationships are ignored. When people are ignored, they become offended and no longer care about completing the task. They stop working on the task because they withdraw from the relationship. This is very difficult for a task-oriented person to understand when, suddenly, they find they are working alone.

Our relationship with God is a perfect example of the opposite of focusing on tasks. God focuses on relationship instead of tasks. It is a spiritual relationship between the spirit of God and your own eternal spirit. It is a relationship between the mind of Christ and your own mind (Philippians 2:1–2, Hebrews 10:16).

The all-powerful God of the Holy Bible does not force us to do anything. He does not force attending church, praying, reading the Bible, or accepting Christ as Lord and Savior. God is the perfect gentleman. He invites! He extends His hand, which is a helping hand. Do you sometimes need help coping with the stress the world brings?

Do you enjoy receiving an invitation to important events from important people? His invitation is one not to be left unopened. It is the most important invitation you will ever receive. His invitation is a process issue leading to a choice… acceptance or rejection of Jesus. A popular T-shirt among fishermen has a picture of a river with some good words of counsel, "The river is calling; don't let it go to voicemail." Do not allow God's invitation to remain unanswered!

If you focused on your relationship with God right here, right now, what would He be saying to you? Is He saying the creation is to be honored? Is He saying His work is holy? Is He saying certain things are to be set aside because they are made holy for His purposes? Is He saying you and I should be set aside for His holy purposes? Is He saying we should set a day aside to honor Him? What is He saying to you? Ask Him, and after you ask, listen for several minutes. Continue to listen until you hear from Him. Do this exercise each day until you hear from God. Show Him you want to be in a relationship with Him. Look for God speaking to you at other times during the day. If you want to draw near to God, you "must necessarily believe that God exists and he is the rewarder of those who earnestly and diligently seek him out" (Hebrews 11:6).

If you do not believe God exists, ask Him to help you with your unbelief (Mark 9:14–29). Continue to ask and seek, and you will find Him (Matthew 7:7). If you cannot find God, ask your spouse or closest friend if you have an issue with pride, which often prevents people from recognizing the reality of God. Or perhaps you are angry with God for some reason. If you cannot find God, it is because something deep within you is preventing a proper search.

Perhaps you are disconnected from God because of painful events in your life. If you desire to get reconnected with God, tell Him about your painful experiences, focusing on the sadness and disappointment (Psalm 30:5,11). The sadness and disappointment are process issues. The emotions and what you do with them primarily determine the outcome. Details of the event are content issues. They are important because they are connected to the emotions, but revisiting the content can generate more hurt and fear. **Do not revisit the experience.** Grieve what you lost: loss of innocence, childhood, relationship, boundaries, sense of self... whatever was taken from you. Take your sadness to Jesus. Abuse is a process of taking something away. Do not allow an abusive experience to take away your relationship with God.

Describe the emotions to Jesus, including what you experience in your body as you feel the emotion. As you do, He will take them and replace them with peace. Identify what you lost, perhaps something taken from you by another person. Ask God to strengthen you (II Corinthians 12: 9–10). **Do not revisit the content**, especially by yourself. It can traumatize you again and again. More detail is provided on this process issue in the four chapters on talk therapy.

Disappointment, sadness, and hurt are prime examples of emotions functioning as process issues. These emotions influence choices made about relationships. People choose to withdraw from interpersonal relationships that are disappointing and hurtful, thinking they can find a new relationship with less or no pain. The new relationship seems better until a major disappointment or hurt occurs, stimulating another withdrawal. The cycle repeats over and over...and over.

This pattern is especially pronounced in romantic relationships. It is the single most important process issue that results in separation and divorce. It is precisely the pattern that occurred in my early attempts at romance. Those relationships all ended in divorce. Fortunately, they did not start with marriage! Attraction to the opposite sex usually becomes intense during puberty, but most of us do not have the maturity at that age to cope with hurt and disappointment. When I broke up with my steady girlfriend in high school, I had no idea I did not know anything about conflict resolution in relationships. Ouch! Disappointment is so painful.

The 31 verses in chapter 1 of Genesis point mainly to supernatural events. They are events in which God spoke, and something was created. If you accepted that God spoke the world into existence, would your worldview change? Write your answer below.

____

____

____

____

The Book of Genesis, Chapter Two

Genesis 2:2: "On the seventh day God ended His work which He had done and He rested." Work projects are to be followed by rest. God does not need rest; rather, He is setting an example for us by resting. The goal of a work project is to finish the task. In this case, the task was the creation of the world, which was no small task. The goal of rest is to refresh and rejuvenate the mind, body, and spirit. Our minds and body have limits, and they should not be pushed to the edge of those limits. The body will break down, and the mind will burn out. The result is you are not prepared for the next task.

Genesis 2:7: "God breathed into his nostrils the breath of life." It is important to recognize after Adam was fully formed, he was not yet a living being, a person. God breathed into his nostrils the breath of life, which penetrated every cell in Adam's body. Every cell, tissue, and organ began to function in the fashion God intended. The lungs begin to inhale and exhale, and the heart started beating simultaneously.

Adam began to hear and see things around him. He had thoughts about what he heard and saw. Each cell began complex physiological processes, which resulted in renewal and cellular growth. This is the beginning of life! It is a beginning orchestrated by the power and wisdom of God. It is a miracle that manifests the love that God has for you (Psalm 139:13). This begs the question. Has this miracle been repeated, and is it being repeated now in the 21st century? Consider the process of conception. A single sperm cell and egg unite to become one. One cell divides into two, two into four, four into eight, and so on. Each of these cells demonstrates the same physiological processes present in the cells of the first man, Adam. This is the beginning of life. These physiological processes define the presence of life.

The breath of life from God suggests God imparting a spiritual nature to Adam and a corresponding desire in Adam for a spiritual relationship. The study of various cultures seems to confirm this. Everything under the sun has been worshipped, including the sun itself. There have been gods of fertility, war, harvest, love, and anything else which replaces the God of the Bible. Does wisdom suggest it is wise to worship the sun, or would it be wise to worship the being who created the sun? Man displays a hunger for spiritual relationship. Humanity is spiritual but unable to agree on what or who should be worshiped. What or who causes all this confusion? The answer to this question is found in chapter 3 of the book of Genesis. The answers to other questions you may have are found in the other 65 books of the Bible. God is the source of all life and all knowledge, and He shares what we need to know. He creates, He communicates, He instructs, and He empowers. All these things He does out of love for us.

Genesis 2:8-9: After planting, the Scripture states, "God made to grow every tree that is pleasant to the sight or to be desired, good, (suitable, pleasant) for food; the tree of life also in the center of the Garden, and the tree of knowledge of [the difference between] good and evil and blessing and calamity" (Genesis 2:9). In these words, we again witness that God is the source of life. Plants, flowers, and trees have their own biological processes indicating the presence of life. When these biological processes cease, the plant dies. Everyone can recognize the death of a plant. The death of a person is even more striking. In each case, the plant or person is separated from the physiological processes that sustain life. Since these physiological processes were instituted by God, we can think of death being a separation from the sustaining power of God. This is consistent with the Greek word *Thanatos,* which translates to the English word *death. Thanatos* has two very different meanings. One meaning is the separation of the eternal spirit from the physical body, what we think of as the death of a human being. The second meaning is the separation of man from God, a spiritual event. Have you noticed that people are more proficient at detecting physical death than detecting spiritual death? And why would that be? Could it be due to distraction, confusion, and deception?

The tree of knowledge of [the difference between] good and evil and blessing and calamity is also mentioned in verse nine. These two trees were placed in the garden for spiritual purposes rather than providing food. They are the key to understanding everything that follows in the Bible and human history. They were the physical means God used to transact spiritual realities. The tree of life is the tree associated with experiencing the life of God, including immortality (John 10:10, Psalm 1:1-3, John 3:16). The tree of knowledge of [the difference between] good and evil and blessing and calamity represents human autonomy. By eating from this tree, Adam asserted his desire to be independent of God.[83]

Genesis 2:15-17: God had instructed Adam to not eat from the tree of knowledge. This is the first protection God gave humanity. Had Adam obeyed this instruction, no other laws of protection would be required. There would be no demand to defund the police because there would be no need for police.

---

83 The Spirit Filled Life Bible, study note for Genesis 2:9

Two principles/process issues stem from this event: 1) God is the lawgiver; 2) When we ignore the law God provides, no law of human origin can contain the chaos and evil results. We have armies and navies to maintain international law, federal marshals to enforce national law, state troopers to administer state law, etc. And yet, the law is continually ignored and disobeyed. The word for law in Hebrew is *Torah*, but it has other meanings: instruction, teaching, direction, and precept.[84] In the later books of the Old Testament, it refers to the law of Moses, but it may not have that meaning here because the law of Moses had not yet been given. It can also mean the instructions of a human parent or some other wise person (Proverbs 18:3-1). This would seem to be the meaning in this context, the wise person being the God of the universe. God is instructing Adam on how he should conduct himself because God knows what is best for Adam. God also knows what is best for you and me.

Genesis 2:18–22: In verse 18, God determined man should not be alone. He makes a helper for Adam who is "suitable, adapted, and complementary to Adam." It seems initially, the relationship between Adam and Eve was dominated by love, joy, and peace. In chapter 3, the story takes a decidedly downward direction as a result of sin.

The Book of Genesis, Chapter Three

Genesis 3:1: "Now the serpent was more subtle and crafty than any living creature of the field which the Lord God had made." This is the reason everyone is deceived. It is the reason that all sin and fall short of the glory of God (Romans 3:23). We all need the indwelling of Christ and the power of the Holy Spirit to overcome the schemes of Satan.

Genesis 3:2–8: Tells the story of the serpent deceiving Eve by suggesting eating the fruit would make her like God. Then Eve gave some of the fruit to Adam, who also ate, resulting in the eyes of both being opened and knowing they were naked. In a desperate attempt to deceive God, they made aprons of fig leaves to cover themselves. When they heard God walking in the garden, they hid from Him.

These verses signal a new era in the relationship between God and man. Prior to these events, Adam and Eve experienced a personal visit with God regularly in the afternoon. Think about what it would be like being in the presence of the Creator of the universe, hearing His voice, asking questions of Him, perhaps listening to His instruction. Notice the serpent did not

84 Vine's Expository Dictionary of Old and New Testament Words

deceive Eve and Adam when God was present. He approached them when they were separated from God. This reveals our relationship with God is protective, a defense, a refuge against the attacks of Satan (Psalm 91:1-16). When this defense is weakened or absent, we are in the same predicament as Adam and Eve. It will result in the same outcome: distraction, confusion, and deception.

From the moment Adam ate the fruit, a stumbling block appeared in the God/man relationship. This block rendered man prone to disobedience/sin.[85] This is referred to as our sin nature. It is an acquired flaw of humanity. It is manifested by thoughts, words, and actions that are independent of God.

Sin is like floating the Colorado River through the Grand Canyon. One minute the river is intense and exciting, while the next minute it is trying to destroy you. Sin is the process issue that leads to a decision point to endure the trials of life independent of God. Think about the word *endure*. It includes the following ideas: suffer, tolerate, survive, put up with, and bear. Are you choosing to suffer through life? Or do you desire a life that produces love, joy, and peace? Independence from God includes the following: loss of His Word to guide thinking, speaking, and behavior; loss of the capacity to take authority over sin, and diminished power to cope with the common maladies and stressors of life.

Since that day, being prone to disobedience has influenced the souls of men to choose to take our eyes from God and put them on whatever fruit Satan is offering. Have you been distracted? Has distraction in your life led to confusion, deception, and poor outcomes? Write your answers in the space below.

____

____

____

____

____

After the fall of Adam and Eve, it is our nature when stressed/tempted to focus our energy on solving the problem in our own strength, leaving very little time or energy for prayer and seeking the will of God. The fruit of Satan always disappoints, as it did in the Garden of Eden. What does this look like? People wander around from relationship to relationship, lack

85 With Christ.org, Free will vs. Volition by Dan Smedra

direction in life, and become slaves to their lusts and other temptations. This results in restriction, dissatisfaction with life, depression, hopelessness, suicidal thoughts, and death (II Corinthians 7:7-10). Surveys of people with suicidal thoughts reveal a common thread. They have a sense of hopelessness deep in their souls. These issues will be explored more thoroughly in the chapter on talk therapy and the appendix.

Sin/disobedience always has consequences. We often unknowingly ask God to apply consequences when we do our own thing. Consequences may be divided into two categories, general consequences, and specific consequences.

Specific consequences are related to the nature of the sin. For example, a married man using pornography will eventually find his wife uninteresting sexually. Someone who manipulates relationships will have few or no close friends. A woman having an affair may develop a sexually transmitted disease. The amount of time between sin and the onset of consequences is difficult to predict. It could be immediate or delayed for years. There is an old saying about sin. It takes you "farther than you intended to go, keeps you longer than you intended to stay, and costs more than you thought you would pay."[86] In the last few verses of Genesis chapter three, you will observe the consequences Adam and Eve experienced, which they were unable to predict. Humanity is continuing to experience those consequences thousands of years later. The specific consequence of Adam's sin was eviction from the Garden of Eden.

The general consequences for Adam's sin were fourfold: 1) a disposition of being in rebellion to God, a sin nature; 2) physical death; 3) separation from God; 4) emergence of self-love and self-will. These consequences were immediate, unchanging, and identical for all humanity.

Sin nature refers to the natural impulse of humanity to rebel and live independently from God. This is described in Scripture using different terms: slavery to sin (Romans 6:16), sinful flesh/the entire nature of man without the Holy Spirit (Romans 8:3), and earthly nature/the evil desire lurking in your members [those animal impulses and all that is earthly in you that is employed in sin] (Colossians 3:5). It was passed from Adam to his children and eventually to you and me through the generations. It does not seem to be passed through genetics. No sin gene has been located in the genome. It seems to be passed spiritually.

You will recall when God breathed the breath of life into Adam, the breath of God penetrated every cell in Adam's body. God put life into Adam,

86 I could not find the origin for this quotation.

including the physiological processes that sustain life. The beginning of life was empowered by God. In a similar fashion, the moment Adam ate the fruit, death entered every cell in his body. Of course, it is obvious that the cells making up the tissues of his body did not die instantaneously. Rather a process was started that eventually would lead to physical death years later, a delayed consequence. The beginning of death was orchestrated by Satan. This is not to say Satan has any creative power because he does not. Satan perverts and distorts every good and perfect gift that comes from God. "The thief (Satan) comes only in order to steal, kill, and destroy" (John 10:10).

The separation from God is a reference to spiritual separation. God instituted a plan to repair this breach in the God/man relationship. That plan is the birth, incarnation, crucifixion, and resurrection of Christ. The first hint of this plan is described in Genesis 3:15 when the Scripture prophesies "enmity" between the offspring of the serpent and the offspring of Eve.

Adam and Eve were created with a disposition to please God. There was no selfish trait in their original creation. Selfishness emerged when Eve and Adam took their focus from God and put it on themselves to satisfy their own selfish desires. Self is focused on one's own thoughts, emotions, plans, behavior, and well-being. Self is concerned primarily about number one, you and me! The principal task of self is to take care of you, to protect you, to satisfy your desires, and to criticize, control, and blame others. Other people are relatively unimportant unless they are pleasing you or interfere with satisfying your desires. The word selfish explains the nature of self. It is part of the corrupt nature noted above. It is difficult to separate the self from self-love and self-will. Self-will and self-loving people are described in II Peter 2:10–22. Only verses 12 and 14 are quoted here: verse 12, "But these [people]! Like unreasoning beasts, mere creatures of instinct, born [only] to be captured and destroyed, railing at things of which they are ignorant, they shall utterly perish in their [own] corruption [in their destroying they shall surely be destroyed]." Verse 14, "They have eyes full of harlotry, insatiable for sin. They beguile and bait and lure away unstable souls. Their hearts are trained in covetousness [lust, greed], [they are] children of a curse [exposed to cursing]!" These scriptures make strong accusations. Before dismissing them, think about the things you hear about on the news each day.

The practice of sin **compels** a denial of Christ because the acceptance of Christ begins a process of separating self from sin. People who practice sin at this level hate Jesus and those who follow Him because they stand in opposition to their evil purposes. They are uncompromising about their evil pursuits. They attempt to destroy anyone who is an obstacle to their plans. This results in a divided culture, such as we see in many Western countries in the twenty-first century. Left unchecked, they will destroy the American Dream.

The words above describe the corrupt nature of man separate from God. In these words, we hear a description of what it means to be influenced by a sin nature. It results in love of self, self-love. The secular definition of self-love in society today has nothing to do with Christian spirituality. The spiritual component has been forgotten or ignored. Instead, the concept of self-love teaches having positive regard and positive emotions for who you are as a person. This is similar to having positive self-esteem. The problem with this concept is self-love and self-esteem are usually based on self-success. Many people do not have opportunities to experience a lot of success in life. These people often experience low self-esteem, anxiety, and depression. An exercise (the mirror exercise) to learn how to love yourself in a Godly fashion will be provided in the chapter on talk therapy and the appendix.

Contrary to self-love is the concept of agape love in the teachings of Christ. Agape love keeps appearing in the texts of the Bible as well as many chapters of this book. It reappears in different chapters because of its vital importance. Agape love is thinking first of the well-being of others. It edifies, builds up, and encourages others to grow to their full potential, even to the point of being more Christlike. A spiritual home is built and framed with the wisdom and teachings of Christ. This home has large windows which allow the light of God to enter and enables the person to see the outside world with eyes of spiritual wisdom (Matthew 7:24–27, Luke 1:78–79, John 8:31-32).

God sees our fallen nature through a worldview of love and truth. Love desires to be in a relationship with us, while truth sees us as people who are deceived, weak, and disobedient (Genesis 3:1, Romans 5:5–6, II Corinthians 12:10-12). God requires us to be righteous to be in a relationship with Him because He is holy. Reconciliation with God is accomplished through the death of Jesus Christ on the cross. All our sin and disobedience are transferred to Jesus, and all His holiness is transferred to us. This is known as the concept of imputation. The ministry of Christ represents the love of God, the truth of God, and the grace of God, all working together for our benefit.

Does your worldview see people through agape love and the truth of God? Give a couple of examples.

Do you manifest grace in your life edifying and encouraging others? Give a couple of examples.

Which of these two types of love, agape love or self-love, were you mostly exposed to during your childhood?

Can you appreciate a connection between the type of love you were exposed to as a child and what kind of love you are able to express now?

Genesis 3:9-10: We learn about God visiting Eve and Adam while they are hiding from God after Adam eats the fruit.

God begins the conversation: "Adam, where are you?"

Adam: "I heard the sound of you walking in the garden, and I was afraid because I was naked. And I hid myself."

This verse describes Adam and Eve experiencing an emotion they did not have prior to their sin. The emotion Adam identifies is fear. They began to experience other emotions around the same period of time, including confusion, guilt, shame, hurt, sadness, and disappointment. Guilt, shame, and fear are emotions associated with sin, often resulting in hiding and withdrawal. These emotions were "gifts" from Satan that entered the hearts of Adam and Eve because of their sin. You might think of these as unanticipated consequences. Do you want to receive unexpected gifts from Satan? Do you have guilt and shame in your life? Do you want these emotions to fill and occupy your mind? Are these emotions restricting joy and satisfaction in your life? Write your answers in the space below.

____

____

____

____

____

<u>Genesis 3:11</u>: The conversation with God continues: God, "Who told you that you were naked? Have you eaten of the tree of which I commanded you that you should not eat?"

The first question in this verse relates to the origin of the thoughts and emotions Adam and Eve had about being naked. There are four possibilities regarding the origin of these thoughts: God, the serpent, Adam, and Eve. Since Adam and Eve covered themselves and hid, their behavior suggests a negative thought about being naked, or perhaps they're experiencing guilt and shame for the first time, or both. We know from other scriptures that Satan is the accuser and deceiver, the father of all lies. Perhaps Satan put the thought into their minds about being naked (Matthew 4:9–10, 16:21–23).

The second question from God regarding their disobedience calls for a yes or no response. Notice neither Adam nor Eve ever answered this question directly (who told you?). They ignore God. They evade His questions. Does that sound familiar? Ignoring God is part of their rebellion. It is part of our rebellion. It is part of our sin nature? Are you ignoring God? How are you ignoring God? Write your answers to these questions in the space below.

____

____

____

____

____

<u>Genesis 3:12</u>: Adam responds to God: "The woman whom you gave to be with me, she gave me fruit from the tree, and I ate."

Adam blames Eve and God for his disobedience. This is the point at which blame and marital conflict entered humanity.

Genesis 3:13: God says to Eve: "What is this you have done?"

Eve answers, "The serpent beguiled (cheated, outwitted, and deceived) me and I ate."

In Eve's response, we have a clear statement about the rule of deception underlying disobedience. Eve blames the serpent for her behavior. Eve and Adam each have a different excuse to avoid responsibility. The meaning of the word *excuse* in this context is a pretense, a belief not supported by facts. It relieves someone from accepting responsibility. Making an excuse is acting in self-interest. When a person rejects the Word of God, Satan is more than happy to insert one of his thoughts. **The mind of man abhors a vacuum.** When this happens, you have left territory that is under the authority of God and have entered the land of Satan, where he has authority. You have given him permission to steal, to kill, and destroy (John 10:10). What areas of your life have you given Satan permission to steal, to kill, and to destroy? What excuses have you utilized to rationalize being in opposition to God? Write your answers below.

____

____

____

____

____

Genesis 3:14: God says to the serpent: "Because you have done this, you are cursed above all [domestic] animals and above every [wild] living thing of the field; upon your belly you shall go, and you shall eat dust [and what it contains] all the days of your life."

In this verse is the beginning of God administering consequences because of Eve and Adam's sin. It seems appropriate that the first punishment was assigned to the serpent. What consequences for sin have you experienced in your life? Write your answers below.

____

____

____

____

____

Genesis 3:15: God continues speaking to the serpent: "And I will put enmity between you and the woman, in between your offspring and her offspring; he will bruise and tread your head under foot, and you will lie in wait and bruise his heel." In this verse, we have a prophecy about a continuous conflict between the "descendants" of the serpent and the woman. Enmity refers to the continuous conflict between the kingdom of Satan and the kingdom of God. This conflict is not about a minor disagreement. It is not about the choice of having your steak prepared medium or well-done or wearing shorts or pants to the picnic. It is all-out war! Satan hates God and everyone who represents God. God hates evil, of which Satan is the sole author. The offspring of the serpent/Satan are his demons and people under the influence of demons. The offspring of the woman are Christ and those who are obedient to his teachings.

Genesis 3:16: God speaks consequences to Eve: "I will greatly multiply your grief and your suffering in pregnancy and the pangs of childbearing; with spasms of distress you will bring forth children. Yet your desire and craving will be for your husband, and he will rule over you." Adam and Eve had not yet conceived, so it is not known what childbearing might have been were it not for their disobedience. Certainly, this prophecy has come to pass; ask any mother. This is a specific consequence of disobedience. All of God's prophecies have come to pass. You will not know the nature or content of God's other prophecies unless you read the rest of the books of the Bible following Genesis.

It is important to note Scripture does not say her craving will be for all men in a general sense, but for a husband. This would appear to be a man who is committed to loving, caring for, providing for, and protecting her. The second prophecy describes the relationship between Adam and Eve. The husband will rule over his wife/companion. The "rule" of a husband over his wife must be understood in the context of other scriptures describing the marriage relationship (Ephesians 5:21–26). Since Eve wanted to be like God but now will be subject to her husband, it suggests the marriage relationship may be conflicted going forward. In this one verse, we observe Eve being separated from two blessings that God desired her to have: 1) an easy, pleasant experience of bringing children into the world, 2) a pleasurable and agreeable relationship with her husband.

Satan is extremely skillful at separating us from the blessings God desires for us. And Satan delights when he deceives us while we blame God for the losses we experience in life (Genesis 3:1). If you are a husband, have you and your wife had a conversation about what it would look like if you laid down your life for her as Christ laid down His life for the church (Ephesians 5:21–26)? And if you are a wife, do you submit yourself to your husband's decision after he has considered your input? Do you show reverence for your husband (Ephesians 5:33)? Does your husband lay down his life for you as Christ laid down His life for the church? Write your answers in the space below.

____

____

____

____

____

<u>Genesis 3:17-19</u>: God speaks consequences to Adam: "Because you have listened and given heed to the voice of your wife and have eaten of the tree of which I commanded you, saying, you shall not eat of it; the ground is under a curse because of you, in sorrow and toil you shall eat [of the fruits] of it all the days of your life. Thorns and thistles shall it bring forth for you, and you shall eat the plants in the field. In the sweat of your face shall you eat bread until you return to the ground, for out of it you were taken; for dust you are and to dust you shall return."

It seems God is saying to Adam, "Life is going to be hard from this point forward." Do you think that prophecy has been fulfilled?

There have been many thorns in my life (at present, the biggest thorn is mastering the word processing app on my computer). There is also a prophecy regarding the flesh of man deteriorating when his eternal spirit is separated from his body at death. This prophecy has also come to pass. It is of interest that God applied this curse to Adam because Adam listened to the voice of his wife. This is not to say a husband should never listen to the voice of his wife. But rather, when his wife encourages the husband to disobey God, he should stop listening.

<u>Genesis 3:20</u>: "The man called his wife's name Eve [life spring]) because she was the mother of all living." <u>Genesis 3:21</u>: "For Adam also and for his wife the Lord God made long coats (tunics) of skins and clothed them."

In this verse, we observe the first shedding of blood. The skin of an animal, used for clothing, is a foreshadowing of the blood of Christ which covers our sins. Do you need to have a covering for your sin?

<u>Genesis 3:22</u>: "And the Lord God said, "Behold the man has become like one of us [the father, son, and Holy Spirit] to know [how to distinguish

between] good and evil and blessing and calamity; and now, lest he put forth his hand and take also from the tree of life and eat, and live forever—"

God is speaking here to Christ and the Holy Spirit rather than Adam and Eve. In the wisdom of God, in an act of mercy, He prevented us from living forever in a fallen spiritual state of mind.

Genesis 3:23: "Therefore the Lord God sent him forth from the Garden of Eden to till the ground from which he was taken."

It is not known if Adam and Eve overheard the above conversation, but God acted quickly, expelling them from the garden.

Genesis 3:24: "So [God] drove out the man; and He placed at the East of the Garden of Eden the cherubim and the flaming sword which turned every way, to keep and guard the way to the tree of life."

In this verse, we observe the broken circle of trust between God and man. In verse 8, fear, and perhaps guilt and shame, prevented Adam from trusting God. Now it is apparent that God no longer trusts Adam and Eve as God places a flaming sword to prevent their return to the garden.

Satan's purpose in disguising himself as a snake and entering the garden was to separate man from God. Satan often assumes a disguise that we fail to recognize, resulting in our making the same mistake as Adam and Eve, which was agreeing to follow the rules of Satan instead of the rules God provided. The rules of God are always given to protect us. As a result of following Satan, their life became restricted. They were unable to resume their physical presence or their spiritual life in the garden. Their life separate from the garden would be more difficult.

Whenever we find ourselves living in the kingdom of Satan rather than the kingdom of God, we will find restriction and difficulty in that part of our life. This is known as demonic oppression. Demonic oppression is an unpopular term in society today. Christians and nonbelievers alike are reluctant to consider the possibility of a demon influencing their thoughts or behavior. Demons are part of "old-school" theology to younger generations. The current fad is being "woke" with sensitivity to social injustice, especially racial injustice. Consider this possibility: **all social injustice is a manifestation of demonic activity**. Take some time now to review areas of your life: spiritual life, relationships with parents, spouse, children, and peers, work, play, etc. Is there any area of your life in which you are experiencing difficulty or restriction? Restriction is often accompanied by anxiety, dissatisfaction, disappointment, and depression. Write your answers in the space below.

____

____

____

____

____

In the review of the first three chapters of Genesis, many process issues are introduced. These process issues often lead to a decision. Each decision you make contributes to the life you are experiencing. Are you satisfied with your life? Are you making good decisions? Do you have a purpose in life? Do you have hope for a more satisfying life? Are you experiencing love, joy, and peace? Do you need a different plan to get where you want to be? There is an old Navajo saying, "If you keep heading in the direction you are going you will probably get there." Are you satisfied with the direction you are going? Answer these questions in the space below.

____

____

____

____

____

The most important process issue has not been noted yet. It is this: **God determines all the process issues!** "For from him and through him and to him are all things. [For all things originate with him and come from him; all things live through him, and all things center in and tend to consummate and to end in him.] To him be glory forever! Amen (so be it)" (Romans 11:36). This idea is very difficult for prideful humanity to accept. Our natural thought processes toward God are similar to Adam's and Eve's in the Garden. We want to be independent of God. We hide from God. Of course, He knows where each person is hiding. And He calls to us just as He called to Adam.

In this chapter, we learned about the character of God, the miracles of creation, agape love, the relationship between love and truth, and the fall of Adam and Eve in the Garden of Eden. This chapter summarizes God's story about the beginning of your story. In the next chapter, we begin a more detailed examination of the strategies of Satan. You have to know the snares of Satan if you want to avoid them (Proverbs 29:25).

The Door to Evil

How does a person enter an evil experience? Short answer, it's easy—just open the door! This chapter provides a longer answer: disobedience to God results in losing God's protection and persistent "opportunities" for demonic influence. This allows the kingdom of Satan to fulfill its purposes to steal, to kill, and to destroy (John 10:10). We see this pattern often because Satan is at work in every heart, including the heart of every believer (Jeremiah 17:9, I Peter 5:8).

In the chapter on the *D words,* we saw how a series of process issues produce a cascading effect that leads to poor outcomes. We must learn to recognize this pattern because we cannot afford the cost of being outwitted by Satan. Every deception leads to loss of some sort: loss of relationships, loss of employment, loss of health, loss of the wonderful life God has prepared for you (Luke 6:38, Ephesians 2:10). Adam and Eve were defrauded of their perfect relationship with God, the perfect relationship with each other, and all the blessings associated with living in the Garden of Eden. **A door point is opened to satanic influence/ demonic oppression every time we disobey God by agreeing with Satan.** We constantly see this pattern, but only when we are looking for it. When we are not looking for it, we are easily deceived. Look for this pattern as you read through the rest of the chapters in Genesis and the following chapters of this book. Deception always has its point of origin at a single source: the kingdom of Satan. This temptation may occur externally through the senses or internally from our individual sin nature we inherited from Adam.

We do not have to wait long to find the next recorded example of deception and its consequences. In Genesis 4:1-16, the narrative of our stories continues. It's important that you read the entire account; however, our primary focus will be verses 1 to 7.

> Verse one: "And Adam knew Eve as his wife, and she became pregnant and bore Cain; and she said, 'I have gotten and gained a man with the help of the Lord.'"

Verse two: "And [next] she gave birth to his brother Abel. Now Abel was a keeper of sheep, but Cain was a tiller of the ground."

Verse three: "And in the course of time Cain brought to the Lord an offering of the fruit of the ground."

Verse four: "And Abel brought of the firstborn of his flock and of the fat portions. And the Lord had respect and regard for Abel and for his offering.

Verse five: "But for Cain and his offering He had no respect or regard. So Cain was exceedingly angry and indignant, and he looked sad and depressed."

Verse six: "And the Lord said to Cain, why are you angry? And why do you look sad and depressed and dejected?"

Verse seven: If you do well, will you not be accepted? And if you do not do well sin crouches at your door; its desire is for you, but you must master it."

In these verses, we have the first recorded example of worshipping God, the offering of a sacrifice to cancel sin, and in verse eight, the first murder in the history of humanity. It is apparent that Cain's sacrifice/offering was not satisfactory in some way. It is probable that God had instructed Cain and Abel on the nature of their sacrifice. Abel brought the fat portions of the firstborn of his flock. This is consistent with other scriptures where God indicates He desires the first and best fruits of our labors for an offering in the Old Testament (Proverbs 3:9-10) and from the heart in the New Testament (II Corinthians 9:7-8). We are told in the letter to Hebrews in the New Testament that Abel's gift was "better and more acceptable" than Cain's because it was prompted by faith (Hebrews 11:4). We do not know what Cain brought, but apparently, he was deceived by not acting in faith according to what God had instructed him.

In these verses, we also have the account of Cain becoming jealous and angry toward Abel as a result of God accepting Abel's offering but rejecting his. When God speaks to Cain about his anger and sadness, he starts with a question, "Why are you angry? And why do you look sad, depressed, and dejected? If you do well, will you not be accepted? And if you do not do well, sin crouches at your door; its desire is for you, but you must master it." In verse seven, in the words of God Himself, we have a description of demonic influence hovering and crouching, waiting to spring. The question is where would sin spring? It seems most likely this is a reference to sin entering the heart of Cain. But notice, sin doesn't tiptoe quietly into the heart of Cain; it springs. Sin is powerful. It takes a person by surprise. It attacks the most vital part of a person's function, i.e., the heart. Not the heart that circulates blood, but the spiritual heart where decisions are made and emotions/ desires originate.

Sin wants to be where it can do the most damage. The battle for your eternal spirit is fought in your mind/ heart. God offered Cain an opportunity to change his thinking and behavior, but Cain refused. Apparently, the heart of Cain was already hardened. His heart would not receive the word of God. Instead, Cain opened the door to his heart, allowing a spirit of anger/ bitterness to influence his thinking, his emotions, his behavior, and his will. He was distracted from the word of God; he was confused. This is the precise moment of deception. The moment we agree with Satan and allow one of his demons to influence our thoughts, emotions, behavior, and will. This is referred to as a **door point**. For Cain, this resulted in love for his brother turning to hatred. It resulted in the eventual murder of Abel. How quickly the mind alters perception. Satan's cash register just rang up another sale. Ka-ching!

In verses 8 to 16, we witness the account of the **consequences** that Cain experienced because of his disobedience. The ground he tilled became resistant to his efforts, he was sentenced to wander the earth, and he was exiled from the rest of humanity (specific consequences). He was also separated from God (general consequences). You see in this narrative the same pattern that we observed with Adam and Eve. **Distraction** leads to **confusion,** leading to **deception/a door point**, leading to **evil desire** producing a **decision** to disobey**,** leading to **consequences** with **emotional and spiritual pain.** In this example, the evil desire Cain harbored in his heart was to end the life of his brother Abel.

Cain said to God, "My punishment is greater than I can bear." Cain was not exaggerating. Being shut out from all human interaction...total isolation is worse than death. However, Cain was again disobedient. He could not bear his punishment. He married, fathered children, and built a city. The Bible does not record any evidence of his repenting. The circumstances of his death are uncertain.

Have you had emotional or spiritual pain in your life resulting from a decision to disobey God? Or have you had this kind of unbearable pain in response to abuse from other persons? Did you blame God for what happened to you at the hands of others? Think about the narrative of Cain and Abel. Was God responsible for Cain killing his brother Abel? Write your responses to these questions in the space provided below.

____

____

____

____

____

There is a sequence of process issues, a cascading series of events, that occurs every time we agree with Satan. Satisfying our evil desires produces slavery to sin (Romans 6:16). This is known as oppression (Acts 10:38). When we agree with Satan, we are saying, "Okay, you have my permission to oppress me in this area of my life." This permission is often given outside of our conscious awareness. That is a very scary thought. In Genesis 4:7, God warned Cain that sin was crouching at the door. Cain didn't get it. Do you get it? We generate bad outcomes when we don't get it. Remember, "Satan is more crafty and subtle than any other creature of the field that the Lord God made" (Genesis 3:1).

One problem for believers and nonbelievers alike is that the demonic realm is unseen for the most part. We cannot see the demonic princes who have jurisdiction over municipalities, states, and nations (Daniel 10:1-13). We cannot see the spiritual war that is being waged all around us (II Kings 6:14-17). Scripture tells us to keep our eyes on the things that are unseen (II Corinthians 4:16-18), but our natural response is to think only about what we can see. Because we are unaware of the spiritual war constantly being waged in our minds and around us, we become susceptible to "sneak attacks" such as occurred in the Garden of Eden. The problem of being unable to perceive the spiritual war is compounded by the various distractions that the world presents to us every day. These distractions separate our mind from the word of God.

Door points to demonic oppression often are opened when the **stress** of life is successful at taking our focus off God. That is the precise moment when the risk is greatest. That is when we fall into the trap of relying on ourselves to cope instead of relying on Christ, the word, and the Holy Spirit.

Think about a child raised in a home with an angry, abusive, alcoholic parent. The focus of the child is constantly on the alcoholic parent: how to be safe from the parent, how to behave to prevent that parent from experiencing a rage, how to protect other family members. These issues are elevated in the child's mind to the level of survival. They occupy the child's attention during the day and are often expressed as unresolved problems through dreams and nightmares. Fear of the parent may be generalized to other people and other settings. School performance suffers from poor concentration. Emotional abuse results in the child experiencing a distorted perception of self. Very few children have the spiritual preparation and maturity to take all this to God in prayer. Instead, they rely on the strategies of the mind to protect themselves, what psychologists call **defense mechanisms**. Children do not understand that Satan is the ruler of this world. Children do not understand why God would allow these things to happen to them. Children do not understand the concept of sinful nature. Children often become angry with God or simply disinterested in spirituality because their life experience suggests having a relationship with God does not protect or help them. While **relying on themselves** to cope, they repeat the mistake made by Adam and Eve in the garden by agreeing with Satan and simultaneously opening door points for spirits of deception, fear, guilt, shame, doubt, confusion, and more. A few of many common thinking errors that result from trauma/abusive life experiences are noted below:

- God does not care.
- God does not love me.
- My parents don't love me.
- Something is wrong with me because God allowed this to happen.
- I'm not going to talk to God anymore because it doesn't do any good.
- I deserve to be depressed.
- I can never trust anyone again.
- The best way to stay safe is not to be in relationship.
- If I could control everyone, I'd be all right.
- If I please my parents/spouse/children/friends, they will like me.
- The harder I work, the more people will like me.
- If I were a boy instead of a girl (or a girl instead of a boy), this would not have happened to me.

- I can control people by using anger.
- Being angry is okay because my father/mother is angry all the time.

Each of these strongly held beliefs, a stronghold, becomes a process issue that leads to decisions about school performance, trust, safety, relationships, etc. A stronghold is a belief based on a lie in which a person has been deceived by Satan (II Corinthians 10:3-5). The longer the belief is held, the more powerful it becomes. A stronghold has been described as a castle of thought. Just as a castle is a fortress that prevents entry, a stronghold prevents the entry of truth. It will allow the entry of further lies and deceptions. These beliefs distort every aspect of a child's existence. In the behavioral science field, they are referred to as cognitive distortions or thinking errors.

Painful emotions may open a door point for demonic oppression. The most important of these include confusion, guilt, shame, fear, hurt, sadness, and disappointment. When these emotions are intense, they may be very painful. Our natural response to pain is avoidance; we fail to process these emotions. This is contrary to the gospel of Christ, which informs us that we should bring all our experience, including our pain and grief, to Christ (II Samuel 30:1-4, Psalm 30:5,11, Isaiah 53:3-4, Revelation 3:20).

A person cannot bring an emotion to Jesus when they're not feeling that emotion. For example, refusing to experience fear and failing to take it to Christ may allow a spirit of fear to linger in your life and influence your thinking and behavior, resulting in an anxiety disorder (Proverbs 1:23-33, 29:25, II Timothy 1:7). Fear is the emotional response to a specific identifiable threat of injury. Anxiety feels very similar to fear, but you are unable to identify the cause. Anxiety comes upon you like a lethal force for which there is no explanation.

A person may respond to fear by engaging or by running away. This is referred to as the fight or flight response. If the stimulus is perceived to be life-threatening, some people will become paralyzed by their fear. The natural response to anxiety is **attempting to avoid the emotion.** You can't outrun anxiety because it has its origin in your own mind. Everywhere you go, anxiety keeps you company you did not invite. This is a process issue that produces disappointment, discouragement, and hopelessness because you cannot fight or run away from something you are unable to identify.

At that point, you may continue to be anxious and disappointed in yourself that you are unable to do anything about it. You may start to have derogatory/ negative thoughts about who you are as a person. This can lead to depression.

There is always a reason you are experiencing anxiety, often secondary to past traumatic experience. Since it is not possible to outrun anxiety, an alternative is to embrace it. This is very difficult if the anxiety is intense, as in panic disorder. Nonetheless, embracing the anxiety, riding the crest of its wave, will teach that anxiety is harmless and will eventually dissipate.

Learning this will take the power out of anxiety. Avoiding situations associated with anxiety exacerbates its power. Avoiding anxiety is often an early/childhood strategy to cope. Avoidance can become a way of life, and anxiety may interfere with recreation, school attendance, school performance, relationships, work performance—with every aspect of your life. When anxiety increases, there is increasing restriction in a person's life. This is how emotions become process issues which lead to decisions with poor outcomes.

Repentance

Repentance is the **spiritual process** that leads to the possibility of a better outcome when you have been deceived. Our understanding of repentance comes from the Greek word *metanoia*, which refers to a change of mind. The mind of man has been hardwired, after the sin of Adam and Eve, to be in rebellion against God. Therefore, the will would have to make an executive decision to please and serve God in order to repent. Scripture indicates that repentance involves other processes and is not simply a change of mind. Since our mind is hardwired to be rebellious, we should expect there will be a **spiritual component** to help with repentance. **Repentance starts with disgust, sorrow, and brokenness** about sin in your life. This produces "a broken and contrite heart" (Psalm 51:17). In this Psalm, King David is repenting from his adultery with Bathsheba and the murder of her husband. A broken and contrite heart is "broken down with sorrow for sin and humbly and thoroughly penitent" (Psalm 51:17, Amplified Translation).

A realization dawns in your mind you will not stop making poor choices relying on self. You confess your self-determination and resistance to have a relationship with Jesus. You begin to read the word of God, change your thinking to comply with the Word, and change your behavior (Job 42:1-6, Joshua 1:8, John 3:14-16, Romans 12:1-2). The spiritual component is your moving toward God while God draws you to Jesus. In a conversation with the Pharisees, Jesus said, "No one is able to come to me unless the Father who sent me attracts and draws him and gives him the desire to come to me, and [then] I will raise him up [from the dead] at the last day" (John 6:44).

God works in our hearts to help us be receptive to Christ.

Repentance involves each member of the Trinity. God draws the nonbeliever to Christ, Jesus instructs through His Word, and the Holy Spirit empowers the process (John 6:44-45, Luke 1:78-79, John 6;63, John 16:7-15). We should not be surprised that each member of the Trinity is involved in repentance when we remember God is relational. Each member of the Trinity relates to the person who is in the process of repentance or accepting Christ.

John the Baptist, Jesus, and the apostle Peter all began their ministries by preaching repentance (Matthew 3:1-2, Matthew 4:16-17, Acts 2:36-38). Repentance must be important!

God blesses obedience. As a result of being reconciled to God through Christ, the believer is released from the penalty of sin (Romans 4:5, 5:15-21) and is free from the power of sin (Romans 6:1-15). Through the grace of God, our sins and penalty have been transferred to Jesus. The righteousness of Christ has been transferred to us. This has sometimes been referred to as "The Great Exchange." There is no longer a need to fear God and no longer a reason to fear death (I John 4:15-18). We begin to live in peace with God. Conflict with God prevents experiencing this peace.

An interesting scripture on obedience producing blessing is Proverbs 1:23-33: "If you will turn (repent) and give heed to my reproof, behold, I [wisdom] will pour out my Spirit upon you, I will make my words known to you. Because I have called and you have refused [to answer], I have stretched up my hand and no man has heeded it, and you treated as nothing all my counsel and will accept none of my reproof, I also will laugh at your calamity; I will mock when the thing comes that shall cause you terror and panic—when your panic comes as a storm and desolation and your calamity comes on as a whirlwind, when distress and anguish come upon you. Then they will call upon me [wisdom] but I will not answer; they will seek me early and diligently, but they will not find me. Because they hated knowledge and did not choose the reverent and worshipful fear of the Lord, would accept none of my counsel, and despised all my reproof, therefore they shall eat of the fruit of their own way and be satiated with their own devices."

In this scripture, the wisdom of God is personified and speaking to us. Here is a paraphrase, my interpretation, of those ten verses: Wisdom is saying, "Listen to me, listen to my instruction about what you are thinking and doing which should change; I want to have a relationship with you to help. When you listen, I will bless you by filling you with my Holy Spirit and opening your mind to understand my Word. When you refuse to pay attention, there are consequences because you have ignored my counsel. Your panic is the consequence you are experiencing because you did not listen. When you do not know how to cope with your anxiety, it is too late to find me. I will not answer because you have relied on yourself, your own defenses ('devices') which do not work." The Hebrew word for devices refers to the plans of the mind. It might include the defenses of the mind which help people cope with unpleasant or painful thoughts, feelings, or experiences.[87]

What instruction specifically is this scripture (Proverbs 1:23-33) referencing? There are several scriptures that respond to this question, but perhaps the best is II Corinthians 7:10, which states this principle: "For godly grief and the pain God is permitted to direct, produce a repentance that leads and contributes to salvation and deliverance from evil, and it never brings regret; but worldly grief (the hopeless sorrow that is characteristic of the pagan world) is deadly [breeding and ending in death.]"

My interpretation of this scripture: God is saying, "Bring your painful experiences to me and I will direct your pain in a way that leads to a change in your thinking, behavior, and protects you from evil. If you rely on your own devices, you will experience a hopeless sorrow which is deadly in its effect."

The above scriptures raise several extremely important questions: When did God speak to me about how I should handle fear/anxiety? Is it true that a loving God could have no sympathy when I find myself paralyzed by anxiety? Why is it too late for me to find God? Why do my own "devices" fail in coping with anxiety/fear?

Here are some answers: God speaks to you about the issues of your life, including anxiety, in the Scriptures recorded in the Holy Bible. Are you reading the Bible? Are you familiar with the teachings provided in Scripture? Are you meditating on what you are reading? Are you following the counsel of Joshua 1:8? "This book of the law shall not depart out of your mouth, but you shall meditate on it day and night, that you may observe and do according to all that is written in it. For then you shall make your way prosperous and then you shall deal wisely and have good success."

Have you been looking up scriptural references provided in this book? If you are not familiar with the process issues that God has created which direct your life, how can you be successful? Repentance is the beginning of Godly wisdom that is mentioned in Proverbs 1:23-33. One reason it is too

87 Psychological defenses are discussed in more detail in chapter three.

late to find God is you have become totally distracted by the anxiety you are experiencing. You deny or have forgotten that God desires to help or do not know how to use your relationship with God to cope with anxiety. This is discussed more thoroughly in the four chapters on Talk Therapy.

Being set free from the power of sin means the believer now has the **option** to resist the deceptions of Satan (James 4:7). What does that look like? We choose to avoid being distracted by his tempting thoughts. It looks like what I speak about in the chapter, *I Can't Believe I Ate the Whole Thing*, when I talk about my problems with weight gain. When I sit down to eat, I confess my addiction to food, ask for guidance, and eat nothing until I hear from God. When tempted to speed, I confess my desire to drive 5 mph over the speed limit and ask for help to resist. When looking at a beautiful woman, I ask for assistance to keep my eyes on her face rather than her figure. I might pray, "Lord help my eyes and my thoughts to honor you while I am with this woman."[88] Am I perfect in my obedience in these efforts? Of course not, but I'm working on them.

God also speaks to you through the consequences of your choices. Do you have a lot of anxiety? Are you a worrier? Does your worry improve your life?

When Christians and nonbelievers refuse to follow the instruction God provides, God experiences sorrow and sadness Himself (Genesis 6:5-6). He does not force obedience; instead, He allows us to experience the consequences of our behavior, including anxiety and separation from Him. It may or may not be too late to find God. God looks at the heart. When He finds a heart that is open to receiving Him and listening to instruction, he will be found! When He finds a heart that has been hardened to love and to truth, the time for repentance may be lost. Your own devices/defenses fail because fear/anxiety is a spiritual problem. Spiritual problems require spiritual solutions, and the best solutions are God's solutions, found in the passages of the Holy Bible. They may be quite different from what you expect!

Oppression and the Cords of Sin

Door points can also be opened in other ways. No words do justice to the influence our culture and peer pressure have on our beliefs, the way we process pain, and our general behavior. The apostle Paul addresses this issue in Romans 12:2 when he writes, "Do not be conformed to this world." Paul

88 Jon Courson's Commentary, New Testament Volume 3, on Romans Chapter 6, Page 921

offers the solution to this problem of worldly influence when he commands us to "dedicate our bodies as a living sacrifice" and adds that doing so is "your reasonable [rational, intelligent] service and spiritual worship" (Romans 12:1-2). Have you considered that obedience to God is an act of worship? Children of God obey out of love for God, not because they think God will hurt them. They do not want to hurt God (Genesis 6:5-6).

God provides Scripture as a yardstick to measure the teachings of the world, and He provides the Holy Spirit to help us separate the truth of God from the lies of Satan (I Corinthians 2:1-16, Colossians 2:6-9). Whenever we disagree with God and agree with Satan, we open a door point to demonic oppression on that issue in our lives (the way we eat, drive, work, cope with emotions, pray, etc.). We consciously or unknowingly place ourselves under the influence of the kingdom of Satan rather than the kingdom of God.

When we are under the influence of the kingdom of Satan and our behavior is governed by his lies, we become oppressed in some way. **Oppression** is a process issue used by Satan to keep us functioning in his kingdom. There are well over 100 references in the Bible to the words oppressed, oppresseth, oppressing, oppression, oppressions, oppressor, and oppressors. Of all these references, only three occur in the New Testament. And of these three scriptures, only one directly refers to oppression being connected to the power of the devil (Acts 10:36-38).

In verse 38, Paul writes, "How God anointed and consecrated Jesus of Nazareth with the [Holy] Spirit and with strength and ability and power; how he went about doing good and, in particular, curing all who were harassed and **oppressed** by [the power of] the devil, for God was with him." In most of these scriptures dealing with oppression, the oppressor is a person, group of people, or nation that is exercising power over another person or group of persons resulting in a **restriction** of some sort. They are prevented from experiencing the abundant life that God desires us to have through the gospel and ministry of Jesus Christ.

What specifically is holding or restricting a person as a result of sin? In Proverbs 5:22, King Solomon writes, "His own iniquities shall ensnare the wicked man, and he shall be held with the cords of his sin." It is the **cords of sin** that bind a person and restrict choices. The cords of sin fall into five important categories: beliefs, emotions, behavior, physiology, and spirituality. These are the five domains of humanity, the core of what makes us human. Satan attacks every part of our personhood.

The Cords of Sin

Beliefs: Sin results in distortions of reality and separation from truth. This is **the cord of fallacy**. Distortions of information lead to an inaccurate worldview and poor decisions.

Emotions: Sin produces confusion, guilt, shame, fear, hurt, sadness, and disappointment. Different combinations of these emotions draw people into the kingdom of Satan and keep them there. These people are looking down and not up. Emotions influence decision-making. This is the **cord of sentiment.**

Behavior: Many decisions are made based on poor information and emotions. Decisions made from distorted reality and painful emotions are often very poor decisions. Dysfunctional behavior is the result. This is the **cord of poor choices**.

Physiology: The Cord of Compulsion. Neurochemical alterations and changes in receptor physiology create a strong predisposition to making the same mistake/behavior repeatedly (Romans 6:16). This is the cord of compulsion.

Spirituality: The Cord of Separation. God, Jesus, and the Holy Spirit are an interwoven lifeline composed of three chords. When this line is cut, you are like the astronaut whose lifeline to the space shuttle has been severed and he finds himself drifting off into space. There is no rescue! This is the cord of separation.

King Solomon instructs, "A threefold cord is not quickly broken." There are five cords of sin that restrict and restrain you in the kingdom of Satan. You will not easily escape. Notice the cord of separation has three strands: God, Jesus, and the Holy Spirit. These strands together are more powerful than the five cords of sin because they form the **cord of relationship with God.**

If you want to know the areas of your life that are being influenced by Satan, there are several strategies you can employ:

1. Pray the prayer of King David in Psalm 139:23–24, asking God to make known to you Satan's deceptions. Be sure to listen for God's response until you hear it. Be willing to pray this repeatedly until you get a definite answer.
2. Ask your accountability/prayer partner or spouse for input.
3. Look for areas of **restriction** in your life.
4. Review a list of difficult life experiences looking for strongholds/door points.

5. Ask yourself, am I experiencing satisfaction in life?
6. Ask yourself, do I have a purpose for life?
7. Ask God, what is preventing me from experiencing love, joy, and peace?
8. Study the scriptures asking the Holy Spirit to guide your understanding of their application to your life.

Where you find oppression or restriction, you will find deception, and where you find deception, you will find Satan or one of his demons nearby influencing you. Our war is not with flesh and blood (II Corinthians 10:3-5, Ephesians 6:12). There is not a devil under every rock, but there is a sin nature in every heart that facilitates the opening of your heart to the influence of Satan. And "the devil roams around like a lion roaring [in fierce hunger] seeking someone to seize upon and devour" (I Peter 5:8). Satan has nothing to do except deceive weak, unsuspecting souls.

A further progression of Satanic influence may lead to demonic possession. When a person becomes demon possessed, instead of being "nearby," the demon invades a larger portion of the heart/soul of the person and controls much of the individual's thought processes, speech, emotions, and behavior. All Christians are indwelt by the Holy Spirit and by Jesus, who gained victory over Satan and his demons by virtue of His death on the cross and subsequent resurrection. This would preclude a true Christian from being possessed by a demon.[89] This book is not intended to explore the process or manifestations of demon possession.

Temptation, which has the potential of leading to sin/disobedience in some way, always has Satan as its point of origin (James 1:13-15, John 8:44). However, it may originate from within our own heart/our sin nature (Romans 7:1-25 and James 1:13-15) or from without, which comes from the world in a variety of temptations. In either case, there is a point of choice, an action point, when we choose with whom we are going to agree and obey. If we repeatedly agree with Satan and are responsive to his deceptions, we become a slave to sin; if we agree with God, the Holy Spirit, and the Gospel of Christ, we become slaves to God (Romans 6:1-23). It is by being a slave to God that it is possible to find love, joy, peace, abundant life here on earth, and eternal life in heaven (Romans 6:22, Galatians 5:22-24). It is only through **slavery**

89 Hostage to the Devil, By Malachi Martin, an authoritative book on demon possession

to God that one can experience freedom from sin (Romans 6:16). This may seem a little odd. Nonbelievers see Christians as being confined and restricted from experiencing pleasure in life, while Christians see nonbelievers as being prisoners of Satan and slaves of sin. One of those two groups is being hoodwinked! There are only two spiritual kingdoms, the kingdom of God and the kingdom of Satan. Which kingdom are you in? If you are uncertain about the answer to this question, go back a few paragraphs to the section on oppression and restriction and work your way through the strategies provided to discover the process of oppression in your life. After finishing a careful review of your life, stop reading, and consider this question for at least 24 hours: which kingdom am I in? Do I want to stay in the kingdom where I currently find myself? Write your answers in the space below.

____

____

____

____

In the next chapter, the process of deception is examined in more detail as to how it is changing our pursuit of the American Dream. The American Dream started in 1585 at Roanoke Island. A review of process issues in our early colonies demonstrates the roots of the problems we are experiencing in living out the American Dream in the 21st century.

Distraction, Confusion, and the American Dream

Roanoke Colony

Building the **American Dream** started with the arrival of the English colonists in 1585 at Roanoke Island off the coast of North Carolina. Hardship forced this group to return to England after several months. A second group of about 100 people went to the island in 1587. They suffered Indian attacks and insufficient supplies resulting in their leader, John White, returning to England for emergency assistance, leaving his daughter and granddaughter Virginia on the Island. A war between Spain and England delayed his return for two years. You can only wonder at the concern White experienced for the people left behind while he was forced to wait in England. When he arrived at Roanoke, there was no trace of the colonists except the word CROATAN, the name of another Island and Indian tribe south of Roanoke, carved into a wooden post.[90,91] One can only imagine the shock, grief, and perhaps guilt he experienced at his loss. **Beginnings** of turning dreams into reality are often fraught with trials, tribulation, disappointment, and great sacrifice. **Maintaining** dreams requires vigilance. The alternative is surrender to the trials and disappointments the world brings…and abandonment of the dream.

Virginia Colony

A third attempt to establish an English presence in North America was authorized by King James I in 1606 through the Virginia Company, which was given exclusive rights by the King to explore opportunities for investments in the New World. Specifically, they were looking for gold, desiring to lay an English claim to territory in North America, and hoping to find "the fabled Northwest Passage through the New World to Asia and the East Indies." England was competing with Spain in each of these pursuits and was lagging behind.

---

90 www.history.com, what happened to the "Lost Colony" of Roanoke

91 www.outerbanksvacations.com, Outer Banks History What does Croatan Mean

However, the Virginia Company was not entirely forthcoming with its investors about their motives for their New World expedition. Instead, they invented a **public relations scheme** in which the expedition was touted as an unparalleled opportunity to evangelize the indigenous population. They lied to their investors. Seeking gold was the object of their expedition. Does lying and the pursuit of wealth sound familiar in politics today?

In May 1607, the Virginia Company landed a group of 104 settlers approximately 40 miles up a river entering the Chesapeake Bay, which they named the James River. They established the colony known as Jamestown. Many of these settlers were gentlemen, men who had come primarily concerned about finding gold or other treasure. They had no interest in the labor necessary to establish a pioneer community. Actual work was not part of their code of conduct. About a quarter of the settlers were laborers, men who were indentured and required to work for the company for up to seven years, after which they were released from service. The rest were tradesmen, including bricklayers, carpenters, soldiers, barbers, fishermen, blacksmiths, children, one drummer, one surgeon, one minister, and "diverse others."

The parson, Robert Hunt, preached every Sunday at services every colonist was required to attend. He worked hard physically and cared for the sick, of which there were many. The gentlemen had the same amount of interest in his sermons as they had in physical labor, little to none. There were no women, thus lacking the moderating influence that wives often have on men's behavior. The settlement was inadequately provisioned. It was located near a swampy area with malaria-bearing mosquitos waiting for flesh, and no fresh drinking water immediately available. They argued about everything; they could not even agree on the need to plant corn in order to feed themselves. Consequently, they bordered on starvation and were dependent on sometimes hostile Indians for food.

In 1607, Powhatan was the chief of 32 named tribes totaling 13,000 to 14,000 natives. The Powhatans occupied hundreds of villages in 6500 square miles along the banks of rivers near the coast. They had their own government, economy, religion, and language. The colonists considered them savages. Some of the colonists stole canoes, grain, and whatever else they wanted from the Indians.[92] John Smith, one of the council members for

92 www.nps.gov/jame/learn/education/classroom/powhatanindiansandtheenglish-historicjamestown.htm

the colony, was prone to shooting an Indian, if necessary, to obtain grain.[93]

When a ship sent to bring additional supplies arrived in February 1608, only 38 of the 104 settlers were still alive. Disease was responsible for nearly all these deaths. As time passed and no gold or other riches returned with the ships from Jamestown, the owners of the London company invented larger and larger lies to stimulate more investment. All this drama continued until May 1610 when a man named Lord De La War brought a ship with provisions and sensible authority, which began a slow reversal of the decline of Jamestown.

In 1610, John Rolfe brought tobacco seeds to Jamestown from Trinidad. Tobacco became the gold long searched for by the settlers. Over the next several decades, hundreds of British ships made the round trip from England each year to transport tobacco. In April of 1614, Rolfe married Pocahontas, the daughter of Powhatan. This reduced hostilities with the natives temporarily.

In July of 1619, each non-indentured man was given 100 acres of land which greatly increased work incentive. A few weeks later, on August 20,1619, the more affluent men of Jamestown purchased 20 indentured laborers. This single act would evolve into the dark story of slavery, which lasted 250 years until the United States Civil War. It is important to note that a large percentage of English colonists came to North America as indentured servants. This will be reviewed in more detail in the chapter on slavery. In 1620 the first census of Jamestown Colony was taken. The population had increased from 38 in 1608 to 928, consisting of "892 Europeans, 670 able bodied men, 119 women, 39 serviceable boys, and 57 children" (most of the youth having been rounded up from the streets of London). There were also 32 Africans and four Indians.[94]

In 1622, a devastating war with the Powhatan Indians killed 25 percent of the European population in Virginia. King James ordered an inquiry of events in the colony while investors literally abandoned ship. King James revoked their charter, and in 1624, Virginia became a royal colony administered by a governor appointed by the Crown.[95] The colony had barely survived, but it did

---

93 The Light and the Glory by Peter Marshall and David Manuel, much of the history of Jamestown and Plymouth colonies provided in these summaries is taken from this book, pages 80-144, a fascinating account of these early colonies

94 www.historyisfun.org, 1620 to 2020 census count

95 www.britannica.com/event/Powhatan-War

survive, becoming the first permanent English settlement in North America.

Plymouth Colony

While the Jamestown Colony was experiencing distraction and confusion, producing chaos and starvation, two nascent Christian groups in England were criticizing the practices of its established church, the Church of England. One group, the Puritans, believed the Church could be purified by working within the church. The other group, the separatists, believed the church was "already corrupted beyond any possibility of purification."[96] Several separatists fled religious persecution in England and relocated in Holland. In 1618, King James issued an administrative order forcing all Puritans and separatists unwilling to accept church authority to leave England. This law from the King, coupled with a decade of extreme hardship in Holland and a desire to spread the Gospel of Christ, prompted the separatists to develop a plan to establish their home and ministry in the wilderness of New England. The separatists were later referred to as pilgrims.

To finance their adventure, they entered into an agreement with a merchant adventurer, Thomas Weston, and other investors in London. This resulted in their being indentured to him for seven years. Weston claimed to share their spiritual beliefs and desire to spread the Gospel, but his true motives were corrupt, cunning, and primarily concerned with financial gain. Weston engaged the captain of the *Mayflower* to take 41 separatists and 61 "strangers" to the New World. The strangers were people unfamiliar with the separatists. Some shared the beliefs and spiritual aspirations of the separatists, while others were looking for wealth.

Hours prior to their departure, Weston presented his pioneer immigrants with a new contract written to his advantage, which they refused to sign. Weston returned to London frustrated and angry, and the colonists left England for the New World without resolution of their dispute with Weston. After seven weeks of storm-tossed, below-decks passage, on November 9,1620, the *Mayflower* arrived at a place English fishermen had named Cape Cod. This area was north of the land included in the Virginia charter. The winds of fortune had driven them 100 miles north of their objective, the mouth of the Hudson River in New York Harbor. They attempted a passage south, but winds and tides made sailing to the Hudson River very difficult. After discussion and prayer, they decided to

96 The Light and the Glory, Pg. 108

stay in the bay of Cape Cod.

When the strangers realized they were staying in a geographical area outside the charter of The Virginia Company's territory, some said they were no longer contractually bound to comply with the laws of the charter. Realizing this rebellious thought process could destroy the colony, leaders of the separatists developed an agreement, later called the Mayflower Compact, which created a set of laws to rule the colony. Two days after their landing, 41 of the 50 men who came on the Mayflower signed the agreement. Two parts of the compact stand out:

1. The colonists would create one society and work together to further it, and,
2. The colonists would live according to the Christian faith.[97]

While exploring the mainland, looking for a site to build, they discovered 20 acres of fertile land cleared and ready for planting. A hostile Native American tribe had lived in this area, but a mysterious plague had decimated the whole Patuxent tribe three to four years earlier. Other tribes were afraid to venture into this area for fear of contracting the disease. They found spring-fed creeks nearby with sweet fresh water and gave this site the name *Plymouth* in remembrance of their departure from Plymouth, England.

New England winters are windy, rainy, and cold, with an average annual snowfall of about three feet.[98] The settlers slept on board the *Mayflower* while constructing buildings in freezing weather. By mid-January, many of the colonists were living and sleeping in the common house, which was also used to care for the sick. By the following spring, 47 of the 102 settlers had died from consumption and pneumonia.

In November 1621, a year after their arrival, Weston sent 35 more colonists to Plymouth on a ship bound for Virginia. However, Weston sent no equipment or supplies, indicating his displeasure with the Plymouth colonists for not agreeing to his revised contract. Feeding 35 additional souls through the winter created a tremendous burden, resulting in half rations for everyone. At one point, the ration of corn was reduced to five kernels per day per person. Instead of supplies, Weston sent an emissary who convinced the colonists to sign his contract. It took an additional 24 years for the colonists to satisfy

97 www.history.com, The Mayflower Compact

98 www.currentresults.com/Weather/Massachusetts/annual-snowfall, average annual snowfall totals in Massachusetts

all the obligations of this revised contract, but they eventually bought out the original group of investors at great cost to themselves. During the first years, the colonists survived primarily because of their ability to endure hardship and through assistance from Native Americans. A native man called Squanto taught them how to fish, hunt, trap, and raise Indian corn. Squanto also played a key role in negotiating peace with local tribes.

The greed of Thomas Weston led to his eventual demise. Without telling his co-investors, he set up a fishing station north of Plymouth Colony. When this came to light, he was expelled from his investment group. As a result of other financial disappointments, he decided to leave London and establish himself in the New World. Upon his arrival, he learned his team of "fishermen" preferred alcohol intoxication to fishing. On his way to investigate this rumor, his boat sank, and he was plundered by hostile Indians, resulting in his begging for assistance from Plymouth Colony. Though colonists had every reason to scuttle him to the bottom of Cape Cod Bay, they gave him a load of beaver pelts and sent him on his way, hopefully never to return.

The colony survived Weston and winter but never became as prosperous as the neighboring Massachusetts Bay Colony, founded in 1628, with which they merged in 1691.

Process Issues and the Fate of Roanoke, Jamestown, and Plymouth Colonies

Now, apply the principles of distraction and confusion to their impact on the development of Roanoke, Jamestown, and Plymouth Colonies and consider parallel problems in society today.

All three of these colonies suffered because of inadequate preparation. It is easy to understand how the first attempt at Roanoke might run afoul of unknown challenges, but it seems the second attempt at Roanoke, Jamestown, and Plymouth colonies did not have a plan to sustain themselves. Plans are process issues because they lead to decision points. While the colonists at Jamestown were starving, English fishing vessels were transporting tons of fish to England for commercial sale. Did the English fishermen with tons of fish on board know about the colonists? Was there any **communication** about their existence or their needs? Communication is a process issue in every relationship. Failure to communicate leads to failed adventures and failed relationships.

There are certain "adventures" in life that turn out better if we have a plan: learning how to hunt, trap, farm, and catch fish were process/survival issues for the colonists. How to support a family, having a successful marriage, a retirement plan, and satisfaction in life are process/survival issues in our modern age.

In the story of Jamestown, there are five groups of people to consider: the Crown, founders of the company, investors, colonists, and Native Americans.

King James was distracted by pride, greed, lust for power, and competition with Spain. The founders and investors were distracted by greed and lies. The settlers at Jamestown were distracted by greed, interpersonal conflict, disunity, sloth, dependence on the natives, and lawlessness.

Only conjecture is possible about what was distracting the Native Americans. Initially, they may have been curious about their European visitors, their ships, and their guns. After they observed the building of a palisade and crude housing, they eventually realized these people were not visitors but were competing for land and other resources. What to do? The colonists did not seem to pose a threat as they were unable to even feed themselves. The natives had no way of knowing how the lust for riches was working in the hearts of these newcomers, the people who sent them, and the many people who would follow.

The ambivalent attitude of the colonists toward the natives, manifested by peace initiatives alternating with hostility, murder, and thievery, certainly added to any confusion the Indians were experiencing. It seems likely the Indians were initially simply distracted from their normal routine. As hundreds of settlers poured in over the next fifteen years, curiosity and irritation gave way to hatred, resulting in the massacre of Europeans in 1622. After a second Indian war in 1644, a treaty was negotiated, ceding much of Native American land to the colony. The tribes under Powhatan had been reduced to about 2000 members by this time.

One process issue overrides all of the above: the **absence of spiritual direction.** This one factor gave birth to all the other process issues that account for the dismal performance of the Jamestown settlers. The authors of *The Light and the Glory* state, "In an age and country where practically all the leaders acknowledged God's existence and thereby considered themselves good Christian gentleman and ladies, hardly anyone was actually living the life Christ calls us to in His gospel. Even among the ministers, who were extolling the need for the thrust of Christianity into heathen lands, hardly any were actually prepared to go themselves."[99]

These groups were distracted from the incredible opportunities that lay before them: the opportunity for adventure, to become landowners, to have families, to experience the fruits of their labor, and to build a satisfying, productive life for themselves. They looked at the beauty around them every day. They touched it. They smelled it. They walked on virgin land but failed to comprehend its value. Instead, thinking they had struck it rich, they sent a ship full of iron pyrite back to London, which was determined to be "fool's gold." Indeed, they were the fools. They were deceived, blinded by their pursuit of gold and the luxury and power money brings. Jamestown suffered and nearly failed because of their **distraction** and **confusion**.

The result of all the distraction and confusion was chaos and starvation in Jamestown. **Chaos** in a culture always produces human suffering. It is difficult to accept the story about the Jamestown colonists failing to plant corn and **depending** on Indians for food during the winter. The pursuit of riches and power blinds people to everything else that is important in life. **Dependency** on others makes people weak, passive, inefficient, lazy, and vulnerable. Is that an issue in society today? Is our government making us weak, passive, inefficient, lazy, and vulnerable? Then, are they taking advantage of our vulnerability?

In Plymouth Colony, the process issues were more favorable to the survival of the colony. The motives of the separatists were partly **altruistic,** i.e., spreading the Gospel, and partly, **self-**centered, looking for a more rewarding, satisfying life. They recognized the potential for disagreement and dissension and reduced that by generating a compact of rules that would govern their behavior. Eighty-two percent of the men on the Mayflower signed this agreement. Women did not vote at that time. Everyone was expected to work. There were no "gentlemen" on board the Mayflower. However, they showed a similar **lack of planning,** resulting in **initial dependence** on the natives. Unlike the settlers at Jamestown, they learned and implemented the necessary skills to survive the first spring and summer after their arrival. They had the advantage of spiritual direction to guide their decision-making. This was manifested in their decision to forgive and assist Thomas Weston, despite his long history of dishonesty and treachery.

Jamestown and Plymouth colonies may be considered from a spiritual perspective. The colonists at Jamestown were primarily motivated by greed

99 The Light and the Glory, Pg.104

and the lifestyle they thought riches would bring. Spiritual concern for themselves, each other, or the Native Americans was practically nonexistent. There was no Thanksgiving celebration at Jamestown after their first year of settlement. At Plymouth Colony, they were motivated spiritually to extend the gospel of Christ and personally to find a more satisfying existence where they could prosper. Their spirituality influenced the agreements they established with one another to govern their behavior in furthering the success of their community. It was at Plymouth Colony where the settlers thanked God for His provision and invited the Native Americans, who assisted them, to join in celebrating our first Thanksgiving. As decades passed, newer settlers became distracted from the mission of the separatists to evangelize. The focus became the acquisition of land and accumulation of wealth.

Variations of the above pattern, Indian wars, reduced numbers of natives, followed by treaties ceding native land, were repeated during westward expansion for the next 300 years. This pattern nearly eradicated Native American life in the "United States." The culture of Native Americans and their possession of lands were diametrically opposed to the objectives of the King, the London Company, and the hordes of immigrants who came to the shores of North America. These were the people in power. **People in power** determine policy, write laws and treaties, administer "justice," and later write the historical account of everything. They are always right in their own eyes.

Continuous disagreement between the colonies and the King and British Parliament over the next 150 years led to our Declaration of Independence and war with Great Britain. Parliament desired to tax the colonies without the colonies having any say in the tax. Britain was experiencing financial stress from seven years of war with France (The Seven Years' War, also known as the French and Indian War), which cemented Britain's claim to territories in mainland North America. Britain expected the colonists to assist in paying for the cost of British troops to protect the colonies from French influence. But Britain erred in not giving the colonists a vote or negotiating power in the process of levying taxes. "Taxation without representation" was the cry of the colonists.

Today, we are walking in the steps of the early colonists and do not know it. Through hard work, private ownership, management, and competition, hundreds of millions of Americans have made the **American Dream** a reality. They became the middle class. This has been the strength and appeal of the United States to people everywhere. But there is a fundamental problem with capitalism, and that is its appeal to the evil desire of lust for greed, power, and control. Capitalism is prone to evolve into a form of government known as an oligarchy: rule by a small group of people who often are very wealthy, powerful, or both. These people consider themselves to be an elite class, separate and above the rest of us. They are controlled by pride, with a result similar to what happened to Lucifer (Isaiah 14:12-20). They are eventually brought down, but often only after they generate a lot of confusion, distraction, deception, and social conflict. "All Tyrannies rule through fraud and force but once the fraud is exposed they must rely exclusively on force."[100] It seems we have arrived at that point in the "land of the free and the home of the brave".[101]

There has always been a natural tension between those who seek to satisfy selfish motives of greed and power and those who are concerned with representing Jesus wherever God puts them. That tension is being manifested by division in our society today, with the divide getting larger day by day. Like matter being sucked into a black hole, the spiritual life of Western Civilization is being sucked into a black hole of deception. The American dream is being sucked in with it. At this writing, it is unclear how much of either will escape (Matthew 16:24-27).[102]

Have you noticed disagreement is often difficult to resolve? Disagreement is a very common phenomenon. Disagreement is a process issue. It often determines outcome. Disagreement is not simply about having a different opinion. People have their own opinion about everything based on their worldview, as discussed in Chapter One. These differences do not necessarily produce conflict. One strategy to avoid conflict is keeping opinions to yourself.

---

100 USANews.Com, George Orwell, 1984

101 www.theglobalist.com, article by Jefferson Morley, The Land of the Free. These words, originally written by Francis Scott Key in 1814 in a poem titled "The Defense of Fort McHenry," were officially incorporated into our national anthem in 1931.

102 The above paragraphs are mostly about process. I have not given details about all the examples of people whose lives have been destroyed. I have intentionally omitted much of the content because there is so much and it is changing so rapidly. If you want to stay up to date on content get on the e-mail list of Intercessors for America, Activist Mommy, Alliance Defending Freedom, Family Research Council, Hillsdale College, News Max, the Epoch Times, Fox News, or similar sources of current events. A book with all this content would fill thousands of pages.

This is helpful as long as no one is forcing you to accept an opinion that violates your beliefs, stimulates fear, or restricts your freedom.

Consider the directions provided by our public health authorities during the recent coronavirus pandemic. Historically, personal choice was the "rule" people followed re: their health care decisions. During the pandemic, a majority of people in most states were persuaded to surrender their choice and conform to the mantra of staying home and taking the vaccine. Those who refused were threatened/punished with ridicule, job loss, loss of medical care, and threats to professional licensure. Instead of quarantining those who were sick, schools and businesses were closed, and much of the citizenry was placed in lockdown. Payments were made by the government to ease the financial stress millions of people were experiencing.

These restrictions on freedom were accepted because of widespread fear of the virus having fatal outcomes. Fear was weaponized to control the thinking, emotions, and behavior of the general population. Now, nearly three years after the early phases of the pandemic, we have not recovered from the draconian measures imposed by our governing authorities. Many businesses have not reopened, students failed to do well with online learning, there has been a pandemic of anxiety and depression, and there are labor shortages in every sector of our economy. When you pay people who are well to stay home from work, many become sick in unexpected ways. This was entirely predictable, but warnings were ignored by those who held power. The governing powers/public health authorities would not listen or engage in discussion.

Communication and **negotiation** are the peaceful processes that resolve disagreement. The Mayflower Compact is a perfect example of how this works. The 16 adult men and 11 women separatists constituted only 27 percent of the 102 would-be settlers on the *Mayflower*. Yet they negotiated an agreement with a large majority of the others containing the following provisions: 1) The colonists would create one society and work together to further it; 2) The colonists would live according to the Christian faith. In these two short sentences are three accords that form three of the five pillars that support our American Republic:

1. Creation of one society
2. Working together to further it
3. Living by an agreed upon set of rules.

The fourth pillar is equal opportunity for all: opportunity for education, opportunity for owning your own home, and opportunity to exercise the inalienable rights of equality and freedom in life, liberty, and the pursuit of happiness.[103] The fifth pillar is a life of society centered in the American family consisting of a father, mother, and children created by their union. These are the five pillars that support the American Dream. Each of these pillars is currently under attack. Each of these pillars is crumbling before our eyes as we observe the process of decay. Many of us experience frustration and disappointment about these events. It seems we are helpless to do anything about it. In reality, most of us are passive or afraid to act. Passivity, helplessness, and fear are **states of mind** which distract, confuse, and create deception. They lead to a decision to do nothing. Inaction is often the result of deception (James 4:17).

These states of mind are promoted by a variation of power dynamics that is dividing the citizens of the United States. In recent years, unity has been redefined by people in power as "agree with our politics or we will punish you." Destroying the lives of people who disagree with those who are in power has become known as "cancel culture." Cancel culture attacks every one of the five pillars supporting our republic.

Cancel culture is hardly new. At the height of Roman power, it is estimated that 40 percent of the population of Italy was slaves. Roman slavery was not based on race. It was based on military power and conquest. Most Roman slaves were captured, purchased, or born into slavery. Financially desperate Roman citizens were known to sell their own children into slavery.[104]

During the Holocaust, approximately six million Jews were murdered by Nazi Germany. Genocide is the extreme result of governments promoting the plague of cancel culture. The people promoting cancel culture in the U.S. seem to prefer slower death by economic strangulation or simply locking people up indefinitely by ignoring legal protections provided by our constitution and state law. Cancel culture destroys the lives of the people who are canceled. There are many ways to destroy a person's life. Cancel culture and slavery have three things in common: 1) use of **force**, 2) the goal to **subjugate** people to those who hold power, and 3) **loss of freedom**.

---

103 www.archives.gov/founding-docs/declaration, paraphrase from our Declaration of Independence

104 www.pbs.org/empires/romans/empire/slaves, the Roman empire: in the first century.

Freedom of speech, freedom of worship, and freedom of opportunity are guaranteed by our Constitution and Bill of Rights. They stand in the way of those who desire to remake America. Cancel culture should be called "destroying the lives of people who disagree with those who are in power." It could be named, *We don't care about you; we will do whatever we want because we are in power and you are not.* It could be referred to as *canceling our Constitution.* It is all of these, but perhaps the best moniker would be *the End of the American Dream.* You can't change the American dream without changing the laws which protect it. That requires a change in the way our Constitution is interpreted, changing the Constitution itself, changing the structure of the Supreme Court to favor the people who hold political power, or simply ignoring the law. Political power can accomplish all of these objectives. Political power **is accomplishing** all these objectives!

The people who are destroying lives through cancel culture refuse to discuss their thinking or behavior. They believe that since they hold power, they can do whatever they want and not be responsible. At this point in time, they are getting away with it! They do not care about the rest of us.

If you are not part of the elite group who hold money and power, you, your life, your family, have no value in their minds. How could this be? There are many reasons:

1. They do not know you. They do not know you as someone with needs, hopes, dreams, emotions, weaknesses, strengths, and life goals. They see you as an obstacle to achieving complete power rather than a person.
2. They do not want to know you. They are totally focused on achieving the goal of complete control of your life.
3. They think of you only in terms of what you can do for them, pay taxes, vote, and cheer for them at their rallies and campaigns.
4. They spend most of their time with like-minded individuals who do not care.
5. They live in the future with plans to accrue more power and money. They are plotting their next plan to deceive.
6. They do not have a healthy spiritual life and do not understand people who do.
7. They do not know God.
8. They make no effort to know God.
9. They have experienced the lovingkindness of God but failed to recognize its source (Psalm 63:3-6,10).

10. They do not have love for their fellow human beings, which is put into the heart of each person who accepts Christ (I John 4:7-12).

Some of these characteristics are very similar to the character of slave owners during our period of Black slavery. Do you want to be a slave to these people? Are you willing to think and act like a slave owner turning human beings into obstacles/things to be manipulated? Answer these questions in the space below.

____

____

____

____

____

What is fueling numbers one through ten above? Answer, **Pride**. I do not know words that adequately describe the insidious, evil desire of pride. The best strategy to understand pride is to observe the worst, most inhumane things that people do to other people. Then look carefully for pride, and you will nearly always find it lurking in the shadows where it is difficult to discern. Consider what Hitler did during the Holocaust.

The thought of our elected leaders not caring about the people who elected them is frustrating and disappointing for the rest of us. American citizens expect to be treated fairly by the people they elect. Fear, passivity, and the defense mechanism of denial are process issues working together to separate citizens from their constitutional rights. Some people are afraid to speak because they fear for their financial and emotional lives. Others think cancel culture is a temporary phenomenon that will change with the next election cycle. Some do not want to be called racists because they are not racists. Some do not perceive a need to defend the truth; they are passive. And some are in denial about the reality of innocent people losing their livelihoods or being accused of hateful racist behavior. They might think, "If I don't say anything, it won't happen to me." Some people who support cancel culture consider themselves social justice warriors defending people who are or have been oppressed. They believe people who disagree with their objectives deserve to have their lives ruined. Instead of advancing social justice, they are waging war on behalf of Satan's demons.

Social justice is not advanced by oppressing other groups of people. These self-appointed social justice warriors **are distracted** from the evil nature of cancel culture. **Cancel** culture is a manifestation of **evil desire** for power and control that destroys the lives of individuals. It perpetuates discrimination and creates a generalized sense of fear in society. It distracts and leads to confusion. Distraction is the initial process issue leading to deception. The above groups of people are all deceived. Was Thomas Jefferson wrong when he stated the rights of men are inalienable? They are only inalienable to the extent that we protect them. We must not be distracted and fail to protect our rights. If we do not defend our rights, we can very easily be separated from them. There is a new declaration originating from our national capital. I refer to it as "The Declaration of Separation". This is the law they are forcing on the American public, forcing it on you.

Cancel culture is joined at the hip with critical race theory and ESG. Critical race theory is the most racist concept to pillage and rape American culture since the enactment of Jim Crow laws after our Civil War.[105, 106] Mark Levin writes the following about the core belief of those who propose and advance CRT: "In other words, America as a land of opportunity and freedom is a fiction, and the citizen-majority that accepts this fiction is made up of mindless zombies, unable to think for themselves…" Do you agree with these assertions? Do you agree America has not been a land of opportunity? Do you agree the citizens of the United States are mindless zombies? If you disagree with these statements, you should be opposed to critical race theory. For more content on CRT, consider reading Mark Levin's authoritative review in his book, *American Marxism.*

It is certainly true that racism continues to exist in the United States. It is equally true no country has completely overcome racist ideology or practice. Asserting critical race theory will abolish racism demonstrates denial, ignorance, and malicious intent. It denies the reality of racism having its roots in our sin nature. It ignores the progress made in race relations since the passage of civil rights laws in the 1960s. It is an example of a spiritual problem requiring a spiritual solution. Cancel culture and critical race theory are destroying the lives of citizens who disagree with those who are in power. They are destroying the American Dream.

ESG is an acronym for environmental, social, and governance. It is a relatively new tool used by those with economic clout to create "a highly subjective political score infiltrating all walks of life forcing progressive

105 christopherrufo.com, The Truth about Critical Race Theory

106 American Marxism, by Mark Levin, Chapter Four, Racism, Genderism, and Marxism

policies on everyday Americans resulting in higher prices at the pump and at the store."[107] For example, we are currently experiencing high gas prices and higher energy prices secondary to current US policy discouraging the development of our petroleum and coal industries. The ESG rating of a company reflects its compliance with policies promoting investing in climate change and radical social policies. They use your money for political purposes instead of producing a return on investment. They do not care about how much financial stress their policies create for you. They are only concerned about advancing their political agenda. ESG is a core feature of the "I don't care about you agenda" which many politicians support today.

The radical people who support cancel culture, critical race theory, and ESG are church phobic, family phobic, children phobic, middle-class phobic, education phobic, prosperity phobic, the rule of law phobic, Constitution phobic, fairness phobic, free speech phobic, police phobic, border phobic, gun phobic, and boundaries phobic. They are not afraid of prosperity, education, or guns to protect themselves. They are afraid for the rest of us to have access to these things. They are distracted and confused about each of these issues. They are angry at, distrustful of, and anxious about the rest of us...the citizens of the United States of America.

They fear everything noted above because they perceive church, families, children, the middle class, education, prosperity, rule of law, the Constitution, fairness, free speech, local police, strong borders, and gun ownership as obstacles to taking complete control. Each of these obstacles is a boundary in their mind they have to violate to secure power. How quickly your mind alters perception! Their own fear prevents governing from a position of love and truth. Instead, they govern through fear and lies. Cancel culture, critical race theory, BLMGNF (Black Lives Matter Global Network Foundation), ESG, public health mandates, and you... the general public are all tools they are using and eventually will discard. Their governing philosophy can be summarized in 12 words spoken by Benito Mussolini in a speech in 1925, "Everything within the state, nothing outside the state, nothing against the state." During the Covid-19 pandemic, fishing was unlawful in the states of Oregon and Washington. Did they think fish were vectors spreading the virus? According to the latest news report (1/11/2023), your gas cooking stove is now against the state.

---

107 ourmoneyourvalues.com, Our Money Our Values-What is ESG: an article and YouTube video explaining ESG

There is a name for people who govern through strategies designed to induce fear. They are called terrorists. At the first international meeting on terrorism in Jerusalem, in July 1979, terrorism was defined as "the deliberate assault on the innocent to inspire fear in order to gain political ends… It was not defined by the ends that the terrorists professed to be pursuing, but by the means they used."[108] This definition of terrorism perfectly fits all the "I don't care about you" (my quotes) strategies being used by radical politicians today. Each of these "I don't care about you" strategies generates fear. Consider the following historical examples: Rome, Nazi Germany, Cuba, Communist Russia, China, Iran, and North Korea. Would you want to live in one of these dictatorships? People who govern in this way do not wear combat fatigues and carry automatic weapons. They often wear expensive suits, and their weapon of choice is fear.

They intend to destroy our families, indoctrinate and alienate our children, create crises allowing them to seize power, and disempower the middle class by destroying our jobs. They will accomplish these objectives by ignoring the rule of law and by **distracting the general public** through accusations of what they are doing themselves. Satan is the accuser (Job 1:8-11, Luke 3:10-14, I Peter 3:16-17, Revelation 12:10-11). When you find yourself accused, look beyond the person hurling the rants and complaints. When they accuse you of racism or some other "ism," they are distracting you from their evil plans and behavior. They must distract you because you are part of their plan. They will use you until there is nothing left of the life you worked for.

Perhaps the worst distraction is all the lies that come from the mouths of our elected representatives. These lies are intended to distract us from their abuse of power. Politicians from both parties are at fault. The reader needs to discern where the greatest fault lies. This is the reason the process of discernment is so important. Each of these lies requires investigation. Practicing discernment reveals who is lying and who is not. These are all distractions that confuse and deceive us using carefully chosen words that confuse. "No weapon is so terrible as a tongue sharpened by the Devil's grindstone."[109] We are living that truth in the U.S. today.

There is a small group of people orchestrating this attack on our rights, but this small group has a large number of followers who support eroding our freedoms and are very aggressive in their approach. The strategies they

108 Bibi, the autobiography of Benjamin Netanyahu, Pg 155, Par. Four

109 The Treasury of David, Psalm 57:4, commentary by Charles Spurgeon

use are producing tremendous pressure on the rest of us to conform. This is a unique type of peer pressure influencing our beliefs and behavior.

The fundamental process issues in peer pressure are **to be accepted or to be safe**. A person or group follows and adopts the attitudes, morals, or behavior of another group to be safe. The pressure can come externally from the group that is being followed, or pressure can come internally from wanting to be like the group. Of course, it could be a mixture of both. When peer pressure becomes generalized to most of the population in a geographical area, it becomes cultural pressure. Peer pressure and cultural pressure are like a hydraulic press crushing a banana. After the press has done its work, the banana is not recognizable. **Cultural pressure can render a group and its culture unrecognizable.** We are witnesses to this process in the United States today.

The end result of cancel culture, CRT, and ESG is persecution of those who disagree with governing authorities. In the history of these United States, persecution was initially focused on Native Americans. Native American culture has largely disappeared as a result. The Europeans who settled the North American continent sought/asked for the obliteration of Native American life. Now, the descendants of those Europeans are having the same experience, i.e., the obliteration of their own middle-class culture and the American Dream. Be careful of what you ask for. What goes around comes around. Remember, the eleven brothers of Joseph sold him into slavery. The twelve tribes of Israel subsequently spent 430 years in Egypt, much of which time was in slavery. Generally speaking, God gives people what they ask for when the request originates from their sin nature. Yet people are often surprised at what they get. This is because it is not possible to predict all the consequences of our sin.[110]

At this point, it seems persecution of the middle class is inevitable. Are you prepared for persecution? The American Dream is the antithesis of persecution. A central element of the American Dream is comfort. The middle class is comfortable. We have exceeded the political slogan of the 1920s, "A chicken in every pot, and a car in every garage". We are accustomed to comfort. Persecution will change everything. We will experience discomfort. Life will become painful. It will be marked by economic pain, social pain,

---

110 www.kingdominbible.com, The Rise and Fall of King Saul by John Hepp, Jr., the sad story of King Saul is another example of being unable to predict the consequences of sinful choices.

conflict, the loss of most of our comforts, and the loss of our freedoms. We experienced a taste of this during the recent coronavirus pandemic. When our radical leaders achieve complete control, they will serve the "full meal deal," which will produce a lot of angst and indigestion for the middle class.[111]

Now, compare Jesus to cancel culture, CRT, and ESG. Jesus humbled Himself by leaving Heaven and taking human form (John 1:14, 3:16). At the end of His three-year ministry, Jesus humbled Himself further by allowing Himself to be crucified to pay the debt owed for the sin of the world (Philippians 2:4-11). Do you know any elected official with that degree of humility?

The Creator of the universe loves everyone equally (John 3:16-17, Romans 5:8). He wants to know you personally. He wants to spend time with you. He already knows your weaknesses but loves you anyway. He desires to hear everything that is happening in your life. He never tires of listening. God desires there be no discrimination (Acts 10:34-35). God desires no one would be lost (II Peter 3:9). It matters not what you have done. When you accept Christ, every sin is transferred to Jesus (Romans 4:11, II Corinthians 5:19). This is the reason the Gospel of Christ is referred to as "Good News." Would you like to hear some good news for a change? Read the Gospel of Matthew! Then read the rest of the Gospels. No program or government-funded strategy will ever replace the goodwill for mankind that originates from God when we accept Jesus into our hearts (Ephesians 4:1-16).

Consider again the Mayflower Compact: 1) creation of one society, 2) working together to further it, 3) living by an agreed-upon set of rules. Our Constitution and Bill of Rights enshrined these three process issues for nearly 250 years. Process issues always determine outcome. It created the American Dream. We need to find our way back to one society, working together, and living by an agreed-upon set of rules. At the same time, we need to work at increasing equality of opportunity and restoring the preeminence of family. You and I are the investors in the American Dream. We must not be like the investors in the Virginia Company who invested in a lie. We must learn to discern the truth.

---

111 An outstanding resource on preparing for persecution is the book, God's Hostage, by Andrew Brunson. There is also a YouTube video series by Pastor Brunson titled, Prepare to Stand. Pastor Brunson was a prisoner in a Turkish Prison for two years. These resources are an account of his overcoming persecution.

Our primary concern is not only the people who are oppressing others; it is also the people who are watching passively as our freedoms are eroded one by one. We are the ones who are responsible for the loss of freedom in our society. We are the ones who are not informed, who do not investigate and discern, who refuse to run for the school board, who do not write our senators and representatives to Congress, who do not vote, who are comfortable, or who are afraid to speak. "We have met the enemy and he is us!"[112]

If you desire to pray about the issues discussed in this chapter, go to Psalm 109 and pray as King David did. Then do something... as suggested in the paragraph above! Just say, "No!" Take your children out of public school. Refuse to provide electrical, plumbing, automotive, and other services to the oligarchy. Stop cooking for them. Stop serving their food. Step out of slavery. If you are a female athlete, stop competing when transgender athletes ruin your sport. Allow them to compete against each other. Unless the general public is willing to be courageous and sacrifice, the oligarchy will take complete control. It is courage and sacrifice, not comfort, that contributed to America becoming the envy of every other nation. It was a process! Process determines outcome.

In the next chapter, an incident with our seven-day-old grandson shifts our focus to frustration and anger. Do babies get angry, or are they simply frustrated? Are anger and frustration the same experience, or are they different? We will examine frustration and anger, provide a rationale for separating them, and explore the process issues that lead people to choose anger to cope with stress.

---

112 This quotation is a parody of a quote by Oliver Hazard Perry during the War of 1812 by Walt Kelly in the Pogo cartoon strip. Perry was bragging about his victory over the British in the Battle of Lake Erie when he reported "We have met the enemy and they are ours".

Lessons from Jack

Everyone was surprised when our grandson's birth weight was recorded at 10 pounds 5 oz. Jack was the fattest baby I had ever seen. His cheeks looked like he was storing nuts for the winter. He had fat deposits in his fingers and toes. I was sufficiently concerned I checked the medical literature for conditions causing fat babies. The only thing I could find was maternal or gestational diabetes. His mother had neither condition, so I diagnosed "fat baby, cause unknown."

Apparently, the pediatrician was also concerned about his weight. He suggested they only give him 6 ounces of milk at his feeding to prevent more weight gain. But Jack seemed to want more. When he was about a week old, he broke the world record for sucking 6 ounces of milk from a bottle. He was quiet for a few seconds after the milk disappeared, and then a cry came out of the deepest part of his infant personality. We cannot know what he was thinking; however, it was not simply his scream that got my attention. His whole body turned red from the top of his head to the tip of his toes. I had heard of people seeing red and/or turning red when angry. I had never observed a person's whole body turn red. As an M.D. working in the field of behavioral science, I was very interested in what was happening.

A lot has been written about the contribution of genetic and environmental factors to personality function. Some argue nature/biology is the more important factor, while others side with environment/nurture. This is often referred to as the nature/nurture controversy. How would you categorize Jack's reaction to the disappearance of his milk?

It seems Jack was experiencing some degree of frustration (an environmental factor related to the absence of milk), which he was unable to express except through screaming, crying, and turning red. Perhaps, because he was a large baby, he had a biological need for a larger-than-average serving. I would suggest he had a desire for more milk based on his experience of enjoying his hunger being satisfied with milk. Was Jack angry? Or was Jack simply experiencing frustration, which is part of life? Are frustration and anger the same phenomena? Is anger innate, or is it a learned emotion? Are anger and frustration process issues? These are interesting questions.

What is a baby communicating with its cry immediately after delivery? Is it saying, "This world is really different from the warm, safe environment I just left," or "I'm not sure I like this. I like floating in warm water better than flailing in cold air"? Is an infant wondering whether it has XX or XY chromosomes, whether it is a boy or a girl? Do incomplete brain growth and immature personality function mean that the infant is not a living being? Write your answers in the space below.

____

____

____

____

____

Two things are certain: the brain of an infant will continue to develop until reaching young adulthood. And the personality of the infant/child will go through a process of development that parallels brain growth and is influenced by life experiences and genetics. Infants are not born with speech, but in older children and adults, speech correlates highly with thought life. So, the absence of speech suggests that infants don't have complex thoughts like comparing life in the uterus to life in their new world.

Frustration and **anger are** both process issues that sometimes determine outcome. Frustration occurs when a person desires to get from point A to point B, but something is in the way, blocking progress or preventing movement to point B. The obstruction itself can influence outcome, but the emotion that is generated by not getting to point B also has a big influence on how things turn out. The emotion can become a process issue. Frustration is not an emotion. It is a process that may generate an emotion. The emotion that is most often generated in response to that process is anger.

Frustration is a process, while anger is an emotion. They are closely connected but are different manifestations of the same event, which is being prevented from reaching point B. Frustration occurs initially, and the emotion often follows quickly, almost simultaneously. The short time lapse is what causes people to assume that frustration is an emotion. The emotional response could be something other than anger. It could be disappointment. It could be amusement about what is preventing progress toward point B.

It could be peace. It might even be love. Can you think of an example of frustration stimulating love? One example is the love parents experience for their children.

When our oldest daughter was one and a half years old, she cried continuously for three hours on a Saturday afternoon; I was unable to figure out the cause of her tears. Her diaper was dry, with no irritation on her bottom. She would not eat. Perhaps she was crying for the company of her mother, but I could not magically make her mother appear. It was frustrating for both of us. She cried. I was curious. As I held her, I felt concerned for her and experienced a Godly desire to resolve her tears, but I had to accept the reality it was her cry. I could not stop it. This is a good principle to remember for anyone crying tears of loss. The love that God has for us is like this. When we do our own thing instead of depending on God, it stimulates pain and sorrow for Him (Genesis 6:5-6).

At the time of this writing (summer 2020), there is growing national frustration with the restrictions in our lives due to the coronavirus. These restrictions are resulting in thousands of small business failures, unemployment, mortgage defaults, homelessness, altered education formats, church closures, restricted opportunities for recreation, diminished social contacts, loss of well-being, and death, to name a few. There is frustration in many aspects of our lives.

Are you able to separate the frustration from the emotions associated with these losses? Loss is usually associated with the emotions of sadness and disappointment. Mental health professionals are reporting increased rates of depression, suicide, substance abuse, and domestic violence. Increased mental health problems suggest people are not handling the stress of these losses in a healthy fashion.[113] The emotions of sadness and disappointment are building up in the minds of our citizenry, producing these mental health issues. As a nation, we are not processing these painful emotions, nor are we finding good solutions to the restrictions. Instead of expressing our sadness and disappointment, we are expressing our frustration to the friends and relatives we are no longer able to visit. Some people are expressing anger instead of sadness and disappointment. It will be noted in the following paragraphs that anger is not a primary emotion. It rarely is a healthy emotion. I am not suggesting anger should be denied. The following paragraphs document the

113 www.thepublicdiscourse.com, The Other Pandemic: the Lockdown Mental Health Crisis

problems with anger when it is expressed. Anger can be avoided when we learn to identify and process its underlying emotions.

In addition to anger, this pandemic is producing another emotion: fear. There is fear of becoming sick, fear of transmitting the virus to loved ones, fear of death, job loss, etc. Newspapers constantly publish the infection and death rate. We hear of someone who contracted the virus and died. Every time we put on a mask or see someone wearing one, it reminds us of the virus. Fear sucks the pleasure out of life and diminishes the effectiveness of our coping strategies. People are on edge and irritated; they become hyper-vigilant to protect themselves from other people who might be carrying the virus. People grow distant from each other. We give up our freedoms, thinking that not getting the virus is the most important issue in our lives. It is important, but its importance is different for each person.

A Historical Look at Anger

The story about anger began at least several thousand years ago. In the 66 books of the Bible, no direct mention is made of when anger made itself known in the range of human emotions. The first Scripture in which the process issue of anger appears is in the 4th chapter of Genesis, verse 5, where it is apparent God did not respect Cain's offering of the fruit of the ground and rejected it while accepting his brother's sheep offering of "the first born of his flock and of the fat portions." Because God was not pleased with his offering, Cain became angry with God and jealous of his brother Abel. God initiated a conversation with Cain, attempting to point him in the proper direction, but Cain refused to listen to God. Instead, Cain appears to have developed a root of bitterness (Hebrews 12:5-15). His hatred of Abel led him to kill his brother.

In the account of Cain and Abel, there are several process issues that draw our attention. The first is the offering of Abel and the offering of Cain. Abel's offering came from the firstborn of his flock of sheep and consisted of the fat portions, which were the most highly prized part of the animal for food. Scripture states that God "had respect and regard for Abel and his offering." Cain was a tiller of the ground, and his offering was from the fruit of the ground. The Lord did not respect Cain's offering, which suggests that Cain may have kept the best part of his crop for himself. Cain did not show respect to the Lord through his offering.

In Genesis 4:5-6, the Scripture suggests that Cain became angry, indignant, sad, depressed, and dejected. In the literal translation, the Scripture describes Cain's facial expression as "fallen;" that is to say, he was looking down.

The use of the words sad and depressed is an interpretation on the part of the translator. Perhaps instead of Cain being sad and depressed, he felt guilt and shame concerning the rejection of his offering. Sadness and depression lead to suicidal thoughts and behaviors. There is no indication in the Scripture that Cain was suicidal. His murder of Abel suggests that he was dominated by the emotion of anger. Cain was unable to cope with the various emotions underlying his anger. He chose to nurture his anger. God instructed him to change his emotions, thinking, and behavior, but he would not listen. Cain was distracted from his behavior toward God and his primary emotions of hurt, sadness, guilt, and shame. Anger and jealousy filled his mind.[114]

Anger became a process issue leading Cain to a decision to kill his brother Abel. How sad! What a terrible outcome for Cain, Abel, and their parents! Abel was dead, and Cain was exiled from his family for the rest of his life. He was an outcast. Adam and Eve lost two children from a single act of violence (Genesis 4:1-16). This was the first recorded act of domestic violence.

The account of Cain and Abel suggests that our emotional life has a connection to our relationship with God. If this is true, then we must consider our emotional life may also have a connection to our relationship with Satan. Whatever God creates, Satan attempts to steal, kill, and destroy (John 10:10). Satan destroyed Adam and Eve's relationship with God in the Garden of Eden. **In this account, Satan is attacking the family unit. Whenever and wherever the family unit is being attacked, look for Satan or one of his demons** lurking nearby.

It is important to note that God did not reject Cain but only Cain's offering. However, when Cain hardened his heart to God, the Lord punished him severely. This suggests God can discern when a heart will never be open to receiving His love, His truth, and His Son, and He acts accordingly.

Questions for the reader:

1. Are you giving from the first fruits of your crop (income) to the Lord?
2. Is God instructing you on any area of your life that you need to change? Are you listening? Are you changing? Is your heart open to receiving correction from God?

---

114 See Hebrews 12:14-15, The writer of Hebrews raises concern about developing a root of bitterness.

3. What does your emotional life suggest about who you are most connected to, God or Satan?
4. Are you in touch with the emotions that often underlie anger: confusion, guilt, shame, fear, hurt, sadness, and disappointment?
5. What does your thought life suggest about who you are most connected to? God or Satan?

Write your responses to these questions in the space below.

____

____

____

____

____

Marital Anger

It seems likely anger first manifested itself through our fallen nature long before the story of Cain and Abel, most likely after Adam and Eve disobeyed God and were banished from living in the Garden of Eden (Genesis 3:1-24). Anger does not promote the righteousness that God requires and therefore anger could not have been present prior to original sin (James 1:20). Since Adam blamed Eve as well as God for his disobedience, an argument about who caused all the turmoil probably started before they left the confines of the garden and found themselves staring at the cherubim and flaming sword which prevented their return. My speculation about the initial episode of anger relates to an **imagined** argument which unfolded just outside the Garden of Eden, something like this:

Adam to Eve: I told you not to go anywhere near that special tree. You were forbidden to touch it, and you just had to have some of that infernal fruit, didn't you?

Eve to Adam: You were supposed to protect me, and you just stood there like a bump on a log when that snake came along and smooth-talked me. You said if we hid in the bushes that God wouldn't find us. Well, He did find us, and please notice whom He called for. It was you He was looking for, not me. Those bushes were prickly, and I got dirt all over me when I was hiding under them.

And by the way, I can't believe you had the nerve to blame this whole mess on God creating me as a companion for you. Do you think God really believed that for a second? I am the best thing that ever happened to you, and you know it. And now we have to wear these skins that are hot and sweaty. I don't like the way they look. They don't flatter me at all. This is all your fault. In the morning, I want you to look around and see what else you can use to make clothing. I am certainly not planning to wear these skins for the rest of my life. You can at least take off the fur and tan the hide. Right now, I am really hungry! Do you suppose you could find something for us to eat?

Adam to Eve: Would you get off my case? And give me a chance to think this through. It seems to me we both screwed up big time. We can both look for food. Life is not going to be as easy now that we're not in the garden.

Eve to Adam: I'll look for food, but don't think you can boss me around all the time. Remember, you are the one who got us kicked out of the garden, not me. So, just get off your high horse and find some food.

Adam to Eve: Yada, yada, yada! (In a louder tone of voice)

Eve to Adam: Yada, yada, yada, blah, blah, blah! (In an even louder voice, if possible)

Writer's comment: Yada, yada, yada and blah, blah, blah has continued for several thousand years without respite.

Now, remembering that Adam and Eve did not have any Scripture or the indwelling of the Holy Spirit, how might Adam and Eve have responded in a Godly way to His discovering their disobedience? That conversation might have transpired like this:

God to Adam: Adam, where are you?

Adam to God: Oh, you know where I am! Say, there is something I need to talk with you about. A little while ago, a snake showed up and talked with Eve. This snake talked about the fruit tree in the middle of the garden which we were not to touch or eat. While she and the snake were talking, I listened very carefully to everything that was

> said. The snake contradicted what you had told me. The snake said we would not die if we ate the fruit, and I began to doubt what you told us. I did not insist that she abstain from eating, and she ate some of the fruit. When I saw her eat, I became distracted from your warning, thinking if she eats and I do not, I might lose her as my helper and companion because you said we would die. So, I also ate some of the fruit. As you can plainly see, we did not die. After I took the first bite, strange things started to happen. I didn't want to be around you. I did not want to tell you what happened with the snake. I wanted to hide from you. What is going on?

I wish Adam had had the second conversation with God instead of the earlier one suggested above with Eve. I would argue that it was not possible for Adam to have talked with God as described in the second scenario, because although Adam had not died physically, he had died to relationship with God after eating the fruit. Adam's new nature prompted him to hide in disobedience from God and to cover his feelings of doubt/confusion, guilt, shame, and fear. He ignored these emotions and chose to express **anger,** which he directed to God and to Eve. He blamed them for his disobedience.

Although Adam did tell God about his fear, he did not ask for help from God to cope with his fear. Instead, Adam acted alone by attempting to deceive God and by expressing his irritation/anger through blame. He shifted the responsibility for his disobedience from self to God and Eve. He was protecting himself by attempting to deceive God, but you cannot deceive God. Relying on anger is often a futile attempt to regain control when we are disappointed or frustrated. People have been following the example of Adam for thousands of years.

A Dissection of Anger

What is anger really, and what are its principal characteristics? Does it have its own process issues? Webster's dictionary defines anger as "an intense emotional state induced by displeasure." This displeasure is secondary to the emotions which accompany being frustrated. The most common emotions that underlie anger are doubt/confusion, guilt, shame, fear, hurt, sadness, and disappointment. These are the same emotions Adam and Eve experienced in the Garden of Eden. These emotions are uncomfortable or so painful that it is natural to disconnect from them. What makes anger so intense are the painful emotions that are underneath. Have you noticed when people become angry with you, their voice becomes loud, and the expression on their faces becomes distorted? This is because emotional pain is fueling their anger.

People often want others to know when they are experiencing emotional pain. There are two common scenarios. The first is when they think you caused the pain. They want you to stop doing whatever they think caused it. The second is when they think you neglected them in some way, and they want the neglect to stop. In either scenario, they are attempting to get your attention, so they raise their voice. You may find yourself shouting back in an angry, defensive posture. In both scenarios, the person who is experiencing pain believes that the other person caused it. This could not be farther from the truth. Whatever emotional pain you are experiencing, you generated yourself, in response to what the other person did or did not do. When people are yelling at each other, the main thing they hear are hurtful comments fueled by anger. We choose to express anger in a vain attempt to control our feelings to produce a better outcome. However, what usually happens is an outcome much worse. Remember, process issues determine outcome. The process issue with anger is that we often make an unconscious choice to be angry instead of hurt, sad, disappointed, or one of the other emotions. Only you can create the thoughts and emotions you have in response to what is going on around you. It is your response. It's your anger.

The word anger has ancient origins in old Norse *angra,* meaning to *grieve*, *vex,* or *distress*, in old English meaning *narrow,* and in Latin, the verb *angere,* meaning to *strangle*. Have you ever felt like strangling someone with whom you were angry?

When we choose to become angry, we often experience a loss of some sort, grief or hurt associated with relationship conflict. We ignore the associated emotions, and then we narrow our focus by becoming angry at the object of our frustration. Then we may feel as though we want to do bodily harm, or strangle that person. All this can happen nearly instantaneously. What a powerful and deceptive process! When mild irritation intensifies to anger, we have thoughts of destroying whatever or whoever is causing our pain. Fortunately, we do not always allow our angry emotions to dictate our behavior because the cost of expressing such rage is high in terms of broken relationships. Rage may actually result in strangulation/murder. The cost is time in prison, a very high price indeed. More often, we raise our voices, say nasty demeaning things, blame or accuse others, become sarcastic, or perhaps withdraw and park the anger inside our mind where it is later accessed in the form of an explosion. It is natural to prefer being angry to being hurt, sad, or disappointed, but it is a response that does not serve our best interest because nine out of ten times **anger is destructive.**

The Destructive Nature of Anger

Destruction is the chief characteristic of anger, and most of us are out of control when expressing it. Destructive anger associated with being out of control can be expressed in different directions: 1) toward others, 2) toward self, 3) toward the environment/objects, 4) toward God. When anger is expressed to others, it tends to impair or destroy relationships. When it is too risky to express anger to another person, our boss, for example, we may displace it to our spouse, children, the dog, our driving habits, or anything else that's handy. When anger is expressed toward self, it may contribute to depressive states, guilt trips, and a variety of stress-related illnesses such as hypertension, peptic ulcer disease, regional enteritis, ulcerative colitis, irritable bowel syndrome, chronic headache, autoimmune disorders, and other medical problems. When anger is expressed toward objects, those objects may be thrown, broken, or totally destroyed. Most importantly, when it is expressed toward God, it results in separation from God.

Being separated from God by anger is similar to what happened in the Garden of Eden when disobedience associated with fear, guilt, and shame separated Adam from God for the first time. **Satan's plan** is to use these emotions, which generate displeasure and discomfort, to separate us from God. **God's plan** is for us to take the emotions of confusion, guilt, shame, fear, hurt, sadness, and disappointment to Christ in contemplative prayer or meditation. Satan's plan and God's plan are in direct opposition. They conflict!

Webster's definition of anger being driven by displeasure prompts us to consider what is unique about the displeasure that generates anger. In order to understand this, it is helpful to return to events that occurred in the Garden of Eden, as told in the first three chapters of Genesis.

After God created Adam, God put him in charge of the garden. God saw that Adam was alone and needed a helper and soulmate. God provided a female companion, whom Adam initially named Woman but later called Eve. Adam and his soulmate were given the task of populating and subduing the earth. They were given the responsibility of ruling over all creation. Following Adam's disobedience, in which he listened to and followed his wife instead of God, God changed certain process issues. Instead of the ground yielding its crop, it became resistant to the production of food. Fear and competition developed between the first couple and the animals.

Eve's disobedience centered on wanting more knowledge, rejecting Adam's leadership, and wanting to be like God, that is, being in control of things. The struggle for control is the story of humanity since Adam and Eve were forced to leave the garden. Eve continues to struggle with Adam, and both struggle with God.

The disobedience of Adam and Eve brought frustration, injury, separation from God, and all the emotions noted above: doubt/confusion, guilt, shame, fear, hurt, sadness, and disappointment. It is these emotions that generate the intense displeasure which Webster references in his definition of anger. Satan wants us to spend our lives in a futile effort to regain the control that was lost in the garden. Are you spinning your wheels mired in the mud of destructive anger while attempting to control others?

Expression of anger represents an attempt to gain control over circumstances that seem important.

When we function independently of God, we are often not in control of ourselves, let alone others or the world around us. Satan is described in the Bible as the ruler of this world. Anger is the emotion Satan wants us to choose to express our frustration and disappointment when we inevitably fail to have control. Satan's plan is for us to choose anger because Satan is a destructive force in the world. When we act out in anger, we are acting on his behalf. His purposes are "to steal, kill, and destroy" (John 10:10). God's plan is for us to depend on Him and for each of us to let go of the **illusion of control**. It's an illusion. It's not reality.

God desires us to bring our displeasure/painful emotions to Jesus rather than to park them somewhere in our minds where they wreak havoc by producing depression or physiological disorders.

What happened in the Garden of Eden suggests that anger is often relational in origin, expression, or both. In the Garden of Eden, Adam experienced disappointment in Eve assuming his leadership role, and Eve experienced disappointment in Adam for choosing passivity rather than protecting her. Adam blamed Eve and God for his disobedience and leadership failure. Eve blamed Adam for not protecting her. Have you experienced blame in your life?

When God applied consequences for their disobedience, they experienced the frustration of loss of relationship with God, loss of relationship with each other, and loss of residence in the garden. That is worse than the worst bad hair day ever! It is not surprising that Adam and Eve were in conflict when they were leaving the garden, as suggested at the beginning of this chapter.

As a result of events in the garden, it is our nature to displace our disappointment and frustration toward God or others. We may find ourselves shouting, using foul language, cursing God or others, and destroying whatever is at hand. It is very curious how the people who profess little or no belief in God blame God for their problems in life or use His name in a profane fashion. This comes from Adam blaming God for his disobedience. Others conclude there is no God because He allowed a frustrating or traumatic experience in their lives. We sometimes believe, as did Adam, that God is responsible for our difficulties, when in fact, we have been deceived just as Eve was deceived. Often, we think we know how to do it better than God. We forget that the world is the kingdom of Satan, and it is his stated purpose to frustrate: to steal, kill, and destroy. We can imagine Satan dancing in the air when we blame God for the nasty things in life that Satan is orchestrating.

Since there is so much displeasure associated with anger, it is curious that we frequently are reluctant to let go of it. This is partly because we hold on to the deception that being angry will result in regaining control. There is also another factor which is operating particularly when anger has relational origins, a second important characteristic of anger:

Anger is sticky!

People do not want to let go of anger. It feels good for a brief period, and it is empowering because of the associated adrenaline rush. For a few moments, we achieve what Eve wanted in the garden--to be like God, all-powerful and all-knowing. Then, after the passing of time, we notice all the pieces scattered around us from the explosion that accompanies anger. We usually feel guilt and shame at this point, but since those feelings produce displeasure, we disconnect from them and store them in our minds, where they predispose to depression or future outbursts of anger.

When our anger is relational in origin, our reluctance to let go of this destructive emotion is related to our unwillingness to let go of the person who hurt or disappointed us. When we perceive injury, we crave justice! This craving is a manifestation of evil desire described in the chapter on the D Words.

We develop an intense desire for some form of compensation for our injury and suffering. Until justice is satisfied, we are prone to hanging on to our anger. Reinforcing our desire for justice is the desire to control. When frustrated or hurt, the need to control the situation sometimes becomes overwhelming. This produces a self-defeating dynamic in which anger leads to loss of control while we are thinking at some level that we will gain control. This process points to a third primary characteristic of anger.

Anger is deceptive!

The deception associated with angry outbursts is a clue to the origin of anger. Satan is the father of all lies, and deception is the engine that powers all of Satan's strategies.

Scripture does not equate anger with sin. In Ephesians 4:26, two cautions are raised about anger: 1) When angry, do not sin, and 2) do not ever let your anger last until the sun goes down. It is a simple thing to counsel someone else to not sin when angry. However, it is very difficult to accomplish in our own lives because there is so much energy associated with being angry and so much deception about how to cope with it. Scripture encourages processing anger before sundown because it appears anger will seek a deeper part of the mind and be stored there during our sleep cycle. When anger is stored in the deeper recesses of our minds, it is more difficult to mobilize and process. The more anger we store, the more prone we are to a small disappointment or frustration leading to explosive behavior. This is what happens in the cycle of domestic violence. Explosions anywhere are prone to creating a big mess. Explosions are always destructive. Explosions at work lead to being fired or, in a worst-case scenario, murdering those you blame for your job loss. Explosions at home lead to hurt, conflict, domestic violence, and divorce. This is why James counsels us to be "quick to hear [a ready listener] slow to speak, slow to take offense, and slow to get angry" (James 1:19). When we depend on ourselves and choose to be angry instead of depending on God, we are prone to sin.

One other observation about anger is important before reviewing coping strategies. The historical roots of anger give us some clues about what is so unique about this emotion. Grief, hurt, sadness, and disappointment are the emotions associated with injury and loss. When we experience injury, our focus narrows, alternating between our own pain (hurt, sadness, and disappointment) and our desire to hurt the person responsible for the injury.

We may focus internally on the emotions of injury, or we may choose to focus externally on the agent we think is causing our pain. When we focus internally, we experience pain and tears, which are uncomfortable. When our focus is external, we experience anger and rage, which feels good because it is empowering. It is impossible to experience emotional pain at the same moment we experience the anger directed externally. As a client observed, "The anger cancels out the other emotions." But it only cancels them temporarily. It only cancels experiencing them at a conscious level. They do not disappear into thin air. This process is very surprising for many people because we alternate between sadness and anger or between hurt and anger very quickly. It happens so fast that it seems like we are experiencing them both at the same time, but that is an illusion. To discover this for yourself, remember a time when someone close to you said or did something hurtful to you. Allow yourself to experience the emotional pain or hurt. You will find it takes all your energy to stay with the pain of the hurt. It demands your complete attention.

This is a blessing, often unrealized, because it gives every person a choice to stay with the pain and tears or choose to become angry. It is often an unrealized blessing because many refuse to feel their pain. It is a little like someone offering a red-hot poker for you to grab that would save your life. You know how much it is going to hurt, so you refuse to take it even though refusing means certain death. It is important to know we can learn to choose. We do not have to be a slave to anger. We do not have to go through life being destructive. Choice provides hope that we can change, if and when we are willing to work on it.

Since the "fall" of Adam and Eve, we have been prone to cope with hurts and disappointments without involving God. But God desires that we bring our injuries, traumas, and the resulting emotions to Christ instead of attempting to resolve them on our own. He wants this to be a conscious decision on our part (Deuteronomy 30:19-20). God is relational, and it pleases Him when we rely on, trust in, and cling to Christ as we make our way through life. Often, at an unconscious level, we choose to store the pain of guilt, shame, hurt, sadness, and disappointment in the recesses of our minds or move on to being angry instead of taking our experience to Christ. With awareness and some work, it is possible to learn to make this choice at a conscious level. This is highly desirable because we have a much-improved chance of preventing the explosions, wreckage, illnesses, and interpersonal injuries noted above when we choose to feel the emotions and take them to Christ or another person. We can learn to choose a strategy that prevents anger and rage. As a Christian colleague once said, "We can learn to do hard things"!

What prompts angry people to turn away from their anger? When they observe the destruction of relationships and other turmoil created by anger, it may lead to a sense of disgust, remorse, and brokenness. These are the states of mind that stimulate a desire to change by turning away from anger to more healthy strategies.

When we observe fear instead of love in the eyes of our children, perhaps we will turn from anger. When our marriage ends in divorce, we may realize the role anger played. When we are unable to hold a job or stop the use of substances, we may turn from our anger. If we are not experiencing disgust about the impact anger is having on ourselves and others, it is unlikely that we will put forth the effort it takes to cope with anger. If you are already disgusted with how anger is impacting your life and the lives of others, and you have been unable to stop your angry outbursts, you are likely going to need some assistance in coping with anger.

Suggestions for assistance include professional counseling, an accountability partner, and other strategies noted below.

Cognitive Interventions: Because anger is destructive and deceptive, the following questions deserve careful consideration. Honest answers to these questions will determine your willingness to take responsibility for your anger.

1. What results are produced by my episodes of anger/rage?
2. Can I live with the results of my anger?
3. Is my anger/rage hurting people I love?
4. Do I say things that are hurtful that I later regret?
5. When angry, do I destroy things, get into verbal or physical fights, or become physically aggressive with family members?
6. Do I withdraw from relationships when angry?
7. Do I become sarcastic when angry or use sarcasm to tear people down in various relationships?
8. Are my episodes of rage associated with the use of alcohol or street drugs?
9. Can I overcome anger by myself?
10. Am I disgusted with being an angry person?

After answering the above, does it seem your expression of anger has had destructive consequences in your life? Has it been hard for you to let go of anger? Have you been deceived by anger? Do you need to learn to manage anger in more appropriate ways? If you have uncertainty about your answers to any of these questions, ask someone close to you to answer each of these questions for you. Give serious consideration to their opinion about how you handle anger.

Affective Interventions: *Affect* refers to feelings or emotions. As noted earlier, anger is not a primary emotion. Underlying the anger are feelings such as confusion, guilt, shame, fear, hurt, sadness, and disappointment. Frustration often generates the emotion of disappointment, which turns to anger. Disappointment is generated by the difference between what you expected and what actually occurred. Anger is an **emotional defense** against experiencing disappointment or one of these other emotions because these feelings are painful.

This is so important it bears repeating: If you are able to get in touch with the feeling that underlies anger, you can block the anger before it is expressed. It is somewhat surprising, but when you stay with the underlying emotions, you will not become angry. You cannot be sad and angry at the same moment in time. You cannot be disappointed and angry at the same moment. When people experience emotional injury associated with a sense of helplessness during their formative years, they "park" these emotions somewhere in the mind and later find it difficult to access them. With all these feelings stored in the mind, it takes only a small injury or frustration in the present to trigger a major explosion. These explosions are out of proportion with the degree of injury and hurt. An explosion in response to a minor irritation usually indicates a lot of stored anger and hurt. It may be an indication of needing professional counseling.

Behavioral Interventions: Anger/rage is associated with a discharge of adrenaline which quickly energizes the expression of anger. For this reason, the first thing to do is to make a choice to leave the setting where something is happening, and you are becoming angry. If you choose to leave, make it known you are leaving because of what is going on within you. Avoid blaming the other person for your angry response. After leaving, you may express this energy in other ways. This requires physical activity such as walking, jogging, or any type of aerobic exercise that exhausts you completely. **Before engaging in aerobic exercise, consult your physician.** You need to choose the option of leaving quickly, or you will find yourself in the middle of a rage, and it will be too late to implement this option. After you are calm, return, engage, communicate, and work toward resolving disagreements.

There is an old saying in psychology: if it is predictable, it is preventable. Considering this principle as it applies to your anger, make a list of trigger words, frustrating experiences, and interpersonal interactions which you respond to by choosing to become angry. Write your responses below.

____

____

____

____

____

Become familiar with these situations and choose to leave before you choose anger as a response. Close your eyes and imagine the above scenarios, and practice various strategies to cope with frustration, hurt, and disappointment. If you prefer to experience rage instead of leaving the situation, it is an indication of a need for professional counseling.

Another behavioral intervention to consider is obtaining an accountability partner, which is a person you meet with weekly to report the number of times and circumstances in which you have chosen to become angry. Share with your accountability partner the impact your anger has had on others and yourself. There is something about bringing your anger into the public eye which stimulates greater effort to control it. Maintaining secrecy about your problem with anger will only perpetuate your difficulty. Choose someone who treasures confidentiality when you confide about anger.

Biological Interventions Most people with anger problems do not have an underlying medical problem that is causing episodes of rage. However, certain historical factors may be a clue to a medical diagnosis. For example, if you have never previously responded with anger or rage and suddenly respond in this way, this history suggests a change in physiology or the onset of a disease process contributing to anger expression. Head injury, seizure disorder, brain tumors, bipolar disorder, and other medical conditions may predispose to anger. **Please, always consult with your primary care physician** to rule out a medical condition contributing to angry outbursts.

Intervention with a variety of pharmaceutical agents may reduce the intensity of anger. Unless there is an underlying medical condition, this is symptomatic treatment and seldom completely reverses or resolves the expression of anger. Becoming dependent on medication to reduce the intensity of anger delays the work that is necessary to stop the choices you make when you become angry.

Spiritual Interventions: This brief discussion will focus on Christian spirituality as a resource to cope with anger. Scripture points out that anger often leads to disobeying the standards that God desires for us and our relationships with others (James 1:20). God promises to help our weaknesses through His strength (II Corinthians 12:9-12).

These principles lead to a simple prayer which is effective for interrupting the pattern of destruction from anger. The prayer goes like this: "Lord, here is my anger coming again, please take my anger from me. May your strength be made perfect in the midst of my weakness" (I John 1:8-9). This prayer should be combined with leaving this situation as quickly as possible. It may be necessary to pray this over and over before you will be able to return to the person or situation. You must pray this quickly, as soon as you start to experience the adrenaline rush when you are frustrated or hurt. This strategy is a form of confession. The word *confess* in Greek is *homologeo*, meaning to speak the same words.[115] Using confession in this way brings us into agreement with God. In the first letter of John Chapter 1:8-9, the apostle notes that when we confess our sin that God will cleanse us… and failure to confess means that we are deceived and in disagreement with God. Does that sound familiar? Are you in disagreement with God about anything, about many things? Write your response in the space below.

____

____

____

____

____

A variation of the above is corporate confession i.e., confessing to the body of Christ. James 5:13-18 describes a process in which an individual may call the elders of the church who will anoint with oil and pray for the person who has offended. This is best accomplished with a small number of people whom you can trust to maintain confidentiality. We are encouraged in verse 16 to confess our sins so that we may be healed. It is a powerful experience to openly admit weakness to a group of fellow believers. It is the opposite of our natural response to hide the things that we do to hurt other people--to keep everything secret. It suggests a willingness and desire to change our heart. God honors prayers of repentance because they honor what Christ

115 Vine's Complete Expository of Old and New Testament Words

did for us on the cross. This may be done after a church service, or you may choose another time and place.

An important part of God's plan for processing anger is **forgiveness**. Forgiveness is making a conscious decision to release anger/resentment and any claim to compensation or apology. This is facilitated by expressing the feelings underlying our anger, often fear, hurt, sadness, and disappointment. A strategy for this is as simple as writing a two- or three-sentence description of the experience in which you were hurt or offended, identifying the feelings associated with that experience, and then describing your experience of having those feelings to another person or to Jesus, and saying, "I forgive." If you continue to hope for compensation or apology, your forgiveness is not complete. If the injury is profound, you may be unwilling to let go of the offense and continue to experience bitterness toward the person who offended you. Therefore, you may need to forgive on more than one occasion.[116] The process of forgiveness provides time to reflect on the feelings that underlie anger and to learn to cope with and express those feelings in a healthy fashion. If you have difficulty accessing the feelings that underlie anger, you may have to work on learning how to recognize emotions in other less-threatening settings. **However, you can forgive and let go of the person or the offense without processing the feelings.**

Forgiveness is a decision of the mind. When we forgive, we interrupt the continuing process of obsessing about the event and how we were offended. This interrupts the process leading to resentment and ends the influence the event has on our thinking, feeling, and behavior. Forgiving and communicating to another person or to Jesus about your hurt or disappointment has a much better outcome than exploding in anger. Forgiveness and communication are both process issues. Jesus is relational. He always wants to hear from us! Process issues determine outcome.

Learning to identify and describe these emotions to Jesus in conversational prayer or meditation is our proper response to His invitation in Revelation 3:20, where Jesus says, "Behold, I stand at the door and knock; if anyone hears and listens to and heeds my voice and opens the door, I will come into him and eat with him, and he [will eat] with me." When life brings an experience, or we enter an experience by choice that results in these difficult emotions, Jesus desires to fellowship, to talk, and mend the wounds of our hearts with

116 The Bait of Satan by John Bevere, an excellent resource for coping with offensive behavior.

His healing love. Notice He only knocks on the door. It is our responsibility to open the door. This process is sometimes referred to as "turning it over to God." If you take it back from God, you have more work to do. Keeping a journal on circumstances, people, triggers for generating anger, and the progress you are making can be very helpful.

Forgiveness is the responsibility of the person who has been injured. It would seem at first that forgiveness is for the person who committed the offense, but actually, it is for the person who is injured. Until the injured person is willing to forgive, he creates a prison for himself made of bricks and walls of resentment. Only the injured person can let himself out of this prison. Forgiveness is the key that opens the prison door (Matthew 18:21-35).

A strategy that is helpful to prepare your heart to forgive is to pray for the person who injured you. As you build up through prayer the person who offended you, your heart will soften toward that person and you will let go of your desire for revenge. If you refuse to confess your anger, refuse to process it, and refuse to forgive, you make a choice to store your anger in the recesses of your mind, where it becomes more intense and energizing, often proceeding to resentment, retaliation, hatred, violence, and recurrent explosions. Refusing to forgive is self-destructive, contributing to the development of physical disease, as mentioned earlier in this chapter. Do not be deceived. Start working on reducing the number of angry episodes in your life and the destructive influence they have on yourself and others, including the people you love.

When examining the topic of anger in this chapter, I often used the pronoun *you*. Perhaps you wondered about anger in my life. I regret to say I have not escaped the curse of anger. It has manifested in two somewhat different expressions, both in the context of family.

My first encounter with anger was in my family of origin. My father was not engaged with the lives of my brother and myself. He was a no-nonsense type of person of German heritage who was the authoritarian figure in our family. He was not physically abusive, but neither was he expressive of love or encouragement. He never said, "I love you" or "I am proud of you." He hurt me through his lack of interest in my activities; my hurt and anger were probably driving the comment I made to him at four or five years old when I said, "I don't like you." That is a very gutsy thing to say to your father when you are five years old. My speculation is that this comment was powered by my anger toward him. Had I stayed in touch with my hurt, I would have gone to him with tears, which might have been more effective in improving our relationship.

He had a temper, but I rarely saw his anger directed at people in or out of our family. He used four-letter words when frustrated. When my brother and I were focused on promoting our sibling rivalry in the back seat of the car, he would raise his voice and threaten to stop the car and invade our territory, but this never happened. There was a razor strap at home, ostensibly kept to sharpen a straight razor, but Dad kept it around as a threat to maintain order. This came out on very rare occasions as one swat on the part of your body people sit on.

My second encounter with anger was in my own family. As an adult, I often raised my voice when frustrated with my children. I also developed the habit of using four-letter words when life's little frustrations would pop up… but not with my kids or wife. This habit surprised me because when Dad used this type of language, I thought there must be a better way to express oneself. It is surprising how much unconscious dynamics from childhood shape our adult patterns of behavior.

One day I was leaving my office and had a pile of things to take to the car. This was back in the dark ages when it was necessary to open the car door with a key. I should have made two trips, but when I got to the car, I balanced everything on one arm while attempting to open the door with my other hand. Most of my papers and books fell into a morass of slushy, muddy snow. The bad words were in the air almost before everything hit the snow. That is an indication of how fast the emotion of anger finds its way to our tongue.

After picking everything up and putting it on the back seat, I felt convicted about my use of profanity. I had a very brief conversation about it with God, saying, "Lord, I can't stand to be this way anymore. Please take my anger away from me." Suddenly a sense of peace came over me. A few days later, while in church, we were going through the liturgy (words of confession and worship set to music), and I found myself saying words with the rest of the congregation, "Unless you confess your sin you deceive yourself and the truth is not in you. When you confess your sin God is faithful and just and will cleanse you from all unrighteousness." That is what happened when I dropped my books and papers. I confessed my profanity, and God removed it and replaced the anger with peace. Now I had a choice. I could become angry, feel powerful, and rely on myself to be in control for a few seconds, or I could turn to God, rely on Him, and be at peace with myself and others. I chose to be at peace for a while.

Stopping a habit that is contrary to what God wants for us often **is a process**. Could God take away all the anger stored up in my mind in an instant with a single confession? Of course. But God is **relational**. He desires that we learn to depend on Him rather than ourselves. I chose to use the tool that God gave me, i.e., confession, and my use of profanity stopped quickly. But then, and this is hard to write about, I thought I had it under control. Pride deceived me. I stopped confessing when frustrated or irritated, and before long, I was again using those same four-letter words that I detested.

Being angry and using foul language were not the only traits I picked up from my father. I perpetuated my father's authoritarianism, his work ethic, and the strategies he used to maintain discipline. I also instituted some new practices that reflected my training in behavioral science, such as positive practice, consequences connected to behavior, and grounding or restriction for major affronts. Our kids still complain about bringing in eight cords of wood every winter to fuel our wood-burning furnace. They insist they brought in every stick of wood by themselves, but I remember the chore a little differently. They learned something in addition to how to bring in and stack wood: they learned how to work! Now they both have good jobs they enjoy, which allow them to support themselves.

Despite the difficulties I had with my father, there were many good times; each week through the summer, our parents invited a different family for a short boat ride from Point Place to Guard Island where we would barbecue and goof off after the meal. There was fishing every Saturday through the summer with two of the nicest men I had ever met, weekends at our summer place on Middle Bass Island in Lake Erie, card parties, family events, social gatherings at church, learning about construction, and a family dinner hour every night. There were many good things; they do not cancel the hurts but mitigate them and provide perspective.

Satan is the Accuser. When Satan is unsuccessful at accusing you, he will accuse others through you. Satan's desire is for us to ruminate on the negative things in our lives. Do not fall into that trap. No families are perfect. If you are unable to find anything positive about your childhood, ask God to help you create experiences in the present that are positive, rewarding, and draw you closer to Him.[117] Focus on these things (Philippians 4:8). Our focus, our

117 Review the meditations of Abigail in the chapter on Talk Therapy for one example of this process

thoughts as we go through our day, are connected to the mood we experience during our day. Learn what the Bible teaches about focus.[118]

My mother's personality was in stark contrast to my father's. She freely expressed emotion and was very loving. She taught me to do the same. She was a stay-at-home mom who took care of the needs of her children. It wasn't easy with two boys. An expression of frustration we would hear from her on "special occasions" was "I'm so mad I could chew nails." That sounded interesting, but I never saw her chew even one nail.

Jack and the First Law of Thermodynamics

The first law of thermodynamics refers to the law of conservation of energy. This is a reference to the principle that the total energy of an isolated system can be transformed from one form to another but cannot be created or destroyed. For example, the energy of an isolated system can be transformed into heat or work. This principle of physics is not ordinarily applied to people. However, at times when I observe Jack, what I see reminds me of this fundamental principle. When Jack is not taking food into his body, in a sense, he is an isolated system. Presumably, there would be a finite amount of energy in his system. Jack uses this energy to create movement when he is silly or playful. He wraps himself in a blanket and pretends he is trying to escape from the restraint of the blanket while laughing, giggling, and making a great deal of noise. It's like he is wrestling with an invisible opponent. But what grabs my attention at these times is this: he is exercising almost every single muscle group in his entire body while thoroughly enjoying himself. *Jack is exercising without having any awareness that he is exercising.*

Several thoughts come to my mind as I observe Jack converting energy into motion: Will Jack continue to enjoy exercising his body as he enters school and sits behind a desk for several hours each day? Will he become sedentary? Will he become obese? At my age (77), I am not able to move my body the way Jack moves his body. I am envious of Jack. The ravages of time have taken a toll on my body.

I am also a bit jealous of Jack exercising without any conscious effort to do so. I have gone through a variety of exercise programs over the past 50 years to maintain strength and flexibility for outdoor sports. There have been medial meniscus tears in both knees. After the first meniscus tear 35

118 bible.knowing-jesus.com, 50 Bible Verses about Focus

years ago, I consulted a sports medicine specialist for a second opinion about surgery. He gave me two options: surgery or exercise to strengthen the muscles around the joint. I chose exercise. A surgical procedure was delayed for 20 years until the meniscus was re-injured. I wonder how many orthopedic procedures could be prevented if people would simply exercise.

The unconscious part of the mind takes care of a lot of important things. But it is not likely to send you a message to exercise. After adolescence, it usually takes a conscious effort to maintain strength, flexibility, and balance. I hear people my age complain about not being able to get out of a chair. How many of these people exercise daily? When a person changes from a sitting to a standing position, a specific set of muscles comes into play in combination that may not be used in any other activities. If you are having trouble getting out of a chair, practice getting out of a chair. If you are having balance problems, see your doctor for evaluation and ask about a referral for physical therapy. Combine this with 20-30 minutes a day of exercising your major muscle groups. This simple proactive strategy will extend the life of your musculoskeletal system by many years. It will extend your enjoyment in life. An exercise program, "Aging Backwards" by Miranda Esmonde-White, works well for many people. I do this in the evening while watching the news. **Caution, before beginning any exercise program, consult with your primary care physician for approval.**

Children Point the Way to Heaven

In this part of the chapter, we draw attention to Jesus using little children like Jack to point to a path leading to heaven. Six character traits in little children are considered necessary to enter the kingdom of heaven.[119] Four of these are taught by Jesus in conversation with His disciples. These traits are being loving, trusting, humble, and forgiving (Matthew 18:1-4). The other two traits, being obedient and teachable, are mentioned by Paul in his discussion on overcoming the slavery of sin (Romans 6:16-19, 12:1-2). Jesus emphasizes the spiritual nature of His Kingdom when saying you must become like little children to enter the Kingdom of Heaven (Matthew 16:24-26). The Kingdom of God is very different from the focus of earthly kingdoms, which are prone to being uncaring, untrustworthy, prideful, and vengeful. These are characteristics of many of our government leaders.

When Jesus instructs His disciples to become like "little children," the

---

119 120 www.str.org, What is the Kingdom of Heaven?

implication is that His adult disciples lacked those traits. Did the disciples have these traits as little children and then lose them? Can you lose character traits such as trust and humility? Can you lose the ability to love others? The short answer is yes. The world, or the culture surrounding us, brings adverse experiences that may distort or destroy our capacity to love and trust. We will examine the impact of trauma on the human soul in detail in the chapters on talk therapy.

The term "Kingdom of Heaven" has something in common with the Greek word for salvation, *soterion.* Salvation does not refer only to life after death but to being rescued from sin while yet living on earth. Entering the Kingdom of Heaven is a reference to the same process issue, being under the influence of God, Christ, and the Holy Spirit while living your daily life. You can enter the Kingdom of Heaven right here, right now, by saying this simple prayer: *Lord, I need you in my heart, I want you in my heart, come into my heart.* Then start reading the Gospels, beginning with Matthew. Visit Christian churches and ask God where you should attend.

Some may read the above paragraphs and conclude that this is a works-oriented plan for salvation because these traits have to be learned. Since Jesus made these statements, they have to be true. But it is not works-related. The learning of these traits is facilitated by adult modeling and empowered by the Holy Spirit. These traits are manifestations of the fruit of the Spirit, which is love, joy, peace, patience, kindness, goodness, faithfulness, gentleness, and self-control (Galatians 5:22-26). When a person follows Jesus, the Holy Spirit enables the person to be more like Him, i.e., loving, trusting, humble, forgiving, obedient, and teachable. We learn from this and many other examples that God forms a partnership with us to bring about His purposes. God invites us to become part of His story. Becoming part of His story means becoming more like Jesus. That is good news for us, and it honors and glorifies God. We cannot accomplish any of these things through our own strength. The Holy Spirit empowers the process of repentance and acceptance of Christ as our personal Lord and Savior.

Do you want to change? In the space below, write where you think you are on a 1-10 scale in developing each of these character traits. Then ask your spouse, parent, or close friend to rate you (a spouse is the best rater). Compare your rating with that of a person who knows you well. Are there changes you should consider?

	Your Rating	Other Rating
Loving:	______	______
Trusting:	______	______
Humble:	______	______
Forgiving:	______	______
Obedient:	______	______
Teachable:	______	______

The six character traits above are the same traits Jesus demonstrated in accepting the Father's will that He be crucified. If you are planning to follow Jesus, you need these traits. If even one of these traits is missing, it will have an adverse impact on your life. Take some time now to meditate on each of these traits and how Jesus demonstrated each one in His crucifixion. Write a summary of your meditation in the space below. Some Scriptural references to facilitate your meditation are John 3:16-17, Proverbs 3:5-6, Philippians 2:4-7, Luke 23:33-34, Philippians 2:8, 12-16, Proverbs 4:10-13, John 12:48-49.

Number One and Number Two

Charney and I were taking care of Jack one day when he was between three and four years old. Jack said he needed to "go potty." We asked if he had to go number one or number two…and, did he need help? He looked at us with a puzzled expression, not saying anything. After a few seconds, he said with a serious tone, "number four." Neither of us was familiar with number four. His response also suggested there might be a number three… and what would that look like? While we were laughing about his response, Jack quietly went to the bathroom and took care of his needs.

I mention this incident to make a point. If a three-and-one-half-year-old boy does not yet comprehend the difference between number one and number two, should four to five year old children be expected to understand the concept of gender? Should children less than the age of reason be making decisions about puberty blockers and genital surgery, so-called "gender affirming care"? These are examples of indoctrination and child abuse perpetrated by people in the educational and medical system. How can you have faith in a medical system which promotes these types of misinformation, misuse, and maltreatment?

There is a rational explanation for what "educators" and medical personnel are doing with our children. They have developed hardness of heart as described in the next chapter. Their attitude toward children is one manifestation of this hardening of heart. There are many others noted throughout this book.

As a result of the hardening of their hearts, God has sent a "spirit of delusion" to them which is making it impossible to see the errors of their thinking and behavior (Ephesians 4:17-22, II Thessalonians 2:9-12). How sad for them! How sad for our children. If parents and our society are not able to stop this fad about being transgender, our children will end up looking like the banana in the hydraulic press noted above, unrecognizable. Here is a quote from the conservative gay community about this process: "Our (gay) community that once preached love and acceptance of others has been hijacked by radical activists who are now pushing extreme concepts onto society, specifically targeting children in recent years."[120] Enough said!

In the next chapter, we will examine the functions of our spiritual/ emotional heart. One of the functions of the heart is to make decisions. It may be more complex than you think.

120 A quotation from the website Gays against Groomers

Affairs of the Heart

In Western culture, love is associated with the heart that pumps blood throughout your body until the moment physical life ceases. It is located inside the left part of your chest. This is your physical heart. The physical heart actually has nothing to do with romantic love except perhaps beating a little faster when you think of your "heartthrob."

There is a different heart. This is the heart that appears on a Valentine's Day card and happens to have a shape somewhat similar to your physical heart. This heart is the center of your intellectual, emotional, and spiritual life, including your expression of the various manifestations of love.

Have you ever wondered where your emotional heart is located? It is different from your physical heart. This chapter is about your Valentine's Day heart, the heart that receives and gives love. This heart has its origin in ancient Hebrew writing in the Old Testament and Greek in the New Testament. There is much more to this heart than its association with love. It has complex functions which determine your satisfaction in life. This is the heart that generates joy and peace, or sadness, anxiety, and depression. It is the center of your decision-making. It is the center of your spiritual function. There are approximately 700 verses in the Bible that contain the word *heart.* Do you think this might be an important concept?

The author of the letter to the Hebrews addresses the question about the location of your emotional heart: "For the word that God speaks is alive and full of power [making it active, operative, energizing, and effective]; it is sharper than any two-edged sword, penetrating to the dividing line of the breath of life, (soul) and your immortal spirit, and of joints and marrow, [of the deepest parts of our nature], exposing, sifting, and analyzing, and judging the very thoughts and purposes of the heart" (Hebrews 4:12). Where is this heart in your physical body?

Where are the deepest parts of your nature? Where is the dividing line of soul and spirit? We must be satisfied with waiting for this knowledge. Scripture does not give a precise location. Some spiritual mysteries will not be clarified until we join Christ for eternity.

It is very important to understand what happened with the human heart in the Garden of Eden associated with the sin of Eve and Adam (Genesis 3:1-7). Adam and his helpmate, Eve, were created with hearts inclined to please God. Then Satan appeared in the garden disguised as a snake. Satan deceived Eve through his words and the appearance of the fruit, suggesting it was good for food and would make her wise like God. Eve was distracted from the counsel of God and became confused and deceived, resulting in an evil desire (pride) to be wise like God. She ate the fruit to satisfy her evil desire.

Then she gave some of the fruit to Adam, who was there listening to Satan's distortions and lies (Genesis 3:1-7). Adam was not deceived about being disobedient (I Timothy 2:14). He apparently ate the fruit, thinking he would lose his helpmate, Eve. Adam had his eyes and thoughts on Eve, thinking he would lose her if he did not follow her example. He was distracted from and confused about the instruction God gave him. He ate the fruit to satisfy his evil desire, which made Eve more important than the word of God. At that moment, everything changed (Genesis 3:8-24). Although Adam was not deceived about his disobedience, he was deceived about the consequences of his disobedience.

The most significant consequence was the change in their nature, forever being inclined to sin and passing this propensity to sin to all future generations. Ouch! This resulted in a break in the relationship between God and the First Couple. However, God instituted a plan of reconciliation immediately (Genesis 3:15) centered around the birth, ministry, death, and resurrection of Jesus Christ (John 3:16).

In Hebrew writing, there are three components to the emotional/spiritual heart: 1) cognition, 2) emotion, and 3) volition, or 1) thinking, 2) feeling, and 3) will. The spiritual heart is the center of these functions, just as the physical heart is the center for the life of the physical body. When thinking about the heart, it is important to consider what is happening in each component. For example, Adam's desire for Eve was stimulated by his thoughts about losing her. This suggests the battle for our heart is often fought in the cognitive part of our mind. This will be discussed in more detail in the chapter titled *Intimacy with Evil.*

In Proverbs 4:23, it is written, "Keep and guard your heart with all vigilance and above all that you guard, for out of it flows the springs of life." The springs of your spiritual life flow from your spiritual heart. Most people put more thought and energy into guarding their wallets than their spiritual hearts.

I. Cognition: This includes the following functions: thinking, understanding, discernment, memory, meditation, dreaming, repository of moral principles, and interpretation of sensory experience. It includes conscious and unconscious functions. We often speak of this part of our heart as our mind. Below are some relevant scriptures generating questions for you to consider:

"This Book of the law shall not depart out of your mouth, but you shall meditate on it day and night, that you may observe and do according to all that is written in it. For then you shall make your way prosperous, and then you shall deal wisely and have good success" (Joshua 1:8).

Question: Are you meditating on spiritual issues that lead to prosperity, wisdom, and success? ______Yes____No

"For man looks on the outward appearance, but the Lord looks on the heart" (I Samuel 16:7).

Question: What does the Lord see when He looks on your heart?

____

____

____

____

____

"Lean on, trust in, and be confident in the Lord with all your heart and mind and do not rely on your own insight or understanding. In all your ways know, recognize, and acknowledge Him, and he will direct and make straight and plain your paths" (Proverbs 3:5-6).

Question: Are you considering the word of God while developing your plans in life? __Yes__No

"The heart is deceitful above all things, and it is exceedingly perverse and corrupt and severely mortally sick! Who can know it [perceive, understand, be acquainted with his own heart and mind]?" (Jeremiah 17:9).

Question: This Scripture supports the concept of an unconscious part of the human mind. There is a portion of your mind to which you do not have direct access that may deceive you. Do you find that concept somewhat unsettling? _____Yes____No

Do you want to know what is stored in the unconscious part of your mind? __Yes__No

We learn from the above scriptures that the functions of the heart are extremely complex. When you consider each of the scriptures, what they mean, and how they apply to you, you are using the cognitive part of your heart. You remember past experiences in your life that contribute to your openness to receive the truth of these experiences. Or, your mind may be closed to these truths because of psychological defenses to stressful experiences. Your thoughts or emotions connected to those experiences through your worldview may prevent your being open to the word of God.

II. Emotion: This is a more elusive concept to define. What is an emotion? According to Webster's Dictionary, it is defined as follows: "an affective state of consciousness in which joy, fear, etc. is experienced, distinguished from cognitive and volitional states of consciousness." What Webster fails to mention is the state of consciousness includes a physical component, something that is experienced in a person's body. Each emotion has its own physical manifestation. Most emotions are experienced in the face, chest, or abdomen (Genesis 4:6). Different facial expressions and body postures are clues to different emotions. There are many small muscles in the face which are used to express these emotions. Guilt, shame, hurt, sadness, and disappointment are usually manifested in the face and chest by a sense of heaviness, a disquiet of the soul. Fear or anxiety may be experienced anywhere in the body, including "butterflies" in the stomach or trembling in the extremities. Why are these things important? It is important to recognize these emotions because God wants us to bring our emotional life to Jesus along with the rest of our life. It is a big part of having a relationship with Him (Isaiah 53:1–6, Revelation 3:20).

There is not a single reference in Strong's Concordance to the word *emotion.* There is one verse with the word *feeling* where it is used pertaining to emotion (Ephesians 4:19). Paul writes, "In their spiritual apathy they have become callous and past feeling and reckless and have abandoned themselves [a prey] to unbridled sensuality, eager and greedy to indulge in every form of impurity that their depraved desires may suggest and demand." Paul is talking of the hearts of nonbelievers who live in the "emptiness of their souls and the futility" of their minds (Amplified Translation, Ephesians 4:17-18). These verses suggest three things about emotion/feeling:

1. Spiritual apathy may be associated with a loss of the ability to feel emotion.
2. The experience of feeling/emotion is different from the desire that is associated with sin. For example, lust is a desire, not an emotion. A person may be numb emotionally and continue to experience Godly desire or evil desire.
3. The evil desire associated with sin may contribute to reckless behavior (Romans 6:16). Have you observed people making poor choices over and over, yet they are unable to change their behavior? Men who repeatedly go through the cycle of domestic violence and their women who are unable to separate from them are examples of this. Angry men are often disconnected from the emotions underlying their anger. Their female partners are often disconnected from the emotions keeping them in the relationship. These are examples of emotions distracting, confusing, and leading to deception. The pattern of deception is noted again below.

Distraction>confusion>deception>evil desire>sin>consequences

Since we are considering the process of deception, consider the following theory concerning the emotional life of Adam and Eve before and after the fall. Before their sin, their emotional life was centered around love, joy, and peace. They may have experienced other Godly emotions such as curiosity, excitement, satisfaction, etc., but they did not experience the following emotions: confusion, guilt, shame, fear, hurt, sadness, or disappointment. These emotions came into existence as a result of sin. Where did they come from? There are only two possibilities, God or Satan. There is not a single scripture indicating Satan has any creative power. In Isaiah 14:14, Satan asserted, "I will make myself like the most High." God must have been amused. He threw Satan out of heaven along with a third of the angels who followed him (Isaiah 14:12).

Although God did not allow Satan to have creative power, He did allow Satan to steal, kill, and destroy (John 10:10). The Greek word for destroy is *apollumi*, meaning to ruin or to lose, not in the sense of being, but in the sense of well-being. It is akin to the English words *pervert*, *distort*, or *corrupt*. So, this theory suggests Satan distorted and corrupted love, joy, and peace as follows: love became anger and hatred, joy became guilt, shame, hurt, sadness, and disappointment, and peace became fear, anxiety, and confusion. These were "gifts" from Satan and consequences which God allowed as a result of their evil desire and disobedience. God is prone to giving people what they ask for. Eve wanted to be wise like God, to know the difference between blessing and calamity. Her evil desire was fully satisfied. Adam elevated his desire to be with Eve above God's instruction about not eating the fruit. His evil desire was satisfied. He remained in the company of Eve, but both of them lost residence in the Garden of Eden. The consequences were tragic for them and for us.

There are many references in Scripture to specific emotions, including love, joy, peace, sadness, guilt, shame, anxiety, etc. Therefore, it is apparent that Scripture does not deny the existence of emotions or the effect emotions have in life. Scripture provides counsel about the context in which emotions occur and how to cope with them. This will be examined in more detail in the chapters on talk therapy.

Secular literature proposes different theories regarding the nature of emotions. Most of them have three things in common:

1. There is a cognitive element to experiencing emotion.
2. There is a physiological element due to the release of neurochemicals in the central and peripheral nervous systems. This produces the sensations in the body described above.
3. The cognitive and physiological elements are a response to a stimulus, an event of some sort.

The cognitive or thinking part of the response relates to how the mind interprets the stimulus considering the context. For example, seeing a grizzly bear behind steel bars 10 feet away at a zoo is very different from seeing one 10 feet away growling and charging at you with its open jaws dripping saliva.

The physiological response occurs in the central nervous system (brain and spinal cord) and the peripheral nervous system, the nerves that extend from the central nervous system to end organs (sensory organs, internal organs, joints, and musculature). In the case of the grizzly bear charging, the stimuli come from the ear hearing the growl, the eye seeing the jaws open and dripping saliva, and the repulsive stench. Your mind determines this context is detrimental to your longevity. The emotion of terror is experienced, and a plan is quickly developed to flee, roll into a ball, or fight. Or you may become paralyzed by fear. Paralysis is more likely absent a plan to cope. If you are paralyzed by fear, you will probably hear a crunch as its jaws close on some part of your fragile skeleton.

There is a discharge of adrenaline to promote fight or flight. Your body responds according to your knowledge of grizzly bear encounters and past experiences coping with fear. Your stomach is doing somersaults, you are drenched in sweat, and your entire body is shaking. Or, without flinching, you draw your 44-magnum handgun and start firing. Or you run like the devil is after you.

All these responses take only a second or two, nearly simultaneously. People with different knowledge about bear attacks and different experiences coping with fear have different responses to the same stimulus. This observation regarding the variance of response informs us that each individual is responsible for their emotions as well as for their behavior. You are responsible for your emotions, so… do not blame others for what you are feeling. Don't blame the bear! Likewise, you are not responsible for another person's emotions, including anger, rage, happiness, well-being, or contentment. You can blame the bear for wanting to end your life if you think it is wise to take time to have that thought.

Have you taken responsibility for another person's emotions? Make a list of these people, identify what you thought you were responsible for, and note how taking responsibility turned out for you and the other person. Write your responses in the space below.

____

____

____

____

____

III. Will: Will is the most difficult of the three parts to describe. It is extremely important because it is the part of the heart that chooses, the part that decides in favor of this or that. In order to avoid confusion about the will, it is important to distinguish between free will and volition. The concept of free will is examined first.

The will of created man has never been completely free.[121] The concept of free will is actually a misnomer. In the Garden of Eden, prior to sin, the will of man was inclined to please God. Adam and Eve pleased God with their thoughts, emotions, decisions, and actions. After the fall, the will of man was inclined towards evil. Adam and Eve could do nothing to please God (Genesis 3:8, Isaiah 53:6, Romans 8:5-8, I Peter 2:24-25). The will of man has never been completely free. However, the cognitive processes of Adam and Eve were not inclined by God before or after their sin. Their thoughts were stimulated by their circumstances, their relationship with God, with each other, and their imagination. Adam and woman did not have free will, but they did have freedom of thought, before and after their disobedience. They were in charge of their thinking processes as we are in charge of our thinking processes. It is in the area of their thought life where the trouble started. The same is often true for you and me.

When Satan appeared in the Garden of Eden disguised as a serpent, he contradicted instructions to Adam from God. Satan's distortions of truth stimulated Eve to have thoughts of being like God, knowing the difference between good and evil and blessing and calamity (Genesis 3:1-6). And when she saw the fruit was suitable and pleasant for food and delightful to look at, it stimulated her imagination to be like God. The thoughts and imaginations which lead to evil desire originated in the mind of Eve. It is not known how long she entertained these thoughts before acting on them, but at some point, they produced an evil desire which was not satisfied until Adam ate the fruit. The process of **entertaining these tempting thoughts** produced the evil desire. A paraphrase of the process described in James 1:13-15: temptation > drawing away by evil desire > conception > birth of sin > death/separation from God. It is a process! If Eve **had said** to the serpent, "I don't know who you are or where you came from, but that is the most ridiculous thing I ever heard," or if Eve had said, "You better talk with my husband about that," or simply "I believe what God says," then you would not be reading a book with the title, "Distraction, Confusion, and the American Dream." Eve was distracted and confused about the instructions from God. She should have responded as Jesus did when He was tempted in the wilderness. Jesus quoted the scriptures. He did not camp out on Satan's temptations.

---

121 www.withchrist.org, Free Will vs. Volition, by Dan Smedra

What did Eve say when God asked, "What is this you have done?" Eve responded, "The serpent beguiled (cheated, outwitted, and deceived) me, and I ate." Eve's evil desire was only partially satisfied. She learned the difference between good and evil and blessing and calamity, but instead of wisdom, the inclination of her will became inclined to evil. This is always the result of evil desire. When Satan deceives, you always get something you did not expect. Sin will take you farther than you want to go, keep you longer than you want to stay, and cost more than you want to pay.[122]

Adam recognized Eve was disobeying but said nothing (I Timothy 2:14). Adam was passive toward the disobedience of Eve. Adam's passivity was the birth of passivity to sin in our nature. Adam apparently was imagining what life would be like in the garden alone without Eve. He entertained this thought in his mind, and it created an evil desire to eat the fruit Eve gave him so their life would continue together. His evil desire was satisfied, but all humanity has suffered from that day forward with a will inclined to sin.

The will is not completely independent. It receives information from the cognitive and emotional parts of the heart prior to the point of decision-making. The will also receives information from God (John 14:26, 16:7-11, Romans 8:14, I Corinthians 2:7-13) and from Satan (Acts 5:3-5). Christ and the Holy Spirit reside in the hearts of all believers (John 14:20, II Corinthians 6:16, Romans 8:11). God has written His law in the hearts of everyone (Romans 2: 14–15, Hebrews 10:16). The heart is the location of our conscience (Psalms 119: 7–11, Hebrews 4:12).

The will takes all this information and decides which desires of the heart it will satisfy. The point of decision-making is also the point where deception may occur. The heart is deceitful above all things (Jeremiah 17:9). A will inclined to evil will distract you. It will confuse you. Obedience to God's word directs you and prevents distraction and confusion (Proverbs 3:1-8, Luke 1:78-79). So, the concept of will implies the inclination of man toward God. It is not free. It is inclined toward disobedience/sin.

Volition simply implies the power of choice. Men and women make all kinds of choices as they live a fallen life. Every person makes dozens of choices every day: where to park the car, what pair of shoes to wear. These choices do not relate to our inclination toward evil. We are free to make these choices because we have freedom of thought. Freedom of thought is often mistakenly confused with freedom of will. They are different processes.

122 www.goodreads.com/quotes, a quote by Ravi Zaccharias

Our will continues to be inclined towards evil until we accept Christ. After the indwelling of Christ and the Holy Spirit, man is enabled to be inclined toward God rather than evil. He can still be tempted, at which time he is "drawn away" from the life of God by his own evil desire, lust, and passions (James 1:13–15). **Therefore, you must guard your heart above everything else in your life** (Proverbs 4:23).

You are made in the image of God, so you should not be surprised that the functions of the heart are complex. Cognition, emotion, and volition interact with love, truth, sin, our relationship with God, and our relationships with each other. Scripture has a lot to say about this. God loves you and joins you to fellowship with Him through grace (John 3-16, Ephesians 2:1–10, Revelation 3:20). God puts love into our hearts and enables us to love others. "Beloved, let us love one another, for love (springs) from God; and he who loves [his fellow man] is begotten (born) of God and is coming [progressively] to know and understand God [to perceive and recognize and get a better and clearer knowledge of him]" (I John 4:7–8).

You may have observed people who are not able to demonstrate love toward others. This might be secondary to not being exposed to loving relationships in their formative years. People who go unloved as children do not understand the process of receiving and giving love. Difficulty loving others can also be secondary to not having a relationship with God and not having the love in our hearts for others that He puts there. Difficulty expressing love might be secondary to emotional or physical abuse. Of course, several processes can operate simultaneously.

God desires us to be holy as He is holy (Leviticus 19:1–2, Isaiah 35:8, I Peter 1:16). Because of His holiness, God does not tolerate evil/disobedience/sin. Sin separates us from God (Romans 1:18). These are truths about God. These truths predict what God will do, and because God does not change, He will respond the same way every time (Malachi 3:6).

Because of these truths, Lucifer was expelled from Heaven, and at a later point in time, God expelled Adam and Eve from the Garden of Eden (Genesis 3:22-24). Lucifer and the "garden couple" were both separated from God because of their desire to be independent of God. God allows disobedience but applies consequences. Satan, Adam, and Eve all experienced spiritual death. This was an immediate consequence. Sin has a similar effect on our relationship with God. But the effect is temporary. God allows an extended period for us to experience consequences and choose a relationship with Him. For reasons that are not clear from Scripture, God responded to Satan's disobedience differently than to Adam and Women. God condemned Satan to a state of permanent separation.

God put into effect a different plan to rescue mankind from evil, which originates from Satan (John 3:16, Romans 3:23–25, James 1:12-15). This plan operates through the keys of the kingdom of Heaven (Matthew 16:19). There are three keys: 1) the key of doctrine, which centers on the moral law of the Old Testament and the teachings of Jesus in the New Testament, 2) the key of authority, and 3) the key of power.

The Keys are the Key

The **key of doctrine** is first mentioned by Jesus while meeting with His apostles in the region of Caesarea Philippi (Matthew 16:13-19). This region is unique for two reasons: it was a Canaanite sanctuary for the worship of the pagan god Baal, and one of the largest springs forming the headwaters of the Jordan River has its source there. Jesus was baptized in the Jordan River. Two forces are symbolized in this geographical area: the forces of evil and the power and authority of God.

This was the background for Jesus having a remarkable conversation with His disciples. Jesus started the conversation by asking this question, "Who do people say the son of man is?" Names put forward included John the Baptist, Elijah, Jeremiah, and one of the prophets.

Then, Jesus put His apostles on the spot by asking the same question to them, "Who do you yourselves say that I am?" Peter stepped up and answered for the group, saying, "You are the Christ, the Son of the living God." Jesus notes Peter had been blessed with this knowledge which had been revealed to him by God. Then Jesus said, "I will build my church, and the gates of Hades (and the powers of the infernal region) shall not overpower it [or be strong to its detriment or hold out against it]." Jesus established three key principles on which His church would be established: doctrine, authority, and power. Christ (the Word) will be the cornerstone of the church. The **key of doctrine** was gradually revealed as follows: beginning in the Garden of Eden, continuing with the patriarchs of Abraham, Isaac and Jacob, the nation of Israel, the prophets, and John the Baptist, all leading to fulfillment in the life, ministry, and gospel of Jesus Christ.

The **key of authority** is reaffirmed in Matthew 18:15–18 and elsewhere. The key of authority has two aspects to it. The first is the authority of God.

Even Jesus was subject to the authority of the Father (John 5:19, 12:49–50). The second facet of this key is the authority that Christ has given us over the powers of the kingdom of Satan (Matthew 16:18–19, Mark 16:16-18, Luke 9:1–2). Both principles are evident in Scripture from James 4:7, "So be subject to God. Resist the devil [stand firm against him] and he will flee from you." This authority also grants us the privilege of building the body of Christ (Matthew 28:18–20, John 14:12-14).

The third key is the **key of power**. At the time of the conversation between Jesus and the apostles at Caesarea Philippi, knowledge had been expanded, and authority and power were added to knowledge. Authority must be invested with power to execute its purposes. The power needed by the church to stand against the gates of Hades is derived from the indwelling of the Holy Spirit (John 3:1-8, 16:5-15). Power is necessary to enforce authority. Power is also necessary for the word/doctrine to be effective (Hebrews 4:12). These are three keys to the kingdom of heaven: doctrine, authority, and power.

The definitions of the word key in this context are as follows: 1) a means of gaining or preventing entrance, position, or control, 2) something that gives an explanation or provides, explains, and provides direction. The three keys are intended to be used together. If one of the keys is not used or misused, the process of building the body of Christ slows or comes to a halt. For example, in sharing the Gospel, it is necessary to understand and present the elements of the Gospel while allowing the Holy Spirit to work in the heart of the nonbeliever. The proper application of authority is to explain the gospel and to humbly witness about how Christ has worked in you to save some part of your own life. If you exceed that authority and become judgmental or exhibit spiritual pride, the opportunity to bring the person to Jesus may be lost. Knowledge and authority both require power to be effective, while power alone results in a lot of activity and spinning wheels but very little progress.

Through diligent study and proper application of the keys, the body of Christ can experience the blessings of God. Each blessing is appropriated through the proper understanding and application of the keys. These blessings include salvation itself, intimacy with God, peace with men, successful marriage relationships, fruitful ministry, being in good health, and having life abundantly. When we neglect the keys, we come under the influence of the kingdom of Satan, which immediately steals, kills, and destroys the blessings God desires us to have (John 10:10). The keys are the key to understanding the plan that God has for your life (Ephesians 2:10).

Notice the word *life* keeps popping up. The gospel of Christ is all about life, spiritual life! Following Satan in the Garden of Eden brought death and separation from God. By accepting Christ as your personal Lord and Savior, you experience reconciliation with God and new life manifested by love, joy, and peace (John 10:10, Ephesians 5:22). Each person must accept Christ to reverse the decision that Adam made in the Garden of Eden.

Idol Worship—An Affair of the Heart

With the doctrine of the keys firmly fixed in our minds, let us focus on love, an affair of your spiritual/ emotional heart. In the 1960s, the sexual revolution started with the mantra "Make love not war." The meaning of these words seemed to be, "Make sexual love at home; don't go to war in Vietnam." A current mantra from the homosexual community is "All love is equal." This sounds good but is a perfect example of word manipulation, deception, and the need for discernment. Is it true that all love is equal? Consider the following. The process of deception is:

Distraction > confusion > deception > evil desire > disobedience > consequences.

This process manifests itself in gay and lesbian relationships as follows: distraction from the Word of God leads to confusion about sexual preference, eventually resulting in the exchange of natural desire (attraction to the opposite sex) for unnatural desire (same-sex attraction), leading to disobedience (an LBGT relationship). The consequences are unnatural desire and separation from God. The unnatural desire becomes an object of worship that replaces the God of creation. This is known in the church as idol worship. Anything can become an idol when it becomes more important than God in a person's spiritual life. Some of the common idols today are sex, power, greed, and comfort. Remember the article by Aldo Leopold, *Thinking Like a Mountain.* The deer herd eventually "died of its own too much" as a result of the wolf population being decimated. Most of us are worshipping the idol of "our own too much," too much stuff, and too many comforts. The country we love is at risk of dying because of our worship of this idol. Process issues always determine outcome, including the outcome of the United States.

Anyone worshipping an idol is worshipping the creature/Satan rather than the creator (Romans 1:25). Idol worship interferes with our being dependent on God and increases dependence on self. These spiritual truths are very difficult for Christians and non-Christians alike. Many Christians are familiar with the concept of idol worship but are in denial about it being an issue in their own lives. Radical activists in the LGBT community hate Christians who hold to these truths. These radical activists entertain an evil desire to destroy the church.

Deception impacts everyone, including yours truly. Years ago, wilderness adventures became my idol. One year, I spent 30 days in various wilderness areas. At the end of the year, when I was writing an annual Christmas letter, I found myself bragging about this "accomplishment." When I was reviewing the letter, I was convicted by the Holy Spirit about wilderness areas becoming an idol in my life. Oops! The pervasive denial of idol worship is a testimony to the power and insidious nature of deception. Deception is everywhere, and it impacts everyone, including the writer and reader of this book.

Love is an Affair of the Heart

In Eskimo culture, there are many words describing differences in the character of snow. The differences in the quality of snow are sometimes a matter of survival. In English, we have several different words describing various types of sandwiches but only one word for love. It's obvious there is a huge difference between a sub sandwich and a peanut butter and jelly sandwich. The English word for love does not distinguish between love for a friend, romantic passion, love for family, love for an activity, or love for apple pie and ice cream. This can create confusion. In ancient Greek, there are several words for love. Each of these words describes a different manifestation of love. Understanding these differences may relate to your emotional and spiritual survival. It is important to remember that every form of love comes from God, including passionate sexual love. But also remember Satan is there to steal, kill, and destroy (John 10:10). Love did not evolve. The God of the Holy Bible instituted love, and His instruction on the subject of love is worth noting (Romans 5:5, I John 4:6-21).

Much of our confusion about love comes from two words in the Greek language, *eros* and *agape*.[123] **Eros** refers to the desire for physical, sensual love. It is the passionate physical attraction that occurs between a man and a woman. This attraction starts during puberty. It is God's plan to be expressed through a sexual relationship after marriage. Eros is the love that attracts

123 www.compellingtruth.org, What is the Meaning of Agape Love?

people physically. Eros between two people of the same sex separates them from God because they follow their own plan instead of the plan that God has for sexual expression. Any process that separates a person from God lacks agape love. It has limitations. There are very few LGBT relationships in people who are Christian. Christians with same-sex attraction often feel anxious or uneasy with same-sex desire because they are indwelt by the Holy Spirit, which convicts and guides believers into the truth. Nonbelievers lack the prompting that comes from the spirit of God. They deny the truth of God. It is of interest that the word eros is not present anywhere in the Bible. However, the concept of eros is present in the Old Testament in the Song of Solomon (S. of S. 4:1-11, 5:1, 7:6-13)[124]

Agape love is the type of unconditional love that God has for every person, irrespective of whether the person believes or does not believe. It consists of affection, goodwill, and benevolence that builds a person into a mature adult. It works together with truth to accomplish this. Agape love attracts; it draws attention because it is relatively uncommon. It also attracts people to Jesus. When people see it, they wonder what is going on. Every person wants and needs to be loved in this way, but many are frustrated in finding it. This is because they are deceived about where to look. They are looking in eros. They will not find it only in eros.

Agape is the love that sustains relationships, including your marriage relationship. Agape has the following characteristics: it endures all trials, is patient and kind, is never jealous, never rude, always gracious, does not insist on its own way, does not keep a record of wrongs, it never rejoices at injustice, it always rejoices when right and truth prevail, it bears up or lasts under all circumstances without weakening, it never fails, and it will never come to an end because it will be experienced for eternity by those who are saved through Christ (I Corinthians 13:1-13). For those who are married or in some other type of romantic relationship, would you like to have a relationship manifesting affection, goodwill, benevolence, grace, forgiveness, forbearance, building you up, and meeting your needs? You are unlikely to find a relationship with those characteristics without agape love. Agape love is hard to find unless your partner is indwelt by Christ. Agape love is the love that prevents divorce. When agape love is functioning properly, every type of relationship will grow stronger over time. It is Jesus, through the power

124 125 If you doubt the importance of passionate romantic love, read the book, Solomon on Sex by Joseph C. Dillow

of the Holy Spirit, who enables Christians to develop the characteristics of agape love.

Other words for *love* in ancient Greek include the following:

Pragma is literally translated as that which has been done or accomplished. It refers to a long-standing love often associated with well-established couples. This type of love is associated with compatibility and a history of life shared that is mutually rewarding.

Storge is the Greek word for love existing between family members, between parents and children and siblings. It is unwavering unless sin produces conflict in the relationships.

Phileo is the love existing in close friendships such as King David and Jonathan (I Samuel 18:1-4).

Ludus is a Latin word that Greeks considered to be associated with flirtatious, playful, uncommitted sexual love between young lovers or in adulterous relationships. People often experience confusion because they fail to discriminate between eros, agape, and ludus love. Ludus love is a distraction from passionate sexual love expressed in a marriage relationship. It results from evil desire. It is always hurtful, although it may provide brief pleasure and gratification (Proverbs 7:1-24, Hebrews 11:25, James 1:13-15). This is what makes it so deceptive and confusing. Young men are often seeking ludus while their female partners are seeking agape and eros through marriage. When two people have different goals for a love relationship, it usually results in a poor outcome.

At a conscious level, young men appear satisfied with their short-term affairs. They are unaware of the process, evil desire, that is reducing their sensitivity to the needs of women. They are focused on satisfying their sexual desire and are not considering how it will hurt their partner. In later years, when these young men are seeking agape and eros, they will lack skill in creating and maintaining an agape relationship. When they experience disappointment in their marriage, they will give up and look for another eros relationship. These men are prone to divorce or having an affair which usually ends their marriage.

Young women get hurt in these uncommitted, flirtatious relationships. Their hurt and disappointment reduce their sexual desire in future relationships. Yet they still have a desire for a husband (Genesis 3:16). After marriage, especially after childbearing, they may find it difficult to give themselves completely to their husbands in a sexual relationship. This may produce tremendous stress in the marriage, leading to divorce.

You may be asking, is any of this true? Well, the first thing you can do to check that out is to examine the romantic relationship/s you have presently or had in the past, looking for agape love. The word of God is prophetic. It predicts that romantic relationships will not thrive or survive based solely on erotic love. This prophecy is corroborated by a divorce rate hovering around 45-50 percent. What aspect of agape love was missing that contributed to conflict or break up with your relationship/s? Read the love chapter in First Corinthians and the verses in Ephesians and First Peter on sacrificial love and respect (I Corinthians 13:1-13, Ephesians 4:21-31, I Peter 3:1-9). These verses will help you identify what is missing in your romantic love life. Write your answers in the space below.

____

____

____

____

____

Hard Hearts

What is a hard heart? The following example originated in the kingdom of Satan and will introduce you to this process issue. As you read this story, consider what idol is being worshiped.

In 1949, scientists at the Hanford Nuclear Reservation in southeastern Washington intentionally released 8000 curies of radioactive iodine (iodine-131) over a 48-hour period of time. This experiment was known by the code name Green Run. The release at Hanford compares to the 15 to 24 curies of radioactive iodine released accidentally in 1979 at the Three Mile Island nuclear reactor accident. Winds carried airborne radiation throughout eastern Washington into northeastern Oregon, northern Idaho, Montana, and Canada. People exposed to iodine-131 can suffer acute and chronic health effects, including thyroid cancer, benign thyroid growths, and overall inhibited thyroid performance. Although Hanford officials were aware of the potential dangers of iodine-131, they did nothing to alert their own workers or people in distant communities of the attendant risks.

Hanford researchers conducted secret studies showing "how high dosage levels of ingested iodine-131 in sheep 'showed virtually complete destruction of their thyroids in those of their offspring'. At the same time, they conducted press briefings in which officials assured the public that 'not one atom' of radioactivity had escaped the facility." On one occasion, they said the facility was "safe as mother's milk" although they knew differently.

Tom Baillie grew up and lived on a farm near Hanford. In 1984 he spoke to a congressional advisory committee showing a map he called "death mile, where 100% of those families who drink the water, the milk, and eat the food downwind of the radiation releases have one common denominator that binds us together, and that is thyroid problems, handicapped children, or cancer."

Despite many such stories, the final draft of the Hanford Thyroid Disease Study released in June 2002 stated, "If there is an increased risk of thyroid disease from exposure to iodine-131, it is probably too small to observe." In 2005, the class action lawsuit, representing about 3500 claimants of health problems, was finally settled after 24 years. Instead of humbling themselves and admitting their abuse of the downwind population, Hanford officials hired attorneys at government expense. They wasted $57 million of taxpayer funds defending this human experiment. Details of the settlement were not made available to the public.

The opposite of humility is the evil desire of pride. We have seen how pride resulted in Satan being kicked out of Heaven and Adam and Eve being thrown out of the garden. Pride tends to obscure the feelings of guilt and shame which should be experienced consciously when we ignore our injuries to others. Guilt and shame produce hiding behaviors that work together to reinforce pride. Hardness of heart works together with pride to deceive sociopaths and politicians to not care about how their behavior impacts the lives of the citizens they represent. They think their lies and other evil acts will not be discovered or punished. They think no one is powerful enough to punish them.

What body of knowledge (cognition) suggested releasing radiation was a wise thing to do? Did pride overcome knowledge as it did with Satan? Did these researchers think they were so much smarter than the public that they could do whatever they desired? Were they responding to evil desire? Were they narcissistic? Did these scientists listen to their emotions, guilt, and shame before they made their decision? Were they deceived? What was the will of the Hanford scientists who intentionally exposed the public to radiation? Was this an abuse of science? Have there been other abuses of science? What was the condition of their heart? Were they ever prosecuted? Should they have been prosecuted? Is the government doing anything similar today? Has the US government become more trustworthy since 1949? Write your responses to these questions in the space below. Your answers are important to your general well-being and survival.

____

____

____

____

____

It seems their evil desire was to conduct an experiment without concern for the health of the downwinders. This constituted obvious abuse of power. Lies often cover for abuse. It should have been prosecuted.

It has been 72 years since the Hanford release of radiation. Do you think the government has stopped lying to the public? Or **is there currently a pandemic of lying?** Ordinarily, we think of science as being informative and advancing culture. When science and technology are used for selfish and/or political reasons, it injures the people it is supposed to serve. It degrades the culture. It produces hardness of heart for the people in charge of the science. Lying by the government about science or politics produces distrust in the people who are governed. The government attorneys delayed justice for the downwinders for 24 years. Many of the researchers would have been retired after 24 years, and some of the downwinders were dead, too late for any assistance or compensation.

This shameful event is symbolic of the government's approach to transparency. The government relishes spending our tax dollars to prevent the truth from coming to light. In the example of Operation Green Run, they wasted 57 million dollars protecting their fragile egos…and preventing prosecution. Deception, abuse, and disease arrived together for the downwinders in the Hanford experiment. Deception and abuse working together is a plan of Satan. Compare that to God's plan for love and truth arriving together as described in the gospel of Christ (John 3:16). Love and truth arrive together because they are intended to work together. When people resist the love and truth that comes from the creator of the universe, their hearts begin to harden. They become slaves to sin (Romans 6:16). Disobedience becomes a way of life. Hard hearts are manifested by interpersonal conflict, anger, personal attacks, threats, dissension, divisiveness, selfishness, envy, and constant lying. You will not find love and truth in persons with hard hearts.

Hardness of heart is described in detail in Ephesians 4:18–19: "Their moral understanding is darkened and their reasoning is clouded. [They are] alienated (estranged, self banished) from the life of God [with no share in it; this is] because of the ignorance [the want of knowledge and perception, the willful blindness] that is deep-seated in them, due to the hardness of heart [to the insensitivity of their moral nature]. In their spiritual apathy, they have become callous and past feeling and reckless and have abandoned themselves [a prey] to unbridled sensuality, eager and greedy to indulge in every form of impurity [that their depraved desires may suggest and demand]." These two verses are an indictment of the hardness of heart. Obedience to the plan God offers has an entirely different effect on the human heart. It produces an intimate relationship with the creator. It generates blessings that no one can predict. Obedience strengthens faith (Romans 8:28). It is an act of worship (Luke 6:38, James 1:17, Romans 12:1). It generates knowledge of His purposes for the believer (Romans 12:2). This is what produces softening of the heart, which is a spiritual process that enables acceptance of Christ as your Lord and Savior (John 6:44–45). God the Father softens hearts for this purpose. The softening process produces a Godly desire to accept Jesus and to follow Him.

"The same sun that melts the ice also hardens the clay."[125] Jesus is the spiritual sunlight to the world that shines on every heart. When it exposes a cold heart willing to be obedient, it melts that heart to join in accomplishing the work of God (John 6:28-29). When it exposes an unwilling heart, it hardens the heart. Every heart starts as a cold, frozen heart because the will of the natural man is inclined to sin (Romans 7:15-25, I Corinthians 2:14, 15:42-44). God desires every soul to be saved (I Timothy 2:3-4, II Peter 3:9). Every heart has the same opportunity. Some respond to the light, but many do not because their hearts are already hardened.

Consider the following scriptures:

Psalm 44:20-21: "If we had forgotten the name of our God or stretched out our hands to a strange God, would not God discover

125 The Bible Exposition Commentary, Old Testament, Isaiah-Malachi, by Warren Wiersbe, pg.120, par. 7

this? For he knows the secrets of the heart."

Jeremiah 17:10: "I the Lord search the mind, I try the heart, even to give to every man according to his ways, according to the fruit of his doings."

Luke 1:78-79: "Because of and through the heart of tender mercy and loving kindness of our God, a Light from on high will dawn upon us and visit [us]. To shine upon and give light to those who sit in darkness and in the shadow of death, to direct and guide our feet in a straight line into the way of peace."

What are your thoughts about God having access to everything that transpires in your mind and heart? Is your heart frozen, or has Spiritual Sunlight begun the melting process? Do you have peace in your life? Write your answers below.

____

____

____

____

____

This chapter has focused on process issues relating to the function of our spiritual heart. The three primary functions are cognition, emotion, and volition. The affairs of the heart determine our satisfaction in life. Since the heart is the center of our cognitive, emotional, and spiritual life, we should not be surprised that it receives information from each of the two kingdoms, God and Satan. But these concepts are difficult to accept because we cannot see the spiritual processes around us. God softens our hearts so that we might understand love and truth coming into the world through the ministry of Christ.

In the next chapter, we investigate the workings of having intimate experiences with evil. Evil desire impacts each part of the heart: cognition, emotion, and volition. This is the reason encounters with evil need to be taken seriously.

Intimacy with Evil

Intimacy with evil is a topic on which I never had lectures in medicine, psychology, or psychiatric residency. Why is that? Could it be a manifestation of deception? Three questions come to mind about evil. What is evil?

Is it possible to have an intimate experience with evil? Does the power of evil change a person during an intimate encounter? Answering these questions is the focus of this chapter. We will start by examining evil in a general way and then look at how it affects the five domains of humanity. Below are some observations about evil.

We hear about evil in our presidential rhetoric. Do any of the following comments resonate with you about evil desire?

- George Washington: "The very atmosphere of firearms anywhere and everywhere restrains evil interference."
- Thomas Jefferson: "Evil triumphs when good men do nothing."
- Abraham Lincoln: "I would rather be a little nobody, than to be an evil somebody."
- Dwight Eisenhower: "War is a grim cruel business justified only as a means of sustaining the forces of good against those of evil."
- Barack Obama: "We know we can't stop every act of violence, every act of evil in the world, but maybe we could try to stop one act of evil, one act of violence."
- Shakespeare: "Hell is empty and all the Devils are here."

From the group of luminaries who have commented about evil, perhaps Shakespeare had the best understanding of evil: If "all the devils are here," should we not be on the lookout for them (Matthew 26:36-45)? But where do you find them?

In the early 1980s, anxiety and depression secondary to sexual abuse were gaining attention in mental health clinics and notoriety in the news media. The diagnosis of post-traumatic stress disorder (PTSD) had made its appearance earlier in veterans returning from the Vietnam War. In 1980,

PTSD was included in the diagnostic manual of the American Psychiatric Association for the first time. It was defined as follows: "The essential feature (of PTSD) is the development of characteristic symptoms following a psychologically **traumatic event** that is generally outside the range of usual human experience. PTSD is considered a type of anxiety disorder."[126]

A social worker with extensive experience with survivors of sexual abuse was leading training at the mental health clinic where I consulted. When she talked about perpetrators of sexual abuse, she was determined that we all understood sexual abuse and rape had nothing to do with emotional intimacy. I briefly stopped listening to her presentation because her statement grabbed my attention. Her comment haunted me.

In the church, you often hear about horizontal relationships and vertical relationships. Horizontal relationships are those with acquaintances, friends, and family. Vertical relationships are a reference to your relationship with God, Christ, and the Holy Spirit. Intimacy can occur in these various relationships. It occurred to me that the vertical dimension has two aspects to it, up and down. Up vertical in this context relates to relationships with the Creator of the universe. Down vertical relates to having a relationship with Satan/evil. So the thought came to me: perhaps it is possible to have an intimate experience with evil. This prompted an inquiry into the process of evil... and its effects on the human soul.

Evil is not easy to define because it is a supernatural force. Evil is like the wind: you cannot see it, but you can see, hear, and feel its effects. Evil can be like a tornado destroying everything in its path, or it can be like a gentle breeze caressing your cheeks on a hot summer day. Evil sometimes feels good. But the wind is the wind, and evil is evil, no matter how good it feels. We are reluctant to admit that there is a part of our heart that wants to steal, kill, and destroy. (Jeremiah 17:9, John 10:10). Evil is the fundamental process issue that takes our eyes from God and focuses them on Satan, his temptations, and his purposes: to steal, kill, and destroy. **Evil distracts!** Evil distracts from the divine purposes and plans of God.

To understand evil, consider the relationship between God and Satan. After Lucifer's rebellion, his name changed to Satan or the Adversary. This is the clue that helps us understand evil. Evil is everything that is adversarial to God and His plan for humanity. In Christian doctrine, evil is "the comprehensive

126 DSM III, Diagnostic and Statistical Manual of Mental Disorders (third edition), 1980

term under which all disturbances of the divinely appointed harmony of the universe are included."[127] The divinely appointed harmony of the universe was disrupted when Satan and the other angels rebelled against God. It was disrupted a second time through the disobedience of Eve and Adam in the Garden of Eden. It has been disrupted continuously since that time through our sin nature inherited from Adam.

Evil may be thought of as anything that is in opposition to the purposes of God. It is divided into two types: 1) physical evil, i.e., a disorder in the physical world, natural phenomena which destroy physical well-being (storms, lightning, wind, floods), 2) moral evil, i.e., the disobedience of mankind to the will of God, referred to as sin. We are unable to see evil in the same way we have difficulty seeing our own sin nature. We are deceived. We only see the manifestations of evil, that is, evil thoughts, speech, emotions, behavior, and circumstances.

Philosophers, psychologists, and other secular writers have a very different understanding of evil from what is described above.[128] They describe evil by describing different types of evil behavior. In psychology, evil events are referred to as trauma. Thoughts about these events often produce a response in the mind that takes the person back to the original experience in some way. When this happens, the person may be flooded with the emotions associated with the original experience: confusion, fear, hurt, guilt, shame, sadness, and disappointment. This is referred to in behavioral science as post-traumatic stress symptoms.

They have no explanation for the origin of evil. They are in denial. They have two objections to the Christian view. First, they object to the supernatural element. They do not see it, so they deny it. They are like the Jamestown colonists who could not see the gold they were walking on. Like the colonists, they put all their effort into fool's gold, theories, intellectual machinations, and other vain deceits (Colossians 2:8).

Secondly, they do not comprehend how an omnipotent, omniscient God who is full of grace, love, mercy, and truth could allow the presence of evil in the world. For the Christian, objection to the supernatural element is overcome simply through faith. Scripture answers the second objection in the book of Romans. "For who has known the mind of the Lord and who has understood his thoughts, or who has [ever] been his counselor?" (Romans

---

127 The New Unger's Bible Dictionary, Moody Press, 1988

128 www.plato.stanford.edu/entries, The Concept of Evil

11:33-34, I Corinthians 2:14). We have never been able to comprehend all the purposes and plans of God. We are like little children who have not reached the age of reason. The thought life and plans of God are beyond our own thought life. We evidence wisdom when we accept His plans based on our faith In Him. Any person who believes he understands God completely is having an acute and overwhelming attack of pride. Most unbelievers deny the existence of God, or they desire to give God advice. Giving the Creator of the universe pointers on moral conduct is a little like a 16-year-old teenager in jail for reckless driving advising his father on how to drive the family sports car.

Many believers think they should have a life relatively free of trauma and illness because of the work they do for the Lord. It is natural to think this, but unrealistic. No one wants to be traumatized. But physical evil and intimacy with evil are realities we face as a result of fallen humanity. Abuse is a manifestation of a fallen world. God hates abuse and every other form of disobedience. But God allows physical evil, storms, and floods, which are evidence of the fallen state of the physical world. He also allows storms in our relationships. This will be discussed again below under the heading, *The Cord of Separation, Spiritual Issues.*

How Groups of People Relate to Evil

People relate to evil in different ways. There are five main groups, although there are no distinct boundaries between the groups. People can move from one group to another.

1. There are people who perpetrate evil. We are all perpetrators (Romans 3:23). But a relatively small group, who possess great power, have a huge adverse influence on society. This small group spends much of their time developing evil plans to take advantage of others. They do not care about the people they are hurting. The concept of fairness is alien to their minds.
2. Persons who have been injured by evil experiences, such as those who have anxiety, depression, or post-traumatic stress. Everyone experiences evil because we live in a world dominated by it (John 14:30-31, 15:19, Romans 12:2, II Corinthians 4:3-4). Some survivors of evil need help to overcome the effects of their exposure to evil.[129]

129 The process of overcoming evil in personal experiences is discussed in the four chapters on talk therapy

3. Many people are entertained by evil. **Evil appeals to the sin nature we all have deep within our hearts.** Hollywood uses knowledge of this process issue in every R and X-rated movie. Their dual purposes are to stimulate your sin nature and separate you from your paycheck. It seems there are more TV shows related to crime than any other genre. We are fascinated with crime. Yet we have taken the Ten Commandments out of our schools, and many are calling for defunding the police. If crime shows on TV did not have a police response, the programs would go off the air. Yet many are saying they don't want a police response in the communities where we live. Is that a deception? Rape, sex trafficking, gruesome murders, and other shocking manifestations of evil dominate our news and Hollywood productions. Pornographic movies and websites use visual stimulation to encourage sexual practices which enslave men and women and destroy marriages. People who are entertained by evil unknowingly support it.
4. A large group of people who attempt to ignore it. This group is large in numbers and passive in their approach to evil. They do not want to be personally involved. They hope to remain aloof from the process of evil. That is not possible because evil degrades the society in which they live.
5. A small group of individuals who actively resist evil. These people are prone to burning out. They often receive very little support from others. Some of them place themselves at great risk in their effort to combat evil (John 15:18-21, Hebrews 12:3-4).

What is wrong with the "picture" that Hollywood portrays? By continually watching productions that shock and horrify, we become desensitized to the effects of evil. Hollywood is using the medium of entertainment to manipulate the way we think about morality and to blur the distinction between love and lust. They deny the reality of a savior and use entertainment to stimulate the rest of us to join in their denial.

If Hollywood producers admitted the existence of Satan, they might have to confront their denial of Christ and His death on the cross. Wisdom suggests caution about using evil to entertain our minds. It may open a door for demonic influence or simply generate unnecessary stress. When I was eight or nine years old, I went with my older brother to see *The Thing,* a movie starring James Arness. I had difficulty getting to sleep for weeks afterward, thinking that an alien was going to jump out of my closet. I also had nightmares about it. Scripture suggests it is better to have our minds focused on the positive aspects of life. "Whatever is true, whatever is worthy of reverence and is honorable and seemly, whatever is just, whatever is pure, whatever is lovely and lovable, whatever is kind and winsome and gracious, if there is any virtue and excellence, if there is anything worthy of praise, think on and weigh and take account of these things [fix your minds] on them" (Philippians 4:8).

What does it mean to weigh something in your mind? It means to ponder or contemplate for the purpose of making a decision. Imagine a balance scale. On one platform of the scale, you put the positive aspects of your decision. On the other platform, you put the negative aspects. Then you observe which platform has the most weight and make the choice that will produce the best outcome. For the scale to function properly, it is necessary to have a measure of what is true and what is false. Without truth, the scale is useless. Confusion is the result. Confusion does not often lead to decisions with good outcomes (I Corinthians 14:33).

Truth and **lies** are process issues that lead to decisions opposite in nature and outcome.

There are two pathways that lead to someone experiencing intimacy with evil. 1) Often, evil is forced on an innocent person--sexual abuse is a perfect example (Matthew 18:6). This results in unwanted intimacy with evil. Since the intent of evil is "to steal, kill, and destroy," the impact on personhood is pervasive and destructive (John 10:10). 2) As populations in Western cultures move farther and farther from Christianity, larger numbers of people actually seek relationships with evil through various practices. They knowingly enter intimate experiences with evil. Their "rewards" gratify the self but harden their hearts to a relationship with God. They pay an eternal price for brief periods of pleasure.

Something intimate is defined as "belonging to or characterizing one's deepest nature, marked by a very close association, contact or familiarity, of a very personal or private nature." In our culture, we talk about emotional intimacy and sexual intimacy with a positive frame of reference. In the chapters on the D words, we learned that desire has two versions: that which is stimulated by God (Godly desire) and that which is stimulated by Satan (evil desire). It seems logical that when evil desire gains access to the most intimate parts of our being, it can generate an experience impacting our deepest nature, our personality, and our very soul. The intimate parts of our being are the elements of our heart: our mind, our emotions, and our will.

The threefold purpose of evil desire, to steal, kill, and destroy, will be experienced in our mind, our emotions, and our will. The secular word that describes this process is **trauma**. Post-traumatic stress disorder is simply a collection of the various manifestations of how our mind, our emotions, and our will are influenced by an intimate encounter with evil desire. These manifestations are referred to as symptoms in medical terms. Anxiety and depression are two of the most common symptoms that bring people in for a mental health consultation and talk therapy.

The rest of the discussion in this chapter will focus primarily on the effects of intimacy with evil. The discussion will focus on depression, but much of what is stated will apply equally to anxiety. The cause of most depression falls into two categories: depression biological in origin and depression which has its origin in traumatic life events, referred to as reactive depression.

It is difficult to know precisely what percentage of depression is biological in origin because the diagnostic system approved by the American Psychiatric Association changes every five to ten years, but my guesstimate would be 5 to 10 percent or less. This leaves 90 percent of depression due to trauma. Biological depression is best treated by discovering the underlying medical problem and correcting it. Prescribing anti-depressants or other psychiatric medications is primarily of help for psychiatric illnesses of biological origin and is relatively ineffective for tumors, endocrine problems, vitamin deficiencies, etc. The best treatment for these conditions is to correct the underlying malady.

Many psychiatrists stopped taking the time necessary to differentiate biological depression from depression due to trauma. Some argued it was not possible to make such a distinction. Others argued that failure to make this distinction results in misdiagnosis and inappropriate treatment. It appears Big Pharma supports the idea that all depression should be treated the same, i.e., with anti-depressants. This would appear to be financially advantageous for Big Pharma, who manufactures and supplies myriads of anti-depressant agents.

This is a multibillion-dollar industry. It also appears the medical insurance industry supports this idea, as they seem reluctant to provide benefits that financially support talk therapy. Big Pharma and the insurance industry have been successful in relegating most psychiatrists to be dispensers of psychotropic medications. Very few psychiatrists offer therapy in the 21st century.

When I started practicing psychiatry during my internship in 1969-70, DSM II was in use, and depression was referred to as a neurosis. This was a concept originating from the work of Freud, which became associated with the idea of mental instability. Depressions that were secondary to life events were also placed in this category. Use of the terms neurotic and neurosis was unfortunate for two reasons. First, no one wants to be considered mentally unstable (neurotic), so eventually, this term was dropped from psychiatric diagnoses.

Second, these terms shifted the emphasis from trauma causing the symptoms to the symptoms themselves. This continued a cycle of changing the classification system based on symptomatology rather than cause.

This neurotic label prevented many people who might have benefited from counseling services from seeking those services. The general population was deceived into thinking that having a need for counseling implied some type of personal deficiency. Nothing could be farther from the truth. **Reactive Depression and anxiety are normal responses to trauma.**

Counseling became associated with the emotion of shame in the minds of the general public. Shame stimulates hiding behavior. People kept their trauma and the symptoms of their trauma to themselves. In these individuals, the emotion of **shame** became a process issue determining a poor outcome: untreated depression and anxiety.

Prescribing anti-depressants for trauma is often ineffective because there is no medication that completely reverses the impact trauma has on the mind, emotions, and the will. Trauma, such as physical injury, sexual abuse, emotional abuse, and spiritual abuse, can impact the mind, emotions, and will in the five categories noted below. The impact of intimacy with evil manifests itself in each of the five domains of humanity. There is no medication that will completely correct faulty thinking, connect us to emotions, change unproductive behaviors, correct physiology, or resolve spiritual apathy.

Now, consider the following: **the five cords of sin** noted in chapter five. These are the process issues that often perpetuate the symptoms of anxiety and depression.

I. The Cord of Fallacy, False Perceptions, and Beliefs: Children especially, but also adults, learn things from trauma/abuse experiences that are not true. These are sometimes referred to as thinking errors, cognitive distortions, or abuse lessons. A girl might think she was sexually abused because she is pretty. She assumes responsibility for the perpetrator's behavior. Most children are unable to conceptualize an adult motivated by evil desire, so children use psychological defense mechanisms such as avoidance, repression, denial, and rationalization to cope with the abuse experience. This girl might attempt to compensate for being pretty by being unfeminine, obese, or masculine as she matures. She might develop a romantic interest in girls who appear less threatening.

When children or adults generalize anxiety associated with the trauma to a broader range of situations, a cognitive distortion known as *generalization*, they may develop an anxiety disorder. For example, an elementary school girl sexually abused by her uncle may determine in her mind that most men are unsafe to be around and sexual behavior is sick and anxiety-producing. This may discourage dating as she matures into young adulthood or promotes anxiety and failure to experience pleasure during marital intimacy. Some common thinking errors are:

- Black and white thinking (people thinking in extremes)
- Catastrophizing/negative thinking (always assuming the worst possible outcome)
- Personalization (thinking you are being criticized or blamed when in reality, the comment or experience is not related to you)
- Mind reading (assuming you know what other people are thinking without asking)
- Isolating (avoiding relationships to maintain safety).

The above are all strategies to maintain emotional and sexual safety.

Each cognitive distortion makes it more confusing for the will to execute a proper decision. People often think, "I must be losing my mind." Many people who seek therapy have this thought. That is a deception orchestrated by the father of all lies, Satan, the great accuser. Actually, experiencing these symptoms is a perfectly normal reaction to trauma. They are defensive reactions to insane experiences. Minor stressors that resemble the original trauma can stimulate these reactions. It's unfortunate and painful, but it's normal to have them. So, many people think there is something wrong with them when the problem resides in their perpetrator.

If reading these paragraphs or any of the questions below are disturbing to you, stop reading and seek professional counseling.

1. Review a complete list of thinking errors/cognitive distortions from

the Internet and note the distortions you have in your own life. What thinking errors will you need to work on to resolve your anxiety, depression, or other mental health problem? Write your answer/s in the space below.

____

____

____

____

____

2. Do you have cognitive distortions influencing your relationships in any way? Write your answers below.

____

____

____

____

____

3. Show the list of thinking errors you downloaded from the Internet to your spouse or closest friend and ask them to check what they perceive are your thinking errors. Compare your list with their list. Note any differences below.

____

____

____

____

____

4. Do you think your perception of self has been influenced by intimate experiences with evil? How? Write your answers below.

____

____

____

____

____

5. The will is the part of your heart that chooses. Have you made choices that did not have a good outcome? Select one experience with a poor outcome. Analyze the cognitive, emotional, and spiritual factors that you considered which produced an unsatisfactory outcome. Before

this exercise, review the chapter "Affairs of the Heart" on cognition, emotion, and volition.

____

____

____

____

____

6. Was there any spiritual input contributing to the choice made above? Would spiritual input from scripture have changed the outcome? Write your answer in the space below.

____

____

____

____

____

II. The Cord of Sentiment, Disconnection from Emotions: Traumatic experiences often produce emotional pain. The feelings of confusion, guilt, shame, hurt, fear, sadness, and disappointment are so strong it seems one cannot bear it. People cope by disconnecting from the emotions associated with the experience. This is referred to as dissociation. They refuse to experience and process the feelings. These emotions do not disappear; they hang out somewhere in the mind. When enough of them are stored instead of being expressed and processed, the person experiences symptoms of anxiety, depression, or some other mental health problem. Clients generally agree that the emotional pain associated with trauma is worse than any physical pain. Each of these emotions becomes a process issue that contributes to poor choices, as described below under behavior.

1. Are you aware of your emotions at all times, including the emotions that underlie anger?
2. What emotion/s most often underlie anger for you?
3. Are you able to connect the emotion/s underlying your anger to specific life experiences?
4. Do you have grief work waiting to be accomplished? Write your answers below.

God has emotions. But God never pushes His emotions into the unconscious part of His mind, as we do. It seems unlikely God has an unconscious mind. When you turn away from the face of God, He is hurt and disappointed (Genesis 6:5-6, Luke 19:41-44, Ephesians 4:29-32). God is also patient. He is waiting for you to come to Him.

III. The Cord of Poor Choices: This refers to behavior resulting from poor decisions. We learn from the above that intimate experiences with evil/trauma impact our understanding, thought life, perception of self, and how we cope with our emotions. We should not be surprised to learn that trauma influences our will, the part of our heart making decisions. Thoughts and emotions are two of the primary process issues that determine behavior. It follows that faulty thinking and emotions outside our awareness would influence the will to make decisions that do not work well. We become distracted by the events in our lives. Distraction leads to confusion, promoting indecision, poor decisions, anxiety, and depression. Guilt and shame lead to secrecy and other forms of hiding. They stimulate our defense mechanisms, such as repression and denial, which are a more sophisticated **form of hiding. Hurt and fear often produce avoidance, anger, or passivity. Sadness and disappointment generate grief.** These processes work together to create anxiety and depressive disorders. Sometimes this mental activity happens mostly on an unconscious level. This helps to understand the scripture in Jeremiah 17:9, "The heart is deceitful above all things, and it is exceedingly perverse and corrupt and severely, mortally sick! Who can know it?" A lack of awareness about how these process issues are working against peace of mind contributes to the turmoil experienced by someone who is anxious or depressed.

Survivors of combat and survivors of rape/sexual abuse have some things in common. They have both been exposed to a process that is generally outside the range of human experience. They are often both diagnosed with Post Traumatic Stress Disorder. They are prone to using alcohol, street drugs, or addicting prescription medications to cope with emotional pain.

Trust is impaired. Symptoms include recurrent distressing memories of the event/s, recurrent agonizing dreams, dissociative flashbacks, and anxiety or stress upon exposure to stimuli that resemble aspects of the events. These are generated by unconscious processes of the mind. The memories, dreams, flashbacks, and anxiety are related to content issues. They are connected to the content of a traumatic experience. They are conveying a message from the unconscious to the conscious mind: "You have had an experience that is waiting to be processed. I will store this intimate encounter with evil until you are ready to process it. But I have to remind you, it is there, waiting for you." This "message" can be highly anxiety-producing.

When you decide to resolve it, do not go by yourself. Go with another person, a Christian therapist, or go with Jesus, who is the best therapist because He is always available for emergency calls and knows precisely what you need. Review the therapy of Abigail and the section on meditation in the appendix for details about this process.

People have very little control over these anxiety-producing symptoms. It becomes very difficult to maintain peace of mind. People think they are losing their mind, but this is a **normal response to trauma**. Some veterans cope by isolating themselves from society, choosing remote environments to "live." Survivors of sexual abuse simply cut themselves off from relationships outside their families. These are conscious decisions of the will. They protect, but they do not resolve trauma. Isolating is like treading water. You don't drown, but you never get to shore where you can get out of the water to enjoy the rest of your life.

1. Do you have repetitive behaviors that do not work well? Make a list below.
2. Where did you learn these behaviors?
3. What beliefs and emotions support these behaviors?

____

____

____

____

____

IV. The Cord of Compulsion, Physiological changes: Severe traumas reset various aspects of our nervous system function and the organs these nerves control. Neurochemical changes and receptor physiology in the brain underlie compulsive behaviors that become difficult to change. Physiological changes manifest a variety of symptoms: the heart beating strong or fast, elevated blood pressure, excessive sweating, shortness of breath, headache, weakness, fatigue, anxiety, sudden mood changes, and a host of other symptoms and psychosomatic illnesses. **These are symptoms of trauma**. However, the connection to trauma may not be recognized because the process issues are working partly or mostly unconsciously.

The symptoms noted above are often not responsive to routine medical evaluation and treatment. If you have seen two or three doctors for the same symptom and consultation is not helping, consider the possibility of unprocessed trauma underlying your problem. Carefully read the therapy for Ruth for an example of this process.

V. The Cord of Separation, Spiritual issues: It is a nearly universal phenomenon for people who experience trauma to question God. Why did God allow this to happen? Why didn't God protect me? Does God even care? Does God know what's going on in my life? If God is all-powerful and all-knowing, why doesn't He stop this? These are all excellent questions. We can only make observations about these questions, not explanations.

There are many other questions we should take to God, questions about the choice of spouse, vocation, lifestyle, etc. When looking for answers, we are wise to search the scriptures first and seek counsel with Christians who are mature in the faith. Continue to study His Word. Continue to ask and listen. God loves for you to come to Him with questions. He will answer you. God wants to communicate with you, but it may not always be the answer you desire. If it is not the answer you wanted, take time to examine your desire to determine its origin. Is it from God? Remember, Satan is the accuser. Do you think he could be putting these questions about God being indifferent into your mind? Does Satan have the nerve to accuse God (Matthew 4:1-11)?

We often pose spiritual questions to unsaved people such as a spouse, friends, or a therapist. This is very risky. When you cannot find an answer in Scripture, these questions should be taken to God Himself. Only God can answer your questions definitively. After appealing to God, take several minutes to listen for His response. Continue to ask God, and continue to listen until you receive an answer (Luke 11:9-13). Sometimes silence is your answer.

Many people do not diligently search for the answers to these questions. Instead, they become angry with God and give up on Him. Do not give up on God. You are being deceived when you give up on God.

Summary

Scripture records the original creation was perfect in the sense it fulfilled the divine purpose for which it was created, a beautiful place for Adam and Eve to enjoy a relationship with God, with each other, and with creation itself (Genesis: Chapters 1 and 2). Many believers and nonbelievers ask the above questions because they do not understand Genesis chapters 1-3 and Paul's reference to it in Romans 8:17-23. Remember, man was made in the image of God, and there is complete harmony among the Trinity. It follows there would be complete harmony in the creation, as God pronounced everything He created as good, suitable, and pleasant.

When Adam disobeyed in the Garden, the entire creation was subjected to futility. The Greek word for futility is *mataiotes* meaning "vanity, emptiness as to results."[130] When used to describe the creation after Adam's disobedience, it means "failing of the results designed, owing to sin." So, the divine will and purpose were thwarted (Romans 8:17-23). God cursed the earth and punished Adam and Eve. All existing relationships changed from being harmonious to being characterized by competition, conflict, and bloodshed (Genesis 3:7-24, 4:1-8; Romans 8:17-23).[131] Eve wanted to be like God. Adam joined her in rebellion. There has been conflict between God and mankind since Adam's moment of disobedience. Mankind was separated from God. Without the indwelling of Christ and the Holy Spirit, mankind continues to be separated from God.

Everything a human being does falls into one of the five categories briefly described above: thinking, feeling, behavior, physiology, and spirituality. We learn from this discussion that intimate experiences with evil impact every aspect of a person's life. Experiences with evil stimulate defensive responses that involve every aspect of our function. This is why trauma should be taken seriously, and people who are traumatized should seek assistance. It is very difficult to resolve trauma by yourself. It is not possible to be objective about any of these issues.

Understanding trauma in this way confronts us with a hard reality. No medication's going to correct faulty thinking, connect us to our emotions, change behaviors, or resolve spiritual apathy. There are medications that raise or lower the levels of various neurotransmitters in the brain and sometimes elevate

130 Vine's Expository Dictionary of New Testament Words

131 answersingenesis.org, Did the Fall Have Consequences on Creation?

mood, promote sleep, and reduce anxiety. However, this is a symptomatic treatment. Medication does not treat the five areas of function which have been damaged and need healing. This partially explains the phenomenon of treatment resistance clients experience with anti-depressant agents.[132]

Every patient, in consultation with their physician, should determine the primary cause of their anxiety or depression. Is it primarily biological or primarily related to traumatic life events? Is it related to intimacy with evil? If the cause is primarily biological, the treatment will focus on biological strategies, with therapy playing a supportive role. If anxiety and depression are primarily related to life events, medicine may diminish symptoms but should not be expected to completely resolve them. It will be necessary to work on the five domains of humanity noted above to resolve these mental health issues. Intimacy with evil is spiritual in origin and requires a spiritual solution for complete resolution.

What do you think you will need to work on to resolve your anxiety, depression, or interpersonal dysfunction? Write your answer in the space below.

____

____

____

____

____

About half of this entire book is devoted to different manifestations of intimacy with evil. We are at risk of not recognizing evil because of its subtlety. In the next chapter, we consider the topic of love, beginning with an examination of evil desire manifesting deception in the practice of prostitution. And contrasting with that, we look at the two most intimate loving relationships, the love between God and His people and between a husband and wife.

132 www.mayoclinic.org, Treatment Resistant Depression

Love Stories

In the summer of 1965, I worked as an apprentice carpenter on a large apartment complex. It was fun and interesting to see the framing go up where earlier, there had been nothing but sand and gravel. The work was physically demanding, and the humid Toledo summers exacerbated getting through eight hours each day. I could not help thinking about the start of medical school in Montreal in September. At the last minute of my last hour, I threw my hammer into the air and declared my career in home construction to be over. A few days later, I was driving to Montreal to begin four years of medical study at McGill University.

My number one priority in Montreal was finding a place to stay. After a full day of walking the streets around McGill University, I found a large apartment with several bedrooms, two baths, a kitchen, and a common room. A lady rented the apartment and sublet the rooms to students at McGill. I developed close friendships with Jean-Claude (Jim), an oxygen therapist at the Royal Victoria Hospital, and Tim, a master's level geology student. Jim was dating Charney, who was in the nursing program at Royal Victoria Hospital. One day when she came to the door looking for Jim, I happened to answer the door. I tried to be cool and just look into her eyes. They sparkled. She was wearing a trench coat which obscured her figure. She later confided she admired my build and thought I would be a good date for a friend of hers.

A few weeks later, Jim asked if Charney could borrow a text from me on embryology for her nursing studies. When she came to pick up the book, she was wearing the same trench coat. I had more time on this occasion to consider her feminine charms. I noticed she had large calves, which were not a turn-on for me. I gave her the book, and a few weeks later, Jim returned it. I did not see Charney again for the rest of my first year at McGill.

Jim played the guitar, which I had wanted to learn for years. Jim gave me access to his guitar and showed me a few cords. He suggested I get really good on the guitar because "No one will listen to you sing." Unfortunately, he was right, but that did not deter my playing. When I went home for

Christmas break, I asked for no gifts except a new guitar. My parents purchased a Gibson LG-1, a medium-sized guitar with a beautiful sound. Once I was back in Montreal, it created immediate problems. After dinner, I would pick up the guitar, thinking I'd play for 45 minutes to an hour and then study. I could not put it down. About 11 p.m., I would start to study for classes and finish around 3 o'clock in the morning. I was up at 7:00 every morning for an 8 o'clock class. I was young… and foolish.

Jim and I spent a lot of time together because of our shared interest in guitar. On one occasion, he asked to talk to me about his relationship with Charney. He said he was looking for advice. He had a "problem" as follows: "Charney will kiss up a storm but won't go any farther." Jim wanted a sexual relationship with Charney, but apparently, she did not. He wanted to know how to get her into bed. I did not answer his question immediately. I thought to myself, this is a problem for Jim but not for Charney. Finally, I said, "If she doesn't want to go to bed, I think you need to honor that." Jim seemed to accept my comment and continued to date Charney for the rest of the year.

Around Christmastime, my geologist friend Tim asked me to work for him the following summer. Every summer, Tim worked for the Ontario Department of Mines doing geological surveys. There were five people in our group: another geologist, and three people like me who cooked and assisted the two geologists in gathering rock samples each day. We were in the Ontario wilderness for 10 weeks and were paid $1000 and travel expenses for the summer. Our food and other necessities were flown in by float plane. I enjoyed camping, and I was assured of having $1000 left at the end of the summer, which would more than cover my tuition at McGill. The grades for my final exams were flown in by float plane, which created a bit of anxiety because the failure of a single course would require my taking a "supplemental" summer course to continue studies the following year. That would leave the geology group one person short for the summer. Tim expressed confidence about my passing the test. The grades came in a tiny envelope about 5 inches long and 3 1/2 inches wide. Tim's prophecy proved correct: I passed everything.

That was a great summer for me. We stayed at a base camp at a department of Lands and Forests' Lodge on Killala Lake. We were there for three weeks off and on and at fly-in drop camps the rest of the time. One of our drop camps was at Vein Lake. One evening after dinner, we saw several moose swimming across the lake. Tim suggested we get in the canoes and have a closer look. We did not consult the moose about this. We were not thinking about the moose's perspective. We paddled right up to within a few feet of a bull moose. The moose were helpless when swimming, but when they could stand on the lake bottom, they let us know they were in "charge." A large bull nearly put his antlers under our canoe to flip it; we set a record for how fast two persons could paddle backward from a disgruntled moose. Tim must have anticipated this outcome because he was laughing on shore while we were making fools of ourselves on the water.

In the middle of summer, Tim asked me to go with Larry, the assistant geologist, on a 10-day canoe trip to gather rock samples. We were to be on two different rivers. After reaching our destination on the first river, we portaged through the bush to a second stream which took us back to our base camp at the lodge. It rained every day for ten days.

On the first river, we were going upstream with our canoe powered by a three-horse motor. There were lots of small rapids, but nothing rated over class II degree of difficulty. We had about 100 pounds of gear, and the three-horse motor barely had enough power to get us upstream through these rapids. Larry asked me to run the motor. On several occasions, I thought the bow of the canoe would be caught in the current and the canoe swept broadside into rocks. But I was always able to compensate by steering the motor one way or the other. One afternoon we were only five or six feet from the bank in the weakest current I could find when the bow started to swing toward the center of the river. I jumped into the chest-deep water, holding the canoe with one hand and grabbing a small willow with the other. Larry jumped in also, and we secured the canoe to the bank while we attached lines to the bow and stern so we could line the canoe upstream through the rapids. Nothing got wet except us.

At the beginning of the summer, Tim had advised me to treat my sleeping bag as if it were life itself. This meant if you were flying to a different location, you never got into a float plane without your sleeping bag. On the river, it meant you rolled up your bag and put it in a plastic garbage bag in case the canoe flipped. One afternoon we came back to our tent and found our air mattresses floating in a pool of water. My sleeping bag was rolled up and stuffed inside a plastic bag and sitting on the middle of my air mattress, floating high and dry. Larry's sleeping bag not been rolled or stuffed. A third of it slipped off the air mattress and now lay in the middle of a small lake inside our tent. Larry assessed the situation quickly and then turned the air blue with every curse that ever left the lips of a Canadian geologist. I was overwhelmed with laughter which I forced back. I wanted to make a comment about his sleeping bag not floating well but I managed to maintain silence. I quickly left the tent for fear of putting my personal safety at risk. Before long, we had a huge fire around which Larry had stretched his sleeping bag. His mood slowly improved while I fixed dinner, and he monitored the temperature of his bag so it did not end up in flames.

When summer was over, I returned to Montreal for my second year of med school. I learned through the grapevine that Charney's boyfriend, Jim, had returned home to Northern Ontario. Their relationship apparently was over, but it never occurred to me to call her for a date. The following spring, I did not have enough money to get back to Toledo for spring break. Most of my classmates were gone for the week, so I was bored and a bit lonely. Charney had graduated from nursing school by this time and was living with some other nurses. I stopped by one afternoon to say hello. She happened to answer the door. Kissing me on the cheek, she invited me to come in. A couple of other nurses were there also, and we talked for a while and played guitars and sang songs. Charney had been in a small country band in high school, and she played drums and guitar. After leaving that afternoon, I had pleasant thoughts about her kiss. I asked her out the following week, and we dated every week until school ended. I had plans to study medicine in Sweden during the summer while she was planning to work at a summer camp in Maine. I thought about her being at camp for 10 weeks with young single male counselors and decided to give her my University of Toledo windbreaker to wear for the summer. This would send a message to any young man with romantic fantasies; Charney was already in a relationship. She was delighted to have it.

In the summer of 1967, the Cold War with Russia was raging. I wanted to study in Poland to learn more about living under a communist regime, I had been accepted by a Polish medical school for study, but the Polish government refused to grant me a visa. I had a reservation on a chartered British flight round-trip from Montreal to London for $100. As time edged closer to my departure date without a Polish visa, I accepted an opportunity in Sweden at the University of Lund. When the visa from Poland finally arrived two days prior to my departure, I was irritated and wondered if this was a strategy of the Polish government to prevent US citizens from learning about communist oppression. I ignored the Polish visa and went to Sweden.

The experience in Sweden was disappointing regarding medical study. Our mentor was a cardiac surgeon who was very knowledgeable and pleasant to work with. However, it turned out that most doctors in Sweden took vacations at the precise time we were there for our study. Since the doctors were mostly gone, there were practically no patients in the hospital. The other students were a young man from Ireland, another from Belgium, a brother and sister from France, a girl from Poland, and yours truly, the only American. There was also a Swedish student thrown into the mix to assist our adjustment to Swedish culture.

My experience in Sweden was mostly social/cultural in nature. The first week we took a day off and went to the beach. There was no bathhouse in which to change into our swimsuits. Natalia, the girl from Poland, said, "Watch me," so naturally I did. She wrapped herself in a large beach towel and took off all her street clothes under the towel. Then she put her swimsuit on while still covered with the towel. I somewhat awkwardly followed her example.

Natalia had relatives in Stockholm whom she wanted to visit. It was 375 miles from Lund to Stockholm. She did not have money for bus fare. She decided to hitchhike and asked me to accompany her for protection.

When we were about halfway there, we were picked up by two young Swedish men. After driving about five or six miles, they demanded money in broken English. Shaking our heads, we said, "No krona" (the Swedish monetary unit), and they stopped and let us out of the car. A few minutes later, they came back and demanded money. These were not the Swedish men you see cross-country skiing in the Winter Olympics; they were short and slender and not intimidating to either Natalia or me. Natalia had no intention of giving them a penny. We were prepared to fight for what little money we had with us. The two men made some angry comments which neither Natalia nor I understood. We made some angry comments back, which I believe they understood. After a few minutes of arguing, they finally left us alone on the highway.

On our return trip to Lund, we had a lot of trouble getting lifts. At 10:30 p.m., we still had about 150 miles to Lund, and light was rapidly fading. At that time, a Swedish law allowed people to stay in jail overnight if they had no other options, so I suggested this possibility to Natalia. She became hysterical, so upset that she had a hard time making herself understood. Apparently, she feared Polish authorities would learn she was in jail in Sweden, and somehow, this would create hardship for herself or her family in Poland. After she calmed down, we agreed to continue hitchhiking. A half-hour later, we got a ride all the way to Lund, arriving at about 2:00 a.m. I was glad it had not worked out for me to study in Poland. Seeing the intensity of her fear of the Polish government was all I needed to know about Marxist regimes.

I left Lund after four weeks with Peter, the student from Belgium. We hitchhiked to Amsterdam, where he left me to return to his home. I stayed in Amsterdam for two days to see the sights. Amsterdam is sometimes referred to as the city of diamonds. I took a tour of the Van Moppes diamond factory. At the end of the tour, they had a display of diamonds for sale. Visitors are allowed to linger in a room to ogle the diamonds. I started to have thoughts about Charney. I cannot recall if my heart was skipping beats, but after about 30 minutes, I asked a salesperson to show me some diamonds. These were not set in rings, just loose diamonds. After another hour, I left the factory with a pear-shaped diamond and $25 to fund my last six weeks in Europe. There was a tiny space in the neck of my guitar for a nut that could be tightened if the neck started to warp. It was covered with a small piece of plastic held by two screws. I put the diamond in the space, wrapped it in a bit of paper, and replaced the cover. It rested there until I got to my medical fraternity house in Montreal. When I went through customs in Montreal, I "forgot" to declare the diamond.

Amsterdam is also known for legalized prostitution. It has many different types of "red light districts." I was staying in the middle of one of these districts. The girls were known as window prostitutes. They were sitting or standing in rooms bordering the street just inside a full-length window. I was very curious about how they'd gotten into a fix like this. I suspected it was a sad story for each of them. I was afraid to ask.

While writing this story, I checked the Internet to learn if this practice is continuing 53 years later. Sadly, the practice continues to flourish. When I was in Amsterdam, I knew nothing of sexual abuse, human trafficking, pimps, or prostitution. I only knew there was a significant risk of contracting a sexually transmitted disease. We studied many of these sexually transmitted diseases in microbiology at McGill. I remembered most of what I had learned, and it was scary and appalling. But it was not as appalling as what was happening to these young women.

While writing this, I wondered about the life expectancy of prostitutes. A study published in 2004 of 1969 prostitutes in Colorado Springs, Colorado, over a 33-year period, revealed 8%, or 152 women, died over three decades. Twenty-one of these women were murdered. The average age of death for those who were murdered was 34 years. The authors stated the risk of homicide is higher for women who prostitute than for any other group of women.[133] This is sobering data but only addresses physical death. It does not speak a single word about the emotional and spiritual states of women who prostitute themselves.

During sex, most prostitutes detach from the sexual act and retreat to a secret place in their minds. They are no longer present in what is happening sexually. However, the unconscious part of their mind continues to be a recipient of the hatred and evil desire that is being expressed by their "partner." This results in emotional and spiritual death in the heart of a prostitute, an outcome worse than physical death in many ways. They become separated from their emotions and from God. Prostitution is a subset of sexual abuse. This is true for women who voluntarily prostitute themselves as well as for those who are trafficked.

There are three criteria for every kind of abuse, whether physical, emotional, or spiritual:

1. Abuse only occurs in human relationships.
2. There is a concentration of power in one person or group who exert power over other individuals or groups.
3. The person or group who holds power uses it to gratify himself/themselves without considering how it affects the other persons or groups.

How does the above definition apply to prostitution? In prostitution, the customer is the individual holding power. The group holding power is the culture that supports the process. When prostitution is legalized, the citizenry is supporting it. In prostitution, all the participants are deceived. The prostitute is distracted by financial compensation. She is deceived, thinking payment justifies selling her body and that she is in control because she determines the fee. She is usually unaware of having opened the door to demonic oppression.

In prostitution, the customer is distracted by his/her sexual lust. The customer experiences sexual gratification for a few minutes. This person is deceived, exchanging an emotional and physically intimate relationship with a spouse for a few moments of sexual passion. Often the buyer is insecure and/or unsuccessful in creating a mutually satisfying emotional and

133 American Journal of Epidemiology, Mortality in a Long-term Open Cohort of Prostitute Women

sexual relationship with a significant other. Every person who pays for sex is relationally challenged in some way. People are rarely aware of opening a door point to demonic oppression. They are not concerned about the emotional or spiritual state of the prostitute.

She becomes an object to be used and discarded. The buyer/perpetrator uses money to gain power over his/ her victim. The citizenry supporting prostitution is distracted by their passivity and their own lust. If they investigated and discerned the evil impact prostitution has on women, some of them would desire to stop it. They are deceived, thinking it is a victimless crime.

All the participants are using massive amounts of denial and rationalization to justify a process that injures everyone: the prostitute, the customer, and the culture. Evil desire fuels every aspect of prostitution. Process issues always determine outcome. Prostitution always has a bad outcome for everyone. It degrades the culture by diminishing the value of women. Why, then, do cultures everywhere support it? Could this be a dynamic contributing to the disparity of salaries between men and women in Western culture? Is paying for the use of a woman's body unconsciously connected to paying less for the use of her mind? Does spiritual apathy contribute to the persistence of this blight on society? The answers to these questions are important but ignored.

Most sociological studies on prostitution have focused on women and their need for financial resources to survive. They do not study the people who are abusing power, the people who have sufficient power to avoid exposure of their evil acts. Prostitution has been rationalized as payment for services, as a profession, but prostitution is a type of rape using financial power to perpetuate the rape. It may be the most egregious example of men failing to protect women.

What was it like for me to walk by the window prostitutes for two days? It was tempting to look. Of course, I was tempted to look. I did look. Men are wired for visual stimulation. Charles Spurgeon makes this comment about the lust of the eyes, "Eyes can generally see what hearts wish."[134] Jesus said this about the eyes, "The eye is the lamp of the body. So if your eye is sound, your entire body will be full of light. But if your eye is unsound, your whole body will be full of darkness. If then the very light in you is darkened, how dense is that darkness?" (Matthew 6:22-23).

While looking at these women, my eyes were unsound. I was flirting with

134 The Treasury of David, Commentary on Psalm 35:21 by Charles Spurgeon

darkness. I was distracted by beautiful women sparsely dressed who were selling their bodies. What that said about my heart was scary (Jeremiah 17:9). But I had choices (Deuteronomy 30:19-20). I chose to focus on the diamond, now in my possession, resting comfortably in the neck of my guitar. Occasionally I would take it out, unwrap the paper, look at it, and think about Charney. I chose to focus on the young lady in Northern Maine who was wearing my windbreaker. I did not know during that time about the word of God written on my heart, which was instructing me as follows: "Whatever is true, whatever is worthy of reverence and is honorable and seemly, whatever is just, whatever is pure, whatever is lovely and lovable, whatever is kind and winsome and gracious, if there is any virtue and excellence, if there is anything worthy of praise, think on and weigh and take account of these things [fix your minds on them]" (Philippians 4:8).

After leaving Amsterdam, I begged for rides in Belgium, France, Germany, Austria, Switzerland, and England for the next five weeks. I slept in fields, bath houses, church yards, and anywhere I thought no one would bother me. Thoughts of Charney provided companionship during my wandering and adventures. I enjoyed travel, but I was at the airport in London early for my departure to Montreal.

Are you aware of the Word of God in your heart? Do you hear it? If you are not hearing it, what is distracting you? What was the focus of your mind while reading these paragraphs on prostitution? What is the focus of your mind as you navigate your way through the superficial customs of the world each day (Romans 12:2)? Is there something "superficial" that is occupying your attention? Or are you concerned with the deeper issues of life? Are you choosing wisely? Write your answers in the space below.

____

____

____

____

____

Ancient Romance

Back in Montreal, seeing Charney for the first time, I realized I'd made a great decision to purchase the diamond. I wanted to see her wearing it. She confided having my windbreaker helped her cope with male counselors at camp. I was a little surprised and extremely pleased to hear her say that. I had developed a design for setting the diamond in her engagement ring. It involved a swirl of small rubies around the pear-shaped diamond. I took the design and diamond to a jeweler, who came back with an estimate of $1200. My heart fell; $1200 was twice the cost of my tuition at McGill for a year. Disappointment can be painful. I adjusted my fantasy for her ring, and the jeweler adjusted his estimate to something I could afford.

During the next few months, we spent as much time together as my studies and her job would allow. I told her she was the woman I wanted to be with for life. She was equally committed. I had the diamond set by Christmas but was anxious about popping the question. I had mentioned I wanted it to be a surprise when I asked her to marry me. She had responded that she was certain she would not be surprised. I took her comment as a challenge. In the spring of 1968, we were taking a walk along Boulevard Saint Laurent in Montreal. This was a quaint area, a national historic site, with all kinds of interesting ethnic shops and restaurants. We had stopped at a German meat market to get something to eat and were walking back to her apartment when I turned to her and said, "Will you marry me?" She said, "Oh, you don't have a ring with you!" I said, "Will you marry me?" and she said yes. I slipped the ring on her finger, and we had a great kiss. Heck, all our kisses were great! Her kisses are still great!

We walked to the apartment she was sharing with a couple of other nurses who happened to be home. We said nothing about our engagement to our friends, wondering if they would notice the ring on her finger. After about an hour of placing her hand in various odd positions, one of the girls exclaimed, "Charney! Is that an engagement ring?" Finally, we were able to share our excitement!

Charney and I attempted premarital counseling with her pastor in Huntington, Quebec, about 50 miles by bus from Montreal. We met one time. It was not enough. Like many couples, there were obstacles to getting the counseling that would have benefited our relationship. But we did not worry about the counseling we did not receive. We were in love. It is of interest that in the Bible, there's not a single word about falling in love. Instead, there is a lot of counsel about entering and maintaining love relationships. Consider this question: Do you think it is wiser to fall in love or to enter a romantic relationship with forethought? There is something about the idea of falling that seems unwise. Every time I fall, I usually end up getting hurt.

We planned an August wedding. I decided not to work that summer since the time was shortened despite not having tuition for my last year. This allowed Charney to go to Toledo with me to meet my parents for a week before the wedding and for a period of relaxation instead of the rush/stress often leading to a wedding ceremony. It also gave us four weeks for our honeymoon. Charney's father gave us $100 for a wedding gift, with which we paid for our entire wedding reception. The owner of Meacham Lake Inn in upper New York State gave us three nights lodging at one of his cabins for our first three days of married life.

We arrived at the border, crossing on our way to the cabin at about midnight. The US customs officer took one look at us and said, "Just married?" When we nodded, he waved us through the border. A "friend" had given us a bottle of champagne for celebration. When we got into bed, we opened it, and it exploded. We and the bed were soaked with champagne. Charney accused our "friend" of shaking the bottle. Providence provided for us as our cabin had a second queen bed.

Our honeymoon did not disappoint. After leaving Lake Meacham, we drove to Quebec City, the Gaspe Peninsula of Quebec, New Brunswick, Nova Scotia, Prince Edward Island, and, lastly, Toledo, Ohio. We had to finish our trip to Toledo to return the car my parents had loaned us for our trip. Having had access to wheels for four weeks, we did not want to return to Montreal without them. So, we used a cash wedding present from my grandparents and made a down payment on a new fire engine red 1968 Pontiac Firebird. Grandma expressed some disappointment about our not putting the money into savings, but we were young. We did not have a savings account. We had a 1968 Pontiac Firebird, which at the time seemed better than a savings account. You can't wash and polish a savings account.

There was one little fly in our honeymoon ointment. Charney was diagnosed with infectious mononucleosis about halfway through our trip. We agreed it was not a good time to stop kissing. It was probably too late for the no-kissing strategy. It was not a great surprise when I came down with mono during my first week at school. I missed two weeks of my obstetrics rotation, which I had to make up during Christmas break.

When we got back to Montreal, two matters needed attention: 1) obtaining tuition for my last year of medical school, 2) learning to be a good doctor while learning to be a good husband to my wife. I worked on the financial part first.

I immediately scheduled an appointment with financial aid to beg for tuition. Driving the 600 miles from Toledo to Montreal, I was preoccupied with how I was going to explain owning a new Pontiac Firebird and not having money for tuition. When Dr. Knowles, the financial counselor, saw my financial statement, he had the same question. He opened the door to his office and said, "Come in, Dr. Trudel." Now, he knew very well I was only a fourth-year medical student. I began to perspire, wondering why he addressed me as a doctor.

It did not take long to find out. After I sat down, he said, "I see from your application that you are driving an automobile that is a better ride than most of our professors have!" He stopped speaking. The silence suggested it was my turn to speak, to explain this conundrum. I was prepared, saying, "That car (distancing myself from the pride and joy it brought me) is an embarrassment (a lie). It was a wedding gift from my grandparents (a distortion of the truth). I couldn't refuse it (another lie)." I completely omitted to mention that Grandma wanted us to put the money in savings. I thought it unlikely he would be in touch with my grandparents. He glared at me over his reading glasses for a few seconds and then stamped the loan approved. I thanked him and left his office as quickly as possible.

Telling lies can be so easy in or outside the marriage relationship. One manifestation of the wisdom of God is that he is not primarily concerned about our being good. Rather, his primary objective is spiritual life—goodness will follow. Do not misunderstand. I'm not suggesting that anyone can or should lie because God will forgive the lie. When I lied to Dr. Knowles, I took the easy way out (Matthew 7:13-14). This was not character-building. The idea that you can sin as much as you want because God will forgive you is known as cheap grace.[135] Cheap grace ignores the requirement of repentance for disobedience. It looks the other way and refuses to acknowledge the suffering of Christ on the cross. It denies the request Jesus made to you and me to pick up our own cross and follow Him (Matthew 16:24-26). Satan says there is no cost to discipleship. That is a huge lie from the father of all lies (John 8:42–45). It is a perversion of the gospel. It's another deception. God knows we can't be good through our own strength (Philippians 2:12-13). God is patient. He is especially patient with husbands and wives, as we will see next.

We each had a secret that we did not confide to the other at the time of our engagement or wedding. We each had an alias, another name that was undisclosed and strictly confidential. My secret name was "Mr. Right."

---

135 The Cost of Discipleship by Dietrich Bonhoeffer

Charney's undisclosed name was "Miss Always Right." Or, it may have been the other way around. When Mr. Right marries Miss Always Right, it is highly probable the relationship will give birth to disagreement. We named our progeny *Argumenta.*

After Argumenta was born, she matured really fast. It was no time at all until she reached adolescence. I would *like* to report that one day I experienced an epiphany and simply confessed to my wife, and she, moved by my openness, honesty, and humility, also cheerfully confessed, But no! Only in our dreams. Remember how pride screws everything up? Our relationship was not an exception to the rule of pride. Pride generated resistance to admit our claims to always being right. But clues to our true identities kept leaking out like gossip at the water cooler. Then, when Argumenta was a teenager, she burst forth with hormones raging amid mutual accusations and evidence that could not be denied. Other couples have different monikers for this brood, such as Conflicta, Discordia, Division, Meltdown, Differences, and many less complimentary terms. Every marriage relationship gives birth to this seed. How long it takes to germinate is highly variable. How high it grows depends on how much you feed it. We decided to cut it off at its root.

We started to practice agape love. Agape love is the antidote for conflict, discord, division, meltdowns, and differences. What does agape love look like? The husband honors his wife by laying down his life for her, and she responds with awe and respect for his sacrificial attitude. A couple of examples: in the course of our 53 years of marriage, we have built three new homes. Each time I created a floor plan, and each time my wife approved the floor plan prior to beginning construction. In the case of our second log home, it took 18 months to come up with a plan we both liked. At our current residence, she wanted a two-car garage. We had never had a garage during our first 40 years of marriage. I did not see any need for a garage. She said it was important to her. We have a large two-car garage. I love It! I wanted a tractor to help take care of our six acres. She did not want a tractor. She did not see any need for a tractor. I said it was important to me. We have a tractor. She loves the tractor…and uses it as much as I do. Oh, if only I had been this meticulous about sacrificial love and communication in every other aspect of our relationship! When a wife experiences love expressed sacrificially, it honors her. It stimulates her desire for her husband manifested by trust, openness, and an erotic, passionate, romantic relationship (Genesis 3:16). Notice you recognize agape love by action! The Holy Spirit empowers this process. You can't do it on your own. Agape love is a process issue. It may determine the outcome of your marriage. An excellent website, Peacemaker Ministries, offers resources for conflict resolution in a variety of circumstances.

When a husband does not love in this way, a wife experiences some combination of confusion, hurt, sadness, disappointment, or anger. She begins to entertain thoughts about her husband not loving her, and not meeting her needs. These thoughts and emotions often are not expressed, and over time, may produce a sense of hopelessness about the marriage. She may experience fear of her husband physically hurting her if they have experienced angry arguments or… fear the marriage will fail. "The fear of man brings a snare" (Proverbs 29:25). Her snare is prone to becoming angry or withdrawing emotionally and physically from the relationship. She begins to look for agape love in all the wrong places, such as erotic stimulation through porn, fantasy lust, masturbation, "romantic" movies, flirting, or an affair.

It works in a similar fashion for a husband when he is not viewed with admiration and awe for what he does for his wife. His snare is becoming angry, emotionally withdrawing, or both. If she responds mostly with anger, the husband may develop a fear of discussing issues and working toward a resolution. "There is no fear in love" (I John 4:18). It is tragic how many married men and women have unexpressed fear for each other. He is likely to seek sexual gratification through an affair, a distraction from the pain of the marriage. Confusion, hurt, sadness, disappointment, anger, and affairs are all **distractions** preventing the resolution of marital stress. Either of the above scenarios may lead to cessation of communication and eventual divorce.

Charney and I began to learn how to communicate our hurts and disappointments instead of expressing ourselves through the destructive process of anger or pretending everything was OK. I confessed anger when frustrated. God honored my dependence on Him, replacing anger with peace. Instead of holding court on who was right, we focused on what was important to each person and how to meet that need. When we could not agree, we looked to the Word of God for direction. At some point, it occurred to us that neither person was right all the time. These things are not rocket science. But, because of deception, we struggled for a while. Fortunately, we were both committed to doing things God's way rather than our way, especially in practicing agape love.

We had the following process issues in our favor: commitment to the relationship, trust, agreement on exclusivity, many common interests, training in behavioral health, early stages of agape love, faith in God, and reliance on His word to resolve differences—and yes, romantic love. Relying on Scripture was the single most important process because it facilitated everything else.

Now would be an appropriate time for confession. Remember, my relationship with Linda ended largely because of my failure to communicate. Mr. Right and Miss Always Right were not thinking about the issues noted above when we were engaged. So, Mr. Right and Miss Always Right married without discussing any of these things. How did that happen? We never had any conflicts during our dating (8 months) and engagement (6 months). Very simply, we were ignorant and distracted by romantic love. This is a common occurrence. Romantic love is very distracting. It distracts from learning the skills of communicating and conflict resolution. It distracts from having financial resources to feed, clothe, and house a family. It distracts from the importance of knowing how to forgive. Romantic love tends to blind people to these realities. Romantic love does not overcome any of these realities for very long after marriage. Romantic/erotic love primarily conquers the need for relationship and physical intimacy (I Corinthians 7:1–9). It does not automatically produce emotional intimacy. It does not build a house or a loving home. It puts a roof on the house but does not finish the interior.

Not too many years after marriage, many women begin to think about having a nest. Charney and I started nesting behaviors the year after we returned from Papua New Guinea in 1971. Having a nest involves two separate processes: building a nest and having chicks. In nature, the nest is prepared first, and the chicks follow later. We thought that sequence was for the birds, so we did it the other way around. Our first child, a girl, arrived on December 28, 1972. I was finishing a year working in the emergency room at Toledo Hospital. We planned to move the following year to Montana, where I was joining a small family practice with two other doctors. We really liked Montana. We thought we would stay there forever. We purchased a 44-acre parcel of land on a small creek a few miles from town. We had been talking about having a log home. Neither of us had lived in a log house, so it was decided to build a small cabin to see how we liked it before investing in a much larger log structure.

I decided I would do the log work. I talked to several people in the area who had built log homes. Everyone agreed it was hard work but not technically difficult. I was doing the log work by myself. I needed a **plan** for raising the logs that was inexpensive, simple, and easy on my body. Each log was about 23 feet long and weighed around 300 pounds before seasoned (dried). I finally settled on a strategy of my own design. Instead of having a foundation consisting of a continuous concrete footer, I had concrete piers at each corner and a concrete pier in the middle of each sill log. When the forms were set for the concrete three quarter-inch bolts were placed in the corner piers pointing to the inside of the cabin. To these bolts, I attached a vertical log 12 feet high with an arm extending towards the outside of the cabin wall. With a triple sheave block and tackle attached to the arms on each corner, it was easy to raise one corner at a time and set each log on top of the one below it. After the log was suspended in air, it was effortless to move it a quarter of an inch or a foot, if needed, to place it precisely where it needed to be. Having a plan in mind, the next thing I needed was logs.

House logs have to be straight logs. A third of the logs brought to our building site were not straight. A logger should be able to determine what is straight and what is not by looking at the tree while it is still standing. Perhaps our logger's desire to help interfered with his assessment. "How quick your mind alters perception." He kindly brought 15 additional logs to compensate for the crooked ones at his expense.

On a good day, it was possible to cut the saddle notches on each corner, raise, and set two logs.[136] When the log work was finished, I subcontracted for the roof, plumbing, and electrical work. It was time for me to take rest.

Building a marriage is a little like building a log house. There are somewhat similar process issues. Start with a good foundation. The foundation for a good marriage is love, trust, commitment, exclusivity, communication, the ability to resolve conflict, agape love, and reliance on the word of God. There is one process issue that stands out from the others. In constructing a house, **you must have a plan for the design and a separate plan for turning the design into reality.** The same is true for building a marriage. It is wise to have a **clear idea** in your mind of **what a romantic relationship looks like before attempting to have one**. Having a healthy plan for romance will prevent a tremendous amount of hurt and grief.

All relationships require hard work. Romantic relationships, especially marriage, require more work because there is more intimacy. You will discover every flaw that has taken residence in your romantic partner. Unfortunately, you will not discover most of them until after your wedding day! At the same time, you will be unaware of your own flaws. You need a plan. Consider the

136 The Owner Built Log House by B. Allen Mackie

plan described in this chapter on love stories. When building a log house, you **never stand under a log when it is being raised**. A dropped log will crush you...end of you and end of project. When building relationships, take all necessary precautions to prevent emotional pain and suffering. Emotional pain ends many marriage relationships. It is referred to as irreconcilable differences...no mention of pain. "How quick your mind alters perception."

Marriage

Most people are strongly motivated to find an opposite-sex relationship in which they can **love** and be loved exclusively. Notice the word love is in bold type, which means it is a process issue. This implies it is necessary to examine love carefully and discern precisely where we might become **distracted** in attempting to find it. Distraction is the beginning of the process leading to deception. Where does distraction start when you are looking for romantic love?

Engagement should not simply consist of slipping a ring onto the finger of your future spouse. It should include a commitment to a process of sharing how each person thinks, feels, and behaves in life. Maintaining secrecy about any one of those three areas is a strike against a successful marriage. Three strikes, and it is likely you will be out of your marriage relationship.

Divorce rates in the US were almost non-existent in the 1800s, began to increase in 1920, and rose sharply during WW II, and peaked at around 50 percent in 1990.[137] Since every couple is assured of some degree of discord, it would be wise to be proactive and do some premarital planning or counseling. Proactive strategies to protect your marriage fall into three broad categories, process issues that must be in place and functioning if a marriage is going to thrive. They include 1) agape love, 2) commitment to communication, conflict resolution, and forgiveness, 3) exclusivity and trust. When these process issues are in place and functioning properly, the marriage will grow in blessing both spouses with passionate love and intimacy.

Let's start this inquiry by considering the persons before us, a man and a woman. **God created men and women equal in His eyes** (Genesis 1:26-28, Romans 3:23, John 3:16, I Peter 3:7). God desires a relationship with men and women equally (Genesis 3:8, Isaiah 53:4-6, Romans 8:28, Matthew 5:1-11, John 11:5). God judges and rewards men and women equally (Romans 2:10-13). Although men and women are equal in the sight of God, He also

137 www.theguardian.com, Divorce Rates Data 1858 to Now: How It Has Changed

created them to be different in many ways.

The differences between male and female sex begin with different chromosome combinations. Each parent donates "a set of chromosomes to their offspring, 23 pairs from each parent for a total of 46. Each of these chromosomes contains genetic information that determines everything from the baby's eye and hair color to the baby's sex. Gender is determined by the sex chromosomes X and Y.

If the Y chromosome is present, the baby will be a boy. A baby with two X chromosomes will be a girl. Gender is fixed, immutable…it cannot change. "The X chromosome has 1000 working genes, and the Y chromosome has less than 100 working genes. Although males have an X chromosome, it behaves very differently when there is another X chromosome present compared to its behavior when a Y chromosome is present. Of the working genes on the X chromosome, 200 to 300 are unique to sex, so only 700 to 800 of the working genes are shared and active in both males and females."[138] So… the genetic constitution or genotype of males and females is different. These genetic influences lead to a nine-month period of growth and tissue differentiation producing a boy or a girl, ending in birth. Over nine months, these genes produce different sexes, different physiologies, and different physical appearances or phenotypes of male and female babies. These diverse genetic pathways were entered into every cell of man who was created from the dust of the ground and every woman who was created from the flesh of Adam. After 18 years, when children are close to maturity, outward appearance, or phenotype, of the two sexes is very different but complementary. The result is men are generally rugged, strong, and handsome, while women tend to be rounded, soft, and beautiful. It seems very unlikely these genetic differences (genotype) and physical differences (phenotype) occurred through a random process. A more plausible explanation is that these complex genetic pathways were put in place by the same God who created an orderly solar system and universe.

In addition to creating different biology, God also established different roles for the sexes. The word *role* is not found in the chapters and verses of most Bibles. The concept of social role has been around for thousands of years, but the word itself came into usage in the last century. Its meaning in sociology is a little scary. In 1936, writing on the "Study of Man,"[139] sociologist Ralph

138 sciencing.com, Differences in Male and Female Chromosomes

139 The Study of Man by Ralph Linton

Linton wrote a chapter on status and role. He contended, "it is obvious that the more perfectly the members of any society are adjusted to their statuses and roles, the more smoothly the society will function" (pages 114-115). The scary part of this is people with money and power, whom sociologists call the elite class, often use their resources to prevent other individuals from improving their status or social position. Historically they accomplished this by controlling access to and the quality of education. But more recently, they have expanded their efforts through control of elections, business, finances, and digital media.[140, 141]

Scripture suggests people can learn contentment with their station in life. At the same time, Scripture is not opposed to improving one's social position (Philippians 4:12-13, Philemon 1:11,16). Consider the apostle Paul; he was born a Roman citizen and became a Pharisee, a persecutor of Christ, an apostle to the Gentiles, a teacher, a worker of miracles, and a martyr for building the church of Christ. The period of persecuting Jesus was the low point of his life. This happened secondary to Paul being deceived (Acts 8:1-3, 9:1-22). His last calling, a martyr, was certainly his highest station in life.

The closest words to the idea of role in the scriptures are the words *chosen*, *appointed*, and *consecrated*. A good example is the prophet, Jeremiah. "The word of the Lord came to me, [Jeremiah], saying, Before I formed you in the womb I knew and approved of you [as my chosen instrument] and before you were born I separated and set you apart, consecrating you; and I appointed you as a prophet to the nations" (Jeremiah 1:5, Acts 14:23, Romans 13:1-2, Ephesians 2:10). Consecration is the process of setting something aside for a sacred purpose. The purpose always points to the wisdom of the plan of God. Jeremiah was "set aside" for the purpose of speaking on behalf of God to the nation Israel. Jeremiah was deeply concerned about his people. He is known as the weeping prophet because of the tears he shed over his people who rejected the wisdom of God (Jeremiah 8:18-9:3). The nation of Israel not only rejected God, but they also rejected Jeremiah.

Questions: Do you think God has called you to a specific role in life? Do the people you elect shed tears over the status of you or your family? Do they show concern about how their policies impact the life of your family? Have you noticed people who represent God today often have an experience of

---

140 imprimis.hillsdale.edu, What is the Great Reset?

141 christianitydaily.com, Intercessors for America Warn about 5 Dangers the Country is Facing

persecution similar to that of Jeremiah? Write your answers in the space below.

____

____

____

____

____

People appointed to power who do not listen to the people they govern do not care about those people. Instead, they are afraid, untrusting, and narcissistic, only concerned about themselves. Author Candace Owens describes this process in her book, *Blackout.* The evidence supporting her thesis is this: politicians, primarily from the Democratic Party have been in charge of our cities for decades, and yet conditions in our cities have continued to deteriorate. The evidence for Owens' assertion is undeniable. **This process issue is destroying the American dream.** It is contrary to the founding documents of the United States Constitution and the hope for a better life.

It happens to work the same way in the marriage relationship. A husband who does not listen to his wife, or does not care about her in the agape sense, does not understand the marriage relationship (Ephesians 5:21, I Peter 3:7, I Corinthians 13:1-8).[142] He is thinking primarily about himself, meeting his own perceived needs. These husbands are deceived.

The God of the Holy Bible appoints married people to roles with specific responsibilities. These roles or appointments are related to the biology of sex, but unlike chromosomal combinations, they are not fixed. They are plastic, the plasticity largely relating to worldview and religious beliefs described in chapter one. God allows people to use their imaginations to distort His love and His plans in countless ways (Romans 1:19-32, Colossians 2:8). The following plan from God for marriage is rejected by a majority of couples in our culture. This is the primary reason the divorce rate is so high.

God has *appointed*, *chosen*, and *consecrated* husbands to be head of the wife, servant leaders, protectors, providers, and lovers. God has *chosen*, *appointed*, and *consecrated* wives to be in charge of the home, companions to their husbands, helpers, teachers, and lovers. The marriage relationship has been set aside (sanctified) to point to the wisdom of the plan God has for marriage. The interaction of husbands and wives executing these ten roles constitutes the largest portion of the marriage relationship. The most important of these

142 www.biblestudytools.com, 30 Bible Verses about Marriage and Love Scripture Quotes

roles is lover, in the agape sense. Everything else springs from agape love. Many people outside the church are not familiar with the concept of agape love. They know something is missing from their marriage but are unable to identify what it is.

Please review the section on agape love in the chapter, *Affairs of the Heart.* Then read Ephesians 5:21-33 before reading the following paragraphs.

Agape love is not romantic love or love associated with physical attraction. The Amplified Bible translation describes agape love in I Corinthians 13:1: "that reasoning, intentional, spiritual devotion such as is inspired by God's Love for and in us." Examples of agape love are provided in the following scriptures: I Corinthians 8:1-3, 13:4-7, Ephesians 5:21-33, I Peter 3:2, 7-8, I John 4:7-13, 15-21. We learn from these verses that **agape love is not simply an emotion**. Agape love is action-oriented… expressed by inaction, things you should not do (I Corinthians 13:4-6), or by action, things you should do (I Corinthians 13:7). It is a **Godly desire** expressed by doing things for another person to improve the character, personality, soul, and life of another individual. It builds people up, as described in the preceding scriptures. It is exemplified by God giving His only Son so you and I might share eternal life with Him (John 3:16). Agape love is an experience, a process. It will determine the outcome of your marriage. Each person in the marriage needs this kind of love. But, **in addition** to the above, the husband and wife each have a unique way to express agape love to each other.

The husband is to love his wife by subordinating his own selfish desires and doing what is best for his wife.

Agape love expressed in this way builds his wife into a better person… and a loving wife. In doing this, the husband is following the example of Christ, who laid down His life for the church. This requires humility on the part of the husband. God's plan for marriage has several goals in mind:

1. Establishing a relationship to meet the emotional needs of the marriage partners.
2. Becoming one flesh in the process of birthing children.
3. Satisfying sexual desires through a relationship sanctified by God.
4. The process of husbands loving their wives sacrificially and wives reverencing their husbands. This results in marriage pointing to the wisdom of God.

5. Husbands' love toward their wives being a sanctifying love.[143] The husband is set aside to belong to the wife, and the wife is set aside to belong to the husband (Song of Solomon 2:16).

"Christ gave himself for the church, so the husband, through love, gives himself for his wife."[144] Husbands should "love their wives as [being in a sense] their own bodies. He who loves his own wife loves himself" (Ephesians 5:28-31). He protects, provides for, nourishes, and cherishes his own body, which are actions he should take toward his wife (Ephesians 5:25-29). With the exception of his relationship with God, his relationship with his wife is more important than anything else. He must treat it as such. It is more important than work, fishing, hunting, male friendships, sports, alcohol, etc., etc. It is the responsibility of the man to lead in the marriage relationship by loving the wife in this way (Ephesians 5:23-24, 31). When the husband loves in this way, the wife has the experience of being loved. This is not a single feeling. It is an experience that generates a variety of feelings, including admiration, security, confidence, respect, awe, and love. This is a spiritual process empowered by the Holy Spirit. The husband is not able to do this on his own. It is described by Paul as a "great mystery" concerning Christ and the church.

The wife, in addition to following agape love described in I Corinthians 13:4-7, demonstrates agape love by expressing reverential fear/awe for her husband in their daily life. What is reverential awe/fear, and where does it originate? This concept comes from the Greek word in Ephesians 5:33, which describes the manner in which the wife is to love her husband. The Greek verb is *phobio*, and the noun is *phobios*. These words imply a reverential fear or awe. This is translated in the Amplified Bible as follows, "you are to feel for him (your husband) all that reverence includes: to respect, defer to, revere him—to honor, esteem, appreciate, prize, and, in the human sense to adore him, that is, to admire, praise, be devoted to, deeply love, and enjoy your husband" (I Peter 3:2). When this happens, the **husband has the experience of being loved.** The reverential fear women have toward their husbands is governed in part by their attitude toward God. It is stimulated by a Godly desire to please her creator in the manner she relates to her husband. It is similar to the reverential fear/ awe she has for her Creator (Proverbs 9:9-11, Psalm 111:10). It stems

143 The Bible Exposition Commentary by Warren Wiersbe New Testament, page 51

144 ibid, commentary on Ephesians 5:25-33

from the reality that it is only God who ultimately meets her spiritual and earthly needs through the mate he has provided for her (Matthew 6:25-34). She must be empowered by the Holy Spirit to accomplish this.

When husbands love their wives sacrificially, and wives express reverential awe for their husbands, these two processes cement the marriage relationship. The relationship becomes hard as concrete...impervious to all the temptations and distractions the world brings against it. If agape love is absent, the marriage may survive, but it will not thrive. Process issues determine outcome. Physical attraction often plays a role in starting a relationship (Song of Solomon 1:9-10, 13-16, 2:2-3, 14). It is not sufficient to nourish and sustain it.

There is a hierarchy in the marriage relationship related to the concepts of sacrificial love and reverential awe. Scripture informs: God is the head of Christ, Christ is the head of the church, Christ is the head of the man, and the husband is the head of the wife (I Corinthians 11:3, Ephesians 5:22-24). The Greek word for head is *kephale.*[145] It refers to "the authority or direction of God in relation to Christ, of Christ in relation to the church and to men, and of the husband in relation to the wife (I Corinthians 11:3, Ephesians 5:23). So, the husband has authority over the wife (Ephesians 5:23-24). **However,** the husband and wife are subject to each other (Ephesians 5:21). And the direction the husband provides to his wife comes to him through the word of God. This means the husband sacrificially loves his wife by laying his life down for her. This produces a reciprocal softness to the relationship (Colossians 3:17-19). Agape love softens her heart and reduces her defenses. Women cannot resist agape love. It stimulates their feminine nature, including their desire for erotic love. Every woman wants an erotic, passionate, love relationship with a man because God put a desire for a man in every woman's heart (Genesis 3:16).

This does not give the husband license to be dictatorial to his wife. Rather he uses his authority to relieve his wife of the stress of decision-making, to protect her, and provide for her and their children. When the husband does all these things, it is natural for her to have reverential fear/awe for her husband.

Most men in modern culture do not love their wives sacrificially, and few women express reverential fear/awe to their husbands. Many men have never heard of this principle. Many women have been abused by men prior to meeting their future husbands. These women have an evil desire to control the men in their lives rather than submit. Demonstrating reverential awe/fear is not on their radar. They may struggle simply to be companions

145 Vine's Complete Expository Dictionary of Old and New Testament Words

to their husbands. They marry for romance, protection, provision, and for their husband to give them children, all appropriate reasons but insufficient to maintain the relationship God desires them to have.

Women have the primary responsibility for managing the home. They are created physically and emotionally to have the primary nurturing role in the home (Proverbs 31:10-31). The wife may contribute to the income of the household through work without neglecting her duties at home (Proverbs 31:16, 24).

Trust and exclusivity are essential to the life of the marriage. Trust is having sufficient confidence that you can rely on the integrity, general character, and strength of another person. Trust is given at the time of taking marriage vows. This is a starting point. It is not the end of the race. In marriage, it is paramount to maintain exclusivity in the sexual relationship. Breaking this trust produces so much hurt, disappointment, and anger that restoration of the relationship may take years. Forgiveness may happen fairly quickly, but rebuilding trust is an extended process. Husbands having affairs not only destroys trust, but it also often destroys the woman herself. She begins to question her femininity. A woman must trust her husband before she will open up emotionally or sexually. When wives have affairs, men are prone to destructive anger and rage.

Distractions

There are many things a couple can do either prior to or during engagement to increase the odds of having a long-term romance after marriage. They include discussion of the following issues: communication strategies, conflict resolution, handling of finances, having children, number of children, parenting strategies, past traumas, secrets, and a host of other topics. Refusing to discuss these issues are all **distractions** from expressing agape love. In the process of discussing these issues and reaching an agreement, each couple will discover their skill level of communication and conflict resolution.

A major distraction is the secular concept of finding a soulmate. This can be a very complicated distraction because of the following issues: 1) defining a soulmate, 2) an existing cultural belief there is only one soulmate, 3) and the question, does God have any role in the process of selecting your mate for life?

Different "experts" have different ideas about what constitutes a soulmate. Some list six criteria, some 10, and some 18 for a soulmate.[146] Some people

146 https://steptohealth.com, Six Keys to Finding Your Soulmate

suggest finding a soulmate requires a leap of faith. Others say having a soulmate is too painful and opt instead for a succession of temporary relationships. Albert Einstein observed this: "Any fool can make things bigger, more complex, and more violent. It takes a touch of genius –and a lot of courage--to move in the opposite direction." Let's do what Einstein suggests and move in the opposite direction. Instead of treading water checking off criteria for a soulmate, consider shifting to an examination of what the Bible says about finding a soulmate. It is much simpler.

The word *soulmate* is not found in the Bible text. Instead, the phrase describing an opposite-sex relationship with mutual love and exclusivity is *covenant relationship*. The English word *covenant* comes from Latin (*con venire*), meaning "to come together." It presupposes two or more parties who come together to make a contract, agreeing on promises, stipulations, privileges, and responsibilities. Covenants are described in the Bible between God and man and man and woman. Marriage is a covenant between the husband and wife and between both of them and God. The covenant criteria originating from the Bible are communication, commitment, permanence, trust, agape love, forgiveness, exclusivity, equal yoke, and obedience to the instructions of God on these issues. These are the same criteria observed in the covenant/ love relationship between God and His chosen people, the nation of Israel.

The love relationship between God and Israel started with God's call to Abraham (Genesis 12:1-3). The promises God made to Abraham in these verses are known as the Abrahamic covenant. Exclusivity in the Abrahamic covenant meant Israel would confine its worship to one God, the God of creation, the God of the Holy Bible. Exclusivity in the marriage relationship refers to one man marrying one woman and confining romance to the marriage relationship. Equal yoke refers to marrying within the Hebrew ethnic group of the Old Testament and marrying within the Christian community in the New Testament. Although God's love for Israel never failed, there were times when Israel was unfaithful to God. The book of Hosea describes Israel's unfaithfulness to God. There is example after example of this in the Old Testament.

So, God defines a soulmate as a person of the opposite sex to whom you are attracted, who shares your belief in the criteria God has established for a healthy marriage. Many times, the husband will lead in the relationship, but the husband and wife must learn to submit to each other. The husband leads at times and other times lays down his life for his wife. When the husband makes a decision for the family, it is only after he has received input from his wife, carefully weighing her suggestions. After he makes a decision, the wife should support it, even if she disagrees. Men want to be honored by their wives, which means being supported by them. When the husband leads in protecting, providing, and expressing excitement and delight in his wife, she will gradually allow him the privilege of discovering who she is.

The first Biblical instruction on marriage is this: "A man shall leave his father and his mother and shall become united and cleave to his wife, and they shall become one flesh" (Genesis 2:24). Notice how early in the biblical narrative this instruction is provided to Adam. God gave this counsel to Adam immediately after He gave Eve to Adam as a companion. Whatever God does, His timing is always perfect. This verse mentions two conditions for a married couple to become "one flesh." The first instruction is for a man to leave his parents. This does not mean simply to leave physically and live in another residence with his bride, but it also means to leave emotionally. God is saying the man is not to bring any emotional "baggage" generated by his formative years into the marriage relationship. Very few men think about this, and fewer men accomplish it. It is easy to say and difficult to achieve.

The second condition is for the husband to cleave to his wife. The word *cleave* has two opposite meanings. One meaning is to split something into two pieces, i.e., cutting one piece of meat into two. The other meaning is to join two things together so tightly they cannot be separated. The second meaning is the way God wants a man to relate to his wife. God wants husbands to hold onto their wives so tightly that nothing distracts their relationship with their wife. Of course, the wife also has to leave her emotional baggage out of the marriage and cleave to her husband. The husband takes the lead in this process as an example for the wife to follow. Have you considered what is in your emotional baggage? Here are some questions to assist you in that process:

- What was the most difficult experience you had growing up?
- What emotions did this experience generate for you?
- How did you process those emotions?
- What did you learn during your formative years about how husbands and wives relate to each other?
- By whom were you loved while growing up?
- Did you have to do anything to earn that love?
- How do you prefer love to be expressed to you by your spouse? Do you prefer affirmation, acts of service, gifts, physical touch, quality

time, or some other manifestation of love?[147]

- Did you have an unmet need during your formative years?
- How will you meet that need in your marriage relationship?

Caution! If you feel overwhelmed by thoughts or emotions connected to these questions, s**top reading** and **seek professional counseling!** These questions may bring up losses requiring grief work. This will be discussed in the chapter on talk therapy.

Answering these questions individually and then sharing the information with your future marriage partner will help you leave your baggage behind and prevent stress in your marriage. Work on one question per meeting with your future spouse, mentor, or therapist. It is not mandatory to get through every question, but there should not be any secrets withheld. Secrets will eventually manifest themselves in the marriage relationship. Most couples will not perceive any need for this because love is blind. Love can also be foolish if it is mostly about sexual desire.

A secondary purpose for working on the above questions is to develop the resource of communication and conflict resolution. Communication is the oil that allows the engine of our relationships to run smoothly. If there is no oil, the engine will break down; it is only a matter of time. In marriage, time may be an asset or your worst liability. It can be an asset as it will afford multiple opportunities to address issues that are certain to make their appearance. It becomes a liability when there is a failure to communicate and achieve a resolution on a particular issue. Continuous disagreement prevents unity and often builds resentment (Matthew 12:25). All relationships require work, but marriage relationships require more work because there is a greater degree of intimacy and more opportunity for conflict. In the Gospel of Luke, the author points out a wise person calculates the cost of a building prior to starting a project (Luke 14:28-30). The "cost" of creating a successful marriage is recognizing areas of dysfunction in yourself and correcting them. Pride and blind love tend to stimulate self-denial in this regard.

First Love

What was it like for Adam when God presented his mate to him? It seems reasonable to assume that Adam thought, "Wow" or perhaps "Double wow." He was excited, perhaps sexually. It is more likely he was excited to

147 The Five Love Languages by Gary Chapman

get to know whom God had created to be a companion for him. When he saw her the first time, Scripture records he said this, "This creature is bone of my bones and flesh of my flesh; she shall be called Woman, because she was taken out of a man." Do you hear an unstated "wow" in his reaction? It also sounds like an intellectual response. This may be a clue to a difference between the way men and women relate to each other.

Adam could not have known Eve was created from his own flesh unless God spoke to him about it. Perhaps God also gave him instruction on the wisdom of getting to know his companion before they mated. This interpretation is consistent with Genesis 4:1, which documents Eve not being impregnated until after they were forced to leave the Garden of Eden. Do you remember when you fell in love with your future spouse? When your fiancé entered the room, you experienced excitement, delight, and pleasure. Attention was focused on each other. When Adam saw the woman for the first time, he forgot all about tending the garden. He took a few days off. He could only see his new companion. Everything else faded into the background. It was a similar reaction for Eve. Very quickly, Satan made his appearance in disguise, and Eve was distracted from Adam and the counsel of God by the thought of becoming like God. Adam was distracted from the counsel of God, thinking he might lose his companion. Distraction is the beginning of the process of deception.

God gave Moses this instruction about marriage, "When a man is newly married, he shall not go out with the army or be charged with any business; he should be free at home for one year and shall cheer his wife whom he has taken" (Deuteronomy 24:5). Wow! A year off. Learning how to cheer your wife and knowing her is the most challenging task every husband will ever have.

The first thing to note in this Scripture is the similarity between this verse and Genesis 2:24, "Therefore a man shall leave his father and mother…" The man is to lead in establishing a relationship where his primary focus is his new wife. The wife should reciprocate. This Scripture suggests 12 months after marriage for the husband and wife to make each other the primary focus in their lives. This will establish a pattern of placing each other first in the marriage relationship. The husband's demonstrating his excitement, delight, and pleasure for his wife stimulates her femininity, including sexual responsiveness. Although not stated, the wife should follow her husband's lead. It takes practice to establish this pattern. Once established, this defeats the purpose of Satan, which is to distract, confuse, and deceive.

Taking a year off is not mandated in New Testament writings. It is not something you have to do. It simply demonstrates wisdom to learn early in your marriage that your relationship with your spouse is more important than work, sports, computer games, pornography, or whatever. Implementing this early is a process issue that will prevent distraction and lead to decisions promoting marital satisfaction.

Two other scriptures support the idea of taking an extended period to maintain focus on your marriage. The first is in Ecclesiastes: "To everything there is a season, and a time for every matter or purpose under heaven" (Ecclesiastes 1:1). In the next seven verses, Solomon gives examples, including a time to build things up, a time to laugh, a time to dance, a time to embrace, a time to love, and a time for peace. It is logical that the time to begin doing these things is the early part of your marriage relationship. A honeymoon lasting a week is not enough time to establish these patterns.

Many men do not know their wives on their wedding day, and vice versa. This is secondary to the reality that people wear a mask during the process of engagement. This mask conceals parts of the person's history and interpersonal style. This mask is removed at some point after the wedding. It might be removed during the honeymoon, at the time of their first disagreement, or some years later. Women must feel emotionally safe to remove their masks. Feeling safe and trusting her husband, she will allow her spouse into her heart and mind and enjoy having him inside her body.

The second Scripture is from Revelation 2:4: "Nevertheless I have this against you, that you have left your first love. Remember therefore from where you have fallen; repent and do the first works. Or else I will come to you quickly and remove your lamp stand from its place— unless you repent." This Scripture references the relationship of the church at Ephesus to Christ. However, there is a parallel metaphor in the New Testament that compares Christ and the church to the marriage relationship (Ephesians 5:25–29). Here, in Revelation 2:4, Jesus chides the church for leaving its first love, i.e., Jesus. The solution He offers in verse five is to remember and do the things they did in their relationship with Jesus at the beginning. This is equally good counsel for married couples.

Consider the following strategy: for the groom, make a list of all the things your bride has said and done during your courtship that contributed to your being in love with her. For the bride, make a list of all the things your future husband has said and done which contributed to your being in love with him. Keep these lists in a box you designate your marital treasure chest along with other items that strengthen your love for each other. From time to time, take out the list that you each made during your courtship and assess how you are doing at continuing the things you did from the beginning of your relationship. Practice these things during your first year of marriage, and if possible, take off an extended period to focus on your relationship. Pray for God to grant you wisdom, humility, and power to continue these things during your marriage. Do these things, and you will defeat Satan when he attempts to put your focus on work, a hobby, or anything else which is of less importance than your spouse. There will always be obstacles in life, making it difficult for you to receive the blessings God has for you.

In the narrative regarding Adam and Eve in the Garden of Eden, Eve became prideful and disobedient, resulting in her taking her focus from Adam. Adam became passive, concerned about losing his companion, and disobedient, taking his focus from Eve. Do not think romantic love conquers all and eliminates the need to protect your marriage relationship. Taking the time to protect your marriage is a process issue. There are content issues that are also important. For a look at content issues, google, "Taking the First Year Off—Start the Marriage Right," a blog by Stephanie Smith, or review "Taking the First Year Off" by Jonathan Dobson. If you are not yet convinced this is a good idea, watch the Hallmark Channel… and notice they have it backward. The process issue in Hallmark movies relates to every man and woman having a desire for a loving spouse. Unfortunately, Hallmark does not often portray the complexity of romantic love after the wedding.

This entire discussion assumes both parties to the marriage are Christian. A question seldom asked is the following: do I see Christ in my future spouse? Is he/she relating to me by expressing agape love? If you find evidence for God in your future spouse, you are blessed. If you do not find God, proceed with caution. Perhaps you do not find God because Jesus has not been invited into the heart of your future mate. Or perhaps you were not looking for God. Perhaps you were distracted by a worldly perspective of sexual pleasure, money, power, escape from an abusive environment, protection, prestige, or something else. These are all distractions leading to deception, which will fail to produce a lasting marriage. Dating and engagement are seasons of a person's life calling for **discernment**.

Marriage Models

Following the principles above leads to a model of marriage relationship referred to as the **complementary/ partnership model**. In this model, two people become partners in a "marriage adventure," with each bringing something to the relationship that is valuable and needed to enhance the relationship. The husband must overcome passivity by leading in the relationship but doing it in a way that models sacrificial love. Most importantly, the husband leads spiritually in the family. The wife must overcome pride by accepting her husband's decisions after giving him input. She sometimes takes the lead in establishing communication at an emotional level. She may need to share her thoughts and feelings to stimulate more openness in her husband. She softens the relationship and takes primary responsibility for the home and children (Proverbs 31:10-31). This model does not suggest a woman should not go to college or work outside the home. It suggests both men and women should be obedient to the leading of God in determining their roles in their marriage.

In **the top-down model** of marriage, the husband assumes the role of a dictator instead of a sacrificial lover. This results in the wife developing resentment and diminishing her emotional and sexual responsiveness. She often becomes unsupportive. She is present but not there. They have both fallen prey to the deception of Satan. A different deception occurs when the wife becomes the dictator. The result is similar, often leading to conflict and divorce. With either of these outcomes, there is always a loser.

The third model of marriage is known as **the 50-50 split**. In this model, the husband abandons leadership, and the wife insists on having "equal say." Equal say sounds good, but Jesus cautioned against this (Matthew 12:25). This model lacks spiritual leadership and may lack protection for the wife. The wife's respect for her husband is diminished because he is not leading. This may impair her desire to be physically intimate. The relationship often becomes directionless, especially after child raising, succumbing to cultural beliefs instead of following the word of God.[148]

Contrast a God-ordained marriage with a "**domestic relationship**" in which people live together. There is an absence of trust, commitment, exclusivity, and reliance on the word of God. There is always some degree of agape love missing. Reliance on the word of God is replaced by reliance

148 The Quest for Authentic Manhood by Robert Lewis, these models are adapted from his writing.

on self. Selfishness does not cement relationships. It destroys agape love. It destroys relationships. Instead of commitment, there is mutual agreement that if the relationship becomes conflicted, either party can say "I'm not putting up with this. I'm out of here." The fear of the relationship ending impairs the process of each person revealing him/herself to the other. This weakens the relationship. Domestic relationships are unwritten agreements to end the relationship at an unspecified point in time in the future. The same is true of many nuptial agreements.

Remember the precaution provided in Proverbs 4:23, "Keep and guard your heart with all vigilance and above all that you guard, for out of it flow the springs of life." The complementary model described above is not popular in our culture today because of pride and deception. Men fail to lay down their lives for their wives, and women do not think they reach their potential by raising children and looking after the home. If you think sacrificial love is easy, consider what Christ did for you on the cross.

The Song of Songs

The book of the Bible that focuses on romance, sex, and marital love is the Song of Solomon, also known as the Song of Songs. It was written by King Solomon almost 3000 years ago. Do not allow the age of the text to discourage you. Romance and love have been around for a long time. Like the other 65 books of the Bible, it is inspired by God. It is useful for the work of sustaining a marriage relationship (II Timothy 3:16).

Solomon wrote approximately 1000 songs, and the title of this book, Song of Songs, indicates its preeminence. It affirms what we learn about love from the relationship between God and His chosen people, Israel. Marital love requires commitment, permanence, trust, exclusivity, equal yoke, agape love, trust, and obedience. The Song of Songs adds romance and sexual love to the mix, which produces an interesting, provocative, yet tasteful perspective on God's plan for the sexual relationship in marriage.

It is written in poetic language and uses ancient imagery and symbols which make parts of it difficult to understand without explanation. A commentary that does justice to Solomon's writing is the book *Solomon on Sex* by Joseph Dillow. A brief review of Dillow's book can be found on the Internet (Solomon on Sex # 1 by Keith Hunt). The Song of Songs and Dillow's book are extraordinary opportunities to review God's instructions on romance, sex, and marriage.

Chapter 4 describes their wedding night. What is Solomon saying to his bride with this comment, "Your hair is like a flock of goats that have descended from Mount Gilead"? What do you think Solomon's bride (Shulammite) means when she says to Solomon, "Oh, I pray that the (cold) north wind and the (soft) south wind may blow up on my garden, that its spices [may flow out in abundance for you in whom my soul delights? Let my beloved come into his garden and eat its choicest fruits" (Song of Solomon 4:16). Dillow has many interesting observations and answers to questions about marital love. Have you thought about prayer being an antecedent to a sexual relationship with your spouse on your wedding night?

When building your marriage relationship, take every precaution to prevent emotional pain and suffering. Emotional pain ends many marriage relationships. It is referred to as irreconcilable differences…no mention of pain. "How quickly your mind alters perception."

Unfortunately, Solomon, the wisest man who ever lived, was deceived just like the rest of us (I Kings 3:7-12). He did not follow much of the counsel that he gave in the books he wrote. This does not diminish the value of his counsel or wisdom. Remember, pride overcame wisdom and knowledge with Lucifer/Satan and overcame knowledge with Adam and Eve in the Garden of Eden. These historical narratives inform us that we need the Holy Spirit to lead us into the truth. Neither Solomon nor you nor I can outwit Satan through our own intellect. Defeating sin is a spiritual process.

The next chapter focuses on something tempting to most of us, the topic of food. It has its own set of deceptions.

I Can't Believe I Ate the Whole Thing

The title of this chapter is taken from a 1972 Alka-Seltzer commercial that captured the minds of the American public. In the commercial, actor and comedian Milt Moss sits on the side of his bed in apparent discomfort and blurts out, "I can't believe I ate the whole thing." His wife, trying to sleep, counters with, "You ate it, Ralph." After a couple of Alka-Seltzer tablets, Ralph's discomfort is replaced by a smile, and they live happily ever after.[149] Have you ever felt so stuffed with food you were uncertain how you got in that condition? I've had that feeling on many occasions. A parody of a famous quote by Julius Caesar sums up the attitude of the average American toward food, "I came, I saw, I ate."

This chapter looks at one of the most common, frustrating, and puzzling process issues that face the average American today: the process of gaining and losing weight. On the surface, these two opposite processes seem very simple: consume more calories than your body uses, and you will gain weight; use more calories than you consume, and you will lose weight. Most people have no trouble gaining weight, but losing weight seems impossible for nearly everyone. These are accepted facts, but knowing these facts helps very little for people who are overweight and desire to slim down. Why is the process of gaining weight so easy while losing weight is weight so difficult? Have you considered this might be secondary to the process of deception? In this chapter, we will examine this question.

Consider the following: According to the US National Center for Health Statistics, 42.5 percent of adults over the age of twenty are obese. If you add the people who are overweight but do not meet the criterion for obesity, the percentage increases to 73.6 percent. Obesity in the US has been described as an epidemic, but a better word might be pandemic because it is problematic in most of Western civilization.

As of this writing, there has been a viral pandemic for the last 19 months that began in Wuhan, China, in December 2019. In 2020, there were 690,000

149 https://groovy history.com, Alka Seltzer I can't believe I ate that whole thing

deaths due to heart disease in the US, for which obesity is a serious risk factor, while there were 345,000 deaths due to the coronavirus.[150] If we followed the same rationale for locking down the country as we did for the coronavirus, the government would force every family to have a lock on the refrigerator door and require permission from the local health authority to prepare meals or have a snack. Do you see something wrong with this picture? The following paragraphs explain these apparent contradictions. Statistics like this tell us what is happening but say nothing about *why* it is happening. Process issues always determine outcome, including the "outcome" of our waistline.

My maternal grandparents, Billy and May, lived 30 miles from our home in Toledo; Dad's family lived a few miles farther. Dad and Mom were both close to their families of origin. Every Sunday after church, we drove to Grandpa Billy's for Sunday dinner, then visited Dad's family in the evening. Grandma May was a marvelous cook. She was old school—homemade noodles for her chicken noodle soup. Grandpa would buy a steer in the spring, tie it to a couple concrete blocks, fatten it up through the summer, and butcher it in the fall. Before long, we would be having Swiss steak with mashed potatoes and gravy for Sunday dinner. Swiss steak refers to the process of "swissing," an English term for tenderizing meat by beating it with a mallet that has pyramidal-shaped spikes on each side. Following this ritual beating, the meat did not look very appetizing. But Grandma made a dark gravy to cover the steak and baked it in the oven on low for 2 to 3 hours before serving. When it came out of the oven, it looked beautiful again…perhaps because it was covered in gravy. There was no visible evidence it had been beaten. Somehow it recovered in the oven. It melted in your mouth, and the gravy was "to die for." I suppose there was a vegetable of some sort, but I never paid any attention to the vegetables. Steak, mashed potatoes, and gravy captured all my culinary interest. *Capture* is the perfect word to describe my relationship because I was a prisoner to Grandma's Swiss steak.

After finishing a normal portion, I would ask for another piece of steak and then another. I ate steak until I was so full I would have to lie down on the couch for an hour or so before I felt like moving again. I imagined what a python experienced after swallowing a warthog. My parents or grandparents never made any effort to discourage gorging myself; they enjoyed seeing me consume what they had prepared. At home, I had the same issue with

---

150 www.jama.com; The Leading Causes of Death in the US for 2020

cake donuts covered in white powdered sugar. Dad would bring home a half dozen donuts every Friday when he got groceries. After breakfast on Saturday morning, they were all gone, and I had often consumed four of the six donuts. I felt a small amount of guilt about this, but the guilt did not stop my binging. Guilt rarely stops an eating disorder; it is more likely to promote unhealthy eating because food consumption often makes a person feel better for a few minutes.

As a teen and young adult, I continued this pattern of having two or three servings of whatever I found irresistible, and there were a lot of foods I could not resist. During my internship in Orange, California, we used to eat at Farrell's Ice Cream Parlor. There was a sub sandwich about 24 inches long and 4 to 5 inches thick on the menu. The sandwich was named a "gastronomical delicatessen epicurean delight." There was no charge for the sandwich if one person could eat the whole thing. After finishing one of these subs, you received a badge that said, "I made a pig of myself." On one occasion, on a bet, I ate the whole thing. I can't believe I ate that whole thing. Contrary to the name of the sandwich, I did not experience any delight. I had the same sensation of being stuffed that I had at my grandmother's house. I did not enjoy that sensation but could not stop stuffing myself.

I never gained excessive weight during my growing years because of my activity level. I did not gain weight as a young adult because of regular exercise. However, when I started my psychiatry training at age 32, I added pounds, and for the next 40 years, I averaged about 25-30 pounds over my high school graduation weight of 200 pounds. My undoing was not snacking, junk food, breakfast, or lunch; rather, it was extra helpings at dinner, two desserts, and snacking between dinner and going to bed. My hunger was generally satisfied at the end of the meal, but a couple of hours later, I would think it would be nice to have another cookie, piece of pie, or whatever. **I was not hungry,** but thoughts about food would lead to more eating. This has been described as head hunger.

What words of wisdom do we find in Scripture about diet and eating habits? *Diet* is the term that refers to the composition or selection of food items contributing to a person's health. Daniel 1:3-20 tells the story about Daniel's diet. Daniel proved to the king that a diet comprised mostly of vegetables was superior to a rich diet of wine and meat. Daniel's diet is similar to a Mediterranean diet which is often recommended to reduce the incidence of heart disease.[151] Daniel's diet needs to be considered in light of the instruction given to the apostle Peter in the New Testament (Acts 10:10-28). A detailed exposition of Peter's vision is found in the study "What is the Bible Diet?"[152] Wisdom also suggests attention should be given to counsel of the medical profession regarding diet. If a person has blood tests showing problems with lipids, it would be reasonable to consider a diet recommended by your physician.

If the reader finds this confusing, simply ask Jesus what foods should make up your diet and listen carefully for His instruction. Listening is the hard part of having a conversation with God. Nothing is more important than learning to wait on God. The human "heart is ever prone to divide its confidence between God and creature (mankind)."[153] When we seek God only, we should be certain to seek Him early. When we seek God as a last resort, we often find we are in a huge mess of our own making.

Gluttony is the sin of eating to excess. Gluttony is about the quantity of food consumed rather than the composition of the diet itself. Scripture says we should be reasonable in the way we conduct our lives (Philippians 4:5). The apostle Paul tells us that our "body is the temple, the very sanctuary, of the Holy Spirit who lives within you." This suggests we should care for it prudently (I Corinthians 6:19).

During my childhood and my early adult years, I had a vague sense it would be good to stop this pattern, but I could not resist the taste of good food (James 4:7). These thoughts are often explained as a manifestation of emotional hunger, eating to cope with stress. Foods consumed in this way are sometimes referred to as comfort foods. I do not disagree with these assertions, but it is equally true that there is a spiritual component to eating in an unhealthy fashion. I did not feel much stress during my day at the office. I enjoyed meeting people and working with them to help solve their presenting problems. However, listening to people describe their abuse experiences for 8 to 10 hours a day certainly could generate some vicarious stress. Was stress alone generating this unhealthy habit? Eventually, I realized that the **thoughts** about having second helpings or post-dinner treats were a manifestation of deception. Ouch! Reality can be painful and embarrassing.

---

151 usnewsandworldreport.com, Mediterranean Diet vs Nordic Diet

152 www.biblestudy.org, What is the Bible Diet?

153 The Treasury of David, Volume II, page 53, Commentary on Psalm 62, by Charles Mackintosh, 1858

I was distorting the primary purpose of food, which is nourishment. What I was doing was not reasonable or moderate. I did not recognize I was living in the kingdom of Satan during mealtimes. I was totally ignorant that I was experiencing demonic oppression in my eating patterns. I did not realize I was opening a door, inviting Satan in, willing to accept the risks of heart disease, stroke, and other consequences.

For the first time, I finally realized this was a **spiritual problem** due to the evil desire for food. It would require a **spiritual solution**. The spiritual component is this: the person depends on food to cope with stress rather than depending upon God. Therein lies the deception.

The "weightiest" precautions about food compulsions come from the book of Proverbs. About 25 years ago, I encountered Proverbs 23:1-3: "When you sit down to eat with a ruler, consider who and what are before you; for you will put a knife to your throat if you are a man given to desire. Be not desirous of his dainties, for it is deceitful food [offered with questionable motives]." These verses confirmed my suspicion that evil desire was a big part of my problem. And then there was Proverbs 23:21: "For the drunkard and the glutton shall come to poverty, and drowsiness shall clothe man with rags." It was primarily through the grace of God I did not experience either of these outcomes.

My highest weight was 235 pounds. My body mass index placed me in the overweight/mildly obese range. Pride prevented me from gaining more because I did not like the way I looked. Is this a context in which pride is constructive???

I set about figuring out a spiritual strategy to stop binging. The first strategy was fasting, beginning with dinner on Friday evening and ending with breakfast Sunday morning. It was not a complete fast; I continued to have liquids such as milk and carbonated beverages. The result was surprising. After fasting Friday night and Saturday, my appetite for food practically disappeared. I also noticed my mind was more focused on spiritual issues. However, this benefit did not carry over to the rest of my week. I am not suggesting that a Christian should not fast. For me, fasting promoted a greater awareness of my relationship with Christ as I navigated through the day. For that reason alone, fasting is highly recommended.

However, I continued to struggle with overeating at times. I meditated on this conundrum and came up with a plan to start the morning with a brief prayer of confession of my inappropriate eating pattern. At mealtimes, I would look at the food that was being served and ask God what He wanted me to eat. I would not eat anything until it was clear in my mind how much I should be eating. Then I prayed for the Holy Spirit to strengthen me to be obedient to what God was asking me to eat. This strategy followed the commentary given earlier, go to God "only and early." Remember, obedience is an act of worship (Romans. 12:1). I was being obedient…part of the time!

Some people might think this a radical strategy, but think about it this way. There is wisdom in having a meal in the presence of God instead of in the presence of Satan. This was helpful in breaking my dysfunctional pattern of food consumption. In behavioral science, this type of strategy is known as a pattern interruption. This changed the focus of mealtime from food to being aware of God's presence during the meal. I liked this strategy, but it created two new problems for me. First, I had to follow my prayer with obedience. Sometimes I did not want to be obedient; I preferred to indulge myself. On other occasions, I did not want to use the strategy at all. This is a good example of how evil desire overcomes knowledge…remember how that worked with Lucifer? Food consumption was not an area of my life that I was willing to totally surrender to God. Not surprisingly, there were some consequences.

I began to monitor my serum lipids. They were always borderline normal. I thought I was getting away with eating in an unhealthy fashion. But in the summer, I spent a lot of time hiking in the mountains of North Eastern Oregon. My backpack weighed about 60 pounds. With the extra 25 pounds, my "packing weight" increased to 85 pounds. I regularly experienced cramps in my calves after hiking 4-5 miles. There were a couple of times when the cramps were so painful I barely managed to get to our destination.

After closing my practice on 12/31/2018, I took another look in the mirror and decided there was no excuse for not losing weight. I implemented the strategy above and, over about three months, was able to lose 20 pounds. Now I have to be very cautious, continuing to talk to the Lord about what I should eat or again find myself looking in the mirror and being dissatisfied with what I see. Remember, "Satan is more crafty and subtle than any other creature of the field."

People who become anorexic have the opposite kind of experience I had. When food enters their mouth, instead of savoring the taste, it becomes repulsive to them. When they look in the mirror, they see themselves as overweight while they are actually emaciated. How quickly their mind alters perception! Sometimes their refusal to eat seems to them the only bit of control they have in life. It is equally helpful for a person with anorexia to confess their dependence on self instead of God and ask God what and how much they should eat at mealtimes. Binging and anorexia are good examples of the content of a presenting problem being different but the process **(deception)** being the same. Anorexic clients often benefit from family/talk therapy.

Is food intoxicating in the same way as alcohol is intoxicating? Food is not usually thought of as an intoxicating substance; however, the pleasure cycle associated with meals may involve neurotransmitters such as dopamine, serotonin, and opioids which play a role in producing food compulsion/addictions. These neurotransmitters produce perceptions in response to eating, somewhat similar to the altered perceptions people experience with alcohol use.[154, 155] People with food compulsions/addictions often make very poor decisions about the composition of their diets, frequently choosing foods that contribute to maintaining their addictions.

Notice this discussion on food compulsions/addictions implicated each of the five domains of humanity: thinking, emotion, behavior, physiology, and spirituality. Satan attacks wherever he finds an entry point. "The devil roams around like a lion roaring [in fiercer hunger] seeking someone to seize upon and devour" (I Peter 3:8).

It is difficult to convey how pervasive the influence of deception is on individuals and society. Satan has nothing to do but separate us from Jesus, our Lord and Savior. Satan is not building a house for his family, watching sports, relaxing on the beach, or exploring nature. None of the activities you and I enjoy bring him pleasure. The only things that bring him any pleasure are to steal, kill, and destroy (John 10:10). He is watching you. He is watching your children and grandchildren, looking for an entry point to deceive. His evil desire is to insinuate himself into our family life, meals, education, sports, movies, television programming, recreation, and vocation...everywhere. He wants to be unnoticed in each of these venues. We must watch for him (Matthew 26:36-45). If we are not watching and praying, we will fall asleep as the apostles did when Jesus asked them to watch while He spoke with His Father about His impending crucifixion. Be discerning! Watch and pray!

On several occasions, you have encountered the phrase "How quickly

---

154 hopkinsmedicine.org, The Cutting Edge Unravelling the Brain Chemistry of Food Addiction

155 KaySheppard.com, the Biochemistry of Food Addiction

your mind alters perception." One of the darker sides of our minds altering perception is the deception of slavery. In the next chapter, we examine the strategies of the mind leading to Black slavery in our culture for over 150 years. While you read, ask this question: do you think slavery has ended or simply evolved?

Deception, Christianity, and Slavery

How did slavery take hold in the United States of America? The separatists on board the Mayflower were highly motivated to advance the Christian faith. One hundred fifty years later, the Declaration of Independence and, subsequently, the Constitution of the United States established a republic, meaning the rights of all citizens are to be protected equally. What happened? A history of slavery in the United States will help us understand how process issues can easily subvert the best intentions. Look for **distraction, confusion, deception, desire,** and **defenses** as you read the following account.

Slavery has been a stain on nearly every dominant civilization in history.[156] Slavery is alive today, continuing its corrupt and depraved practices in the twenty-first century. Historically, when one culture conquered another, the dominant culture enslaved those who were conquered. This historical fact suggests the exercise of power is an essential component, producing slavery. The result for cultures dependent on slavery is a temporary accumulation of wealth, sloth, idleness, and eventual deterioration from within. Having others do our work appeals to our selfish nature. Everything might seem wonderful for a period of time, but there is a subtle decline in everything that is good. Cultures that promote and live off the work of others always end by being conquered by themselves. The USA will not be an exception to that process issue.

An elite class is currently attempting to wrest power from the people of the United States. If they are successful…the result will be some form of slavery taking power over the middle class.

We learn from this cycle of dominance the three main process issues which generate and maintain slavery are power, greed, and sloth. Accumulation of power stimulates an evil desire to control others to gratify the passions of those who are in control. Power, greed, and sloth **distracted** each of these conquering cultures from treating slaves as human beings.

The Roman Empire is a prime example of subjugating conquered

156 www.equip.org, Christianity and black slavery

peoples.[157] Judea was under Roman authority at the time of the birth of Christ. Rome was hated by the people they conquered. The Hebrew people in Judea were no exception. The Romans used the process of crucifixion to punish those who resisted their authority. Seeing people dying slowly on a cross instilled fear in the general population. The Romans used fear to control the people they subjugated. **Fear is the ideal means of control** because it produces **submission without eliminating the population upon which the dominant culture depends.**

Bible scholars have noted during the three years of Jesus' ministry He never spoke directly against the practice of slavery. However, His teaching emphasized the love God the Father has for all people. The Gospel of Christ calls all people to model God's love by treating others the way they would want to be treated. This is known as the "golden rule" governing all relationships. This teaching rules out the practice of slavery in its many forms.

The apostle Paul gave several instructions to guide the relationship between masters and slaves, recognizing slavery was a harsh reality (Ephesians 6:5-9). Paul's letter to Philemon demonstrates the benevolence Christians should have toward an escaped slave and the preference for the slave being in a state of freedom (Philemon 1:10-19). I would add this: a careful look at the teachings of Jesus and the apostles reveals Jesus was primarily interested in the spiritual state of humanity rather than their position in life, including physical slavery (Matthew 16:24-26, Philippians 4:9-14, I Timothy 6:6-21).

Jesus came primarily to deliver us from the slavery of sin (Romans 6:16-23). This is the context for God giving His only Son as a sacrifice for the collective sin of the world (John 3:1-21). Understanding this context is crucial for understanding the ministry of Jesus. How would you describe the spiritual state of the culture in the town or city where you live now? Write your answer below.

____

____

____

____

____

Slavery sanctioned by the Christian church waxed and waned following the ministry of Jesus. The most egregious period of US slavery by Christians

157 www.spartacus.educational.com, Slavery in the Roman Empire

was the period of slavery coincident with the establishment of agricultural plantations largely worked by slaves in the 17th, 18th, and 19th centuries. Some Christian leaders and pastors rationalized their support of slavery by quoting Old Testament Scripture. In particular, they focused on the story of Noah cursing his son Ham (Genesis 9:20-27) and passages that appear to support the buying and selling of servants (Leviticus 25:44-46).[158] The reader should study these references in the light of the New Testament theology noted above.

In the history of the United States, there are two principal groups/cultures to consider: the enslaved peoples from Africa and the Native American tribes. The primary culture that perpetrated Black slavery came with Europeans who settled in North America. Native Americans had enslaved each other for hundreds of years following intertribal wars. Immigrants continued the process of enslaving Native Americans. Between two and five million Native Americans had been enslaved by 1880.[159] Extermination through slaughter, relocation, and disease played important roles in obliterating Native American culture. Over 300 years, the cultures of the indigenous tribes were slowly canceled by westward expansion.

In the case of Africans, many were sold into slavery for profit by African kings following tribal wars. The culture of people left behind was interrupted by the loss of husbands, wives, and children. Those who were sold endured a below-decks transatlantic trip to North America, being sold on the auction block, further separation of families, and various indignities and cruelties from the hands of their "masters." Their culture was left thousands of miles behind in Africa. Slaveowners sometimes took sexual advantage of female slaves. The remnants of Native American and African slave culture were reduced to skeletons of their former nature.

It is thought the first enslaved Africans arrived in North America as part of a Spanish expedition to establish an outpost on the Atlantic coast in present-day South Carolina in 1526. Not long after their arrival, those Africans launched a rebellion and effectively destroyed the Spanish settlement.[160]

In 1619, settlers in the colony of Jamestown, Virginia, traded food for 20

158 www.kingscollege.net, the religious defense of American slavery before 1830

159 www.brown.edu, Colonial enslavement of Native Americans

160 www.smithsonian, Misguided focus on 1619 as the beginning of the history of slavery in U.S.

Africans who had been seized by the British from a Portuguese slave ship.[161] These Africans became indentured servants, working four to seven years for the colonists. After their servitude finished, some reportedly stayed in the colony, some went to England after obtaining freedom, and some may have continued in servitude.[162] It is important to realize that indentured servitude was a common strategy employed by people who desired to come to the colonies but could not afford passage or supplies after their arrival. The twenty Africans joined a population of largely indentured servants at Jamestown whom the Virginia Company of London had transported and sold into servitude. The 1619 Africans were not slaves. It was a series of laws passed in Virginia between 1660 and 1680 which created the legal foundation in which "Africans had indeed been marked off by race in law as chattel to be bought, sold, traded, inherited, and serve as collateral for business and debt services."[163] The passage of these laws paralleled the growth of tobacco as an important cash crop for the colonists.

To put Black slavery in the US in a historical perspective, consider these statistics:

- The Black slave trade shipped 12.5 million Africans to the New World between 1525 and 1866.
- Of the 12.5 million who left Africa, only 10.7 million survived the passage to the Americas. The fact that 1.8 million perished during the passage is stark testimony to the evil nature of the slave trade.
- In some respects, those who perished during transit were the lucky ones. According to historian Henry Louis Gates Jr., about 450,000, or about 3.5% of the 12.5 million African slaves, arrived in the United States. The other 96.5 % went mostly to the Caribbean and South America.[164]
- The large number of slaves in the US at the time of our Civil War was due to propagation, not transportation. According to the 1860 US census, there were 3,950,528 slaves in the US out of a total population of 31,183,582.[165]

---

161 www.history.com, First Enslaved Africans Arrive in Jamestown Colony

162 www.ancientplanters.org, Who Were the Indentured Servants?-Order of descendants

163 www.theguardian.com/us-news/2019/aug/14/slavery-in-america-1619-first-ships-jamestown

164 www.The root.com, How Many Slaves Landed in the US

165 www.snopes.com, Did only 1.4% of white Americans own slaves in 1860?

- The Europeans who came to the North and the South came from countries where slavery/servitude had been in practice for hundreds of years in various forms.[166] They brought with them a work ethic, a spiritual ethic, and the ethic of servitude. The work of carving a home from the American wilderness was daunting. There was an unending supply of land and resources but a shortage of laborers. A small minority who could afford it bought indentured servants or slaves to clear and work the land. For the next 240 years, the numbers of immigrants, slaves, and tobacco production increased together. The culture of the North became more independent of slavery and supportive of abolition, while the culture of the South embraced slavery to support their agricultural practices.

In the Declaration of Independence, Jefferson wrote these famous words, "all men are created equal." These words became more contentious as people moved westward and formed new territories and states. The conflict over slavery was reflected in new legislation and the courts. The Three-fifths Compromise, reached during the 1787 United States Constitutional Convention, allowed slaves to be counted as three-fifths of a person for the purposes of legislative representation and taxation.[167] The result gave Southern states a third more seats in Congress and a third more electoral votes than if slaves had been ignored but fewer than if slaves and free people had been counted equally. Politics rule! Politics rule because it is a process issue.

In 1857, the US Supreme Court ruled 7-2 in the Dred Scott decision, determining that slaves and their descendants, whether free or not, could not be American citizens and thus had no right to sue in federal court. Congress was also banned from outlawing slavery in new US territories.[168] Again, politics rule!

Abraham Lincoln, a promising leader of the fledgling Republican party at the time, opined on the decision by pointing to the fact that the Supreme Court had often overruled its own decisions and said, "We shall do what we can to overrule this."[169] Civil war broke out a few months after Lincoln was elected president in 1860. On January 1,1863, Lincoln signed into law the Emancipation Proclamation, legally freeing the slaves.

Lincoln's perspective on spirituality and slavery is partially expressed in this quote from his second inaugural address ten days before he was shot: "Both

166 idhi.library.cfc.edu/, Slavery before the Transatlantic Trade. African Passages

167 168 www.blackpast.org, The Three-fifths Clause of the US Constitution (1787)

168 www.thoughtco.com, The Dred Scott Decision

169 The Lincoln Reader by Paul Angle, Pg. 223

(North and South) read the same Bible and pray to the same God, and each invokes His aid against the other. It may seem strange that any men should dare to ask a just God's assistance in ringing their bread from the sweat of other men's faces. But let us judge not that we be not judged. The prayers of both would not be answered. That of neither has been answered fully. The Almighty has his own purposes."[170]

This is a fascinating statement by Lincoln. He seems to be saying the North and the South have the same God and Bible, but each may pray inappropriately, for their individual causes, for self-vindication and self-gratification. God has His own purposes, different from either the North or the South. For that reason, the prayers of neither the North nor the South were answered completely. It is strange for men to ask assistance from a God who loves justice to continue the master/slave relationship. Do not judge in order to avoid spiritual judgment. Lincoln was very careful not to condemn either the North or the South.

Lincoln apparently **discerned** there was deception among **Christians** in the North as well as the South. It was Lincoln's profound ability to **discern**, to **communicate** using common language to common people, and his **concern** for common people, that separates him from many other American presidents. Do the politicians you vote for have these three traits? Do they care? Do they value you? Do they use you? Write your answers in the space below.

____

____

____

____

____

The Civil War ended 25 days after Lincoln was assassinated, but the fight for Black freedom continues to this day. Slavery had been legally abolished, but racial prejudice could not be abolished by presidential decree. Attempts to abolish racial injustice through any political strategy are only partially successful. Racial injustice is the result of the universal sin nature of mankind. It is a spiritual issue that originates in the heart. Attempts to change this through politics often result in reverse prejudice manifested by affirmative action, political correctness, cancel culture, critical race theory, and worse. Reverse prejudice is discrimination against members of a group formerly dominant and powerful in favor of members of a minority or historically disadvantaged group. The target (content) of discrimination changes, but

---

170 www.owleyes.com, Lincoln's Second Inaugural Address

the process is the same. The result is division, the perpetuation of conflict, and the absence of social progress.

The process issues have not changed since Lincoln's speech. Deception is a universal phenomenon north and south in the United States, north and south of the equator, everywhere! Christians do bad things, including a history of promoting slavery. Everyone is prone to being deceived. *Do not confuse Christians with Christ.* People who confuse Christians with Christ become distracted from the true character of Jesus. Confusion about Jesus is the result. In their confusion, people reject Christ. This is a perfect example of how distraction and confusion produce deception.

It takes a decision in the heart to abolish racial prejudice. Changing the heart belongs to the domain of spirituality. This is the subject of different chapters, "Affairs of the Heart and Intimacy with Evil". The process issue behind most of the above is this--**politics rule.** Instead, it should be the **golden rule** articulated by Jesus as follows: "And as you would like and desire that men would do to you, do exactly so to them**"** (Luke 6:31). If everyone was following the Golden Rule, there would be little need for politics.

The three main process issues underlying politics are the same ones that fueled slavery: **Greed, sloth, and desire for power.** These are the process issues that distracted and confused wealthy arrivals from Europe. Although people who could afford slaves constituted a small percentage of early immigrants, they wielded a great deal of **power**. Money is power!

Unfortunately, **greed, sloth, and power** were not the only spiritual process issues at work supporting slavery. The evil desire of sexual **lust** prompted male slave masters to rape/sexually abuse female slaves. **Pride** and **envy** stimulated the pursuit of larger and larger numbers of slaves to gratify the self. And then there is **anger**! Without **restraint** provided by law, slave masters were free to vent their **anger** on the backs of their helpless slaves. There was a great deal of frustration written on the backs of slaves. Frustration often leads to anger, which is destructive. In this short paragraph are **examples of six spiritual issues functioning as process issues promoting the deception of slavery.** These process issues largely determined the outcome for millions of individual slaves.

Slavery is a disgusting lesson in the dynamics of **abuse**. Regretfully, we are all abusers at some point in time because of our sin nature. We are all in the same boat…and there is no first-class passage. We are all traveling below deck, like the slaves to sin we are.

Remember the elements of abuse:

- Abuse exists only in human interpersonal relationships. Chairs do not abuse couches. Highways do not abuse sidewalks.
- There is a concentration of power within one person or group which exerts power over other individuals or groups.
- The person or group that holds power uses it to gratify himself/themselves without considering how it affects others.

Consider the three necessary elements that comprise abuse. Briefly review your own life and, using one or two sentences, describe examples of when you were abused or when you were the abuser (we are all abusers at times). We thank God He does not keep a record of wrongs and is willing to forgive (I Corinthians 13:5, Mark 1:4, I John 1:8-9).

____

____

____

____

____

Many relationships have a **power gradient**, where one person or a group of people hold most of the power in the relationship. Examples include slave owner/slave, boss/employee, parent/child, older sibling/younger sibling, uncle/niece or nephew, grandfather/granddaughter or grandson, pastor/parishioner, government/ citizen, rich/poor, teachers/students. If you do not pay attention to the power gradient that exists in relationships, you will not understand the events that influence outcome in relationships. Whoever holds power has greater responsibility for how power is used. People often use power as their worldview instructs rather than according to the golden rule.

There are only two possibilities for a source of spiritual instruction: the Kingdom of God and the kingdom of Satan. The God of the Holy Bible is all-powerful but does not force obedience. In the Kingdom of God, we find a God who administers love and truth with grace, mercy, and justice. Love and truth are process issues that build people up and set them free. In the kingdom of Satan, we find a fallen disobedient angel who lies, steals, kills, and destroys (John 10:10). These process issues tear people down and enslave them to sin. Satan only has the power over your will that you give to him. No one can say, "The devil made me do it." The devil cannot make you do anything. Satan only deceives. You may think you are doing wonderful things when in reality, you are serving the source of all evil (Matthew 7:19-23).

Powerful people can use their power and influence to build up or destroy people. Observations of their behavior reveal which kingdom is influencing their choices. People who lack power either resist evil desire or become slaves to the people who wield power (Romans 6:16, James 4:7). Proper use or misuse of power stems from **worldview** and **spiritual beliefs**. Worldview is discussed in detail in the chapter on Newton, Hawking, and Darwin.

Did most slave owners have conscious awareness of the appalling acts they were committing? Probably some did, and some did not. Psychological defense mechanisms protected slave owners from the guilt and shame of owning and demeaning slaves. **Rationalization, repression, and denial** were certainly alive and well in the minds of most slave owners. (R**ationalization**: excuses which justify thoughts, speech, or behavior; **repression**: forcing disturbing ideas or memories into the unconscious; **denial**: refusing reality by denying that it exists).[171] These secular concepts from the field of psychology confirm the truth stated in Scripture: "The mind is deceitful above all things, and it is exceedingly perverse and corrupt and severely, mortally sick! Who can know it [perceive, understand, be acquainted with his own heart and mind?]" (Jeremiah 17:9, Matthew 13:15). How sick can the human mind be? The evils of slavery answer that question.

These defense mechanisms are process issues themselves because they lead to choices that are abusive. These unconscious process issues contributing to choices make it very difficult to understand and unravel human behavior. Slavery is an excellent example of conscious and unconscious process issues producing abuse. Are those conscious and unconscious processes continuing to have the same influence in the first part of the 21st century? Have Black people escaped the slavery that oppressed them prior to the Civil War? Have they been released from the Jim Crow laws that followed the Emancipation Proclamation for the next 150 years?

Black author Candace Owens considers these questions in her book, "Blackout." She personally and insightfully describes her experience of being Black in the twenty-first century: "I began to believe that the world was happening to me, that I was a tragic Shakespearean figure doomed to fail because of the unfortunate circumstances of my childhood. This quite naturally led me down a path of liberating myself from any concept

---

171 www.psychologistworld.com, 31 Psychological Defense Mechanisms Explained

of personal responsibility." She goes on to say, "But with time, what was supposed to feel like freedom began to feel like bondage. I was pretending that a life with no rules made me feel free, when in reality it made me feel insecure." In these few words, Owens describes a different form of slavery. A "bondage" produced by "the unfortunate circumstances of my childhood."

A large part of her book focuses on the concept of personal responsibility. Her escape from bondage began when her family was invited to live with her conservative grandparents when she was nine years old. Her experience with her grandfather and grandmother planted seeds that did not bear fruit until more than a decade had passed. Much of her book describes the journey from slavery to freedom that Black people must take today. Looking at her book from the perspective of "process," it seems that she is writing about deception. She escaped the evil desire influencing her from within and from without. The same route of escape is available to other Blacks who choose to take it.

In her first chapter she makes the following assertions:

1. "By 1868, the Ku Klux Klan, less than two years after their inauguration, had infiltrated the Democratic Party's campaign for the presidential election." The slogan for the Democrats during that "race" was "Our Ticket, Our Motto, This Is a White Man's Country, Let white men rule." In other chapters, she details how the party referring to themselves as Democrats have created a new form of slavery, the Democrat plantation, for black people while claiming the "higher moral good" for the Democrat party.
2. "The glorification of victimhood is exclusively promoted from the left."
3. "The sad truth is every policy they (Democrats) promote invariably harms Black America."

A process observation must be made at this point. It seems it would be wise for the higher moral good of our country to be established by the Creator of moral good rather than by either the Democrat or Republican party.

Owen's book is a great read. You will discover that the content producing Black slavery today is different from plantation slavery and Jim Crow slavery. She refers to Black slavery today by the term "the Democrat plantation," meaning Blacks are doing the work for Democrats and getting nothing back. I would assert the fundamental process issues are similar. They are the process issues of money, power, sloth, denial, rationalization, pride, and abuse that combine to produce deception and continued slavery. These are the tools of deception. The dynamics of Black slavery offer a historical perspective on the pressure exerted by politics, economics, and cultural bias. Do you think we are experiencing anything like this in the US today?

Does this describe cancel culture or critical race theory? Write your answers in the space below.

____

____

____

____

____

I would assert the content has changed, but the process is similar to what happened in plantation slavery. At that time, plantation owners used their financial power to purchase slaves, maintain slavery through physical power (chains, beatings), discourage black education, and routinely break up black families on the auction block. Currently, Democrats are purchasing the votes of blacks and discouraging independence through government handouts, providing misinformation about what will help Blacks, failing in educating Black children, hurting Blacks in urban areas by defunding police, promoting the abortion of Black babies, and ignoring the absence of fathers in Black families. The plantation has shifted from a rural agricultural plantation to an urban, inner-city plantation. Tobacco was the product during plantation slavery. The product produced by the Democrat plantation is votes. Political power has always been the most important process issue supporting the existence of Black slavery—plantation slavery then and the Democrat plantation now.

A final thought about slavery: eventual rebellion is the nearly universal response of humanity to slavery. There is one exception to that rule. There is one form of slavery people are willing to accept without much fuss or resistance. That would be slavery to sin. It is a testimony to the deceptive nature of Satan's strategies (Genesis 3:1).

The next four chapters provide examples of process issues in talk therapy. It is important to be acquainted with these process issues as the stress of modern culture results in many seeking some type of professional counseling to cope.

Talk Therapy, Introduction

We are born dependent on others. Many of us will die dependent on others. Between birth and death, God gives each of us an opportunity to grow into a person who loves, works, procreates, recreates, and teaches others something about the process. To succeed, we **must take responsibility** for ourselves and find direction for our journey from the word of God and empowerment through His Holy Spirit.

When our hearts are wounded by others, we often flee from the dangers of relationships and develop a variety of dependencies: dependencies on others, our psychological defenses, alcohol, street drugs, work, sports, technology, or some other strategy. These dependencies delay or prevent the process of growth. They take a strong hold on the issues of our hearts. We become stuck. We may live for years or even decades languishing under the influence of these deceptions. A book about process issues sounds somewhat theoretical in nature. You may wonder if the theory is valid and what it looks like in real-time. This chapter will introduce you to what happens in therapy. The following three chapters provide case examples that illustrate process issues facilitating life change.

Therapy starts with a process of evaluation. The client brings a problem, and the therapist evaluates the problem in the context of the five domains of humanity: thought, emotions, behavior, physiology, and spirituality. The therapist determines which of the domains is contributing to the presenting problem. Is it simply a thinking error? Are emotions involved? Does behavior need to change? Regretfully, it is often the case that all five domains need attention in the process of recovery. Injury to the soul by another person or group can impact every aspect of a person's life. This chapter will help you understand the processes involved in change. Unfamiliarity with therapy prevents many people from starting the healing process.

The most common symptoms of injury to the soul are the various manifestations of depression and anxiety. They are psychological manifestations of underlying process issues in the five domains gone awry. After therapy— when thinking, emotions, behavior, and spirituality are all functioning well, often the underlying physiology will change, and the depression and anxiety will remit. Pharmaceutical companies want people to buy into their mantra that it is always necessary to take medicine to restore physiological function to normal. As stated earlier, changing the physiology through medical prescription without changing the thinking, emotions, and behavior will usually only produce a partial remission of depression or anxiety. On the other hand, if the presenting problem appears to be biological in origin, the specific cause needs exploration and correct diagnosis. Medication may be required to improve the underlying physiology. The process of evaluation determines whether treatment should start with a prescription for therapy or one for the pharmacist.

Talk therapy has a variety of different approaches to help people change. When problems are complex, often, there are many different ideas about solutions. Such is the case with talk therapy. Every form of therapy that works has certain things in common. These include **good listening skills**, validation of feelings, pacing and leading, problem focus, unconditional positive regard for clients, healthy boundaries, and strategies that promote change the client is willing to accept. When the client gives up the strategies/defenses he has been using, the therapist must provide new strategies/tools that work better than the old ones.

Validation refers to understanding and accepting expressions of the client as they describe their experience, including their emotional responses. Validation enhances the therapist-client relationship. It promotes a strong bond. It piggybacks onto the process of listening to the client.

Pacing refers to meeting the client where the client is and spending some time there with the client before attempting to lead the client to consider new strategies.

Problem focus is about focusing on the client's presenting problem and not issues the therapist has observed that might benefit from attention. When therapists bring up issues the client does not perceive as problematic, clients become defensive and may stop therapy. There is a delicate balance in therapy on this issue. It is often wise to ask a question such as "How is that working for you?" Questions may stimulate new awareness of a problem the client had not considered.

Unconditional positive regard is what it sounds like: respecting, honoring, and desiring to facilitate positive change for the client.

Boundaries are relational lines that protect the client and therapist. The therapist has primary responsibility for maintaining boundaries. In therapy, there are physical boundaries (the space between client and therapist), emotional/ sexual boundaries, time issues, social boundaries, political boundaries, and spiritual boundaries.

Time issues relate to the therapist and the client each being on time for appointments, finishing on time, and clients not contacting the therapist after hours unless there is a true emergency.

Social contact is unwise outside the therapy meeting. The reason for this is each type of relationship has a different set of boundaries. Most people, including most therapists, are unable to keep track of more than one set of boundaries.

Client permission is necessary to address political/spiritual issues or anything poignant for the client; the client should agree with the therapist about the need to go there.

Many people who seek therapy have never had a single relationship in which somebody listened to them. It may seem strange to you to have to pay someone to listen, but many clients are grateful that somebody is willing to do this simple thing. The desire to have someone listen to your story is symbolic of the spiritual need you have for God to listen to your story. God knows your story before you speak a word. His desire is for you to open your heart to tell Him so He can facilitate the process of healing (Psalm 30, Psalm 42, Revelation 3:20). Sometimes, a client will need to talk with a therapist first before trusting a conversation with God. This happens when trust has been completely destroyed by prior trauma. For some, it is easier to trust someone they can see. Of course, it should be the other way around, trusting God first.

There has been cultural prejudice against seeking counseling services for decades. People believe their friends or family will think less of them if they go to therapy. Unfortunately, that is sometimes true. Cultural bias about counseling has diminished in recent years, but it continues to be an obstacle for many. The following paragraphs summarize some of the important process issues after therapy begins.

Reality overcomes fear, shame, and pride the moment an appointment is made. But they are only subdued for the moment. They will pop up off and on throughout the therapy in different forms: refusal of homework, refusal to examine thinking errors, refusal to reconnect to feelings, and refusal to work at changing behaviors, often preventing progress in therapy. Clients may continue therapy despite a lack of progress because they desire a safe relationship. They depend on their own defenses instead of trusting the therapist to point them in the direction they need to go. When the meeting becomes conversational instead of change-oriented, the therapy is on the road to nowhere. This needs to be addressed during a meeting. Questions to bring this up for discussion are: *Do you think you are making progress? What were your thoughts? What were your feelings?* or *What is preventing you from doing_________?* or *What was it like for you to do_________?* Reconnecting to emotions is a difficult part of therapy. Trauma produces painful emotions of confusion, guilt, shame, fear, hurt, sadness, and disappointment. These emotions are often associated with a sense of helplessness that was experienced during the trauma. Clients want to avoid that sense of helplessness. These emotions work to prevent seeking help.

The goal of emotional work is to get reconnected to emotion in a general kind of way. The above emotions are part of living in a stressful world. It is natural to experience these emotions as you cope with trauma. It is not natural to go through life unable to experience hurt, sadness, and disappointment. Is it difficult? Of course, no one desires hurt, sadness, and disappointment. But, because of sin, life is peppered with these emotions. The **goal of therapy is to experience these emotions without reliving the trauma in your mind.** It is **not helpful** to relive the trauma. Experiencing the terror of a brutal rape for a second time would simply reinforce the injury to your soul.

The confusion stems partly from your mind's attempts to make sense of what happened. You are unable to understand what happened because it is out of the range of normal experience. Confusion produces uncertainty about what to do. Should you seek help or attempt to disconnect from the experience?

Guilt and shame produce the behavior of hiding, just as they did for Adam and Eve when they hid in the Garden of Eden. Guilt and shame deserve special mention. There are two common scenarios. First, you are a survivor of trauma. Any guilt or shame associated with the trauma belongs to the perpetrator, not you. Do not be deceived. You were drawn into intimacy with evil in some way by a perpetrator (Matthew 18:6). Satan wants you to think you are responsible. He uses guilt and shame to accuse you…to keep you in his kingdom…under his influence, in a depressed or anxious state of mind (Revelation 12:10). Jesus despised and ignored the shame of the cross because it did not belong to Him (Hebrews 12:1-3). Follow the example of Jesus!

Young women may blame themselves for date rape because they allowed themselves to be alone on a first date. She thinks, how could I be so foolish?

The young woman may need to change her dating behavior, but she is not responsible for a rape. Everyone makes mistakes. Do not be hard on yourself. Do you know anyone who has not made a mistake? These are all accusations coming from the great accuser, Satan.

The second scenario is when you hurt someone through your own speech or actions. Do not hang around with guilt and shame (I Corinthians 1:4-8). Send it back where it came from. Stamp it parcel refused. Guilt and shame are your bitter enemies. Simply confess your misdeed to Jesus (I John 1:8-9). Be transparent by asking the person you offended for forgiveness.

One reason Christ is described as our Savior is because He desires to relieve us from the burden of sin. He saves us from the burden Satan wants us to carry around for the rest of our lives. Jesus carried that burden for us on the cross. It has already been transferred to Him. His righteousness has been transferred to us to take the place of our sin. This is known by the term imputation (Romans 4:11). It has been referred to as the "The Great Exchange."[172] It is "Good News" for believers![173]

People rarely get disconnected from the emotion of fear as they do with other emotions. Being able to recognize fear is necessary for survival. Fear and anxiety are different manifestations of the same feeling. Fear is stimulated by something outside your physical body… something you are aware of through sensory experience. Anxiety feels very similar to fear but is generated internally by your mind with uncertainty about its origin. It may be connected to a past trauma that has been repressed. Not knowing its origin can render it more distressing and lead to cyclic anxiety attacks or panic disorder. Fear originating from traumatic relationships is often generalized to other relationships. Different types of anxiety disorders may make their appearance. The life of the person becomes more and more restricted.

The emotion of hurt occurs when there is an injury to the soul, an attack on personhood. The injury may be to their thought life, emotional life, physical body, or spiritual life. These injuries also produce sadness and disappointment, the emotions associated with loss. Trauma is always associated with loss: loss of love, relationship, spouse, security, innocence, stability, childhood, job, confidence, and the list goes on. There may be so much loss it seems as though nothing is left (review the therapy of Ruth).

Because of emotional pain intrinsic to guilt, shame, hurt, sadness, and

---

172 www.ligonier.org, The Great Exchange

173 www.bibleoddyssey.org, The Good News of the New Testament

disappointment, people become fearful of their own emotions. The prospect of sharing their heart with a stranger may be overwhelming. When hurt, sadness, and disappointment are not expressed, they contribute to depression and anxiety disorders. People mired in these emotions are often desperate when they finally call for an appointment. These painful emotions are all **distractions** that pave the way to confusion, deception, and a decision to delay seeking help.

There are different degrees of being disconnected from emotions. A very mild form of this can be observed in general conversation. For example, at a city council meeting, someone may ask, "How do you feel about raising the sales tax by 0.1% on the sale of alcohol products?" And the respondent may say, "I don't feel it's fair to put so much of our tax burden on people purchasing alcohol." Most of the time, a person asking a question of this nature does not want to know what emotion you are feeling (disappointment or irritation) about the tax, but rather, what your thoughts are about it. And in this example, the person responding is not describing his emotions; he is not stating feelings about raising taxes. He is stating his thoughts. This type of communication indicates a mild disconnect between thoughts and feelings. There are moderate degrees of being separated from emotions as well. These people may be aware of suppressing emotions when they are hurt or disappointed. They have a choice about whether they will experience an emotion or ignore it. When a severe loss occurs, they are **tempted** to suppress the associated grief. More severe degrees of dissociation turn three-dimensional life (thoughts, feelings, and behavior) into two-dimensional life (thoughts and behavior). A life devoid of emotion is lifeless, which is why clients may describe feeling "dead inside." This degree of dissociation will nearly always prevent grief work. Feelings of sadness, disappointment, guilt, and shame are stored in the mind, where they contribute to chronic/intermittent depression and unconscious decision-making.

Every emotion has a physical component that is usually experienced in some combination of three different places: the face, the chest/heart, and the abdomen. Fear is an exception to this rule as it can be experienced anywhere; sometimes, the whole body may be shaking at the same time in response to fear. If there is/was fear or panic, take the emotion to Jesus. Ask Jesus to help keep your focus on Him. You do not have to re-experience the event. If you keep your focus on Jesus, you should not experience the event. After you identify *where* you are experiencing the feeling, and the physical sensations, describe what you are feeling to Jesus. Your face may feel tight, your chest heavy, butterflies in your stomach—describe the physical sensations. As you describe them, He will take them from you and replace them with peace (Isaiah 53:3-6, Revelation 3:20). There is no emotion you cannot take to Jesus. You may start by describing the fear you have about experiencing your feelings. It is necessary to open your heart to Jesus before He can heal it.

A similar strategy of relying on Jesus during an anxiety attack is to have a continuous dialogue with Jesus about exactly what you are experiencing, including your thoughts and the physiological signs you are experiencing. It might sound something like this, "Lord, I am really scared; I think something terrible is going to happen. I'm short of breath. My heart is beating fast. I feel numb all over." Continue to describe to Jesus what you are experiencing, your thoughts and physical sensations, until the anxiety has subsided. Talking to Jesus brings you into His presence, where you are more likely to experience peace. As the anxiety diminishes, it will be easier to focus on Jesus. You will learn that when you allow your anxiety to take you to Jesus, He can bring good out of the experience for you (Romans 8:28). This will change your perception of anxiety. Notice these strategies all have one thing in common: keeping your focus on Jesus and not on yourself or your circumstances. It is extremely helpful to have Jesus at your side when facing difficult life experiences.

Pride may be a defense against guilt and shame. Pride is not a simple emotion such as hurt, sadness, or disappointment. It is not a sin to feel hurt, sad, or disappointed. Pride is a sin of the flesh. Pride is an example of evil desire. Pride is a sin because a person's focus is removed from God and put on the self or some object the self has acquired. All sin falls into three categories: the lust of the eyes, the lust of the flesh, and the pride of life (I John 2:15-16). Pride has many different manifestations, one of which is the thought, "I don't need help," or "I can take care of this myself."

We learned in the chapter on the D words that pride overcomes knowledge and wisdom. Pride resists instruction. Pride impairs a person's spiritual function. Part of our spiritual function is caring for our own body (I Corinthians (6:18-20, Ephesians 5:29). Proper care of your own flesh would preclude the possibility of suicide. People who make serious suicide plans or who attempt suicide are always deceived. They think they know more about what is happening in the present and future than the God who created the universe. They do not have a relationship with God or do not know how to use the relationship to cope with their circumstances. The issue of suicide is discussed in more detail in the appendix.

In therapy, the other side of pride is that which exists in the therapist. People who seek the role of caring for another person's physical, emotional, or spiritual health are prone to vanity. Their increase in knowledge often increases pride (I Corinthians 8:1). Higher education may actually decrease the ability to establish a validating, empathic, objective relationship with a client. Humility is the opposite of pride and vanity. Therapists should be humble because they suffer from many of the same problems as their clients. Recognizing everyone will need help through life facilitates the client's willingness to share their story. Therapists who constantly interpret clients' behavior send an indirect message that they are smart and the client is not. This is similar to governments that give handouts to people who are capable of holding a job. The message is we will take care of you because you are unable to care for yourself. These messages foster dependency on the therapist or the government. It is more helpful to ask questions, make observations, and tell stories that stimulate clients to understand their own behavior.

When thinking errors reinforced by guilt, shame, and fear are held for years, they are not usually surrendered quickly. Something has to replace deception in the mind of the client. **The mind of man abhors a vacuum.** The best option is to replace the lie with the truth of God (Luke 11:24-26). The client may accept the truth with the mind fairly quickly but becoming comfortable emotionally and spiritually with a new worldview may take longer. Both therapist and client must be patient with the process.

We should take traumatic experiences to someone. Allowing these experiences to percolate unexpressed or unprocessed in our minds is not healing. Jesus should be considered as your therapist or co-therapist. You can communicate with Jesus in prayer or meditation (Isaiah 53:4, Revelation 3:20). Tell Him very briefly what happened, your thoughts, and your grief. You **do not have to relate traumatic detail** or the emotional reactions to the experience. Of course, He already knows everything, but He wants to hear it from you because God is relational.

Multiple traumas/abuse experiences/adverse child experiences always require **forgiveness** at some point. Many will need encouragement from the therapist to engage in the process of forgiveness. Forgiveness is described in the scriptures in Matthew 18:21-35. Have a look at those verses now to determine if you can answer the following questions: 1) Is forgiveness an act of the mind, a cognitive act, or does it require emotional work? 2) Is forgiveness primarily for the benefit of the person injured or his perpetrator? 3) How do you know if you have completely forgiven someone who has hurt you? Answer these questions in the space below.

____

____

____

____

____

In Jesus' parable of the unforgiving servant, the process of forgiveness is explained. A careful reading of this parable suggests the King made a cognitive decision to forgive. There is no evidence He experienced emotional turmoil in the process. Of course, this is a metaphor regarding God forgiving the sins of everyone who accepts Jesus as Lord. The forgiveness of God is based on the sacrificial death of Christ on the cross. God does not have to think about forgiveness or work through any emotional issues to forgive. You do not have to process your emotions about an event in order to forgive. When you forgive, you turn the person who offended you over to God. Jesus is demonstrating through this parable that you and I need to **make a decision in our minds** to forgive those who injure our souls.

Paul writes about what happens when the process of forgiveness is stalled. (Hebrews 12:15): "Exercise foresight and be on the watch to look [after one another] to see that no one falls back from and fails to secure God's grace (unmerited favor and spiritual blessing) in order that no root of resentment (rancor, bitterness, or hatred) shoots forth and causes trouble and bitter torment, and the many become contaminated and defiled by it." *A root of resentment, rancor, bitterness, or hatred* is the prison that is referred to in Matthew 18:34. God puts you in this prison because you are refusing to forgive your "brother from your heart his offenses" as God has forgiven you. Bitterness and hatred are emotions that distract and confuse, creating deception and evil desire. The evil desire is to seek revenge for the hurt you have experienced. Refusal to forgive opens a door point to demonic oppression. Spiritually speaking, you have agreed with Satan that the best course of action is to refuse to forgive. God does not refuse your evil desire, but God applies a consequence, which is a prison of bitterness which contaminates and defiles the people around you. You possess the key to getting out of your self-imposed prison. The key is forgiveness. People who have been hurt in different ways often believe that forgiveness is for their perpetrator. It is the opposite.

You do not wait for the perpetrator to apologize, compensate you financially, or do anything else that you are tempted to think might cancel their offense. You know you have forgiven when you no longer believe the perpetrator owes you something. Praise God! You got out of prison! In reality, forgiveness is primarily for the person who has been injured.

Forgiveness does not automatically lead to reconciliation. The perpetrator must repent of his hurtful behavior in order for there to be a full restoration of the relationship. God does not expect you to stay in an abusive relationship. The person who was offended must establish and maintain appropriate boundaries to prevent additional injury. Sin complicates relationships immensely.

The most important process issue about therapy is, does it work? Does it help people achieve their therapeutic goals? Does it produce change? Most therapists would say "yes." This is because therapists observe change, and clients often express gratitude for change. Cognitive behavioral therapy has many studies documenting its effectiveness.[174] But some clients do not have that outcome, even after two or three attempts at therapy. There are many reasons for failed therapies, including diverse therapeutic approaches, variation in skill level of therapists, boundary violations, etc. If you desire to review different types of therapy, there are many resources available.[175]

One study revealed 12% of male therapists and 2.6% of female therapists had sex with their clients.[176] In my opinion, that will always produce a failed therapy. Therapist/client sex eventually destroys trust even when the client desires a sexual relationship. Some male therapists have argued that sex with clients can be helpful to the client. They are deceived by their lust. It should be noted that many liability insurance companies refuse to insure therapists against liability claims for having sex with their clients.

In the following therapies, the **names of all clients** have been changed to protect the privacy of clients. Some content issues have also been changed to protect privacy. Clients have graciously given permission to use their stories to help others. Pseudonyms are used, which are taken from the books of the Bible. Detailed notes are taken about content when gathering history

---

174 www.webmd.com, Does Cognitive Behavioral Therapy Treat Depression

175 topics/therapy/psychotherapy-approaches, Different Approaches to Psychotherapy

176 www.psychologytoday.com, Sex with Patients Revisited

during meetings. Although process always determines outcome, content gives important information about process issues that will have to be addressed during treatment. When clients reveal their innermost thoughts and feelings, they expect the therapist to remember their stories.

The stories that follow are transformational in nature. This means the person was able to make at least some changes to achieve his therapeutic goals. Reading these stories might open possibilities for you to consider making changes in your story. **These stories may stimulate difficult emotions. If you find you are experiencing guilt, shame, hurt, sadness, disappointment, or other emotions that produce anxiety, depression, or other unwanted symptoms, you should stop reading immediately and seek professional counseling.**

Bibliotherapy, the provision of literature or other written resources, is the first 'tool" provided for clients. This begins with the disclosure agreement clients sign at the beginning of the first meeting. You may find a copy of this in the appendix. The first therapy illustrates process issues we have discussed earlier: distraction, confusion, deception, and how quickly trauma can alter perception in the mind.

Timothy, A Study of Distraction and Confusion

General History: Timothy was a fourteen-year-old white male who came from an intact family with one sister who was two years his senior. His father had a well-paying administrative position. His mother had a degree in education and did substitute teaching after Tim and his sister started school. The earliest experience Tim could remember from his life was his first day in kindergarten. He recalls his mother walking him to school that day. Tim denied any childhood abuse. He described his relationship with his father as good. His father enjoyed sports, and Tim excelled in sports. He described his mother as loving and outgoing. He attended church off and on with his parents. Tim was looking forward to high school. He wanted to try out for basketball. Tim had not had any experience with formal dates, mostly because he lacked wheels. He was attracted to girls but denied having a heartthrob at the time of our meeting. He was masturbating secretly to women he saw on television programs (fantasy lust). Timothy asked his parents if he could see a counselor. He did not tell them the reason initially. Surprisingly, they agreed without pressuring him for the reason. I met with Tim only five times.

Meeting # 1, Dialogue: His parents had planned a camping trip for the weekend with his cousin's family. They had only one child, Steven, who was a year older than Tim. Tim was looking forward to spending the weekend with Steven and his family.

Tim and Steven were sharing a tent while each couple had their own tent. His sister was at a sleepover with a girlfriend for the weekend. It was a hot night, so Tim was using his sleeping bag as a blanket instead of crawling inside and zipping it up. What follows is his account of what happened.

"I woke up when I felt a hand on the outside of my pajamas. Steven said, 'Don't say anything… just enjoy yourself.' I thought *I'm not going to enjoy myself because I'm not turned on by you.* Then he stimulated me sexually. I was really surprised at how good it felt. After a short time, I don't know how long, I had an orgasm. Steven said, 'Don't feel guilty about this…it was my idea.' Then he asked me to do the same for him. I said 'No.' Steven said, 'It's not a big deal…I just wanted you to know how much pleasure you can get.' I asked him if he was gay. He said, 'No, it was just about pleasure. Please don't tell your parents.'"

I complimented Tim for saying no to Steven. "That took a lot of courage."

Tim continued, "We had one more night in the tent together. I said, 'If anything happens again, I will tell my parents.' He said, 'No problem.' I did not sleep well that second night."

Tim told me he did not know if he could believe Steven's comment about not being gay. But Tim's primary concern was not about Steven. It was about his own sexuality. Because he had an orgasm with another guy, he thought he might be gay. **How quickly your mind alters perception.**

Homework: I gave him a small book to read, *The Bare Facts*, By Josh Mc Dowell. This is a primer on sexuality for teenagers. Tim was very anxious about his sexuality. This concern had replaced his normal thought life of sports, girls, and school. I was hoping I could get him to change his focus. I asked him to take opportunities to look at teenage girls/young women and make some notes about what attracted him.

Meeting # 2, Dialogue: At the second meeting, we reviewed his homework assignments. He said the book helped him realize how little he knew about sex. He said it wasn't any one thing about girls; rather, it was their overall shape that got his attention. He said his attraction to the opposite sex had not changed. He denied having any attraction or sexual thoughts about young men. He denied having any nightmares about his experience with Steven. He did not have any dreams about the sexual pleasure he experienced with Steven.

We discussed the criteria for abuse. He wrote them down. I asked him who had power in the relationship. He was uncertain. He said he was not afraid of Steven physically. I suggested that Steven had more experience in sexual matters, and that gave him an edge in the power dynamic. Also, he approached Tim at a vulnerable time. I suggested it was unlikely Steven was concerned about Tim. Rather, Steven stimulated Tim hoping Tim would do the same for him. Steven was really concerned about his own sexual gratification, not Tim's. Had Steven been concerned about Tim, he would have asked permission to pursue a sexual relationship. I asked Tim if he thought Steven was a perpetrator. Tim said he needed some time to think about that.

Homework: Examine the criteria for abuse and think about Steven's motivation. Abuse Criteria:

1. Abuse only occurs in relationships.
2. One person or group holds most of the power in the relationship/s.
3. The person or group with power gratify/s himself/themselves and is not concerned about how their behavior impacts others.

Meeting # 3, Dialogue: We focused on Tim's feelings about his experience with Steven. Tim could only identify the emotion of anger. I commented he had a perfect right to be angry. I expressed curiosity about what specifically he was angry about. He said, "I think Steven took advantage of me." I agreed. I asked what emotion that generated. He could only come up with anger. I asked him what emotion he felt about seeing a psychiatrist. He said it was embarrassing. I asked him to close his eyes and notice where he felt the embarrassment in his body. He said he felt it in his chest. I asked him to close his eyes again and see himself with Steven…then to check and see if he felt any embarrassment about his experience with Steven. After a minute or so, he nodded, "Yeah, the same feeling is there." I asked him to stay with the feeling and describe it to me. He said it felt sort of heavy. I asked him to stay with the feeling for a couple of minutes, describing to me what he was experiencing… to determine what would happen. After a short time, he said the feeling "kind of went away." Then I gave him a list of seven feelings (confusion, guilt, shame, fear, hurt, sadness, and disappointment) and asked if he could identify other feelings. In addition to anger and embarrassment, he identified hurt from the list. I thanked him for his willingness to work on, to process, his feelings. I asked him if he was angry with God because of this experience. He said, "I can't see this has anything to do with God." I agreed.

Homework: Work at staying in touch with the feelings underlying his anger about what happened with Steven.

Meeting # 4, Dialogue: We focused on boundaries. I defined a boundary and noted that abuse always involves a boundary violation. I explained three types of boundaries (physical, emotional, and spiritual) and asked Tim which boundaries Steven had violated. He picked "physical." I agreed. Then I asked what boundary was violated that produced his embarrassment and hurt. He seemed confused about the question. He finally said, "Physical." I said, "That is one way to look at it. Another possibility is one behavior by Steven violated all your boundaries, physical, emotional, and spiritual. He didn't say anything.

Homework: same as for meeting # 3

Meeting # 5, Dialogue: At the beginning of our fifth meeting, Tim said he reported to his parents the incident with Steven. His father called his brother, and there were some heated words on the telephone. Tim's uncle apparently thought it was just normal teenage stuff, and no one had to make a big deal about it…the same words Steven used. Then Tim said this would be our last meeting. He said, "I am no longer concerned about being gay." His parents did not want him to see a psychiatrist "forever." Near the end of our meeting, Tim thanked me. I noted his courage and strength in coping with everything and expressed appreciation for his doing homework. Finally, I said he was welcome to return any time there was a need.

Tim was not reading the Bible regularly, so it did not occur to him to search the Scriptures for a solution. The therapy was very short, which did not allow me to focus on spiritual issues. Some people are concerned that the therapist will drag out the treatment as long as possible for financial gain. His parents seemed to have this concern, or perhaps they were embarrassed about their son meeting with a psychiatrist. Therapies often end prematurely from the perspective of the therapist, but from the perspective of the client, they usually end on time. A third party, such as a parental couple or an insurance company paying for the therapy, complicates the termination process at times, as it did with Tim.

Discussion

Tim's life history suggested stability and relative freedom from trauma until the incident with Steven. A question to consider is: did Steven sexually abuse Tim? Steven was a year older than Tim, and apparently, his sexuality had been stimulated early and inappropriately. His age and his knowledge about sexual stimulation conferred power with Steven in his relationship with Tim. Remember our definition of abuse: 1) abuse only occurs in relationships among people, 2) one person or a group holds most of the power in the relationship/s, 3) the person or group holding power uses it to gratify himself/themselves without considering the impact on others.

So, let's consider how Tim's thinking and emotions were affected by Steven's behavior. Tim's thought life changed from school, sports, and girls to having doubts about his sexual identity. He was distracted and confused.

The change in his thought life was generating anxiety. The fear of man brings a snare (Proverbs 29:25). The snare for Tim was the thought of being gay.

Tim identified anger, embarrassment, and hurt, but mostly he was in touch with his anger. Notice how quickly he lost his emotional stability and experienced distraction and confusion about his sexuality. This process issue needs to be stated again and again, **How quickly your mind alters perception**. Tim had one same-sex experience, and he was immediately questioning his sexuality. People in the LGBT community know this will happen, which is why they are pushing the concept of gender fluidity and gender experimentation. As soon as evil makes its appearance, **demonic accusation/distraction, confusion,** and **deception** start. Accusation is a form of distraction.

The accusation Tim was struggling with: *You must be gay!* Intimacy with evil spawns a fertile field in the mind for demonic oppression. Tim's focus in life was altered to thinking about his experience with Steven. The mind of man abhors a vacuum. When Tim stopped thinking about the usual things in his life, the accusations of Satan poured into his mind to take their place. Instead of looking up to God, Tim was looking down at the accusations coming from the Kingdom of Satan (Psalm 7:13, Ephesians 6:16, Revelation 12:10). **How quickly your mind alters perception**. This process issue cannot be overstated. **Altered perceptions lead to thinking errors, and thinking errors contribute to poor life choices.**

So, you decide. Was Tim sexually abused? Write your answer in the space below, explaining your opinion.

____

____

____

____

____

A second question to consider is how Tim would cope with Steven's behavior. Here are several possibilities:

1. He could ignore what happened with Steven and continue with life as though nothing happened
2. He could inform his parents and ask them to intervene with his uncle
3. He could talk with other people or a professional counselor to get additional perspectives
4. He could search the scriptures to find what guidance they would provide.

5. He could report what happened to the police.
6. He could get into a physical fight with Steven to aggressively establish a new boundary.

Tim chose option three initially and later option two.

A third question is how Tim would determine if he was gay. He chose option three. Tim made good choices.

Now, consider Tim's experience from a more general perspective. Sexuality is usually awakened in the early teen years when the juices, primarily testosterone and estrogen, start to flow. These hormonal changes produce physical changes in both sexes referred to as puberty: in boys, the development of facial and pubic hair, voice change, and increased musculature; and in girls, development of pubic hair, breast enlargement, widening of the hips, and the onset of the menstrual cycle. It is important to distinguish sexual **awakening** from sexual **stimulation.** They are not the same. Awakening takes place inside the body, secondary to hormonal changes. Most sexual stimulation originates outside the body working through the senses of sight, sound, touch, and to a lesser extent, smell, and taste. The timing of **awakening** is a natural process orchestrated by God. The timing is generally perfect. The timing of stimulation is orchestrated by man, and as such, is often prone to error. God's general plan for sexuality is for most stimulation to begin at the time of marriage. However, there is an exception to this generalization. When the juices start flowing, boys begin to visually notice girls sexually, and girls notice boys. Young men notice the hourglass figure of young women/chicks, and girls notice the muscular development of young men/hunks (the terms chick and hunk may have a bit of mold on them).

Since God is omniscient as well as omnipresent, it seems very likely He anticipated young men and women noticing each other sexually. This attraction of the sexes to each other prepares the way for marriage at a later point in time. Sexual awakening and sexual stimulation are both process issues. They render the person prone to take their eyes off spiritual matters and put their eyes on sexual gratification. This leads to a decision point for every teenager. How am I going to treat sexuality going forward? Am I going to handle it, or will it handle me? This may often be more of an unconscious decision than a conscious one. Unconscious decisions often take us by surprise.

What happens when arousal and orgasm begin prior to marriage? Let's consider Tim and Steven. Tim and Steven both stimulated their sexuality prematurely through masturbation. Steven also engaged in oral sex with other male teenagers. Are there potential problems associated with premature stimulation of male and female sexuality? Here are some issues:

1. Control/mastery of sexual attraction
2. Risk of falling into pornography or other counterproductive sexual practices
3. Emotional injury
4. Comparisons of premarital sex and marital intimacy
5. Bonding
6. Spiritual injury/separation from God
7. Risk of developing sexually transmitted diseases.

Control and Mastery of Sexual Attraction: We live in a culture where the only way to avoid sexual stimulation is to stay in a darkened room by yourself with your eyes closed on intravenous feeding. Modesty in dress is a historical oddity. Sexual attraction is an issue in which everyone will experience the process of **temptation**. The definition of *tempt* is to entice or allure, to do something often regarded as unwise, wrong, or immoral. So, what is unwise, wrong, and immoral about looking at a beautiful woman or a handsome man? Nothing if it does not stimulate sexual thoughts or fantasies. What happens in your mind depends largely on what you are looking at. If you are looking at the person's face, particularly the eyes, your mind will focus on the verbal and non-verbal communication being expressed. You are focusing on the soul of a person.[177] If you are looking primarily at their sexual anatomy, you will be having sexual thoughts.

Jesus said this about our eyes: "The eye is the lamp of the body. So if your eye is sound, your entire body will be full of light. But if your eye is unsound, your whole body will be full of darkness. If then the very light in you [your conscience] is darkened, how dense is that darkness?" (Matthew 6:22-23). A person's conscience is darkened when he opens a door point to demonic oppression. At that point, you are entering the kingdom of Satan, where his purposes are to steal, kill, and destroy (John 10:10). It is very dark in the kingdom of Satan. Without light, you have no idea the direction you are taking or what you will stumble over. When you experience the fruits of darkness, you become a slave to darkness. "Do you not know that if you continually surrender yourselves to anyone to do his will, you are the slaves of him whom you obey, whether that be to sin, which leads to death, or to

177 A quote from Shakespeare, "The Eyes Are the Window to the Soul"

obedience which leads to righteousness (right doing and right standing with God)" (Romans 6:16)? If you do not master sexual attraction, it will master you. One morning you will awaken and discover that you are caught in the trap of sexual perversion discussed in the following paragraphs. It will be too late. It is very unlikely you will escape from this snare through your own efforts.

You will lose interest in the person who is with you and begin to think about that person as a sexual object. This prevents meaningful relationships. The **choice** you have is either to gratify yourself sexually through a feast of stimulation or learn to guard your eyes and mind by refusing to look at someone sexually. This is not easy. The battle for your soul will be fought in your mind (Matthew 11:12, Hebrews 12:1-4). You cannot defeat Satan by yourself (Genesis 3:1). You need to be empowered by the Holy Spirit to accomplish this (John 16:13-14, Acts 1:8, Romans 8:9, II Timothy 1:7).

Pornography or other Counterproductive Sexual Practices: Gratifying self and objectifying others leads to pornography, masturbation, prostitution, and other sexual practices that are never truly satisfying. They produce momentary pleasure but cannot produce satisfaction because they are performed alone or with a partner who is also struggling relationally. The content issues are unique to each person, but the process issue is often similar. Many of these strategies are a defense against relationship anxiety about having an age-appropriate, long-term, committed, heterosexual relationship. Their decisions about the choice of sexual object are often made unconsciously. Their decision allows them to control their anxiety while temporarily satisfying the drive for sexual pleasure.

Infants who do not experience a mother's loving touch develop failure to thrive. People who engage in these sexual practices do not thrive relationally or spiritually. They are separated from God in this area of life. They live a life of pleasure but may lack meaning and purpose in their life. Consider the anatomy of a man and a woman. It is a no-brainer to recognize that they are made for each other sexually. Everyone knows this, but fewer and fewer people are willing to say it.

Emotional Injury: Young men and women who have a series of heterosexual or homosexual relationships are simply seeking sexual gratification. They become insensitive to the emotional needs of their partner. Women are often pressured into a sexual relationship for a variety of reasons and experience hurt and disappointment when their "boyfriends" move on. This may impair their ability to experience sexual intimacy after marriage.

Comparisons of Premarital Sex with Marital Intimacy: The fallen nature of man has many different manifestations. Making comparisons is one of the more deadly aspects of our sin nature. It is the **process issue** driving the sin of envy, one of the infamous seven deadly sins. In Western culture, we compare everything: appearance, clothing, intelligence, homes, the vehicles we drive, our gardens, lawns, bank accounts—and yes—our sexual partner if we have had more than one. The problem with comparisons is they usually lead to discontent. If they do not lead to discontent, they lead to pride. Discontent leads to looking for a different relationship that we think will satisfy our desires. Pride produces faulty thinking: *I deserve something better than the relationship I have.* Discontent and pride produce affairs. Comparisons nearly always prevent healthy communication which could improve a relationship. Comparisons kill relationships. In our minds, we do not accept the thought that we killed our marriage relationship, so we have another word for it. We call it no-fault divorce. Deception and denial work well together to steal the blessings God desires for us.

When a woman discovers a boyfriend or husband is doing porn, she immediately compares herself to the pictures he is fantasizing about. She wonders, *why am I not able to satisfy this man's need for sexual pleasure?* She is hurt and angry but more likely to express her anger. This process is always destructive to the relationship! Anger wants to destroy the object of its wrath.

Bonding: Oxytocin, dopamine, and serotonin are released by the brain in both men and women during romantic encounters, including sexual union and orgasm. Oxytocin is the hormone released during breastfeeding by stimulation of the nipple. It stimulates the breast to release milk for the baby. It is thought to play a major role in bonding between mother and child. It seems to have a similar effect in romantic relationships. Oxytocin has been described as the love hormone and the cuddle hormone. It draws two people closer together. This appears to be true for same sex as well as heterosexual relationships.[178]

Having multiple sexual relationships prior to or after marriage generates a plethora of these bonds. This produces **confusion** about being in a long-term committed relationship. It weakens commitment. It produces **relationship dilution,** that is, difficulty experiencing satisfaction from a single, committed, heterosexual relationship. When something is diluted, it loses its strength or flavor. It becomes weaker, like adding too much water to Kool-Aid. When

178 www.livescience.com, Oxytocin, Facts About the Cuddle Hormone

Kool-Aid loses its flavor, you don't like it and don't drink it. You throw it out. Relationship dilution leads to a cycle of throwaway relationships. Is this what you want for your life? Do you want to model this pattern for your children? Do not allow yourself to be deceived.

Distraction >Confusion, > Deception > Evil Desire>Disobedience>Consequences

Getting hooked on sexual stimulation distracts from God's plan for your sexual life. It produces an evil desire for multiple sexual partners. Confusion and relationship dilution destroy commitment. Marriage fails without commitment because all relationships have ups and downs. Commitment sustains the marriage during the down times.

Spiritual Injury/Separation from God: Satan and the angels who followed him were thrown out of heaven as a result of their disobedience. All **sin** separates us from God. This process issue was established at the time of Satan's rebellion. We see the same process issue in the Garden of Eden at the time of Adam's rebellion. Adam and Eve were thrown out of the garden. God does not change (Malachi 3:6, Hebrews 13:8). Our disobedience and rebellion have the same result: we are separated from God. The reason for this is related to God's perspective on sin. God is holy, and sin/disobedience is viewed as rebellion. Rebellion, from God's perspective, is the same as witchcraft (I Samuel 15:1-23). God perceives the same demonic element in rebellion as exists in witchcraft.

It is difficult for people in modern Western culture to appreciate the implications of sin, especially witchcraft. Much of our understanding of witches comes from Harry Potter books and movies, the pagan religion of Wicca, or board games such as Dungeons and Dragons.[179] These three pursuits have one thing in common, they draw on demonic assistance or power in some way. However, they attempt to present themselves in a pleasant, entertaining, non-threatening fashion to the participant.

Every Christian is indwelt by Christ. When a Christian engages in sexual sin with another person, he joins Christ in that process because they become one body. The apostle Paul writes about this in First Corinthians 6:15-17: "Do you not see and know that your bodies are members, bodily parts, of Christ (the Messiah)? Am I therefore to take the parts of Christ and make

179 There are many articles, pro/con re: dungeons and dragons on the Internet, google <a christian evaluates dungeons and dragons>

[them] parts of a prostitute? Never! Never! Or do you not know and realize that when a man joins himself to a prostitute, he becomes one body with her? The two, it is written, shall become one flesh." (Genesis 2:24).

Sexual sin removes non-Christians farther from the presence of God and the direction that is provided by His Word. The heart of the non-believer becomes hardened, the word of God becomes meaningless, and he is prone to becoming a scoffer, a person who is hostile to God, a person who hates God.

Sexually Transmitted Diseases: No one wants a sexually transmitted disease. Although I have encountered several people who derived great pleasure from seeking sex to transmit a disease back to a different member of the sex from which it originated. Very few people are thinking about sexually transmitted diseases when they are having casual sex. Often, they are overwhelmed by sexual desire and sexual arousal. This may be true more often for men than women. The process of sexual desire/arousal distracts from the risk of STDs. The common deception is that sexually transmitted disease only happens to other people, or *I will take a chance*. This deception is reinforced by organizations such as Planned Parenthood that teach using condoms will prevent the transmission of sexual disease. Actually, the use of condoms only provides greater protection against sexually transmitted diseases that are passed by genital fluids, such as gonorrhea, chlamydia, trichomoniasis, and HIV infection. It does not provide absolute protection against any STD. Most men do not like using condoms as it diminishes their pleasure. They will lie about their intention to use one.

It is estimated that two-to-five percent of condoms fail, most often due to human error in application.[180] Moreover, condoms do not provide any protection from STDs that are passed from skin-to-skin contact, such as genital herpes, human papillomavirus (a cause of cervical cancer), syphilis, and chancroid. For these reasons, practicing casual sex places your health and future sexual relationships in marriage at risk. Some sexually transmitted diseases can infect a fetus in utero or at the time of delivery; for example, gonorrhea can produce blindness and other infections.[181]

Wisdom Guiding Sexual Development: A simple model of sexual response is divided into four parts: attraction/desire, arousal/stimulation/excitement, orgasm, and resolution. The following remarks are confined to

---

180 www.livescience.com, Safety First, Fourteen Common Condom Use Errors

181 For a complete review of STDs that can be transmitted to your baby in utero go to the Center for Disease Control website.

attraction and desire as they are the important process issues for our discussion.

Each of the phases above is a result of different degrees and types of stimulation. The attraction may occur very early in child development. Remember my attraction to Mary Beth in second grade? I was attracted to her pretty face, softness, and pleasant personality. There was no sexual desire because I had not experienced a sexual awakening yet. Attraction is greatly magnified when the hormones begin to flow. This leads to sexual desire. Other terms for sexual desire are sex drive, sexual urges, sexual thoughts and talk, longing for sexual activity, and sexual appetite.

After sexual awakening, adolescent boys and girls begin to experience sexual attraction/desire. Desire is one of the words used in Scripture that has diametrically-opposed meanings. Godly desire is inspired by our Heavenly Father, while evil desire is inspired by Satan. The purpose of Godly sexual desire is threefold: 1) to cement the bond or soul tie between a man and woman through sexual union after marriage, 2) to become one flesh through the creative process of having children, and 3) to experience sexual pleasure in the context of marriage. All three of these purposes work together to create and maintain the family. God's plan is for teenage men and women to sublimate their sexual desire by practicing agape love in opposite-sex relationships. In this context, the word *sublimate* means: to divert the energy of a (sexual or other biological impulse) from its immediate goal to one more socially acceptable and morally correct.

Practicing agape love prior to marriage is what prepares men and women of any age for a marital relationship because it is agape love that sustains marriages. Agape love is sacrificial love. The man does what is best for his wife...what builds her ups and strengthens her. He honors her. She realizes his eyes are for her only. She reciprocates. He leads, but they also learn to submit to each other. Remember my relationship with Linda. My relationship with her continued for 18 months, which is a long time for a high school relationship, even in 1960. I was not aware of the scriptures on agape love. I was intensely aware of enjoying being with her at the moment and sharing those moments with her. I desired to do things to strengthen our relationship. When I was with her, my focus was completely on her, and other things faded into the landscape. She reciprocated. That is what the Scripture is referencing in Genesis 2:18 in regard to God making a suitable helper/companion for Adam. We were practicing a form of agape love without any knowledge of the theology.

A criticism often heard about waiting to have sex until marriage is something like "Christians don't know how to have fun." That is a major deception. It is important to recognize God is not a prude. Read Dillow's commentary, *Solomon on Sex*, in chapter four of the Song of Solomon. It describes the consummation of their marriage on their wedding night. The verb *consummate* means to bring to a state of perfection, to fulfill, to bring to a state of completion, as in an agreement. In the last verse of chapter four, his bride, Shulammite, says to Solomon, "Oh, I pray that the (cold) north wind and the (soft) south wind may blow upon my garden, that its spices may flow out [in abundance for you in whom my soul delights]. Let my beloved come into his garden and eat its choicest fruits." My commentary on that verse: the cold north wind is stimulating, but the south wind is often soft and gentle. Shulammite is saying to Solomon, "Stimulate me sexually in a gentle, loving fashion so that I am prepared for you to come inside me where you will be ravished, where you will experience the joy of sexual union with me." The word *ravish* means to transport with strong emotion, especially joy. Do you want a joyful and perfect end to your wedding day? Follow the plan God has for you, and you and your partner will both be ravished every time you make love, not only on the day you are joined in marriage.

Grand Larceny: The word *ravish* has other meanings: to seize and carry off by force, to rape or violate, to rob or plunder. The words *rob* and *rape* are familiar to us. We understand their meanings. The word *violate* has the following meanings: to break or infringe upon a law, promise, or instruction; to disturb rudely, such as to violate someone's privacy; to assault sexually; to treat irreverently or disrespectfully, such as to violate a church. It is derived from a Latin word *root,* which means to treat with violence. Do not treat sexuality irreverently, disrespectfully, or violently.

The word *plunder* has the following meanings: to rob of goods or valuables by open force; to rob or fleece; to take by pillage, robbery, or fraud. Satan's plan is to distract young men and women from agape love and focus on erotic/sensual love because he knows that erotic love will never sustain a marriage. Satan's purposes are to **steal**, kill, and destroy (John 10:10). Satan wants to steal the beautiful sexual relationship a man and woman are intended to have in marriage, a relationship of knowing and being known, of giving and receiving love. This is grand larceny!

After marriage vows, the other phases of sexual response, arousal, and orgasm, are to begin. The age of marriage can vary tremendously depending on the man, woman, and the culture. Some never develop the level of maturity to sustain a marriage relationship. This is reflected in divorce rates of approximately 50 percent. A strategy for Christians to consider in selecting a mate is to ask their friend's pastor for a reference prior to engagement. For a non-Christian, a similar strategy is to ask the opinion of several friends about the "marriage potential" of your future mate. The point is to get some objective counsel prior to engagement and marriage. It is true that love is blind.

Cultural Trends: We live in a culture where sexual education and stimulation are gradually changing in favor of earlier and earlier onset. This took off in the 1960s with the onset of the sexual revolution. At the time of this writing, there is a movement in the educational system of the United States to begin the introduction of sexual education in kindergarten. This is presented to the public as comprehensive sexual education. In Washington State, comprehensive sexual education in schools is mandatory as a result of state legislation passed in 2020. In other states, it may happen as a result of an administrative rule from the office of the superintendent of public instruction.

The appropriate time for sexual education is when sexuality is in the process of being awakened, at the time of puberty. Introducing the subjects of sexuality and gender issues in kindergarten steals the innocence of our children. It forces them to begin an unwanted premature journey to adulthood.

The concept of starting sex ed in kindergarten or earlier has its origins in an organization known as SIECUS, which is an acronym for the sexuality, information, and education council of the United States. SIECUS was founded in 1964 by Mary Calderone, a former medical director of Planned Parenthood. Planned Parenthood is an organization that promotes a culture of death through abortion. At the time of this writing, Planned Parenthood has videos on its website that claim the use of condoms prevents sexually transmitted diseases. The Centers for Disease Control has this statement on their website about the theoretical and empirical basis for protection from condoms: "Condoms can be expected to provide different levels of protection for various STD\s, depending upon differences in how the diseases or infection are transmitted." Planned Parenthood appears to be concealing information regarding risk that is important for individuals who are sexually active. This suggests they are promoting some agenda other than the sexual health of the audience who is watching their videos. What do you think that that agenda would be? Write your answer in the space below.

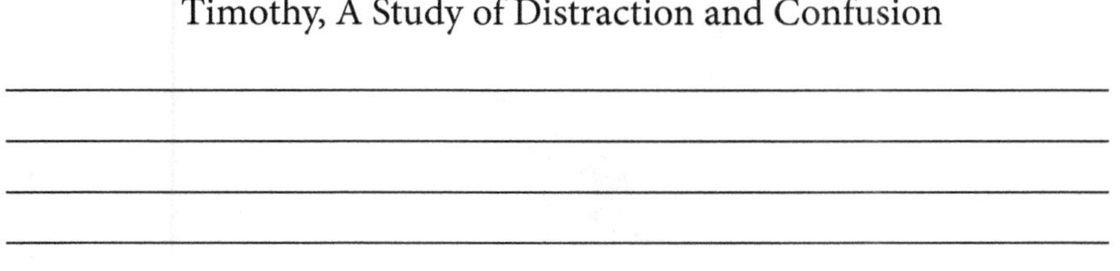

God's Plan for Sexuality: Attraction to the opposite sex increases, and sexual desire begins *after* sexual awakening. It is God's plan for sexual arousal and orgasm to be delayed until marriage. Sexual attraction is primarily the result of visual and tactile stimulation, which may be reinforced by peer talk. When sexuality and sexual pleasure are stimulated inappropriately before sexual awakening or marriage, or in an inappropriate way such as masturbation, same-sex stimulation, premarital sex, and pornography, it leads to dysfunctional patterns of sexual gratification in adolescence and adulthood. These patterns often later produce marital dissatisfaction and divorce.

Sexual union and marriage should be delayed until the man and woman are emotionally and spiritually prepared for a committed relationship. Sexual activity prior to marriage is associated with the risks noted above, including **relationship dilution**. If agape love is not occurring prior to marriage, it is unlikely to magically appear after your wedding day. There is an old saying, "A wedding does not a marriage make." Follow the plan that God has for marriage, and you will find a relationship that grows stronger, richer, and more passionate as the relationship matures.

The next therapy focuses on coping with the pain of loss. The concept of meditating with Jesus is introduced. The chapter about Ruth illustrates the process of grieving and the obstacles encountered in the process of recovery.

Ruth, Recovery from Abuse and Loss

Meetings 1, 2, 3, Personal History: Ruth was in the autumn of her life when she decided to seek counseling for long-standing depression. She had an arthritic condition of uncertain origin, and she wanted to know how much depression was contributing to her arthritis and inability to function.

She was depressed during childhood, and her mother arranged for psychiatric counseling. She remembers the psychiatrist saying nothing. Ruth said nothing in response. Finally, Ruth asked the psychiatrist how she, the psychiatrist, was doing. The psychiatrist said nothing. After five meetings, Ruth stopped counseling.

Her parents divorced secondary to her father having an affair when Ruth was in grade school. She and her mother moved to be closer to her mother's parents. "The house was depressing; I did everything I could to get out of it." Her mother never dated or remarried, and she constantly worried about Ruth's father sending their monthly check for financial support. Ruth remembers being overweight, having low self-esteem, and being afraid during her childhood. She was sexually molested by a male cousin on a single occasion. It was sexual touching, but she thought she would get pregnant. She did not report it to anyone. She had suicidal thoughts as a teen but never made an attempt. In high school, she was a supergirl in clubs, band, drama, and cheerleading. Her activities kept her out of the house, but she continued to feel alone and depressed.

She denied suicidal thoughts/plans at the time of our meetings. She recalled her worst depression was during her first marriage at age 19 and after she married her second husband at age 32. Eventually, she discovered her first husband was having multiple affairs, and she divorced him. Both husbands were several years her senior. She married her second husband because of the strength she received through her relationship with him. Neither husband communicated well. Her depression as an adult was associated with a pervasive sense of hopelessness, increased sleep (an escape), weight gain, low energy, and mood that was down from the time she awakened until sleep. Her self-talk was accusatory; "You are fat, no fun, unable to do anything right." At one point, an M.D. diagnosed her bipolar because of her father's suicide and two nephews with that diagnosis. She was prescribed "heavy meds" but did not tolerate them. She stopped them. She states she was depressed most of the time until an M.D. prescribed risperidone a couple of years before our first meeting. Risperidone improved her mood but did not resolve her depression. My formulation? Her depression was due to adverse childhood experiences, multiple traumas, and not biological in origin.

She had received the "gift of faith" many years earlier. She stated prior to that point she considered herself to be "amorphous…lacking a core." She described a constant prayer life but little study in the Bible because she did not like to read. She was willing to discuss spiritual issues as they applied to her presenting problems.

Ruth was spiritually hungry because she found the Scriptures confusing, was uncertain if God kept His promises, and was "mad at God" for allowing her to think she was pregnant for months after her childhood sexual abuse.

Commentary: It is difficult to convey the impact abuse and loss have on the life of a child. It affects each of the five domains of humanity: thinking, emotion, behavior, physiology, and spirituality. Abuse and loss steal the normal life a child should have and replaces it with a life no one wants (John 10:10). As you read the stories of Ruth and Abigail, look for problems in each of these domains.

Portions of our meetings were spent discussing questions she would bring relating to these and other spiritual issues. Here are three strategies used to address the kinds of questions that were bothering Ruth:

1. Pointing to scriptures relating to her question,
2. Telling stories, therapeutic metaphors similar to her situation, which contained a solution to her question, and
3. Introducing Ruth to a more intimate relationship with Christ.

In reviewing Ruth's therapy, you will see that all three strategies were used at different points in time. The most-helpful strategy was offering an opportunity for a more intimate relationship with Jesus. Of course, all three of these strategies work toward that purpose. I met with her 59 times over 24 months.

Meeting # 4: Dialogue: I suggested the short answer to her presenting question about depression contributing to her arthritis was, yes, it probably is contributing. But I could not give her an estimate of how much it was contributing. I suggested there were other issues that needed attention which might diminish her depression…then we would have a better understanding of the dynamics. At this meeting, I gave her the handout to read titled *Overcoming Depression and Anxiety*. You may review this in the appendix.

Homework: Review the handout on overcoming depression.

Meeting # 5: Dialogue: She stated she had not read the handout. We discussed it during this meeting. Homework: What area would she prefer to start working on in therapy?

Meeting # 6: Dialogue: Since she had indicated on two separate occasions that she did not like to read, I introduced her to the process of meditating with Jesus. Prior to the first meditation, three scriptures are reviewed which provide a rationale for meditating. There are many more than three, but these are sufficient for most clients. They are John 14:21, Colossians 2:3, and Revelation 3:20. In John 14:21, Jesus is speaking about manifesting Himself to people who love Him. The Greek word for manifest is *emphanidzo*. It has several meanings, but the one most pertinent is **"to make visible and present oneself to the sight of another."**[182] In Colossians 2:3, Paul writes, "In him all the treasures of [divine] wisdom (comprehensive insight into the ways and purposes of God) and [all the riches of spiritual] knowledge and enlightenment are stored up and lay hidden." In Revelation 3:20, Jesus is speaking, inviting "anyone" to listen to Him, to open the door of his heart, and to have fellowship with Him. These three scriptures together suggest spending time meditating with Jesus may provide healing and direction in the process of recovery.

Ruth did not express any questions or reservations about meditating. I asked her to close her eyes and visualize me and to let me know if she was able to accomplish this. She said "Yes." At this point, I asked her to visualize Jesus and I gave her a couple minutes. After she indicated seeing Jesus in her mind's eye, I asked her to "look into His eyes and see the love He has for you, experience his love." I said nothing for a couple of minutes. Then, I said, "Notice the peace that comes from being in His presence." She said nothing. Then I asked her if she was experiencing anxiety or depression. She said, "No." I suggested, "You are at peace because your focus is on Christ rather than on things that come from the world." Things that come from the world include abuse and other stresses.

182 Word Wealth, The Spirit-filled Life Bible

When it was time to finish the meditation, I asked Ruth to take as much time as she needed to thank Jesus (Psalm 116:17), praise Him for the opportunity of fellowshipping with Him (Hebrews 13:15), and gradually return to my office by looking around and reorienting herself.

After reorientation, the client is asked to share the nature of the experience as they are comfortable doing so. Ruth said it was a good experience for her. Clients generally are willing to discuss their meditation as they like to share their progress and relate how Jesus interacted with them. Most meditations in the office last 15 to 20 minutes. At home, they might be longer…or shorter..

Were you surprised to learn Ruth did not experience significant anxiety or depression while meditating? Instead, she experienced peace. She looked up at God, and her mood changed. Wow! For years, Ruth had been under the influence of a spirit of fear (I Timothy 1:7). She was afraid to experience sadness and disappointment from her childhood. Think about the implications of experiencing peace for treatment of various psychological maladies, including substance abuse. Substance abuse is a defense against painful emotions and depressing, stressful thoughts and accusations from Satan. The substance is used to disconnect from these thoughts and feelings. Meditating with Christ is a healthier strategy to cope with emotional pain and the accusations coming from the kingdom of Satan. There is more information about meditating with Jesus in the appendix.

Meditation can be used to correct thinking errors, facilitate grieving, change behaviors, and grow stronger in faith. These are big steps forward from using marijuana, cocaine, methamphetamine, heroin, or prescription meds to cope with grief.

Homework: to practice meditating with Jesus. She followed through with that suggestion. She meditated with Jesus at home or in my office for the next 22 months.

Meetings # 7-9, Dialogue: We focused on current issues in her life, including her weight, her husband's health, and many spiritual questions she wanted to discuss. She experienced confusion re: things she read in the Bible. For example, she thought if she prayed to Jesus, she was neglecting God the Father, a thinking error. She wanted to lose weight. I suggested Daniel's diet, confession of poor eating habits, exercise, daily reading of Proverbs 23:1-3, and not eating anything at mealtime until she had a conversation with God about what and how much she should have. She liked these suggestions but, at later meetings, indicated difficulty following through. She did not lose significant weight during her therapy.

Homework: Implement the suggestions noted above, continue meditating.

Meeting # 10: Dialogue: She spoke about her mother's health. "I saw her daily the last year she was dying. I felt I should be doing more. I felt nothing when she died… a little sadness. What I miss the most is her unconditional love." Ruth added, "I had no emotion at the time of my parents' divorce. I fear being emotional." There were no tears during this discussion.

Homework: Continue meditating with Jesus.

Meeting # 11, Dialogue: She meditated again with Christ. The focus was on love and peace. Near the end of the meditation, I asked her to request Jesus to take her to a place and spend time with her there so she could get to know Him better. Post meditation, she said, "That was lovely." She did not provide detail. I did not ask for detail because it was likely to be content related.

Homework: Meditate on God's love at home.

Meeting # 12: Dialogue: She described her meditations at home. She stated, "I'm having trouble seeing His face. I do well with His holding me. I talk with Him. It's comforting and relaxing. I love it." She meditated again in the office. I asked her to allow Jesus to pick an experience she associated with fear and describe her fear to Jesus until it was replaced with peace. She said, "I have no fear because I'm with Jesus. I have been working on it already." She began to cry (the first tears I had witnessed) and opened her eyes prior to my asking her to end the meditation. She closed them again at my request and started to talk about missing her mother. Her tears became a stream. I asked her to put her tears in Jesus' bottle (Psalm 56:8). Post meditation, she said, "I'm shaking inside…the emotions."

Homework: Continue to meditate at home.

Meeting # 13, Dialogue: She commented about our last meeting, saying, "I had a rush of wanting to cry." She said, "I don't cry at home because my husband will not hold me. He does not know how to help with my sadness." She also talked about being nervous regarding all the promises that the Bible makes. "Are they true?" I responded she would need to discover that for herself.

Meeting # 14, Dialogue: Ruth talked about medical issues and…need for orthopedic surgery. Homework: Review the exercise program "Aging Backwards."

Meeting # 15, Dialogue: She said, "I figured something out…I've been carrying a heavy sadness with me for years. It has prevented normal function." Later, she said, "After my cousin molested me, I was silent for a whole year. I thought I might be pregnant." She was angry with God for not taking that thought away from her. She said, "God is flawed." I responded that God "does not swoop down on a white horse to take all our troubles… rather He invites us into a relationship with Him and through repentance, the study of His word, and relationship with Him, He works in our heart to heal our wounds" (Psalm 30:1-12, II Corinthians 7:10, Revelation 3:20).

Ruth continued. "It never occurred to me to tell [my mother] about my cousin. My mother never had time for me. She was so busy working to support us. Other people were getting more from her than I was."

My commentary: One of the first things to repent of is our **natural inclination to depend on our mind** to protect us instead of God. Depending totally on our mind generates defense mechanisms and simultaneously opens door points to demonic influence. Every one of our defense mechanisms diminishes our ability to depend on God and reinforces our habit of depending on self. Self gets bigger, and God gets smaller in our minds and in our lives.

Anger toward God is a defense mechanism, as it covers the disappointment people experience when God does not do what they expect and hope, i.e., protect them. For people who are so angry they abandon God, it might be helpful to ask, "How can you be angry at a person who does not exist?" Or asking the client to consider the implication of being angry with God.

Ruth thought she could not go to her mother to talk about being molested. God did not stop her perpetrator. She thought she had no other resources. She was confused. She did not realize her being molested was the result of evil desire on the part of her cousin. Being molested came from Satan, not God. In her confusion, she concluded God was flawed. This was a thinking error.

Distraction>confusion>deception>evil desire>sin>consequences

Ruth was distracted by being molested. She was confused about God. She allowed the thought, *God is flawed*, to camp out in her mind. This deception created an evil desire to criticize and distrust God. The consequence was to delay taking her sadness and disappointment to God and to struggle with depression and anxiety in her adult life.

At this meeting, she discovered the answer to her presenting question: her depression was contributing to her inability to function. She discovered this on her own. Self-discovery is always preferable to interpretations by a therapist. Self-discovery contributes positively to self-esteem. Interpretations, even when correct, imply the therapist is clever and the client is not. Many interpretations miss the mark.

Homework: Continue to meditate.

Meetings 16-29: Over the next 15 meetings, we focused on Ruth grieving losses: childhood, her relationship with her mother and father, lack of intimacy in both marriages, and other content issues: Ruth said, "During summer visits with my father, he left me at bars while he chased women. I **hurt everywhere** a year after I married my second husband. He put me down constantly. I never saw worth in myself. I have no core except through my husband. He was solid…representing security for me."

Commentary: I thought her comment about hurting everywhere might explain her undiagnosed arthritis… emotional pain manifesting as arthritis. I did not say anything. She had already concluded her depression was contributing to her inability to function.

At another meeting, she said, "Jesus is my Father now" (Psalm 27:10, 68:5, John 14:18).

Commentary: God is willing to be your Father if you will allow it. She did much of her grief work while meditating with Jesus in the office or at home or just thinking about her losses during the week. While meditating, Jesus showed her the sadness He felt when these things were happening to her. She "followed Him" (my quotes) by allowing herself to feel sad. She continued to fear being emotional for many more meetings but worked at it consistently despite her **desire** to avoid emotional pain. During these 15 meetings, I gave her tools to facilitate her work. The book, "The Difference a Father Makes," by Ed Tandy McGlasson, helped her appreciate how a loving father relates to boys and girls growing up. Reading it facilitated her recognition of what it meant to lose her father to another woman and later to suicide. Reading it also facilitated more grief work. I gave her the Doorbell Exercise, the Father's Love Letter, and the mirror exercise as tools to use at home. These are available for review in the appendix.

Homework: Continue exchanging old defenses with recovery tools and her relationship with Jesus. Think about psychological defenses being tools of Satan to draw you into his sphere of influence. They delay or prevent dependence on Jesus.

Meeting # 30, Dialogue: She provided additional detail re: life with her single mother. "I'm remembering more of what it was like in the house. "Mom lived in a state of fright. She was not demonstrative. Living in a home with so much sadness… we did not talk. All my business with school activities was my way of coping with the sadness at home. I wanted a new coat… mom said no… I cut off the bottom of her coat. I picked at my finger. I ate out the inside of cakes. I never thought it bothered me not having a father, but it affected me in different ways: I always had to have a man in my life, yet I was uncomfortable around them; I thought men were no good, I thought I was bad, I saw women as victims, I saw myself as a victim, it was difficult to enjoy intimate sex with my husband, my husbands were always many years older than me. I see all these past experiences in a distant kind of way."

My commentary: She had repressed some of these experiences, and they were slowly returning as she continued to grieve. As the memories returned, she would process them with Jesus.

Homework: continue to meditate.

Meeting # 31, Dialogue: She said, "I cried this week thinking of my past." She was having trouble with the mirror exercise. She forgot to work on it or misunderstood the instructions. When she did do it, she did not believe what it said about God's relationship with her.

Homework: Continue practicing the Father's Love Letter and Mirror Exercise.

Meetings # 32-35, Dialogue: Much of our meeting time was spent with my encouraging her to continue the process of change which had started.

Homework: Continued from above.

Meeting # 36, Dialogue: She said, "I am ready to give up." She cited the stress associated with several relatives and friends who were not doing well in life, saying, "I'm surrounded by so much sadness…taking it on."

Commentary: I responded by talking about my work, "I am surrounded by hurt and sadness in the office eight hours a day, and I do not take it on" (Romans 12:15). "It does not belong to me. It's not my hurt and sadness. It's a boundary issue. I weep with my clients when they are weeping and rejoice with them when they are rejoicing. I leave it all at the office. Do not take what does not belong to you."

She continued. "I was born to be depressed. I have heaviness in my heart.

I take it to Jesus…but I am weary. I don't love me. How can you be a God of love and allow something like the holocaust? The Father's Love Letter ignited my disbelief."

Commentary: I observed, "You are not doing the mirror exercise. It would help you learn to see yourself the way God sees you." I reflected to her a summary of what she said and added, "You refuse to take your deep pain to Him. God is not flawed." Then we explored Job 33:13-14 and Lamentations 3:31-37, the essence of which is this: God speaks repeatedly; He is sovereign in all things; man disregards what God says; God is compassionate; He does not explain His decisions; man should not complain about consequences for his sin. Then I shared the ups and downs from a story in my own life and how God worked it out over several years. God is patient with us. We need to learn to wait on God.

Homework: Consider the patience of God, be patient with yourself and with God, and persevere.

Meeting # 37, Dialogue: She started by saying her meditation on Lamentations 3:31-37 "solved the holocaust issue for me," then she added, "I have accepted that God is not flawed. I have accepted that God is sovereign. I was arrogant [**pride**] last week."

Commentary: I responded, "Your faith has grown in the last week." Homework: Meditate at home.

Meetings #38-44, Dialogue: Review of several past content issues stimulated more grief work. She spent a lot of time during meditations having Jesus hold her, simply experiencing His love.

Meeting # 45, Dialogue: During meditation with Jesus, she worked at processing the time she and her mother left her father after the divorce… they were taking a bus trip to their new life. I suggested she ask Jesus to "help you remember what you were thinking." She said, "I'm sitting with Jesus on the bus. There was the three of us. I wish I had known that He was with me then." I suggested she tell Jesus what she was thinking about leaving her daddy. She responded, "I can't remember times with Daddy. Jesus says, 'I was there with you.' He says that over and over." I instructed, "Ask Jesus what is preventing you from engaging?" She responded, "Avoidance of sadness and pain at all costs."

Homework: Continue meditating on her relationship with her father.

Meetings 46-51, Dialogue: Her husband is terminally ill. She worked intermittently on processing her relationship with her father, grieving losses for the next seven meetings. When she expressed fatigue from grief work, we addressed current issues. She forgave her father at the end of this series of meetings.

Homework: None. She was supporting her husband as he was terminally ill. Meeting 52, Her husband passed. She worked on processing that loss.

Homework: Take your grief to Jesus.

Meeting 55, Dialogue: She said, "I see the difference between grief and depression. I think my depression has lifted. I think it is lifted because I am released from my father. That heavy cloud is gone. I'm still grieving the loss of my mother." Note: the client is the final arbiter of how much grief work is necessary for recovery. At times, Ruth would choose to avoid grieving, and at other times she would choose to pursue it. Having a choice in this regard indicates significant progress. **Grief work and forgiveness** are necessary keys to unlocking the doors of depression. Each client does this at a pace unique to them.

Ruth was starting to make plans to move. She experienced some anxiety regarding her depression recurring, but it did not. We had only a few more meetings before she moved. She continued to meditate with Jesus, but now she was meditating on things happening in the present. The process of change was working.

Homework: She will determine what she needs to work on.

Meeting # 59, Dialogue: At our last meeting, almost exactly two years after beginning, I encouraged her to use the tools now in her possession to help with the move and the adjustment to her new life. I had telephone contact with her for 24 months after her move. During these calls, she indicated she was continuing to grieve losses from years earlier. She was doing well at the time of my last contact.

Discussion

Ruth's therapy was focused primarily on assisting her in reconnecting to feelings of sadness. There was one loss after another in her life: her father, childhood, mother, and two spouses. She was phobic about experiencing the pain of these losses. Her willingness to have Jesus share her grief was a tremendous asset that facilitated her recovery work. People who meditate with Jesus or take their lives to Him in prayer experience the "peace of God which surpasses all understanding" (Philippians 4:6-7). So…don't attempt to understand the peace referenced in the last sentence. You must experience the peace of God in order to understand it! The peace of God "guards your heart and mind" in a way that allows you to encounter the pain of loss in a healthy way without further injury to your soul. When you draw close to God, He will draw close to you (James 4:8-9). Ruth had experienced distance in her relationship with God for several reasons noted in her history. Consider all the obstacles Ruth had to overcome in order to strengthen her relationship with God. Satan will provide an endless list of reasons for being upset with God or not going to Jesus. A wise person once made this observation: "While you wait for God to answer, Satan is quick to speak." Satan speaks accusations that keep you depressed or anxious while separating you from God.

Meditating with Jesus was a major tool for Ruth in her recovery work. It helped close the distance between herself and God. It gave her a venue where she could experience the peace of God while at the same time pursuing the processes of reconnecting to feelings of sadness, grieving her losses, and forgiving people who were responsible for hurts in her life. After the first meditation, it is often helpful for the client to repeat the experience of focusing on the love of Christ. This can be facilitated during a meditation in the office by asking the client to have Jesus put His arms around the client and hold the client while experiencing His love. Some meditations may need repetition, such as experiencing the love of Jesus and grieving losses. Grieving is a process. When someone is stuck in therapy, meditation can be helpful to demonstrate a path forward. For example, if a client is having difficulty feeling sadness about a trauma, have the client ask Jesus to show the client what emotion He is experiencing about the trauma. Then ask the client to follow Jesus by **experiencing the same emotion while keeping the client's focus on Jesus.** Everything can be taken to the process of meditation that would ordinarily be addressed in conventional talk therapy: thinking errors, emotional blocks, behaviors, physiology, and spirituality, whatever has been impaired as a result of prior injury to the soul. For example, if a client is having difficulty gaining spiritual insight into a thinking error, have the client ask Jesus to share what He thinks about the belief of the client or what the client should learn from the experience. **This does not mean it is necessary for the client to revisit the trauma;** Jesus simply relates His perception of what the client needs to understand or do.

During meditation, the therapist says very little because the client needs time to accomplish whatever recovery work **Jesus is facilitating**. While the client is doing his recovery work, the therapist is observing and praying for the client. The client can be instructed to let the therapist know when he is finished with something and ready to move on. At the end of meditating, time is often allowed for the client to spend some time with Christ just "hanging out." These are always unique and special times for the client. In the therapy detailed next, you will see how Abigail experiences these principles through her meditations.

From a global perspective, Ruth's therapy consisted of addressing her thinking errors about God and making a decision to use her relationship with Jesus to give up her old defenses in order to grieve many losses. My formulation of her depression was reactive in nature. I suspected she would experience fewer depressive symptoms as she accomplished these processes.

This raises an important question: Is there support in Scripture for the concept that we generate our own "depression" as well as other symptoms by using defenses we develop to cope with evil? Quotation marks are around depression since Strong's Exhaustive Concordance does not have a single reference to that word in either the Old or New Testament.

In the chapter on the D words, in the account of Cain's jealousy toward Abel, we learned that what we think of as depression is really deception that comes from looking down to the kingdom of Satan rather than up towards the kingdom of God. When God speaks to Cain about his anger, a better, more literal translation for Genesis 4:6 is not "Why do you look sad and depressed and dejected?" but rather "Why has your face/countenance fallen?" When people look down, they experience restrictions in various areas of their life: their thought life, emotional life, behavior, physiology, and relationship with God. When Cain looked down into the kingdom of Satan, the devil was looking back at him and saying something like, "No more joy for you, buster. You belong to me now. You screwed up big time!" However, it seems likely the only thing Cain experienced in his mind is the last part, the accusation, "You screwed up big time." Satan is laughing every time his spiritual cash register goes, "Ka-ching." Satan is always the accuser. The problem for Cain was that **he could not see the devil looking him in the eye.** And, of course, **that is the same problem for you, Tim, Ruth, and me.**

What support does Scripture lend to the above hypothesis? In Psalms 42 and 55, King David writes about his state of mind in response to his experience of intimacy with evil. Spurgeon postulates it is the evil of being driven from Jerusalem, being unable to worship in the temple, and being ridiculed for putting his trust in God. This happened twice to David. The first time, he was a young man when he was forced to leave by his jealous father-in-law, Saul. The second time, he was in the twilight of his life when his son Absalom rebelled and attempted to replace David as King. Spurgeon suggests both Psalms are related to Absalom's rebellion.[183]

In Psalm 42:5, David writes, "Why are you cast down, O my inner self? And why should you moan over me and be disquieted within me?" David is inquiring about what is happening to him. Making an inquiry about the reason we are not doing well is an excellent idea. It could be practicing the process of discernment. It could be having a consultation with an M.D. about the cause of chest pain or some other symptom. Or it might be entering the process of therapy. David is tearful in mourning yet not clinically depressed! He is not depressed because his focus Is on God. He **is looking up while coping with his present circumstances.**

Consider the following commentary on Psalm 42:5 by 17th-century Presbyterian pastor Christopher Love: "In our translations the words are translated and rendered passively 'why are thou cast down?' Yet in the original, they are rendered actively, reading 'why bowest (or pressest) thou down thyself, my soul? And why tumultest thou against me?'"[184] The English language 375 years ago is a bit dated. It might read something like this, "Why is my mind bowing down and why is it, my mind, creating turmoil within me and against me?" Please think about these words. David is saying **he is creating the turmoil** in his own mind. The implication is that it is David's responsibility to change the thoughts and emotions in his mind. He is not pleading with his persecutors to stop. He is not blaming the people who are persecuting him. Perhaps he realizes that because of their evil desire, they will not stop. You and I might find ourselves in the same position as David. For that reason, it is important to understand David's response.

An important question to ask is, to whom is David's mind bowing down? Answer, Satan. When we bow down to Satan or keep our gaze fixed on his kingdom, he steals, kills, and destroys (John 10:10). It seems likely that when David wrote these words, his countenance had fallen similarly to what Cain experienced. However, unlike Cain, David decided to put his trust in the

183 The Treasury of David, commentary by Charles H Spurgeon

184 The Treasury of David, commentary by Christopher Love

Lord, as indicated in the second part of verse five: "Hope in God and wait expectantly for Him, for I shall yet praise Him, my Help and my God." If we could only learn to respond to stress and trauma as David did, **recognizing its origin and looking for a spiritual solution from God.**

In Psalm 55, different content is found than in Psalm 42. In Psalm 55, there is a strong emphasis on an intimate friend and adviser betraying David's trust and a more detailed description of the evil involved. And the tone (process) of Psalm 55 is different. The tone in Psalm 42 is one of tearfulness and grief, but in Psalm 55, the tone expressed is dominated by fear.

The difference in content as well as process suggests these psalms may have been written about different events. Perhaps Psalm 42 is David's writing about his escape from King Saul. David was in his twenties during much of his time running from Saul. David was young and strong, at the peak of his physical prowess. He had killed a lion, a bear, and the Philistine warrior Goliath. Despite Saul's intent to kill him, David showed little sign of fear during this period of his life. He had the opportunity to kill Saul on two separate occasions and would not raise his hand against the King whom God anointed. David had a reverential and worshipful fear of the Lord, which is the beginning of wisdom (Proverbs 1:7).

When Absalom rebelled, David was in his early 60s. He was an old man, and his strength was waning. He lacked confidence that he could survive the rebellion. He feared for his life. He sent Joab to command his army against the forces of Absalom instead of going himself. In verses two to five of Psalm 55, David prays the following to God: "Attend to me and answer me; I am restless and distraught in my complaint and must mourn [and I am distracted] at the noise of the enemy, because of the oppression and threats of the wicked; for they would cast trouble upon me, and in wrath they persecute me. My heart is grievously pained within me, and the terrors of death have fallen upon me. Fear and trembling have come upon me; horror and fright have overwhelmed me." In verse two, David says to God, "I am restless and distraught in my complaint and must mourn." Commentary by J. A. Alexander on this verse: the literal translation of these words is, "I will suffer to wander in my thinking, I will let my mind wander, or my thoughts rove as they will." David is lost in his own thoughts about his circumstances. Focusing on these thoughts produces suffering. Suffering is what happens to us when we "wander" through our own thoughts about intimacy with evil. David allows himself to become distracted. Distraction is the beginning of deception. The difference between David and most of us is he recognizes he is distracted, verse three, and calls upon God to save him, verses 9,16-19, 22-23. Do you want to suffer? It is essential we learn to follow David's example to change our focus from thoughts about the event to thoughts about God.

Let's review briefly the first two therapies we have examined in light of the above discussion. Tim allowed his thoughts to wander around the idea that he might be homosexual. He was anxious, angry, and hurt about his experience. He was confused. He wisely sought counseling to explore the changes he was experiencing in his thought processes. He suffered only for a short period of time because he asked for help.

Ruth wandered around the thought of being angry with God for allowing her to think she was pregnant after her childhood sexual abuse. She repressed her feelings of sadness and disappointment about her losses, not wanting to experience the pain of these emotions. This prolonged her suffering and delayed her healing for many years.

When my high school love (Linda) seemed to be losing interest in our relationship, I wandered around the thought, *it would be less painful if I broke up with her, instead of her leaving me for college.* I was so wrong…so deceived.

When prostitutes wander around the thought that the only way to be financially secure is to sell their bodies, they suffer physically, emotionally, and spiritually as a result of their deception. **When we "wander" in our own thinking,** we open a door point to demonic oppression. That is a repulsive and unacceptable idea, so we deny it. Satan wants us to suffer and blame God for our suffering. We accept the suffering that results rather than the truth about its origin. We would rather say we are depressed or anxious because our culture supports those ideas. The above examples are all thinking errors, the results of wandering around lost in our thoughts when we should be taking direction from God.

Many people think they understand anxiety and depression because they suffer from it. Most people who are depressed and anxious are familiar with the symptoms but not the process issues generating and maintaining the symptoms (Proverbs 3:5-8, Psalm 147:3-6).

When things were going well for young King David, he wrote poems and songs about his life to the Lord. It was natural for him to take his problems, his emotions, and his grief to God. He often started with **praise** and ended with **thanksgiving**. Praise and thanksgiving are process issues that invoke blessing from God. God turned David's mourning into dancing (Psalm 30:1-

12). Ruth followed the example of David during therapy, learning to take her grief to the Lord. Her depression gradually remitted.

So, the answer to the question of whether there is Scripture to support the idea we are responsible for our state of mind, is yes! There is a saying in Al-Anon that goes something like this: "We are not responsible for the storms of life but we are responsible for the weather in our minds." If you take nothing else from this book, remember you are responsible for your state of mind. Failure to take responsibility for your thoughts and emotions results in failure to change.

This does not relieve perpetrators of the responsibility for their behavior. It does not mean you have to continue to be in a relationship with a perpetrator. It means **we are responsible for how we respond to evil** in our thought lives, emotions, behavior, physiology, and spirituality.

Ruth struggled with using some of the tools and making progress in getting in touch with her emotions. However, she bought into a major process issue in therapy--**the only way out is through.**[185] When clients engage in **therapy** and **accept it is a process**, it is often a matter of time until goals can be achieved. "Do, or do not; there is no try."[186]

In the next therapy, look for the thinking errors Abigail experienced as a result of her mind wandering in its own thought processes. You will find a detailed exposition of how Jesus helps a person escape intimacy with evil.

185 An observation from therapist Byron Kehler

186 Yoda, from The Empire Strikes Back

Abigail, A Meditation with Christ

Personal History: Abigail was a middle-aged, married, white female whose presenting problem related to family turmoil. Her twin boys, David and Johnathon, both had surrendered to the influence of alcohol and street drugs. Abigail had been raised in an alcoholic family. Seeing her sons, David and Johnathon, prisoners of alcohol, she could not tolerate the emotional pain. The last time she had lunch with Johnathon, he became verbally abusive. She had discontinued her relationship with both of them prior to our first meeting. Her preoccupation with her adult children was interfering with her relationship with her husband, Joshua. She felt guilty about taking all her emotional issues to Joshua. At times she described herself as being "mechanical." She was aware of disconnecting from her emotions at times. In our meeting, she was tearful talking about her relationship with her sons.

Abigail's formative years were a narrative of one instance of emotional abuse after another. She was frightened of her mother, Martha, who came from an alcoholic family. Her mother was angry and controlling. Her mother was sexually abused by two different family members. She married an alcoholic. Alcohol was a source of frustration and rage for her mother. She vented much of her anger about alcohol to Abigail's father. Her father did most of his drinking at bars, arriving home intoxicated. On one occasion, Abigail recalls her mother saying to her dad, "If you come up the stairs, I'm going to splatter your brains all over the stairwell." She made Abigail watch her when she was hateful toward her husband. Her mother hated her own sexuality and attempted to induce in Abigail her attitude about sex. She told Abigail, "Sex is a dirty thing. You will lay there and take it. You will have sex only after you are married, or I will kill you and the man who did it to you." A few days prior to Abigail's wedding, her mother canceled it because Abigail's fiancé was not well off financially. She hid Abigail's wedding dress. Abigail got married wearing street clothing.

Her father was loving and attentive when not drinking. "He never raised his voice to us. He was encouraging and protective. He brought home gifts for me and Mom, which irritated Mom."

I saw her 26 times over eight months. Shortly after our first meeting, Abigail began to meditate with Jesus every day and continued almost daily throughout her therapy, writing a summary of each meditation for my review. Her meditations with Christ were beautiful, profound, and filled with spiritual truths that should guide every therapy. Notice how Jesus does something to build her up in each meditation. Love builds up (I Corinthians 8:1). Jot down the process issues you discern in each meditation. These meditations were usually reviewed at the beginning of the next meeting. After the meditations, one or two highlights of the meeting will be noted under dialogue. There may be therapist commentary after some meetings. As you read her meditations and the summary for each meeting, look for problems in the areas of thinking/cognition, feeling/emotion, behavior, physiology, and spirituality. Scriptural references are provided to assist with this. **Make notes** about the content and process issues she is working on in each meeting. What are her struggles? Her obstacles? Is there anything distracting her, producing confusion and deception? Abigail's therapy is unique because she documented it so carefully. Recovery tools introduced during her meetings are described in detail in the appendix.

Meeting # 1: Dialogue: Abigail described relationship problems with her two sons. Her sons were not honest with her. They had a secret life centered around substance abuse and lied to her about it. While intoxicated, Johnathon was verbally abusive at times. When asked how she was handling the pain, she responded, "It's hard. I pray and cry. I push the feeling down. I don't want to deal with it." At the time of our first meeting, she had no contact with either of her sons.

I challenged her decision to discontinue her relationship with her sons. We reviewed the parable of the prodigal son, a story about a rebellious son who asked for his inheritance before his father passed and spent it all in a foreign country. When the money was gone, he came to his senses, returning home looking for employment and sustenance in his father's house. His father saw him coming, ran to greet him, and celebrated his return, restoring him to full sonship (Luke 15:11-32). I suggested God's relationship with us is very similar to her relationship with her two sons. We are often disobedient, causing God sorrow and grieving the Holy Spirit (Genesis 6:5-6, Ephesians 4:20-32). God patiently continues to love and invite his children to be in a relationship with Him. I encouraged Abigail to do the same…to meet her sons where they are, to do what she could to build them up without enabling, and to speak the truth in love while patiently waiting for a change of heart (Acts 17:15-34 [an excellent example of pacing], I Corinthians 8:1 [love builds up], Ephesians 4:12-15 [speaking the truth in love], Galatians 5:22-23 [patience as a fruit of the spirit]). She listened, considered, and implemented these suggestions. Because she had said, "I pray and cry," I asked if she would take her tears to Jesus. She closed her eyes and visualized Jesus. Tears were streaming down her face. Post meditation, she said, "All I could see was compassion."

Homework: I asked her to start looking up… taking her focus off the things her sons were doing, to continue to take her tears to Jesus, and using a concordance to do a word study on hope and trust.

Commentary: Abigail's post-meditation description of seeing "compassion" in Jesus suggests she was engaged in taking emotional pain to Him. An important process issue for clients to appreciate is that Jesus suffers with them. He is not a disinterested objective observer. His pain did not end when He died on the cross.

Notes: ____

____

____

____

____

Meeting # 2, Home Meditation: "Jesus and I stood on the edge of the canyon. I could not see the bottom. There was a wide chasm to get to the other side. Jesus took my hand and said, 'Nothing is too difficult for me. Trust me.' We stepped over to the other side. It was so easy!"

Compare: Philippians 4:13.

Home Meditation: "Jesus and I were walking together. People were throwing mud at me. It was not sticking to my white dress. Jesus held my hand and said, 'Stay close to me. What they do won't harm you. Keep your eyes on me. They did the same to me. Don't fret. Trust me.'"

Compare: Psalm 91:1-16.

Dialogue Abigail commented about her meditation at our first meeting, saying, "I left (the first meeting) understanding the compassion of Christ. He is suffering with me."

Therapist Commentary: Recognizing that Jesus suffers when you are suffering often changes the perspective of a client who has been abused. It addresses the thinking error, "God doesn't care," that clients often hold.

She did the word study that was assigned, mentioning Proverbs 14:12: "Hope deferred makes the heart sick." David had texted her, "I love you, Mom." Abigail continued, "I had lunch with David and reported my meeting with you. David cried." I asked her to put a question to Johnathon, "What was it like to grow up with me as your mother?"

Homework: Have a conversation with Johnathon.

Commentary: A recurring theme in Abigail's meditations is Jesus asking her to keep her focus on Him. When we take our focus off Christ, we are prone to wander in the kingdom of Satan. Make a note each time Jesus mentions focus and add them at the end of her therapy.

Notes:____

____

____

____

____

Meeting # 3: Home Meditation: Jesus and I walked past an old, dilapidated house. He said, "Don't let the past ensnare you. Continue going forward. Better days are ahead. Don't look back."

Compare: Proverbs 29:25, Isaiah 43:18-19, Romans 12:2, II Corinthians 5:17, Hebrews 12:1-3.

Home Meditation: "Jesus showed me a big, beautiful flower. He said, "This is you. I see you as beautiful." I said, "Flowers are planted in dirt; I see dirt." He said, "I see beauty. Don't focus on the dirt."

Compare: Philippians 4:8.

Dialogue Abigail reported on her conversation with Johnathon. "I mentioned I'm in counseling. I told him I had learned that Jesus was suffering with me. Johnathon said nothing. Then Johnathon told me of his experience of growing up in our home. 'Being raised in a Christian home… it was shoved down my throat. I was forced to go to church. I was teased in school. You don't know what that was like. I'm not an atheist; I ask God to help me through the week.'" Abigail replied, "He heard me. I asked for forgiveness… He gave it. Two to three hours after our meeting, he called and said, 'I wouldn't trade you. You are the best mom. Everyone makes mistakes.'" Abigail commented to me, "It bothers me greatly, my being pushy."

Meditation during our meeting: I asked her to tell Jesus every dream she had for her sons. She became tearful. I asked her to identify where in her body she experienced the feeling associated with her tears and describe it to Jesus. I encouraged her to put her tears in Jesus' cup. Post-meditation, she said, "Jesus was chuckling. He said, "I have better dreams for them." He pulled the bottle back, and put His hand on my head, stroking my hair and soothing me. He said, "More will come as I sit before Him."

Homework: To continue to meet with David and Johnathon.

Commentary: Jesus counsels Abigail to not focus on her past abuse. Focusing on the past tends to keep the client in the past. Therapy is not about reexamining or reliving the trauma. It is about **addressing the damage in the five domains of humanity.**

Notes: ____

____

____

____

____

Meeting # 4: Home Meditation: "I was in a rowboat. There was a big rope attached to it. Jesus was standing on the shore, pulling me to Him. He said, 'I have drawn you to myself, and I love you. I am using you. Continue to draw near to me. I will reveal myself through you.'"

Compare: John 6:44, 14:21.

Home Meditation: "Jesus held me as I cried lots of tears today. He showed me my heart… a hard black case was over it. As I cried, the case cracked, and a new heart was revealed. I needed to forgive Martha for her meanness. He showed me how I have been the same with Joshua at times and how forgiving he is to me and so patient. Joshua has been so good to me. I must be the same to others. God is so good."

Compare: Proverbs 28:14, Ezekiel 36:26, Matthew 19:1-12, Ephesians 4:17-24, Matthew 18:21-35, Hebrews 3:7-19.

Dialogue I suggested she might explore with Johnathon his meeting with a substance abuse counselor.

Homework: Approach Johnathon regarding substance abuse counseling.

Notes: ____

____

____

____

____

Meeting # 5: Home Meditation: "Jesus and I were sitting in a big, overstuffed chair. We were reading a book. There were little sparkling drops falling on us. He was smiling. I said, 'What is that?' He said, 'Mercy drops.' I was giggling and wiggling my toes. He kept smiling."

Compare: Psalm 145:8, Luke 1:78-79.

Home Meditation: "Jesus and I were sitting on a river bank. It was so peaceful." Jesus said, 'As often as you come to me, you will have peace. Stay close to me to have peace.'"

Compare: Philippians 4:6-7.

Dialogue Abigail met with David and shared a dream. In her dream, there was "a big old white house. David was inside on his hands and knees, being shaken. I was on the outside unable to get in. He was saying, 'Help me, Mom.' I said, 'I can't get to you. Jesus can help you.' He said, 'I will, I will.' David thanked me for sharing the dream."

Abigail mediated during our meeting. She started by experiencing the love of God expressed through Jesus' eyes and the Peace of God by being in His presence. I asked Abigail to relate every thought to Jesus she had about withdrawing from her sons. After she shared these, I asked Jesus to show Abigail the disappointment she experienced in her family of origin…and to describe her disappointment to Jesus, putting her tears in His cup until the disappointment was replaced by peace. Tears began to stream down her face. I suggested she ask Jesus to put His arms around her to comfort her. She said, "His hands are there, with a balm."

Post-meditation: she made these comments: "My dad's love was unconditional. I had to perform to get love from Mom. I feared Mom and Dad would split up. I don't think I deserve compliments."

Homework: Take your fear to Jesus.

Notes:____

____

____

____

____

Meeting # 6, Home Meditation: "A beautiful time with Jesus tonight. Lots of tears; been a long time. Jesus opened me up, and there was a big yellow squishy thing inside me. It was like a fatty tumor. I asked Jesus what it was. He said, 'Rejection.' The word rejection was written on it. He showed me I have a core of rejection because of the way my mom rejected me. I always had to work hard for her approval. She never accepted me. I have felt I need to work/perform for others for their approval. Jesus took the tumor. He is healing me of rejection. He closed the wound in me. He stitched it off with gold thread. He reminded me of my dad's approval of me just for who I am, not for what I did or did not do. Thank you, Jesus!"

Compare: Ecclesiastes 3:1-8, 7:2-3.

Home Meditation: "I took little white porcelain bowls to Jesus and laid them at His feet. The bowls were full of thanksgiving for all the things He has done and been doing in me. He was smiling. It was amazing. I have so much to be thankful for. God is so good!"

Compare: I Samuel 15:1-23, Psalm 51:15-17, Ephesians 5:1-2.

Dialogue She started by saying, "I need to separate my childhood from my sons' issues. I'm still dealing with my past pain. It makes the present more difficult." She described (at home) taking her tears to Jesus about several childhood traumas and asking Jesus to "help me not to take my childhood pain to the boys."

Homework: Continue grieving the loss of her childhood.

Notes: ____

____

____

____

____

Commentary: Review Psalm 95:1-7. In verse two of Psalm 95 is the word *thanksgiving.* Note from the Spirit-filled Life Bible: "The Hebrew word for thanksgiving is *todah,* meaning thanks, thanksgiving, adoration, praise. This word is derived from the verb *yadah* to give thanks, to praise. The root of *yadah* is *yad,* "hand." Thus, to thank or praise God is 'to lift or extend one's hands' in thanks to Him."

In the Old Testament, God looked at the sacrifice for sin that was made by the priest with raised hands on behalf of the person who sinned. In the New Testament, God looks at the heart of the sinner rather than raised hands. Anyone can raise their hands. Only God can enter and live in the human heart… and change it. Abigail was giving thanks for the blessing of healing. The sacrifice she is making is forsaking dependence on herself and depending on Christ. Her tears and dependence on Jesus reveal her renewed heart occupied by Jesus. This is pleasing to God, which Jesus expresses to Abigail on multiple occasions.

Meeting # 7, Home Meditation: "Jesus and I were walking through a grove of trees. I was holding His arm. He said, 'Stay in my presence. You must press through and stay in my presence. It is my greatest gift to you. So much draws your attention away from me. You must press through, for I have so much for you.' There were so many **distractions**... I kept holding His arms tight."

Commentary: We learned in the chapter on the D words that distraction is the beginning of deception. The deception, in this instance, would be to allow her mind to be distracted from her time with Jesus.

Compare: Psalm 88:13-15, I Corinthians 7:32-35.

Home Meditation: "Jesus held me as I wept lots of tears. I don't feel worthy of His goodness. He said, 'I don't have to work or perform for it.' His goodness is always there for me. Wow!"

Compare: Ephesians 2:8-9.

Dialogue She continued to focus on her twin sons. Johnathon's verbal abuse continues to produce separation. She wants a break from experiencing sadness and disappointment. Meditation in the office on these issues: I suggested Abigail ask Jesus to show her the love He has for Johnathon. "Jesus showed me He loves both (of us) the same. When I express that love, Johnathon will know he is accepted. It's a spirit of pride that is separating me from him."

Homework: Take your emotions re: Johnathon to Jesus.

Notes:____

____

____

____

____

Meeting # 8, Home Meditation: "I ran and jumped into Jesus' arms. He held me laughing. He said, 'I am so pleased you enjoy your time with me. That pleases me more than anything.'"

Compare: Matthew 7:21-27.

Home Meditation: "Jesus and I sat on a big porch. My leg was in a cast. The cast had past memories written on it. Jesus was gently removing the cast.

He said, 'You won't be crippled by your past. I'm setting you free.' He was gentle and patient. I was crying."

Compare: John 8:30-32.

Dialogue "Johnathon and I apologized to each other after the last time we talked. Joshua holds me when I cry and prays for me. I need to focus more on Joshua."

Homework: consider Joshua's love language, stay in the present, and start the doorbell exercise.

Commentary: During our first eight meetings, Jesus is not having Abigail relive prior traumatic experiences. Instead. He is teaching her about the process issues God has put in place to promote healing: experiencing His love, expressing that love to others, grieving, forgiveness, looking up, being transformed by the renewal of her mind, replacing deception with truth, resting in His peace, trusting and relying on Him rather than self-generated defense mechanisms, having a relationship with Him, i.e., spending time with Him through the study of His Word, conversation, and meditation, and following Him. **In our relationships with our clients, we should follow Him in the strategies He uses to promote healing.** This does not include reliving the exposure to evil.

Notes:____

____

____

____

____

Meeting # 9, Home Meditation: "The Holy Spirit came to me and took me by the hand. There was a mist and a glowing light. We danced and twirled in freedom. I told Him I wanted a renewed spirit and refilled to reach the lost, to pray effectively once again. He came to me. It was amazing!"

Compare: Proverbs 1:23, John 14:26, Ephesians 5:18-19.

Home Meditation: "Jesus stood watching me dig with a small shovel. I was working hard. He said, 'You don't need to work for my goodness. You did that as a child… always working to receive. What I have for you is free and abundant.' He held out His hand to me. The words goodness were written on them, pouring out to me. I put down my shovel and received His goodness. I cried."

Compare: Luke 6:38, John 10:7-10.

Dialogue: This meeting largely focused on taking her personal history, which ordinarily is done at the second meeting. I changed my custom to meet her need.

Homework: continued from the last meeting.

Notes:

Meeting # 10, Home Meditation: "Jesus held me and washed my face. He said, 'My radiance is on you. I washed you so you would reflect me.'"

Compare: Proverbs 4:13-19, Isaiah 60:1, II Corinthians 3:16-18.

Home Meditation: "Jesus clothed me in a beautiful gown. He was smiling at me and told me I am beautiful. He makes me beautiful. He loves me."

Compare: Psalm 139:13-16, Ecclesiastes 3:11, I Peter 3:3-5.

Dialogue: Abigail described grief work she was doing at home…taking things to Jesus "that broke my heart" connected to her "childhood, my boys, and not serving Christ." She is realizing "my happiness is not found in my boys, or anything…it is found in my relationship with Jesus."

Homework: Continue using the doorbell exercise to process current stressors. Identify thinking errors. **Commentary:** Over 40 years, several female clients have had the experience (while meditating) of Jesus clothing them in a gown… usually a white gown…while He is saying, "This is the way I see you, beautiful and without sin." That is good news for all of us.

Notes:

Meeting #11, Home Meditation: "Jesus was pushing me on a rope swing. The ropes went way up in the air into the clouds. You could not see the ends and could not see what they were attached to." Jesus said, "You need to trust me, even when you can't see."

Compare: John 3:16, Romans 10:9-10.

Commentary from the Spirit Filled Life Bible: The Greek for "believe, *pisteuo,* is the verb form of pistis, 'faith.' It means to trust in, have faith in, be fully convinced of, acknowledge, rely on. *Pisteuo* is more than credence in church doctrine or articles of faith. It expresses reliance upon and personal trust that produces obedience. It includes submission and a positive confession of the Lordship of Jesus."

Compare: Matthew 7:21-29.

Dialogue: Abigail noted, "Insecurity, loss of identity, are big problems. At times it's hard to believe God loves me like He does others." She was introduced to the Father's Love Letter and the mirror exercise today.

Homework: Continue work on the doorbell exercise and start the Father's Love Letter and mirror exercise.

Commentary: Faith in Jesus produces salvation. Salvation includes continuing a relationship with Christ after death which **started during life on earth**. The knowledge that Jesus is the Son of God saves no one…it's all about a relationship. There is a lot of confusion about this in and out of the church.

Notes:____

____

____

____

____

Meeting # 12, Home Meditation: "Jesus and I were fishing. I was catching fish and giving them to Him. He was smiling. We were working together. He was using me, and I want it to be used. Awesome!"

Compare: Matthew 4:18-20.

Home Meditation: "I carried a big rock to Jesus. It was on my back. I laid it at His feet. It turned to sand. I lay my burdens down, my disappointments, frustrations, and sadness. Jesus takes care of me."

Compare: Matthew 11:28-30.

Dialogue: Abigail related that when she was pregnant, her mother wrote her physician indicating Abigail was not healthy enough to have her baby. Abigail was enraged. In meditation at home, Jesus showed her she was still angry with her mother. She gave her anger and hurt to Jesus. She reported she was doing the mirror exercise but did not believe it… at the end of the exercise, she was saying to herself, "Yeah, right!"

Homework: To confess her disbelief and doubt prior to doing the Father's Love Letter and mirror exercise. Ask her spouse how he sees her relevant to the Father's Love Letter. Continue the doorbell and mirror exercise.

Commentary: Survivors of constant putdowns and emotional abuse find it difficult to see themselves the way Jesus views them. Renewal of their minds about this is a process that sometimes takes several months.

Notes:____

____

____

____

____

Meeting # 13, Home Meditation: "Jesus and I were in a rowboat heading to the falls. He was gently rowing, not at all fretful even though the falls were so close. He said, 'Your life feels like this, out of control, but I am in control. Rest in me. Trust in me; have no fear. I'm taking care of things.'"

Compare: II Timothy 1:7.

Home Meditation: "Jesus was flying a kite. I was on the kite. He said, 'I'm taking you to new heights. I am holding you. Hold on to me.' I was smiling as I soared."

Compare: Proverbs 3:5-8.

Dialogue: Abigail reported, "I have not been doing the mirror exercise. I have not confessed seeing myself through my mother's eyes. I see myself as brown and dirty. I don't feel worthy. It comes from my mother."

Homework: Continued from the last meeting.

Notes:____

____

____

____

____

Meeting # 14, Home Meditation: "Jesus showed me climbing glistening stairs. He was at the top. As long as I kept looking at Him, the climb was easy, but when I looked down… the stair step I needed to take was higher and harder. He said I must keep my eyes on Him."

Compare: Jeremiah 29:11-14, Matthew 7:7-11, 15:8.

Home Meditation: "Jesus held me on His lap. He had a soft, brown robe on. I cried hard. He had tears falling off His beard. They were falling on my head. He was stroking my head, and He said He weeps with me. He feels my pain. He shares my pain. I was thinking of David. His birthday is tomorrow. No family time. Jesus reminded me of a time when I was eight or nine. I hid in my closet with my blanket off my bed. I just wanted to be alone to get away from the pain in our family. I thought nobody would come looking for me. I didn't think they would find me. When I was found, they wanted to know why I was hiding. I said I wanted to be alone. Jesus showed me when I hurt, I try to closet it, hide it, to handle it alone. But I can't. Jesus showed me He is with me in my pain—always has been. Wow!"

Dialogue: Abigail said, "I'm still not doing the mirror exercise." I responded to her refusal by 1) quoting Yoda's famous quote from Star Wars, "Do or do not, there is no try"; 2) citing Philippians 4:13: "I can do all things through Christ who strengthens me"; 3) citing James 4:7: "So be subject to God. Resist the devil [stand firm against him], and he will flee from you." After our discussion, she responded, "OK, I'll do it." I asked about her grief work. She said, "His presence comes quickly. I go to Him. I open up. It frees me up. I thought I could make things better by doing things…I have to trust God."

Homework: Continue grief work and the mirror exercise.

Commentary: When Jesus refers to searching for Him with your whole heart, He means with your mind, emotions, and will. When distractions appear, and they certainly will, you must will yourself to persist in what He is asking you to do. The Holy Spirit will enable you to do what you cannot do on your own…the **key of power.**

Notes: ____

____

____

____

____

Meeting # 15, Home Meditation: "I asked Jesus to show me where I am with Him. He showed me standing in front of Him. He was holding a big red heart; it was decorated really pretty, like a valentine's heart. It said, "Be mine." I just kept looking at Him and thinking about it. My husband got up so I didn't have time to process it." **Compare:** Exodus 35:5, Deuteronomy 11:13.

Home Meditation: "I asked Jesus to show me where I am with Him. He told me why He held out the heart to me yesterday. He wants me to receive His love for me. He showed me a little girl pulling a red wagon. It had a house, a broken heart, and David in it. Jesus was in front of me. He wanted me to let go of the handle of the wagon and come to Him. **As I was letting go, I was growing into a woman.** I was crying… I cried real hard and long. I don't think I'm fully there yet, but I'm getting there. Jesus came up behind me and enveloped me in a big hug. I feel safe, secure, and loved."

Compare: Romans 5:7-8, Ephesians 3:14-19.

Dialogue: Abigail reported she has started reading the Father's Love Letter once a week. She is still not using the mirror with the letter as suggested (the mirror exercise). I asked if she was oppressed (demonic restriction) in this area of her life. Her answer: "Yes." She stated, "It is easier to believe for others. Jesus cared more for their spiritual needs." I suggested her thought pattern was related to deception and provided a plan to help her: 1) confess those thoughts; 2) take responsibility; 3) cast out the demon of lies; 4) replace that thought with the word of God; 5) start to use the mirror and prayer as previously described.

All these suggestions were made in the context of a lengthy discussion on Mark 6:35-52, focusing primarily on verse 52 and the Greek word *logizomai*, meaning *consider*. In this account, the apostles did not recognize Jesus during the storm because they had not **considered** or understood the meaning of the miracle which Jesus had performed a day earlier. Similarly, Abigail did not understand the nature of her thoughts because she had not considered their origin, i.e., from the kingdom of Satan. *Logizomai* has several different meanings: reckon, count, charge with, reason, decide, conclude, think, suppose. Each of these meanings provides a subtle distinction on the meaning of the word *consider*, which is the key word in Mark 6:52. Other words which might substitute for *consider* would be the English words *understand* or possibly, *discern*. Discernment adds the element of **investigation** or **inquiry** to the **thought process**. Abigail's **thought processes** might go something like this: *Why does Jesus care more for the needs of other people as compared to my needs? It would be* **wise** *for me to look into this question and* **reason** *it through.* **Suppose** *these thoughts are coming from Satan. They sound like the kind of thoughts Satan would* **desire (evil desire)** *to fill my mind because they take me away from Jesus and the word of God. I have been* **thinking/** *blaming Jesus for these thoughts. Jesus loves everybody… and His love is manifested through action/caring for people. I should* **charge** *Satan* **with** *these thoughts, not Jesus. I* **conclude** *these thoughts are a* **deception**. *My* **decision** *is to rely on a* **spiritual solution** *for what began as a spiritual problem.* **Praise God!**

Thought processes are pivotal in the role of producing deception. This is easily traced to Eve's deception in the garden of Eden (Genesis 3:13). Satan is the father of all lies (John 8:30-45). Lies distract. Distraction is the first step in the process of deception. Lies distract from the truth. Because all lies proceed from the heart of Satan, it is paramount for believers to recognize Satan's evil desire…to steal, kill, and destroy (John 10:10). We must use caution and discernment in deciding the information allowed into our minds.

The meditations of Abigail noted above beautifully document the role Jesus/The Word of God plays in producing mature Christians (Ephesians 2:8-10, 4:11-15).

Thoughts coming from Satan (the accuser) have the following characteristics: They are mostly accusations: accusations of weakness, incompetence, ugliness, stupidity, inferiority, worthlessness, and on and on. Satan's thoughts are all negative and demeaning. They tear you down and condemn. We are prone to generate guilt and shame in response to Satan's thoughts. His thoughts bind you to his kingdom and separate you from God, family, and friends (II Timothy 3:1-4, Revelation 12:10). Satan's evil desire is for you to be alone, separated from the people who would build you up. Many people who commit suicide think they are alone without hope!

Thoughts that come from God are uplifting…they build you up because love builds (I Corinthians 8:1). These thoughts are gentle, patient, encouraging, healing, relationship-stimulating, and **truthful**. They may convict and stimulate repentance, but they never condemn! They take you to places that are beautiful, healthy, exciting, and filled with people who love you. Consider the meditations of Abigail as an example.

Use these criteria to determine from where your thoughts originate. When you find thoughts coming from the kingdom of Satan, ignore them. Study and memorize scriptures that introduce you to the truth.

Homework: Work on the Father's Love Letter and the mirror exercise together.

Notes: ____

____

____

____

____

Meeting # 16, Home Meditation: "Jesus showed me a big table with lots of food on it. There were people there and some empty chairs. He knows I'm dreading the holidays. He said to lean on Him and He would get me through. He said I'm too weak, and I can't do it without Him. I leaned into His arms and rested my head on His chest. He held me."

Home Meditation: "Jesus showed me a canyon. It had lots of steep, sharp points sticking up. Each point had a name on it: disappointment, bitterness, frustration, negativism, sadness, doubt, fear, anger, discouragement, lack of faith. He showed me a big arch going over the canyon. He was on the other side. I was standing by the arch. The arch was faith. My first step was to be trust. He showed me I can only come over the canyon by trusting Him, by keeping my faith in Him. Before He showed me this, He wrapped me in a big goose-down blanket and held me tight. He said, 'I understand you; take comfort in Me; I am holding you.'"

Dialogue: Abigail reported, "I do the mirror exercise from time to time. When I look in the mirror, I don't feel the heaviness I did (earlier). Maybe I don't feel approved by Him. I never felt approved by Mom. Before I went on my first date with Joshua, I had to clean the whole house."

My observation to Abigail: "Instead of being **carefree**… you had to be **careful** with your mother".

Homework: Ask Jesus to help connect your tears to losses in your life.

Notes: ____

____

____

____

____

Meeting # 17, Home Meditation: "Jesus showed me sitting inside an old-fashioned washtub crying real hard. I was crying, the tub was full of tears, and there were lots of small, galvanized buckets all around me full of tears. Jesus was holding me and crying too. He said, 'I share your tears, and I am with you in your tears.' I told Him, 'I'm frustrated, disappointed, and discouraged with my sons.' He said He understood. I need to trust Him. Lots of tears."

Compare: Job 16:20, Psalm 56:8, 126:3-5.

Home Meditation: Jesus showed me playing in the fountain; the spray was shooting way up. He was standing to the side, watching me. I was dancing and twirling around and laughing. He said, 'Stay close to Me, and you would be refreshed. Don't let your mind get bogged down. When you get caught up in negative thinking, it's like walking in mud, and it will bring you down.' Jesus wants to refresh me. I have to take captive my thoughts and bring them to Jesus."

Compare: Psalm 30:11, II Corinthians 10:3-5.

Dialogue "The mirror exercise is better. I actually bought a dress yesterday." She meditated during the meeting. I asked her to look in the mirror (part of the mirror exercise). She reported, "I saw a little girl looking in the mirror, me. Over my right shoulder was a gift. I said, 'That gift is perfect.' Jesus said, 'That's what you are.'" I asked her to open the gift in her meditation. She said, "I don't want to open it…it's too perfect, the wrapping."

Commentary: You might wonder what is therapeutic about someone playing in a fountain and dancing. Children growing up in an abusive environment often have very few normal childhood experiences. Their focus is on staying safe and surviving. Playing and dancing exert healthy emotions and behavior. It provides a platform for the person to transition to more adult patterns of thinking, emoting, and behaving.

Homework: Work on opening the gift while meditating.

Notes:____

____

____

____

____

Meeting # 18, Home Meditation: "Jesus and I were walking up a stream. There were big round rocks we were stepping on. They were really slippery. The word *doubt* was on them. Jesus started carrying me. There were alligators in the river. When I started to doubt, the alligators would open their mouths. Each mouth had a different word written on it: fear, disappointment, discouragement, frustration. They would snap at me. Jesus said, 'Trust Me. You must trust Me.'"

Home Meditation: "I was sitting at Jesus' feet handing Him cards. There was nothing written on the outside, but they were puffy like they had a lot on the inside. He smiled at me and said, 'I received your request.' I laid my head on His knee and rested."

Dialogue: I asked her about the gift box she received during her meditation in our last meeting. During a meditation at home, she opened it. "It was me inside the box."

We discussed the concept of imputation, her sins being transferred to Jesus, and His righteousness being transferred to her. She said, "I'll have to work on that."

Homework: Study and meditate on Romans 4:8-13. This is homework for you also.

Notes:____

____

____

____

____

Meeting # 19, Home Meditation: "Jesus and I were having tea. He was pouring tea into my cup. The tea set was so beautiful. I said I should be serving Him. He said He delights in me, and I am a delight to Him. He said He is pouring out His love to me, and I am to receive it. He said, 'Delight in Me for who I am, not what I do, for I delight in you, not for what you do but for who you are.' Wow!"

Compare: John 15:10-11.

Home Meditation: "Jesus and I were walking through a forest. It was sunny and so beautiful. He was holding my hand. I said, 'It is so beautiful, oh, so beautiful.' He smiled at me and said, 'You're so beautiful. You only see the beauty in the forest, but there are flaws. There are flaws in you, but I only see the beauty. This is how I want you to be. I'm teaching you to see the beauty in others, to touch others for Me. I am doing a beautiful thing in you.' He leaned down and softly kissed my cheek. I smiled and said, "Thank you, Jesus."

Compare: I Corinthians 13:5.

Dialogue: Her sons are both continuing alcohol abuse and other dysfunction. Discussion around these issues. **Homework:** What is God's plan for coping with disappointment with family?

Notes:____

____

____

____

____

Meeting # 20, Home Meditation: "Jesus held me in the palm of His hand. His hand was so big… I looked so small. He said, 'Life has been hard for you. I have always held you here. When adversity comes, I cover you with my hand. I hold you. I have always been with you, and I always will be.' I cried. I reflected on my childhood, not feeling like I had a family, losing mom and dad, losing our house, bankruptcy, my boys and the lives they are living not serving the Lord, and Joshua's health over the years. It has been hard. Jesus has been with me. I do know this. I want to remember the good things."

Compare: II Corinthians 1:1-10.

Home Meditation: "Jesus and I were on the road. He was walking ahead of me. It was a long road, and He was walking real slow. I was running to catch up to Him. There were big rocks in the road tripping me up. I would fall down and jump back up. My dress was dirty and torn, but I kept running to Jesus. He would look back at me and smile. I kept running and falling down. The rocks had words like sadness, disappointment, and frustration on them. Jesus turned around, and I jumped into His arms and He held me. He said, 'Even though you stumble and fall down you keep coming to me. I see your struggle, and I see your heart. I'm pleased with you, and I love you. Don't give up.' I cried lots today. It's been a while. The boys have pulled back… I don't hear much from them."

Compare: Proverbs 14:10, Revelation 3:20.

Dialogue: "I'm crying less… it's a release, a weight lifted. The mirror exercise is becoming more real, less negative. In meditation, I smile now when Jesus tells me I'm beautiful. I have more tenderness and compassion for the boys. I'm not shutting down like I used to."

Homework: Continue mirror exercise and taking disappointment to Jesus.

Notes:____

Meeting #21: Home Meditation: "Jesus and I were on a beach in a blanket. We were the only ones there. It was so beautiful. Jesus was feeding me grapes, and He was putting oil on me. He said, 'The journey has been long, and it is not over yet. I am refreshing you. I am giving you the oil of joy, the joy of Me to be your strength. You must lean on Me… you have a way to go.'"

Compare: Isaiah 61:1-3.

Home Meditation: "Jesus was standing in front of me. I was holding my heart... it was wrapped in a black cloak, and it was wrapped around me, too. Jesus said I'm still trying to protect my heart. He said He suffered for my pain, disappointments, and frustrations on the cross. Everything and everyone I care about and cry out to Him for, He suffered for. The work was done on the cross for them. I need to trust Him. I slowly unwrapped the cloak and gave it to Him. He put it on His shoulders, and I saw the cross behind Him. He said, 'I bear it all. Trust me.' I cried a lot."

Compare: Luke 18:9-14.

Dialogue: "I get disappointed with the boys. I want to shut down, but I have not. I have mercy and kindness to them. I pondered forgiveness. I would never have treatment for cancer...I won't have a physical. You won't change my mind."

Homework: Meditate on your stronghold regarding medical care.

Notes: ______________________________

____

____

____

____

Meeting # 22, Home Meditation: "Jesus and I were walking down a road holding hands. We were wearing white gowns. The road ahead was very peaceful and beautiful. When I looked behind me, there was chaos. I was holding a black bag, and it was dragging on the ground. It held heavy chains in it. The chains were my boys and the words and sadness I have for them. Jesus said, 'Let go of them, for they are dragging you down. You need to trust me.'"

Compare: Proverbs 5:21-23.

Home Meditation: "Jesus and I were sitting together under a plaid blanket. There were little sharp forks falling out of the sky. They were trying to hit me in the head but Jesus was protecting me. He said, 'These are the negative thoughts you have.' I need to stay close to Him and keep my mind on Him so they don't rob me of my peace and joy."

Compare: Isaiah 54:17, Ephesians 6:11-17, II Thessalonians 3:1-3.

Dialogue: Abigail started by saying, "The root of any problem is broken expectations... which can mature to anger and bitterness. If our expectation is to glorify Jesus, they, the expectations, will be exceeded. My expectations for the boys is they are saved. Since they are not, I got angry with Johnathon. He cancels plans. I blew my cork. My emotions do not mean anything to Johnathon. He gets hard as granite."

I suggested to Abigail, "Speaking the truth in love and expressing emotions is good for you…and Johnathon."

Homework: Continue working on disappointment.

Compare: Ephesians 4:12-15.

Notes: ____

Meeting # 23: Home Meditation: "Jesus and I were in a tornado. We were standing still. He was holding me. There was so much stuff flying all around us. There was peace with Him; I wasn't afraid or upset. I know He was keeping me safe. He set me down in a big beautiful field of flowers. The flowers all had words on them: *peace, joy, provision, love, laughter, restoration.* It was beautiful."

Compare: Psalm 34:14-15.

Home Meditation: "Jesus was holding beautiful glowing treasure out to me. It illuminated us. He said, 'I have so much good for you. Do not doubt; all I have is yours.' He was smiling, and I was, too. I was touching His hand and looking at the treasure. It was amazing."

Compare: Proverbs 2:1-7.

Dialogue: "I read the handout on anger. I'm farther along. I have waves of sadness. It does not weigh me down or shut me down. I can stay present with the sadness. I am not looking back on my childhood as much. Jesus said, 'It's up to you' about annual physicals."

Homework: Have a conversation with your husband about yearly physicals.

Notes: ____

Meeting # 24, Home Meditation: "Jesus was doing heart surgery on me. I was watching Him. My heart was open, and He was removing a small rock. He said He is healing my heart and giving me a new one. He reminded me of a time when I was so cold and rejecting of Johnathon because of his substance use…at a basketball game. I gave him a look; he left with slumped shoulders. I did not see Johnathon for a long time. Jesus is healing me so I can freely love without fear of hurt. I cried lots. It was refreshing."

Compare: I John 4:19-21.

Home Meditation: "Jesus and I were walking together. I had on a torn gown… it was worn out. The word *bitterness* was written on the gown. I was leaning on Jesus and walking wearily. He said, 'You are bitter about the boys drinking. You show that bitterness to them and others because of the pain alcohol has brought to your life. You must give me your bitterness, and I will give you my sweetness so you can respond in loving ways.'"

Compare: Matthew 16:14-15, Hebrews 12:15.

Dialogue: Abigail reported, "I'm doing OK with my emotions. I recognize who I am in Christ. I am special in His sight. He trusts me with words of prophecy about my life. People see changes in me. I have more joy, more fun, and laugh more. Ladies are kissing me on the cheek at church. I can receive it. It's sweet. I had to be **desperate** before seeking help. I had no life."

Homework: Continue meditations.

Notes: ____

____

____

____

____

Meeting # 25, Home Meditation: "I was walking on a railroad track. It was really foggy behind me. The tracks were disappearing when I looked back. Jesus said, 'The past is behind you, and a brighter future is ahead. Better days are just ahead.' I was walking over a trestle in the mountains. It was beautiful. There was a big curve in the tracks ahead of me. I couldn't see where it was going, but Jesus said better days are ahead for you. I wasn't afraid."

Compare: II Timothy 1:5-7.

Home Meditation: "Jesus was carrying me up a mountain. We were laughing and smiling. I looked down… it was a long way. Jesus said, 'You have come a long way. You have done well. Keep holding onto me, and you will make it all the way.' The way ahead of us was beautiful."

Compare: Jeremiah 29:11-14, Ephesians 2:10.

Dialogue: Our meeting was largely conversational, an indication Abigail was preparing to terminate therapy. **Homework:** Choose what you will work on for the next meeting in four weeks, our last.

Notes: ____

____

____

____

____

Meeting # 26, Home Meditation: "Jesus and I were sitting together. There were little tiny flowers all around us. I was sitting on His lap giving Him the little flowers. He was laughing and taking them from me. Then He gave me bigger flowers. It was fun. We left."

Compare: Philippians 4:8.

Home Meditation: "Jesus showed me this faucet. He said, 'You don't do my works; I do my works through you. It's your job to stay open like the faucet. Open a little drip, open some a trickle, open up a flow; it's up to you. I want to use you; you want to be used. Be open.'"

Home Meditation: "Jesus stood before me smiling real big." He said, 'I know your heart; you love me. I know you desire to be used by me. I am using you. I know the times you fail. I don't focus on them, for I truly see your heart. Don't focus on these times you fail. That's a trap of the evil one. Focus on me.'"

Compare: Matthew 16:24, Romans 12:1, Ephesians 2:10.

Home Meditation: "Jesus and I were at a large water container. We were having a water fight. We were laughing. He said, 'I have cleansed you; I have made you whole. You are free.' We had so much fun. He said, 'Rejoice in me.'"

Compare: Psalm 16:1, John 8:31-32.

Home Meditation: "Jesus and I were on a high mountain looking out at all the beautiful lakes and fields of wildflowers. He said, 'I have brought you to new heights, and I am showing you beauty… the dark days are behind you. Enjoy this time. Rejoice in me.'"

Dialogue: Abigail commented about her journey/therapy. "Tears have become my friend." There were mutual expressions of appreciation and goodwill for eight months of therapeutic relationship.

Homework for the reader: Using a good concordance, find a Scripture/s that matches or compares with the meditation above.

Compare: ____

Notes: ____

____

____

____

____

Discussion

Abigail sought counseling for assistance in coping with her two sons who were stuck in a cycle of substance abuse. Eight months and 26 meetings later, both sons were still stuck. They were using alcohol to **mood-alter** and to **escape** unwanted thoughts or memories. Although her sons were continuing to use, Abigail had stopped using… but it was not alcohol she stopped. She stopped using the defenses she had used for years to cope with the pain of her childhood. She stopped using the defenses of dissociation (shutting down), avoidance, and rationalization. Seeing her sons in the prison of substance abuse stimulated the repressed pain of her childhood. She also had pain being stimulated by her two sons. She could not bear it, so she severed her relationship with them. She did not know it, but she was walking in darkness in that **part of her** life despite having accepted Jesus as Lord and Savior. The solution for being surrounded by darkness is a spiritual solution…stepping into the light. She accomplished this largely through fellowship with Jesus in her meditations. She reconnected to emotions, grieved, practiced forgiveness, corrected thinking errors, confessed her disobedience, and began to see herself as a treasured possession of Jesus. Wow! That is a lot of progress… and a lot of work.

She realized she needed **to separate the emotional pain connected to her children from the pain of her relationship with her alcoholic father and abusive mother**. When pain from childhood is taken to adult relationships, it often produces problems in the relationship with the adult. This is known as a transference reaction. The emotions, thoughts, or behaviors are transferred from the hurtful childhood experience to an experience the adult is having in the present. This is very common in women who were sexually abused as little girls. It may produce difficulty in having normal sexual responsiveness/pleasure in marriage relationships. Transference reactions may account for part of the difficulty some women have achieving orgasm. The source of the problem is often unconscious, making it more difficult to recognize and resolve.

Abigail lived the scriptures in Romans 12:1-2, written by Paul for every believer: "I appeal to you therefore, brethren, and beg of you in view of [all] the mercies of God, to make a decisive dedication of your bodies [presenting all your members and faculties] as a living sacrifice, holy (devoted, consecrated) and well pleasing to God, which is a reasonable (rational, intelligent) service and spiritual worship. Do not be conformed to this world (this age), [fashioned after and adapted to its external, superficial customs], but be transformed (changed) by the entire renewal of your mind [by its new ideals and its new attitude], So that you may prove [for yourselves] what is the good and acceptable and perfect will of God, even the thing which is good and acceptable and perfect [in his sight for you]."

The psychological defense mechanisms we develop as children are a big part of what Paul is writing about. The world relies on defenses. We learn to rely on defenses as we encounter trauma during our formative years. Sibling rivalry, marital arguments, antagonism and antipathy in our workplaces, and other relationship problems are all fueled in part by defensive reactions. You will not find peace in your life as long as you insist on defending yourself whenever you find yourself in disagreement with someone. Disengagement from difficult relationships requires discernment re: your role and the role of the other person.

In our first meeting, Abigail mentioned she had discontinued her relationship with her sons. That decision was challenged because her reason was to avoid the emotional pain stimulated by their behavior. It tapped into the reservoir of pain associated with her family of origin. Children often do things to cause emotional pain to their parents. That process starts when children are young and do not know the difference between right and wrong. They have not reached the age of reason. This is a process of maturation that takes a dozen or more years. Children need a certain measure of structure to learn what is appropriate and what is not. This structure should come primarily from parents. The pain children stimulate for parents may stop as children mature or it may continue indefinitely. Scripture provides counsel on how to cope with the fear, hurt, disappointment, and sadness that we generate in response to what children do. The meditations recorded by

Abigail document the plan God has for dealing with these emotions, which is taking them to Christ.

So...are there any criteria for breaking off relationships with family, friends, or colleagues? There are scriptures providing guidance on this question, but it is complicated. Scripture suggests three categories:

1. Believers or non-believers who pursue **blatant sin and have a hardness of heart** (Exodus 7:1-14, Psalm 1:1-3, Proverbs 22:24, 24:21-22, I Corinthians 5:1-2, 11, II Corinthians 6:14 -18, II Timothy 3:1-5).
2. Believers or non-believers who entertain an **evil desire to entice you to join** their wicked plans (Proverbs 1:10-20)
3. Believers or non-believers who **continually abuse you emotionally or place your property or physical life at risk** (I Samuel 18:6-16, 19:1-12, 20:30, 25:3, 14, 25, Proverbs 1:10-18).

So, the **criterion for separation is the nature of their disobedience/sin,** not whether they believe or do not believe. These three somewhat different circumstances have something in common. There is an absence of both love and truth. Love builds people up, and truth sets people free. When you find neither love nor truth in a relationship, your risk of injury rises dramatically.

These criteria are "tempered" by the instruction provided to apply love to stressful, hurtful, abusive experiences (Luke 15:11-32, I Corinthians 13:4-8). This is what makes the process complicated.

Let's apply these criteria to Abigail's relationship with her sons. Alcoholism is a blatant sin, and both children appear to have had hardness of heart regarding their substance abuse. However, they were not making any attempt to entice Abigail to join in their alcohol use. There was occasional verbal abuse by one of her sons, but her property or life was never at risk. Her love for her children and her Godly desire for them to repent prompted her "to bear up under anything and everything, to believe the best of every person, and to hope under all circumstances, to endure everything without weakening" (a paraphrase of I Corinthians 13:7). Abigail re- established her relationship with her sons and learned to rely on Jesus to cope with her past and present pain. Abigail did not agree with her sons' substance use, but it was not necessary for her to disengage. Ups and downs in those relationships continued...as they do in all relationships. It is difficult to predict what will happen in the future. Christians have hope in situations like this because all things are possible with God (Matthew 19:24-26).

Perhaps you are thinking... *God knows the heart of everyone. He judges the heart. It's not so easy for you and me to judge another person's heart.* That is true... it is not easy. But, we can observe behavior (Galatians 5:19-21), look for spiritual fruit, and listen to their speech (Luke 6:43-45, Galatians 5:22-23). These observations give us clues about what is going on in a person's heart. It is a process of **discernment.**

You might also think God wants you to spend time with a non-believer so you can be a witness to him for the Gospel of Christ. There is a question you must answer first. Do you have the spiritual maturity to be around this person without being enticed to join in his sin, e.g., pornography or substance abuse? Do people who know you confirm you have that kind of spiritual maturity? Be cautious!

And there are contexts in which it is difficult to avoid relationships with immoral people, such as supervisors, co-workers, or neighbors. Paul writes, "I wrote you in my previous letter not to associate [closely and habitually] with unchaste impure people—not [meaning of course that you must] altogether shun the immoral people of this world, or the greedy graspers and cheats and thieves or idolaters, since otherwise you would need to get out of the world and human society altogether! But now I write to you not to associate with anyone who bears the name of [Christian] brother if he is known to be guilty of immorality or greed, or is an idolater, [whose soul is devoted to any object that usurps the place of God], or is a person with a foul tongue [railing, abusing, reviling, slandering], or is a drunkard or a swindler or a robber. [No] you must not so much as eat with such a person" (I Corinthians 5:9-13). In this Scripture, Paul introduces a practical consideration. A Christian cannot completely separate from non-believers as we live in a world dominated by sin. But be careful, be discerning, because Satan is "more subtle and crafty" than you (Genesis 3:1).

Jesus spoke on the issue of association/separation. He said decisions for or against Him would divide families—fathers from sons, and mothers from daughters. He asserted no relationship should interfere with a person's relationship with Him (Matthew 10:32-37, 19:29). Any object, activity, or person more important than a relationship with Christ becomes an idol that is worshiped in place of Christ (I Peter 4:1-5, I John 5:18-21). One process issue is this: **The Word of God always divides**. It separates believers from those who refuse to have a relationship with Jesus.

The Unique Nature of Therapy

Every therapy is different, which is apparent from the three presentations we have considered. If there were 100 or 1000 different client presentations, each would be unique because each person is unique. However, the process issues are the same in every therapy. The process issues always relate to the five domains of humanity: **thinking/cognition, feeling/emotion, behavior, physiology, and spirituality.** Ruth's presenting problem related to depression. She wanted to know how much her depression contributed to her arthritis. She experienced fear at the prospect of feeling sad. Ruth had family issues, but she did not make them a focus of our meetings.

Abigail's presenting problem related to family turmoil and loss of relationship with her sons. She described herself as "mechanical" at times and "shut down." This description usually refers to being relatively or completely disconnected from emotion. Notice the following: this discussion about presenting problems is totally focused on what is going on in the client. It is **what is happening within the client's heart** (mind, emotions, and will) that determines the symptoms in response to the stress of trauma. If someone is experiencing depression, it is because some combination of their thoughts, emotions, and behavior is stimulating physiological changes in the brain that are experienced as depression. And, if someone is experiencing the sense of being mechanical and shut down, it is because some combination of their thoughts, emotions, and behavior are producing physiological changes in the brain, producing a separation from emotion.

One process issue to promote healing for Ruth and Abigail is identical… reconnecting to their emotions. Abigail's defenses were not working when she was in the presence of Jesus because she reported that when she prayed about her sons, she would also cry. Perhaps she felt safer when in the presence of Jesus through prayer…or meditation. In our first meeting, when she visualized Christ, tears began to stream down her face.

Abigail continued to meditate and send copies to me after our meetings ended. She had learned to **fellowship with Christ** (1 John 1:5-10, Revelation 3:20). It is noted in the scriptures that Jesus spoke with authority when He was teaching (Matthew 7: 28-29). Abigail learned He speaks with the same authority during meditations. There are many opportunities to have time with Jesus. These include traditional disciplines such as fasting, silence, solitude, prayer, confession, study, meditation on the word of God, service, and others. Service is sometimes overlooked as a means of spending time with Jesus

(Matthew 25: 33-46). In these verses, Jesus informs us that when we feed the hungry, clothe the poor, and perform other acts of love in obedience to His gospel, it is the same as doing it for Jesus Himself. He promises to remember these acts of love. This type of love attracts people to Jesus and softens their hearts to accept Him as Lord. These are some of the good works that Christians do who believe Jesus is Lord of their lives (Ephesians 2:10). The word *Lord* in this context means: owner by right of purchase. We have been purchased by the death of Christ on the cross.

When practicing the above disciplines, you are either **doing something that Jesus would do or spending time with Jesus, or both**. The purpose of the disciplines is to know Jesus more intimately and/or to "grow up in every way and all things into Him who is the head, [even] Christ (the Messiah, the Anointed One" (Ephesians 4:15). Jesus did not gather hundreds of His disciples together and protest the oppressive rule of the Roman occupation in Judea. He interacted with individuals to meet their physical/worldly needs, emotional needs, and spiritual needs. This is the model that is offered for us to follow. Will you follow Him?

There are many important process issues evident in Abigail's meditations. A process issue that spoke to me was noted in meeting number 26. It was the meditation in which Jesus showed Abigail a faucet, and Abigail heard Jesus speak these words in her mind: **"You don't do my works; I do my works through you. It's your job to stay open** like the faucet. Open a little drip, open some a trickle, open up a flow. It's up to you. I want to use you; you want to be used. **Be open."** This meditation prompted me to ask myself, *how open to be used by God am I, really?*

Which of the process issues in her meditations speak to you? How open are you to being used to perform the works of God? What is the work of God? (see John 6:26-29) What is preventing you from being more open? Write your answers below.

____

____

____

____

____

In the next chapter, the book takes a small break from more serious discussions. Chapter 17 is a brief account of our year as medical missionaries in the Territory of Papua New Guinea. However, process issues never take a break. Look for some interesting parallels between process issues in Papua New Guinea and the United States of America.

The Land that Time Forgot

Charney and I decided to migrate to a warmer climate when I graduated from McGill University in May 1969. On July 1, I found myself at Orange County Medical Center in Orange, California, starting a rotating internship. Charney had found a job working in surgery and recovery in a different hospital. Thinking twelve months ahead, I applied for and was accepted for the Berry Plan, which allowed finishing specialty training before entering military service. I was planning to do internal medicine, but during my year of internship, I lost interest in being an internist. I wrote my draft board in Ohio, informing them I was dropping out of the Berry Plan. We thought I would be drafted immediately after finishing my internship and sent to Vietnam as a general medical officer.

Late in the spring, I received a letter from my draft board. They had "decided" they would not draft me since I was not applying for an internal medicine residency. When Charney came home from work, I said, "I got a letter from the draft board; do you want to see it?" She took it with trembling hands. Her frown turned into a smile, and she asked, "Is this a miracle?" We both thought so. She said, "What are we going to do?" I said, "I've been thinking about the mission field." She said, "Let's talk about it." Very quickly, we were looking for an organization to place us somewhere in a medical mission. This chapter is simply a recital of disconnected incidents that occurred during our year in Papua New Guinea. Process issues get even more interesting in a country like Papua New Guinea, a land that time forgot.

Appetite for the Mission Field

The World Brotherhood Exchange wanted to place us in the Cameroons in West Africa because we were both somewhat fluent in French, which is spoken there. Six weeks before we were to fly to the Cameroons, the World Brotherhood Exchange called and asked, "Would you go to Papua New Guinea?" Without exploring that option in any way, we said "Yes." Neither of us knew where the Territory of Papua New Guinea was located, so the next day I went to the library and checked out three books. I opened the first book and saw the title of a chapter, "They Cooked Him with Sago and Ate Him." This is a reference to the unexplained disappearance of Michael Rockefeller in 1961. Rockefeller and a Dutch anthropologist were studying art and culture in a remote aboriginal area of New Guinea known as the Asmat.[187] When their raft overturned some distance from shore, Rockefeller decided to swim for shore, using an empty gas can for flotation. He was never seen again. Subsequent inquiries suggested he made it to shore and was captured, killed, and perhaps cannibalized by a local tribe. What a tragedy for the Rockefeller family! It was our first introduction to the culture of Papua New Guinea.

Cannibalism was still practiced in remote places in TPNG in the early 1970s. There was a very rare neurological disorder known as kuru which was contracted by eating human brains. I had never heard of this disorder in medical school or internship, but I would learn more about it during our stay in New Guinea. Kuru was an interesting disease from a medical perspective, but the thought of cannibalism did not increase our *appetite* for spending a year where we could be eaten. [188]

Located in the Southern Pacific Ocean, Papua New Guinea is the second-largest island in the world. It is part of a larger geographical area known as Melanesia, which is composed of approximately 2000 islands. Melanesia lies between Australia to the South, Micronesia to the North, and Polynesia to the East. At four degrees South of the equator, the climate of Papua, New Guinea is tropical with little seasonal variation. Average temperatures range a few degrees on the higher side of 80 degrees Fahrenheit on the coast. Precipitation averages about 80 inches per year, but some combination of meteorological conditions forced 95% of that total to fall at night on our tin roof. The noise could be deafening. After a few weeks, we rarely heard the rain at night despite its continued drumbeat. This is a phenomenon known as *accommodation*, a strategy of the mind in which newly acquired sensory information is ignored when it is not useful to address a new or unfamiliar situation. Adapting to other aspects of New Guinea was more challenging.

---

187 Wikipedia.org, Michael Rockefeller disappears in the Asmat

188 YouTube.com; Deadliest Journeys-Papua, New Guinea, How Safe is Papua, New Guinea for Travel, and other YouTube videos for more information about "modern" culture and travel in Papua, New Guinea

Welcome to Papua New Guinea

A few months before we arrived, the hospital administrator was bitten by a New Guinea death adder. Its venom contains neurotoxins, anticoagulants, and myotoxins resulting in paralysis, blood clotting, and destruction of muscle tissue. These bites are usually fatal without the administration of anti-venom. Paralysis begins as soon as 30 minutes after a bite.[189] The administrator did not realize he was bitten, but when he became weak and experienced partial paralysis, one of the mission doctors correctly diagnosed what was happening and immediately administered the anti-venom. He survived. A death adder had been reported between our residence and another house about 70 yards away shortly before our arrival. I never took a step in the grass without looking to see what I was stepping on.

We lived in a three-bedroom house with electricity and running water. There was a large water tank that collected rainwater and distributed it to buildings on the hospital compound. A week or two before our arrival, a local villager had thrown feces into the tank. This was not recognized until people started getting sick with diarrhea and fever. The whole system had to be drained and sterilized before it could be used again. These were some of the tidbits of survival information in our "welcoming packet."

Our salary was $200.00 per month, and after four months, we had saved enough money to purchase a 175cc Honda motorcycle. Two wheels were better than none, but riding around could be dangerous. There were only 50 miles of paved roads around Madang at that time. There was no map for dirt roads, so it was necessary to keep track of the turns you had made in order to find your way back to Madang. Otherwise, you would be spending the night in the jungle. While there were no large predatory mammals in New Guinea like lions or tigers, I always felt a bit of anxiety when alone. The New Guineans we had contact with on the coast were friendly and a bit shy toward white people, but the men from various tribes could be murderous.

Yagaum Hospital, Our World for One Year

The World Brotherhood Exchange placed us at Yagaum Hospital, a mission hospital about eight miles from the city of Madang on the Northeast coast of Papua New Guinea. This hospital was a remnant of the 119th Field Hospital American Army, World War II, and had been relocated from Finschhafen,

189 www.kingsnake.com, Dangerous Snakes of Papua New Guinea

200 miles south of Madang. Dr. Teddi Braun and his wife opened Yagaum Hospital in 1950 and were both still at the hospital when Charney and I arrived in August 1970. There was a church on campus that held services in English and Tok Pisin, the lingua franca/official language of New Guinea. I had studied Tok Pisin prior to arriving so I could take a medical history with the help of a native nurse.

We started work immediately after our arrival. Medical work in New Guinea was very straightforward: take a medical history, examine the patient, order lab tests/X-rays, formulate a diagnosis, and prescribe treatment. We had a lab staffed by an American lab tech that could do most basic tests. The X-ray machine came with the army buildings from Finschhafen. It reminded me of the much earlier machines such as those used by Madame Curie during WW I, but, in reality, it was probably only 30 years old or less. There was a surgical theater and a nurse anesthetist who provided anesthesia. There was little or no appendicitis, peptic ulcer disease, hernias, or gallbladder disease in our catchment area. The most common surgical procedure was C- sections for complicated pregnancies. The most common cancer was oral cancer due to the ubiquitous abuse of chewing betel nuts to get high. There were no coronary artery diseases or heart attacks among the natives. You rarely saw a New Guinean villager who was overweight. I wondered if they even had a word for obesity in their native languages.

My duties were the pediatric ward, daily census between 20-35 patients, and adult women, 8-12 patients. Charney also worked full-time. We made rounds on our patients every day, rotated evaluating native outpatients, and staffed an outpatient clinic for private paying patients from Madang. Most obstetrical deliveries were performed by midwives. Doctors were called if there was a complication. There were two other physicians at the hospital: Nate, a family doc like myself, and Keith, a middle-aged orthopedic surgeon. I was 27 years old, and Nate was two years my senior. All three of us were relatively relaxed about working at a mission hospital. The bulk of our work was related to infectious and tropical diseases. We saw nearly every type of tuberculosis described in the medical literature, including one case of tuberculous meningitis. In New Guinea, there was often a surprise waiting somewhere in a jungle village. It might take two weeks for the family to get the person to the hospital, and they could be near death by the time they arrived. This chapter provides an account of a few of those surprises. The process issues in Papua New Guinea have unique parallels to certain process issues in the USA.

We worked hard for eight hours a day, but when off duty, we wanted to do something to take our minds off the mission, malnutrition, malaria, and other maladies being treated at the hospital.

Canoe Evangelism

One unexpected development occurred when I contracted with Siar Village to purchase a tree to make an outrigger canoe. The start of this project produced a serious medical complication. Several New Guineans from the village joined Nate and me in cutting down the tree, which was about three feet in diameter. We had a chainsaw borrowed from the Lutheran shop in Madang. I had never used a chainsaw, but I thought it might be fun. I did all the work on the big tree. There was a much smaller tree, about ten inches in diameter, needing to be cut down for the large tree to fall on. Nate asked for the chainsaw, and I took a break while he felled it. Everything seemed to go well. We loaded the two 14-foot-long logs onto the mission truck, and the logs were taken to Siar to be made into canoes.

A few days after this logging exploit, Nate called and asked me to come to his house. He was barely recognizable. His skin was thickened and inflamed on his face, neck, torso, and upper and lower extremities, and he was itching and scratching like a man possessed. The only area spared from this affliction was the part of his body covered by shorts during our logging operation. After I examined him, he said, "What do you think this is?" I thought carefully. I had never seen anything like this, but it looked like an allergic reaction of some sort.

Some missionaries are famous for profound comments or pithy sayings connected to their work. I became somewhat infamous for my response about his medical condition. I finally said, tongue in cheek, "I don't know what you got, but I'm sure glad you got it, and I don't." This response was not characteristic of the type of empathy that medical missionaries are expected to display. My sin nature had made an unexpected appearance and was on full display. Fortunately, we were both laughing. Nate explained, "The tree I cut down had poisonous sap, and the chainsaw sprayed it everywhere. The New Guineans knew the tree was poisonous and didn't say anything." We wondered why they didn't say something. New Guineans could be shy, particularly about instructing white folks. Or maybe they assumed we knew the tree was poisonous.

Nate was taking large doses of Benadryl to reduce the itching, but it wasn't working. I suggested intravenous steroids to reduce the inflammation and itch, but he refused to take steroids orally or via IV. He was unable to work for nearly 2 weeks. At that time, he was continuing to overdose on Benadryl. He called and wanted to go fishing on Saturday. Nate had an 18-foot Hewescraft aluminum boat with a 60-horse Johnson motor on it. The amount of Benadryl he was taking was adversely influencing his mental faculties. He hit a dock when we were starting our trip and put us on some rocks a bit later. After the second incident, I insisted on running the boat for the rest of the day. We survived, which was always the goal in the back of my mind while in Papua New Guinea.

A fringe benefit of having Siar villagers make the canoe was an arrangement by which I could keep the canoe at their village. It was located on a natural inlet from the ocean completely protected from storms. Every time I went fishing, I would leave one or two fish with the village chief, Phillipus. One day I was at the village working on the canoe when one of the men came up to me and tapped me on the shoulder. It startled me because I was focused on my work. He said nothing but pointed to a coconut tree overhead. There were about half a dozen coconuts at the top. I didn't understand at first that he was telling me to move the boat. I suddenly recalled Nate telling me that a common cause of paralysis in New Guinea was head injury from falling coconuts. I thanked him profusely and moved both myself and the boat. Love can be expressed in many different ways, but sometimes it is most effective without words.

I would like to report that my game plan to have Siar build the canoe was a strategy to get to know them, build a relationship, and tell them about Jesus. But, no! It was just about fishing. However, God had a plan for Siar we did not know about. Siar Village was a thread in the tapestry of our life for the next 50 years.

The Operating Room

One of the nurses invited us to join her on a trip to a number of villages to monitor pregnant women, as they had no way to get to our hospital for routine exams. This was a walking trip that lasted three or four days. We crossed rivers by wading; there were no bridges. River crossings were always exciting because of possible encounters with freshwater crocodiles. We ate village food, which was basically potatoes without any butter, salt, or pepper. Their dwellings were single-story, one-room, no toilet, built on log stilts because of heavy rain accumulations. Access was provided by a log with notches cut for steps. We slept in a guest house on bamboo floors with no mattresses. We learned the true meaning of corduroy the first night on one of these floors.

In one village, the nurse examined a woman whose water had broken a few days earlier but failed to start labor. The uterus became infected, and the baby died. Our nurse made arrangements to have this patient brought to our hospital, where a C-section was scheduled to remove the baby. Keith was doing the surgery, and I was assisting. After the abdomen was opened, sterile cloths were placed around the uterus so the remainder of the abdominal cavity would not become contaminated by pus coming from the uterus. As a surgical assistant in undergraduate school, I assisted with several surgeries to drain abscesses when working in the operating room. I had some idea this was not going to be pleasant. I started to breathe through my mouth a moment before he made the incision into the uterus. The pus poured out. Apparently, the odor was overwhelming because Keith fainted. He dropped to the floor. Now he was contaminated. He would have to change into a new gown, gloves, and mask before continuing. One of the nurses looked after him while I delivered the baby, still breathing through my mouth.

After three or four minutes, Keith stood up. Instead of changing into fresh, sterile operating garb, he said, "Terry, would you finish this operation?" I was surprised when he fainted, but now I was shocked. I was at a loss for words. If I had time to think about it, I would have said, "No, I'll carry on until you change." But there wasn't any time. The patient was lying there under anesthesia. This was not a time for discussion. I finally responded to Keith's question. "Sure" was all I could muster. I closed the uterus, put in a drain, closed the abdominal cavity, and got a couple of cultures to determine the nature of the infection. I was still breathing through my mouth. When the skin was closed, I began breathing normally again. I was thankful I had worked as a surgical assistant for a couple of years at Toledo Hospital while I was in undergraduate school. Did God know I would be going to the mission field? Of course! God provides what you need to accomplish His Work (II Corinthians 9:8-9).

The cultures grew only pseudomonas bacteria sensitive to gentamicin. When I got the report from the lab, my heart fell. I doubted we had a course of gentamicin in our pharmacy to treat her. Checking with the pharmacist, I found there was enough for one course of treatment. I was surprised we had any gentamicin at all because a lot of our antibiotics were donated by pharmaceutical companies. She did not develop any post-op fever, septicemia, or peritonitis. No complications. Sometimes having nothing is a good thing. Praise God.

Payback

Tribal customs varied a great deal from one language group to another, but one custom observed throughout much of the country is known as payback. We would think of it as revenge murder. It was explained to me this way: a person from one tribe is offended by someone from another tribe. The tribe which is offended picks someone from the offending tribe and marks him for death. The person who is chosen to be murdered may have nothing to do with the original offense. The tribe planning the murder waits for an opportune time and then disposes of the person marked for death. Months or longer periods could pass before the execution is performed. At this point, the village suffering a murder chooses someone from the other village and marks that person for death. This cycle could go on for years.

Siar Village had made peace with another village to end this process of payback. The district missionary informed us we were invited to attend the ceremony. This was a tremendous honor. We did not know anyone from the other village. This celebration would have a feast, singing, and dancing. The three of us were the only White people among two very large groups of Black villagers. We were sitting on the ground watching a long line of male singers/dancers parading about 20 feet in front of us. Suddenly a native warrior broke from the line and ran toward me. He raised his spear and thrust it toward my forehead. The point of the spear stopped about an inch and a half from the point between my two eyes. Without saying a word, the warrior returned to the line of dancers. I had not moved a muscle. This was not because of courage on my part; there was simply no time to escape his onslaught. Charney later said she thought for a moment she would return to the United States a widow. We thanked God for His protection and mercy.

The warrior's face was painted, so recognition was not possible. The villagers from Siar never offered any explanation. I did not ask for one. There are times in life when you are helpless to stop injury to yourself. God may be protecting you at these times. You can't see the hand of God, but it is there. Think about what Jesus said to Abigail during one of her meditations in the last chapter.

Have you experienced anything like payback in your "civilized life" here in the United States? Have you been attacked emotionally or physically without reason? Is payback in Papua New Guinea similar to cancel culture in the USA? Have you been caught up in a cycle of payback? What did you do? Do you think God protected you? How would you know? Write your answers in the space below.

____

____

____

____

____

Crocodiles and Beaches

If we were not on call over the weekend, we would find something to do on Saturday that would take us away from the hospital compound for a few hours. Sometimes we would swim at a beach near Madang.

There was a sign at the beach that said, "Saltwater crocodiles sighted here in June 1969." The date was September 1970 for our first swim. I had read about saltwater crocs in one of the library books I checked out in Orange, California, before leaving for New Guinea. They are known to grow to a length of 25–30 feet and weigh over 3000 pounds. Their jaws have a snapping force of 4000 pounds. Ouch! If a large croc gets hold of you, it is end of story. I wanted to see one of these behemoths, but not at the beach where Charney and I were swimming. A crocodile is harder to spot in the water than a shark. As I entered the water, I thought, "Oh joy, now I have to look out for sharks and crocs. What a crock!"

A few years ago, we were on a vacation trip to visit missionary friends in Bangladesh. They took us on a five-day commercial boat trip to the Bay of Bengal, where we were looking for tigers to photograph. We saw tiger tracks while exploring the jungle, but no fur. One afternoon, Charney and I were lounging on the deck when one of the crew approached very excitedly. He pointed to two crocodiles resting on a white sandy beach 75 feet from the boat. You could see a path in the sand each one had made from its resting position to where they entered the water. We got binoculars out. The smaller one was about 17 feet long and lay right next to the larger one, which was 25 to 26 feet long. It was grotesque. All its features were distorted by its gigantic size. I wondered if the smaller one, which was probably a female, was taking an unnecessary risk hanging around such a monster.

Large male crocs will fight for territory. Saltwater crocs share waters with killer whales and great white sharks between Papua New Guinea and Bangladesh. If you are interested in what these crocs can do in a fight, there are interesting videos on the Internet. These are R-rated for violence. Large crocs, great whites, and killer whales do not have complex relationships. It is all about power. There is a lesson there for all of us… recognizing what power can do in a relationship.

Obstetrics

One afternoon I was seeing private patients from Madang when a midwife reported a native woman in labor was not having good contractions. Her water had broken. They had started a Pitocin drip to stimulate labor, but the nurse did not think the patient was having good contractions and reported the cervix was not dilating.

She wanted to schedule a C-section. This nurse was anxious at times when making difficult clinical decisions. I had several more patients to see, but I thought I should take an hour to evaluate this patient's labor before scheduling surgery, so I canceled the clinic.

The patient's vital signs were satisfactory. On examination, the cervix was soft and about three to four centimeters dilated. The fetal heartbeat was regular. I started to monitor the Pitocin drip. Her contractions seemed satisfactory. The nurse was adamant about doing a C-section. Ninety minutes later, the cervix had dilated to 5 centimeters. The fetal heart remained stable. I thought labor was progressing satisfactorily. The nurse was upset that I had not agreed to treat this surgically. If anything went wrong with this delivery, it would be the end of my practice of medicine in New Guinea. I stayed with the patient until she delivered a healthy baby about three and a half hours after my first evaluation. I went home.

I was having a bite to eat, thinking about dodging that bullet, when I got a call from the nurse. She reported the placenta had not separated from the uterus. Uterine massage and pulling gently on the chord had not resulted in the delivery of the placenta. Back to the delivery room. I very gently put my hand inside her uterus and felt for the placenta. It was attached to the uterine wall for 360 degrees. Her blood pressure was stable, and she was not bleeding significantly. I started to dissect the placenta from the uterine wall with my fingers. I had never performed this procedure. It must be done very carefully, or it could result in a perforation of the uterus. I worked on this for about 20 minutes. It is strange how some life experiences seem to fly by, but others seem like they will never end. This one seemed like an eternity. When the placenta was finally delivered, examination revealed it to be intact. There was no residual on the uterine wall. We gave her some Pitocin to facilitate the contraction of the uterus. I went home a second time, and after relating to Charney everything that happened, I slept.

This story is illustrative of a stumbling block that exists within the church. That block is sin. Sin is always associated with demonic oppression. The process of oppression is evidenced in our lives by restriction in one or more of the five domains of humanity. My mistake was not going to this nurse the next day and having a conversation with her about the events surrounding this delivery. My anxiety about generating more conflict with the nurse was restricting my ability to communicate. Of course, she could have come to me, saying we need to talk. I suspected initially she was anxious about the welfare of this patient. After the delivery, like me, she was anxious about discussing our difference of opinion.

I was on the young side of life and not experienced in working through conflict in a clinical setting. This midwife was middle-aged and had delivered hundreds of babies. I had delivered perhaps a dozen. It seems her critical judgment and behavior were restricted by pride and anxiety. The church is composed of imperfect people who make mistakes, particularly in complex relationship issues.

When people outside the church observe this kind of behavior, they often conclude Christians act the same as they act, so they think, what's the point? What they don't see is that a Christian is on a journey. What has changed is that a new Christian is no longer traveling by himself. He has Jesus, the Holy Spirit, the Word of God, and the fellowship of believers to help him find his way. If you have ever felt totally alone, consider talking to someone who has discovered the benefits of having a relationship with Jesus. Return to the therapies of Ruth and Abigail. They will help you understand what it means to be in a relationship with Jesus and how He leads you during the journey.

The destination at the end of the journey is not heaven. The goal is to be more like Jesus. Becoming more like Jesus and leaving selfishness (the self) behind should be the goal of every Christian. A new Christian will generally be working on different things than someone who has been in the church for twenty years. Any person who follows Jesus will discover that it is Jesus who takes him to heaven. No one gets there by himself (Matthew 24:30-31,

I Thessalonians 4:13-18). You can't find the way by yourself. There are too many distractions. Failure to resolve interpersonal conflict is a stumbling block inside the church. It is a distraction. Conflict disrupts unity. Unity is necessary for ministry. Unity happens when people are being led by the Spirit. The Holy Spirit does not contradict Himself.

Psychiatric Practice in Papua New Guinea

One Saturday, Nate invited me to go with him to Kar Kar Island to visit the missionary who was providing medical services for the natives there. He asked if it was okay to bring along a native pharmacy assistant from our hospital. I said okay. The three of us started the 30-mile trip by boat on a beautiful sunny day with calm seas. Although the ocean was quiet, the pharmacy assistant was not. When we were about 7 miles from shore, he became agitated. He and Nate were having a conversation in Tok Pisin, which I could not understand. After a few minutes, Nate informed me that our passenger was schizophrenic, not taking his medication, and thought we were out to get him. I looked at this man carefully. His muscles had muscles I had never seen in an anatomy book. I thought this guy could throw both of us out of the boat, and there were nasty sharks in these waters. Nate asked my opinion about continuing to Kar Kar or returning to Madang.

Since we had 23 miles to get to Kar Kar, I voted for a quick return. When we got to shore, we had the problem of getting him back to the hospital. He would not go with us. We did not want to leave him in Madang in his state of mind. Another New Guinean saw our struggle and came to help. Unfortunately, he started to help the man we were fighting because he thought we were attacking this fellow. Now it was two against two. I have always enjoyed a fair fight if I'm not losing. Finally, he realized we were attempting to help the pharmacy assistant. Eventually, the three of us were able to immobilize him and get him back to the hospital.

Cargo Cult

One night I was on call for our emergency room when a nurse called and said there was a patient for me. She would not tell me the nature of the problem; she said I needed to see for myself what was going on. The patient was a young native male about 18 years of age who had taken a hunting knife and performed a circumcision procedure on his penis. He likely did this thinking circumcision was a Christian ritual that resulted in being blessed with all the material possessions white people owned that natives did not. This concept came from a distorted view of Christianity known as *cargo cult.* These thoughts were going through my mind as I looked at his penis. He had done a good job of removing his foreskin. Unfortunately, three or four bleeders were pumping blood and adding to his main problem, which was pain. The bleeding had to be stopped. I gave him a shot of Demerol for pain and put pressure on the bleeders for several minutes, but they simply bled through the gauze. I thought about taking him to the operating room and tying them off under anesthesia. That seemed like an excessive intervention for such a small amount of work. The last option was to put a tie on each bleeder right there in the ER. This would exacerbate his pain briefly but would take only a minute for each one. I was saddened about his condition, but what saddened me the most was thinking about his confusion regarding Christianity. This young man presumably thought the ritual for obtaining material possessions was the surgical operation of circumcision.

A Catholic missionary related a similar but more disturbing story about the cargo cults. An entire village had accepted Christ and was asking a Catholic priest to baptize them. On the appointed day, the priest and a couple of additional people from the church came to the village. After everyone was baptized, one of the village leaders said something like, "You have Jesus; now we will have our savior." They brought out a villager and attempted to crucify him in front of the priest. Fortunately, they were able to stop the misunderstanding. They stopped the crucifixion, but the belief in the cargo cults continued. Belief in the cargo cults has been a major obstacle to the evangelical work in various Melanesian cultures.

What is the cargo cult? The core process **issues** that promote the cargo cult have been around for several thousand years. We learned about them in the chapter on the D words. Satan was kicked out of heaven because of **pride and envy**. He wanted to be like God. He wanted to be powerful and equal to God. Adam and Eve were forced to leave the Garden of Eden because of pride and envy. Eve wanted to be like God. Wanting to be powerful is an issue in every culture. Pride and envy stimulate people with animistic beliefs to search for the proper ritual they believe will make them more powerful or prosperous. They will do anything to obtain the ritual.[190]

The cargo cult may also be understood from the perspective of idolatry/idol worship. Idol worship is the worship of something other than God,

190 mysteriousuniverse.org, The Strange Cargo cults of the South Pacific

something that takes the place of God. It could be an object, an activity, a belief, money…anything. There are three idols worshiped in the cargo cults: 1) the spiritual being of a deceased person, 2) the ritual, and 3) the material goods or sociological/political power. **Pride** and **envy** are the process issues stimulating deception and evil desire. There are usually four components:

1. A population with a cultural belief in animism, a belief the spirits of dead ancestors can facilitate life in the present.
2. Contact by that population with a more prosperous or powerful culture, stimulating envy.
3. Conviction the dominant culture has a ritual to obtain material goods or power and is withholding it.
4. Lack of understanding that the dominant culture has more goods or power because of work and technology, never having seen a factory or production line.

There are two major perspectives on the cargo cults: missionary and anthropological.

Missionaries perceive the cargo cult phenomenon to result from a misunderstanding of Christian doctrine. The perspective of missionaries is based on observations made during long periods of time interacting with native populations.[191]

The perspective of some anthropologists is quite different. They believe indigenous populations have an entirely different experience in social change movements which missionaries do not comprehend. They question the objectivity of missionaries, whom they describe as outsiders. These anthropologists believe indigenous populations who desire to improve their socioeconomic status to be activists working in a "social change movement." They note missionaries have described indigenous populations involved in the cargo cults as "mad/crazy, irrational, primitive, heathen, and lazy."[192] These anthropologists believe missionaries have applied a label, cargo cult, to these native people, which is a "negative stereotype." This would be like putting a ketchup label on a bottle of red wine. If someone only looks at the label, they make false assumptions about what is inside the bottle. They would not realize what was in the bottle until they opened it and put some

191 Road Belong Cargo by Peter Lawrence

192 Kago, Kastom, and Kalja: the Study of Indigenous Movements in Melanesia, chapter 6

on a hot dog. These anthropologists think they know what is in the bottle, and missionaries do not. The perspective of these anthropologists is based on interviews with native people who had firsthand knowledge of the cargo cults. The question is, are these interviews valid?

Anthropologists are correct in stating indigenous populations have an entirely different experience improving their socioeconomic status as compared to missionaries. The same is true in talk therapy. The client is the one with all the heartache. The client must do the work. The therapist observes and points in a direction helpful to the client. The fact that the client must do the work does not prevent the therapist from understanding what has to be done to produce change. The same principle applies to missionaries attempting to help native populations.

Anthropologists do not seem to realize they are also outsiders. Have they considered how the process of studying the phenomenon of social change might change the reporting of the phenomenon? This is known as the Hawthorne effect.[193] It is the process where human subjects of an experiment/survey change their behavior or perception of an event because they are being studied. This is one of the hardest natural biases to eliminate in a study design examining human behavior. It may account for all or part of the well-known placebo effect. Or, in the case of interviewing natives about an event that occurred two decades earlier, their perception of cargo cult behavior may have evolved, which could influence what they say about it.

Why is any of the above important to those who live in the United States of America? One reason: I have observed many clients who hold religious beliefs that combine Native American spirituality or other religious doctrine with Christianity. This suggests the mixing of religious doctrines is not an uncommon phenomenon across widely divergent cultures.

This finding would lend credence to the missionary theory that cargo cult belief is promoted by the mixing of native spirituality with Christianity.

During 25 years of consulting at a residential treatment center for alcohol and drugs, I evaluated about 2200 patients, most of whom were challenged socioeconomically. During the evaluation, each client was asked these questions: "Are you a spiritual person?" and "Tell me about your spirituality." It was surprising to learn some of these clients were Satan worshippers. Some worshippers of Satan had performed various rituals to destroy the lives of people they hated.

193 www.wellmind.com, The Hawthorne Effect and Behavioral Studies

This is a common practice in Papua New Guinea. It is called witchcraft. Many people I evaluated in Oregon were unwilling to talk about their experiences in the Church of Satan. Other clients reported every form of religion between Satan worship and orthodox Christianity. Some people described it as liberating to choose parts of this or that religion and put it all together to have their personal brand of religious practice. This experience supports the theory postulated by missionaries that the cargo cults are a mixture of native and Christian spirituality. This observation begs the question: what is the common process underlying this panoply of spiritual persuasions? Answer: deception. Native populations in Papua New Guinea are deceived largely because there is a profound lack of awareness of how work and technology produce the comforts and machines modern cultures enjoy. People in the United States already possess comforts and machines, so what contributes to their deception? Answer: the process issues of pride, envy, greed, and power.

The process issues are the same. The content regarding the rituals is different here from those in Papua New Guinea. Rituals used in the United States to satisfy greed and power are control of access to education, refusal to share wealth, control of information, suppression of truth, the perpetuation of dependency on government, threats, cancel culture, critical race theory, ridicule, anger, accusation, indoctrination, lies, secrecy, and silence. The cargo is the same: material things or power. The idols are the same: spirits of the dead, rituals, goods, money, and power. This is what we worship here instead of the God who created the universe. Worshipping Satan, idols, material goods, and power inevitably produces social disintegration and conflict. Do you observe those processes active at present in our society? If you looked at the 50-minute YouTube video on the Culture of Papua New Guinea, did you see evidence of social disintegration and conflict in the video?

Evil desire always demands more—more comforts, more possessions, more money, and more power. This desire is never completely satisfied because Satan is stimulating the perceived "need." These people plot and strategize in secrecy and refuse to discuss their schemes when they are discovered. Instead, they accuse those who disagree or refuse to obey. Their evil plans have focused on Black populations, Whites, Orientals, Native Americans, Latinos, and whoever opposes their schemes. When the government does something you should be doing for yourself, the indirect message is: you cannot succeed through your own effort; there is something wrong with you. Ronald Reagan understood this and made the following comment: "The most terrifying words in the English language are 'I'm from the government, and I'm here to help.'"

A second reason cargo cult behavior is important is to compare the phenomenon in Papua New Guinea with what is happening in our own backyard. Are there people here who rely on spiritual representations of dead ancestors to provide them with direction and the necessities of life?

While doing research on this topic, I discovered videos and reporting that members of the Black Lives Matter Movement communicate with spirits of the dead to assist decisions. One cannot help but wonder how many of their policy decisions were determined after they allegedly communicated with a dead relative. If you doubt members of BLM are engaging in necromancy (communicating with the dead) you may do a Google search which will confirm this.

Please note I am not criticizing the general concept that Black lives are important. My wife and I acted on the belief Black lives matter when we went to Papua New Guinea in 1970. We did not go to burn their villages and intimidate the natives who lived there (Matthew 25:31-46). Where is the love in burning, looting, and intimidation that has been part of BLM activities? It is vital to separate the concept of Black lives being important from the movement known as Black Lives Matter Global Network Foundation, BLMGNF. This organization is perverting the compassion Americans feel for Black people who do not have equal opportunities for success.

The organizers of BLMGNF and the institutions who support them want political power. Power has different manifestations. There is the power of the wind. You can't see it, but you can feel its effects. Political power is like the wind. You can't see it, but you feel its effects. They want power over our families, work, recreation, and spiritual lives. People who focus on accumulating power are often people who have not learned to **trust**. They do not trust God and do not trust the people they control. The dynamics are like those that instituted Black slavery in the United States. Greed motivates, while pride reinforces greed. They become their own god and cope with underlying fear by taking control of people. This produces increasing restrictions in the lives of those they control. The result will be similar to what it was for Black plantation slavery, total control and economic slavery.

Radical activists who support BLMGNF rely on defense mechanisms of projection and denial to live with themselves. Many of them have hard hearts.

They deny the reality of their destructive, oppressive behavior and project their evil desires onto the people they control. This requires a constant pattern of distorting the truth (deception), commonly known as lying. "How quick your mind alters perception." They are the most racist people on the planet but accuse everyone else of being racist. They are deceived, and people who accept their lies are also deceived. Many of the people who march with them believe they are supporting a social justice movement. Supporting a new class of discrimination does not advance social justice. Others refuse to stand up for the truth, perhaps thinking *this too will pass.* The cost to our individual freedom and opportunity is enormous.

Political power is intended to flow from the people to their elected representatives, who administer power in the best interest of those who elected them. BLMGNF is not an elected body of government. They are self-elevated and self-appointed to a position of power. They abuse power to advance their own interests. They want the races to be in conflict because disunity weakens our republic, making it easy for them to take control. What we should be promoting in the USA is moving towards equality of opportunity. We have made progress but have been moving too slowly! We must do better! We must correct the inequality of opportunity that has continued for so long. We need equality of opportunity for women, for all minorities, for everyone. The very fact that we do not have equality of opportunity is stark testimony to the existence of deception in our culture.

A major tenet of BLMGNF and other Marxists is equality of outcome. There is not a single country in the history of the world in which its citizenry experienced equality of outcome. Equality of outcome is contrary to human nature. It is contrary to biological science. Take a hard look at yourself and your gifts. Are you the same as everyone you know? Do you have the same gifts as everyone else? Equality of outcome produces stagnation of the economy. It reduces the incentive to compete, which reduces the quality of product. Loss of quality results in failed businesses and unemployment. Do you like to go to a restaurant that provides good service and great food? Or do you want to sit for an hour waiting for a burger and fries that are cold on arrival? Competition produces unequal outcome. Businesses with quality product grow while those with poor product fail. Equality of outcome reduces the incentive to work for wages because everyone is rewarded equally. A large social experiment of this nature in the modern era was in the Union of Soviet Socialist Republics. What did their people say? They said something like this:

"They pretend to pay us, and we pretend to work." [194] The social experiment in Russia was known as communism. One of its founders was Karl Marx. Here are some of his thoughts about government and its relationship to the people who are governed.

- "Keep people from their history, and they are easily controlled."
- "The meaning of peace is the absence of opposition to socialism."
- "The Communists everywhere support every revolutionary movement against the existing social and political order of things… they openly declare that their ends can be obtained only by the forcible overthrow of all existing social conditions."
- "Religion is the opium of the people."

The first three quotes above sound a lot like what we are hearing from those who support critical race theory, which is more racist than any existing institution they are attempting to destroy.[195] The last quote above by Marx is uniquely deceptive, flawed, and misleading. Religion is not the opiate of the people because opium disconnects people from reality. Jesus was religious. Read one of the Gospels describing His ministry, and you will see that **Jesus was totally connected to people and to reality, including the reality of His crucifixion on a cross.**

The BLMGNF organization is Marxist, racist, anti-truth, anti-capitalist, anti-family, anti-police, unforgiving, and power-seeking, and promotes the abortion of Black babies.[196] How can an organization which promotes the abortion of Black babies care about Black lives? BLMGNF desires to establish moral truth on race issues for the rest of society. The definition of higher moral good should be established by the Creator of the concept of higher moral good, the God who created the universe. If they achieve their goal of turning the United States into a Marxist regime, they will not care about anyone but themselves. Marxist leaders are always dictators.

What can we do? First, please separate BLMGNF from the history, success, and beauty of Black lives. When large numbers of well-meaning people march to support BLM, they provide an opportunity for radical elements to destroy public and private property, loot, and terrorize the general public. The general public includes Black people. "You can't correct historic acts

---

194 I was unable to find the source for this quote.

195 www.ifa.org, The Ungodly and Divisive Ideology of Critical Race Theory.

196 https://townhall.com, Top Ten Reasons I Won't Support Black Lives Matter

of racism by promoting acts of racism in the present."[197] If you are truly concerned about Black lives, find a point of entry to a Black family and enter their life in a way that blesses the family.

The process issues to cope with BLMGNF relate to what happened in the Garden of Eden. There, Eve was deceived, Adam was passive, and they both gave little thought to the consequences of their actions. Do not repeat what happened there. Be discerning, be proactive, and consider your future if you do nothing. Instead, join and support Intercessors for America, The Family Research Council, Alliance Defending Freedom, Hillsdale College, Students for Life of America, Activist Mommy, and similar organizations. Get on their e-mail lists. They offer many opportunities, content issues, on how to be engaged. Being proactive for the security and prosperity of your country is an important process issue.

Evil acts do not have their origin in a particular racial group. Evil has its origin in the human heart in persons of every race. Evil acts always originate from the process of deception. This process is described in detail in the chapter on the D words.

A Sweet Good-bye

Siar Village occupied a special place in our hearts. We decided to invite Phillipus, the village chief, and the men who built our canoe to dinner before leaving New Guinea. To our delight, they accepted the invitation. This was a unique event. We had native staff and native nursing students around every day, but it was not often that a village chief and a group of village elders were invited to dinner at Yagaum Hospital. We wanted to honor them as they honored us by inviting us to their peace ceremony. We were not disappointed.

We thought that was the last time we would hear from people at Siar. Forty-eight years after leaving New Guinea, we were sitting at a church service when they showed a video presentation on evangelism in Papua New Guinea. A native evangelist was speaking to a large group of people about the Gospel. It was taking place at Siar Village. Charney and I looked at each other and started laughing. Our hearts leaped with joy. Perhaps God wanted us to know His plan for Siar was starting to bear some fruit. God is so creative…and patient. Forty-eight years!

Some languages have more than one word to say goodbye. Some words mean a permanent goodbye and others mean goodbye until I see you the

197 A comment from a Black person speaking about racism.

next time. On the morning we left Papua New Guinea in August of 1971, the hospital staff formed a line for each person to say goodbye to us individually. One of the native male nursing students asked me if we would return to Papua New Guinea. I could not answer yes, even though a part of me wanted to say that word. I was not sure what we would be doing in five or ten years.

When our plane was in the clouds on the way to Australia, our minds were still on the ground at Yagaum Hospital. I happened to glance at Charney. The sun was illuminating the side of her face closest to the window. I took a picture of the side close to me, a silhouette of Charney with clouds in the background. There was sadness visible even in the silhouette. We had it framed, and it hung in our house for 35 years, taking us back to Papua New Guinea whenever we looked at it.

The next chapter investigates and discerns the subject of same-sex relationships.

The Conundrum of Homosexuality

Unlike previous chapters there will be a lot of content in this chapter. As you read these stories, look for deception, desire, defenses, and the process of discernment. We turn to the cultural pressure that LGBT activists are exerting on Americana today and our response. A very brief history of homosexuality follows.

Notice how the culture influenced homosexual expression and how its expression has changed over the centuries.

The beginning of same-sex relationships is uncertain. An early recorded instance is the account in Genesis 19:1-5: "It was evening when the two angels came to Sodom. Lot was sitting at Sodom's [city] gate. Seeing them, Lot rose up to meet them and bowed to the ground. And he said, 'My lords, turn aside, I beg of you, into your servant's house and spend the night and bathe your feet. Then you can arise early and go on your way.' But they said, 'No, we will spend the night in the Square.' [Lot] entreated and urged them greatly until they yielded and [with him] entered his house. And he made them a dinner [with drinking] and had unleavened bread which he baked, and they ate. But before they lay down, the men of the city of Sodom, both young and old, all the men from every quarter, surrounded the house. And they called to Lot and said, 'Where are the men who came to you tonight? Bring them out to us, that we may know (be intimate with them).'" This would have been approximately 4000 years ago. It is apparent from this account that same-sex relationships have been going on for a long time.

Historians have considerable disagreement regarding the prevalence of homosexuality in ancient Greek culture approximately 2500 years ago. The concept of sexual relationships in ancient Greece was very different compared to modern thought. "Greek men did not discriminate when it came to sex—to them, any sexual activity was just sexuality, not homosexuality or heterosexuality. They framed it more in terms of 'giving' and 'receiving.' Unless you were a woman, however, it was looked down upon to enjoy receiving. Interestingly, those men who enjoyed 'receiving' were stigmatized within Athenian society and were *kinaidoi,* men who allowed other men to penetrate them. This was a degrading word, suggesting that in ancient Athens, the so-called open-minded Greek city-state of antiquity wasn't gay-friendly at all." [198]

There seems to be agreement on one issue: there was no word in the Greek language for homosexuality or heterosexuality. There also seems to be agreement that the most common form of homosexual expression was through the custom of pederasty.[199] Pederasty was a Greek rite of passage from early adolescence to adulthood for both young boys and girls. Much more has been written about the experience for boys. It has been touted as a mentoring type of experience in which a young man, 20 to 30 years old, would court an adolescent boy with gifts and other forms of attention to gain acceptance of the relationship. The boy was free to say no and could wait for another older male to offer a proposal.

It was preparation for manhood, including military service. The older male was dominant and the adolescent submissive. Many of these relationships were mentoring in nature rather than sexually oriented. The percentage of men who were able to control their passion is not known to historians. For adolescent girls, the purpose of the mentoring relationship with older women was to help them become good wives and mothers.

During the Roman Empire approximately 2000 years ago, same-sex relationships related to a complex cultural norm pertaining to the concept of conqueror and conquered. Approval or disapproval of same-sex acts was based on the social status of the people involved.[200] Latin was the language of Rome, but no word in Latin corresponds to homosexual or heterosexual. A Roman law, *Lex Scantinia*, was introduced around 149 BC; it regulated sexual behavior, including same-sex relationships.[201] A sexual relationship between freeborn men was punishable by death. But a freeborn man could have a sexual relationship with male prostitutes, slaves, and other men belonging to an inferior social order.

An Austro-Hungarian journalist first used the term homosexuality/ homosexual and heterosexuality/ heterosexual in a letter to authorities

198 www.ancientorigins.net, Homosexuality in Ancient Greece—One Big Lie (under the section, Only Seeing Sexuality)

199 https://stmuhistorymedia/ancientgreek, Ancient Greek Pederasty: Education or Exploitation

200 www.thoughtco.com, Homosexuality in Ancient Rome

201 www.heritagedaily.com, Roman Sex, Sexuality, Slaves and Lex Scantinia

protesting the prosecution of individuals with same-sex attraction in 1869.[202] This was an attempt on his part to abolish the pejorative terms of sodomite and pederast relating to homosexual acts.

In the postmodern period of approximately the last 75 years, assumptions about sexual behavior in general and homosexual relationships, in particular, changed radically with the onset of the sexual revolution in the 1960s.

In the following paragraphs, I am referring to radical gay activists. I am not referencing the average gay or lesbian person.

On June 28, 1969, New York City police raided The Stonewall Inn, a gay club in Greenwich Village in New York City. At the time, homosexual acts remained illegal in every state except Illinois. The Stonewall Inn was operated by the Mafia, who paid police officers to "look the other way." This raid sparked several days of protest and violent clashes with the police.[203] It stimulated an aggressive stance by the homosexual community to assert gay rights, which has persisted to this day.

Gay activists identified three groups opposed to the LGBT movement: religion, the law, and the American Psychiatric Association. They attacked the American Psychiatric Association first. In 1970, gay activists invaded and disrupted the convention of the American Psychiatric Association. Gay activist Frank Kameny organized disruptions at psychiatric meetings for three years. Kameny was a Ph.D. astronomer who was fired from his position at the Army Map Service in Washington, DC in 1957 because of his same-sex preference. On June 7, 1971, Kameny wrote a letter to the psychiatric news threatening the APA with not only more but worse disruptions. In his letter, he wrote, "Our presence there was only the beginning of an increasingly intensive campaign by homosexuals to change the approach of psychiatry toward homosexuality or, failing that, to discredit psychiatry." An APA task force, led by Robert Spitzer, M.D., was appointed to study the issue. His group recommended the elimination of homosexuality from the diagnostic manual.

Lesbians Kay Lahusen and Barbara Gittings wrote a book about what happened to the American Psychiatric Association titled *Making History*. They have been quite open about the reality of the harassment of the A.P.A. Kay Lahusen: "This was always more of a political decision than a medical decision." Barbara Gittings: "It was never a medical decision—and that's why I think the action came so fast. After all, it was only three years from

---

202 www.lgbthistoryproject, How Male Sexual Desire Became "Homosexuality"

203 www.history.com, Stonewall Riots

the time that feminists and gays first zapped the APA at a behavior therapy session to the time that the board of trustees (APA) voted in 1973 to approve removing homosexuality from the list of mental disorders. It was a political move." **Politics rule**.

The rule of politics is the process issue that allowed gay activists to take over and change traditional American culture. The Live Leak website details the strategies used by these radical activists.[204]

Are these activists terrorists? Terrorism is generally defined as a person or group of people who use unlawful violence and intimidation against civilians in pursuit of political aims. After reading this article at Live Leak, you can decide if radical LGBT activists meet the definition of domestic terrorists. Whether terrorists or not, it is clear they have concocted a conspiracy to attack psychiatry, the law, Christianity, our children, and our culture in general.

How can such a small group exert so much power? A small group of activists seized power while the APA and the church surrendered power. Over several decades, LGBT activists elected or appointed members of their movement to positions of power in various national professional organizations, government positions, periodicals, school boards, legislatures, and judgeships. They have been supported by most liberal newspapers and many corporations. Laws were changed to decriminalize homosexuality. They began an organized attack on Christianity using the same tactic they used with the American Psychiatric Association: intimidation. Many have responded to fear by avoiding truth and love in their lives. As a result, we have politics. Politics Rule.

Let us take a moment to consider what life would be like if politics did not rule. Will Rogers opined, "If you ever injected truth into politics, you have no politics." However, observation suggests it would be more accurate to say if you injected truth into politics, what you get is conflict between those who pursue truth and those who seek power to control our lives. Most people who thrive on politics do not listen. Instead, they ignore voters or actively work at silencing people who disagree. Silence is what the LGBT activists wanted from the American Psychiatric Association and the church on same-sex attraction. They silenced the American Psychiatric Association completely. Objections to LGBT lifestyles from the church became muted.

I would add something to Rogers' quote. You must inject both **truth and**

---

204 www.liveleak.com, How Homosexual Terrorists Got Homosexuality Removed from the American Psychiatric Association's Diagnostic and Statistical Manual

agape love into politics if you desire to see transparency in government and policies that benefit the citizenry. Truth and agape love are needed in every venue. If you inject truth and love into marriage relationships, you would observe an end to divorce. If you injected truth and love into business interactions, you would see an end to fraud. If you injected truth and love into contact sports, you would see an end to brawls in the hockey rink and on football fields. Our lives would be more fruitful and peaceful if we had more truth and agape love influencing our thinking and behavior. Much of the time, we have neither truth nor love in our relationships. Churches have forgotten **agape love and truth are supposed to arrive together.**

Radical LGBT activists are not interested in truth and agape love. They are consumed by hatred and bitterness. Hate? What's going on with that? What happened to the love they talk about so much? Hatred is a destructive manifestation of anger. They attempt to destroy anyone or any organization opposed to their ideology. They have attacked Christian bakeshops, flower shops, innkeepers, professors, chaplains in the military, school teachers, and Christian speakers/writers, examples of which can be found on an Internet search. They accuse everyone of hate who is in opposition to their agenda. Hate is the opposite of love. What happened to opinion, discussion, and search for the truth? Answer, distraction, confusion, and deception!

The Southern Poverty Law Center, which supports the LGBT agenda, maintains a list of organizations that have been designated by LGBT activists as hate groups. Many of the organizations on this list are not hateful in any way. They simply disagree with LGBT propaganda. Hate and homophobia are words LGBT activists use to manipulate public opinion. Not concerned with truth, LGBT activists have changed the meaning of hate and homophobia. There is an appropriate use of the word *homophobia* which refers to people fearing being around homosexuals. The meaning of this word has been misconstrued to mean disagreeing with the radical homosexual agenda. Radical LGBT activists have become political because politics rule, and they know it. **Political correctness** is the process issue determining much conflict in U.S. society today. Half the country accepts political correctness, while the other half thinks it is ridiculous and childish. In reality, opposing the gay agenda is simply having a different opinion.

Radical LGBT activists are not concerned with reality. They deny the reality that sex is determined by the XY or XX chromosome combination.[205] They

205 www.acpeds.org,Gender Ideology Harms Children

insist homosexual, bisexual, and transgender persons are "born that way" despite lacking a single shred of genetic evidence. Beliefs based on bias and life experience need to be evaluated on the basis of truth. Biology based on actual science is true because the science of biology was established by God when He created the world. The word of God is truth (Psalm 119:142, I Corinthians 6:9-13, John 18:37, II Timothy 3:16).

LGBT activists wielding political power have successfully supported legislation in about half of our states, making it unethical for licensed therapists to facilitate counseling a minor with gender confusion to become straight. In the last 10 years, they have used their accumulated power to change educational curricula to favor their agenda, specifically to promote gay, lesbian, and transgender relationships. They want to control our thinking. They are changing our culture through power and leverage. Yet they deny the possibility of power and influence in the world having an impact in the development of their individual sexual expression. Isn't that a little odd? How can they conspire to influence the thinking of our culture yet fail to realize their thinking about sexuality is also subject to the influence of their individual life experiences? Answer, **deception**! Their thought processes about change defy logic. That informs the rest of us, the general public, about the origin of homosexuality. It is a problem of a mind whose worldview about sexual identity and expression has been determined by some combination of life experiences. It is gender confusion. Think about the therapy of Timothy.

The results of radical LGBT activists accruing power are political agendas and lies that advance those agendas. LGBT activists have an agenda. Parts of the agenda are constantly changing. For example, there was a period of time when the primary agenda was to accomplish the legalization of homosexual marriage. The parts of the agenda that change are mostly content issues. They morph into process issues when they are accepted by American culture and influence our thinking, decisions, and behavior. Current agenda items relate to taking over our legislative bodies and the introduction of homosexual curricula in our school systems. Their *ultimate* agenda has three purposes:

1. to gain complete political power over American culture;
2. to use political power to promote the recruitment of American youth to the practice of homosexuality;
3. to use this power to normalize the concept of homosexuality in the minds of Americans.

They are already experiencing success with these goals. They have the support of institutions like the American Psychiatric Association, the American Psychological Association, big business, social media, and the liberal press. They have taken over the rule of law. They continue the process of eroding the influence of the Christian church on American culture. They use threats, ridicule, anger, intimidation, misinformation, secrecy, and silencing to accomplish their objectives. They obscure these objectives through the use of misinformation and clever manipulation of words. They disguise comprehensive sexual education curricula as AIDS prevention. They accuse people of discrimination who do not feel safe with transgender boys and men in female sports, locker rooms, showers, and bathrooms. This is not discrimination; it is simply a matter of common sense, privacy, and safety.

Radical LGBT activists have something in common with the elite group of oligarchs who are destroying the American Dream. They don't care about the rest of us. They don't care for the same reasons the oligarchs don't care. They don't know us and don't want to know us. They have experienced the lovingkindness of God but failed to recognize the source. It is doubtful the oligarchs care about the LGBT community any more than they care about the middle class. They are using the LGBT community and Black Lives Matter activists for their own political purposes: to divide the citizenry, to continue the subjugation of minorities, to destroy the middle class, and to distract the public from awareness of their evil plans.

Origins of an LGBT Lifestyle

Each set of life experiences produces a different outcome. This explains why we have LGBT, and not only LG or BT or just G. Men who are attracted to the same sex have a set of experiences that lead to same-sex attraction. Women who have same-sex attraction have a different set of experiences. These experiences lead to a worldview that includes a preference for same-sex attraction, bisexuality, transgender expression, or something else. Some people have a set of experiences that lead to being asexual. They do not have an attraction to either sex. They have no interest in sexual activity. Is this genetic? Are they missing X and Y chromosomes? Absolutely not! There is no evidence for it being genetic. Asexuality is often seen in women who have been raped or had other sexual abuse experiences. Their development of sexuality is arrested. These women started with heterosexual attraction, which was "taken" from them through sexual abuse.

Remember what Scripture states about the goals of Satan: "The thief comes only to steal, kill, and destroy" (John 10:10). Each person who develops an LGBT orientation has had an encounter with the "thief," also known as Satan. The set of experiences we have in life is a major player in producing our worldview, including our view of self. Our self-view includes our gender identity and sexual preference. LGBT activists claim that being LGBT is their identity. There are many examples demonstrating LGBT orientation does not have to remain a person's identity.[206]

The apostle Paul also refutes that contention. Paul states his identity is joined to the identity of Christ (II Corinthians 5:17, Galatians 2:20, Ephesians 1:4-9). For this reason, a Christian who experiences same-sex attraction should never accept an identity of same-sex attraction in any way. His identity comes from being in the Kingdom of God. His identity does not include being LGBT. That thought is simply a deception of the mind, a temptation that needs to be resisted (James 4:7). Remember, your mind is quick to alter perception, and the first part of deception is being distracted from what the word of God states about an issue.

The word of God says that Eve was created for Adam. That was true in the Garden of Eden and continues to be true today. God does not change (Malachi 3:6, Hebrews 13:8). Paul is also implying the identity of the nonbeliever is being influenced by the kingdom of Satan, so it would be accurate for a nonbeliever to say his identity is connected to same-sex attraction because that's what Satan wants him to believe. The nonbeliever, in his arrogance, is saying consciously or unconsciously, "Bring on the deception. I can handle it. I will take my chances on being wrong." These different origins of sexual identity demonstrate a process issue previously discussed, which is, "**The word of God always divides**" (Matthew 10:32-39). People in the Kingdom of God follow Jesus, and people in the kingdom of Satan follow his demons. They are going in different directions. They have different outcomes. Have you noticed that?

Paul does not leave a person with an LGBT identity without hope. He provides a solution for anyone deceived by evil desire. Paul points to salvation offered through Jesus Christ (Romans 7:24-25). The Greek word for salvation is *soterion.*[207] It has several different meanings: deliverance, preservation,

---

206 www.pfox.org, Parents and Friends of Ex-gays and Gays; www.u-tube.com/ Homosexuality and the Christian Faith by Rosaria Butterfield

207 Vine's Complete Expository of Old and New Testament Words

soundness, prosperity, happiness, rescue, and general well-being. It can mean material and temporal deliverance from danger and apprehension. It has application to nations, individual persons, and to spiritual and eternal deliverance granted by God to those who accept His Son Jesus as Savior (John 3:16). This is an example of love in action, of building people up. It is a manifestation of the love, grace, and mercy of God.

The rescue that Paul is talking about is intended to begin here and now, during our life on this earth. God desires everyone to be rescued from sin. Every Christian has been rescued. This does not mean that Christians do not lapse or do not sin. Satan deceives everyone. It simply means they sin less as they become more obedient to the law of God. This process is known as sanctification (I Peter 1:1-6). The deliverance or rescue continues at the time of our physical death and lasts for eternity. That is good news.

Paul raises caution about the influence of the world: "Do not be conformed to this world (this age), [fashioned after and adapted to its external superficial customs], but be transformed changed by the [entire] renewal of your mind [by its new ideals and its new attitude], so that you may approve [for yourselves] what is the good and acceptable and perfect will of God, even the thing which is good and acceptable and perfect [in his sight for you.]" (Romans 12:2). This Scripture is divided into three parts: a caution, a directive, and an outcome. The caution: don't let the world shape you; the directive: change the influence of the world by developing new attitudes and ideals that come from the Word of God; the outcome: discovering the perfect will of God which is acceptable and perfect for you. If you listen to the caution and follow the directive, you will have a good outcome. What a wonderful example of **process issues** God created to work together for our benefit. This is easy to write about but can take some time to accomplish, sometimes a lifetime. However, they give hope, and we should not allow hope to be taken from us. Do not wait to be rescued! Ask Jesus into your heart now!

Paul identifies the principal process issue that powers homosexual expression in Romans 1:17-32. Only verses 21–25 are quoted here: "Because when they knew and recognized Him as God, they did not honor and glorify Him as God or give Him thanks. But instead, they became futile and godless in their thinking [with vain imaginations, foolish reasoning, and stupid speculations] and their senseless minds were darkened. Claiming to be wise, they became fools [professing to be smart they made simpletons of themselves]. And by them the glory and majesty and excellence of the immortal God were exchanged for and represented by images, resembling mortal man and beasts and reptiles, therefore God gave them up in the lust of their [own] hearts to sexual impurity, to the dishonoring of their bodies among themselves [abandoning them to the degrading power of sin], because they exchanged the truth of God for a lie and worshiped and served the creature rather than the Creator, Who is blessed forever! Amen (so be it)." These words of Paul state same-sex attraction is a spiritual problem. Therefore, it requires a spiritual solution. Remember, God is in the business of providing spiritual solutions.

Exchanging the glory, majesty, and excellence of the immortal God for images resembling man and beasts is what Christian teaching refers to as idol worship. In his letter to the Romans, Paul is referring to worshipping objects/statues instead of God. The reader may be wondering what idol worship has to do with same-sex attraction. It seems Paul is saying that the hearts of these people had been hardened to the wisdom of God. They perceived themselves to be wiser than the Creator of the universe; therefore, God darkened their minds and allowed them to pursue sexual lust in their hearts. These were consequences for their disobedience. In the broad sense, an idol is anything created by the hands or mind of man to which divine honor is given. With LGBT lifestyles, being gay or lesbian is honored instead of giving honor to the true God. Money, sex, and power are three of the common idols that replace God in modern society. When a person pursues their own ideas about sexual expression, sexuality becomes an idol. That person is now living in the kingdom of Satan and will eventually experience consequences for that decision.

Christians attracted to their own sex often struggle with the following question: is it sinful to experience same-sex attraction? There is a yes and no answer to this question. One answer is no; it is not sin if it is the first or second time you find yourself attracted to the same sex. The first time a Christian finds himself tempted by thoughts of same-sex attraction, the appropriate response is to resist that thought and put it out of one's mind (James 4:7). In that example, you have faced temptation and responded in a Godly way. However, if at any point the person dwells on the temptation and/or imagines an erotic component to the relationship, a door point is opened to evil desire and sin (James 1:13-16). The threshold between evil desire and sin is traversed in a moment. Few teens have the knowledge and spiritual maturity to respond in a Godly way to sexual temptation. It's not that this is a particularly difficult concept, but rather, it is not modeled or taught in the church as it should be (Hosea 4:6).

Many teenagers or young adults have not been prepared to cope with same-sex attraction. So, a second answer to the question is yes, it should be confessed as sin, if a door point has been opened through any romantic/ erotic thoughts. This is the same dynamic or process issue that applies to heterosexual temptation. When the average teenage male looks at a young woman, he's often looking at her body and thinking about her body sexually instead of who she is as a person. Teenage boys have not been prepared to cope with heterosexual attraction. They would be wise to keep their focus on the anatomy of a young woman above the neck. "The eye is the lamp of the body. So if your eye is sound, your entire body will be full of light. But if your eye is unsound, your whole body will be full of darkness. If then the very light in you [your conscience] is darkened, how dense is that darkness?" (Matthew 6:22-23). In clinical practice, I have never encountered someone practicing an LGBT lifestyle who did not start with romantic/erotic thought processes directed to their own sex.

It follows there is one intervention absolutely essential to reversing LGBT practice, confession of same-sex attraction. This should begin very early in the process of unraveling all the other issues. It is a very straightforward process for a Christian, consisting of a simple prayer when experiencing same-sex attraction: *Lord, please take this fleshy desire away from me.* This prayer may need to be repeated and should be accompanied by leaving the area where you are experiencing the temptation, if possible. This should be prayed whenever same-sex attraction is experienced (I John 1:8-9). When same-sex attraction begins to diminish, it introduces hope for change in the therapy process. This comes from the client having the experience of seeing God working at his side, facilitating the process of recovery.

Another pathway of treatment is an examination of worldview, including serious consideration of the role of adverse child experiences/trauma in creating sexual preference. Sexual abuse, child/parent relationship disturbance, cultural pressure, or fads can individually or collectively conspire to create a worldview, including confusion regarding sexual preference. This does not interfere with sexual awakening but results in a substitute object for sexual gratification. If the trauma is intense or continuous, it may lead to no preference, asexuality.

Since the process of creating a worldview is often partly or mostly unconscious, people do not connect these confounding experiences to their sexual preferences. Unraveling these influences may involve grief work, forgiveness, correction of thinking errors, emotional work, changing behavior, etc. Assisting the client to have some understanding of how the past is related to the present may increase motivation to work in therapy.

There are three common errors Christians make when attempting to have a conversation with a person from the LGBT community. The first is refusing to listen to their story. Every person has a story and it is honoring when you put your agenda aside and listen to what they have to say. The second error is accepting their story as truth. These Christians abandon the process of discernment perhaps to be perceived as loving or accepting. Stories that are true are filled with examples of repentance. For example in my own story, related in earlier chapters, I repented of the belief that abortion was an acceptable strategy for an unwanted pregnancy, repented of anger, of being Mr. Right in my relationship with my wife, etc. When there is no evidence of repentance the process of deception is alive and well. The third error is forgetting that only the Holy Spirit can convict a person of sin. These Christians put the emphasis on argument rather than relationship. When argument becomes more important than relationship, the conversation usually ends quickly. Our responsibility as Christians is to create relationships characterized by agape love and to witness how God has worked in our own lives to change and bless us. It takes time to accomplish this. These errors are all deceptions. Sometimes they are all working at the same time to destroy the opportunity of having a healthy relationship with a member of the gay community.

Now, there is another facet of same-sex attraction needing exploration.

The Other Side of the Coin

Same-sex attraction is like a silver dollar lying on the kitchen table. The side facing up attracts your attention. You do not know what is on the other side unless you turn it over. Christians have often only noticed the side of same-sex attraction that intersects with their theology about sexuality. Christians should be equally concerned about the welfare of the homosexual community. This part of the story is poignant and tragic.

This is a reference to the constant abuse/bullying to which people with same-sex attraction have been subjected. Bullies identify a physical characteristic or character trait to ridicule in acting out their own unresolved anger or insecurities. Obesity, speech impediments, intellectual function, socio-economic status, physical deformities, race, ethnicity, religion, gender orientation, anything can become a target of **abuse** by bullies. Abuse often generates fear and hatred in the person abused.

It is important to realize people who experience fear and hatred are responsible for those emotions. They are consciously or unconsciously generating these emotions. They are not processing the experience (read again the therapies of Ruth and Abigail). The bullies are responsible for their behavior, and their targets are responsible for their reactions and emotions. Fear or hatred are emotions indicating victim mentality. Did Jesus experience fear or hatred when He was crucified? We do not know if He experienced fear, but He ignored the shame (Hebrews 12:1-4). He asked the Father to forgive his persecutors because they were acting in ignorance (Luke 23:33-36). Jesus demonstrated survivor mentality, not victim mentality. We cannot do this in our own strength (II Corinthians 12:10). But through empowerment by the Holy Spirit, Christians should follow His example. We have to learn to do hard things. Many Christians are seduced by a life of comfort.

Bullies are always acting in ignorance. They do not understand their own behavior because they are deceived. The story next is a tragic example of this process.

On October 6, 1998, Aaron McKinney and Russell Henderson left a bar in Laramie, Wyoming, with gay University of Wyoming student Matthew Shepard. Henderson drove to the outskirts of Laramie while McKinney began to beat Shepherd with the butt of a .357 Magnum revolver. Shepard was robbed and beaten until comatose, then tied to a fence and left for dead. The next day, he was discovered alive by a mountain biker. Matthew Shepard lived for five days but succumbed to his injuries on October 12,1998. McKinney and Henderson were quickly apprehended, and eventually, each received two consecutive life sentences for the murder of Matthew Shepard.

In McKinney's statement to police about the murder, he made several derogatory statements about people with same-sex attraction. His cohort, Russell Henderson, denied any motivation relating to gender discrimination. This murder shocked the town of Laramie, the state of Wyoming, and the nation.[208] In the following legislative session, a hate crimes bill failed to pass in the Wyoming House on a 30-30 tie vote. The crime that shocked the nation seemed to focus mostly on the gruesome physical assault of Matthew Shepard's body. Another way to look at this is a crime of sexual abuse manifesting by a physical assault. It is sexual abuse because it was related to his expressed

208 www.bbc.com/news/world-US-world, Matthew Shepard: The Murder that Changed America

gender. Assault is the content issue, while **hatred and abuse because of sexual orientation** are the primary process issues. Bullying or harassment for sexual orientation should be prosecuted as both a hate crime and a crime of sexual abuse. Perhaps there should be a separate trial and sentence for each aspect (process issue) of the crime.

There is a process issue at work in Matthew Shepard's life, as well as the lives of his two killers, which resulted in his death. What is it? It is the same process issue determining the Columbine High School shooting described next.

Here is a different type of hate crime. In 1999, the Columbine High School shooting resulted in the deaths of 12 students, one teacher, and two student attackers.[209] The Columbine shooting created a "Columbine Generation" in which six subsequent mass shootings (defined as four or more victims dying from gunfire in a single incident) and 40 more active shooter incidents occurred over the next 20 years. Twenty of these incidents followed the pattern of Columbine. The shooters had the following in common: "They were 'in crisis,' had 'experienced trauma,' and were 'actively suicidal and expected to die in the act.'"[210] Three other characteristics seem highly probable: having **relationship problems**, a sense of **hopelessness** about improving their situation, and **hatred.** Two criminal justice professors studied all 46 incidents. They made the following recommendations: "No notoriety for mass shooters in media coverage, and a paradigm shift from homeroom security to holistic violence prevention in schools including mental health, supportive environment, strong relationships, crisis intervention, and de-escalation."

After the Columbine shooting, this writer attempted to facilitate the establishment of an anti-bullying program in a local school district. The school administration noted that teachers were so busy with other responsibilities it was unlikely they would take on the additional responsibility of helping implement an anti-bullying program. Nothing was done at that time, a repetition of what happened in the Wyoming legislature following the murder of Matthew Shepard. The degree of passivity that exists in the United States of America defies logic. Our sin nature overcomes logic. Passivity, part of our sin nature, began in the garden of Eden when Adam stood by and watched his mate be deceived by the serpent.

---

209 The Journals of Rachel Scott, Adapted by Beth Nimmo and Debra K Klingsporn

210 https://theconversation.com, Colorado Shooting Eerily Recalls Columbine Massacre

The school environment poses a particularly fertile set of circumstances that promotes abuse. There are many students with diverse characteristics and a relatively small number of adults to supervise them. Teachers cannot prevent hurtful remarks in the hallway or other places in the school environment. Students, working with teachers, must take responsibility for stopping harassment and abuse. Students always know who the bullies are. They have learned to report suspected school shooters, but they need to take responsibility for reporting emotional and sexual bullies. The school environment belongs primarily to the students, not the teachers. Students must learn to just say no to passivity. They need to find the courage to do the right thing. Finding courage is a hard thing when the culture you live in does not support that ethic.

Students do not realize that as a unified group, they have tremendous power. On November 3, 2021, several hundred students from Oakland Technical High School left their classrooms and marched two miles to school district headquarters to protest a learning environment dominated by sexual harassment and sexual assault.[211] It was alleged a very small number of teachers were participating in promoting a sexualized learning environment. At the school district, the students "took turns speaking out about being groped, abused, or otherwise harassed on campuses." Schools like this would cease to exist if students refused to attend. Students, supported by parents, must play a role in establishing and maintaining a healthy school environment. Students and parents need to learn the meaning of the word *no* and use it.

Hate crimes serve multiple purposes. They attack emotionally, spiritually, and/or physically to destroy the person/group who is hated. If you want to understand hatred, think about what Henderson and McKinney did to Matthew Shepard. People who hate have an evil desire to destroy the object of their hatred. Their hateful acts are an external expression of anger raging internally. This includes LGBT activists who hate everyone opposed to their ideology. They express their hatred through cancel culture and their attacks on the church.

Columbine-type rampages draw national attention to the shooters. They often relish their presumed attention in a fantasy life prior to the shooting. They feel weak internally and compensate for that by holding a gun in their hand and using it to destroy the objects of their hatred.

All bullies intend to intimidate, to strike fear, into the class of people attacked. Sexual intimidation is particularly egregious because of the degree

---

211 www.mercurynews.com, Oakland Students walk out of Class to Protest

of physical intimacy with evil. Everyone in the class that is attacked becomes a survivor. If you have not directly experienced an attack of this nature, it is not possible to imagine what it is like. Schools must be safe for everyone, or learning for everyone will be impaired. Any words this writer would use to describe the experience of bullying or sexual abuse over gender issues would be inadequate. You are encouraged to take advantage of the internet to hear LGBT students describe their encounters (google "LGBT high school students share their experiences" or google "videos of interviewing LGBT high schoolers." Please look at one or both videos before reading further.

What is the process issue that drove the murder of Matthew Shepard and the Columbine shooting victims? It is the process of deception noted below.

Distraction>confusion>deception>evil desire>sin/ disobedience>consequences

Remember, one of the fundamental character traits of God is to be relational. The murderers of Matthew Shepard were distracted from their relationship with God by a set of circumstances generating hate in their hearts. Matthew Shepard was distracted from his relationship with God by a set of circumstances producing same-sex attraction. Through no fault of his own, Shepherd encountered the hatred of McKinney and Henderson waiting to be expressed. It was a perfect storm of deception. The consequences were death for Shepherd and life in prison for McKinney and Henderson, poor outcomes for everyone, including the people of Wyoming, you, and me.

Thirty-two years after the death of Shepard, instead of blatant murder, hate is expressed by destroying the lives of people who are hated. This is accomplished through emotional attacks, control of information, suppression of debate, and destroying people economically. It is called **cancel culture**. The people who perpetrate cancel culture are separated from their relationship with God, just as McKinney and Henderson were separated from God. They **rationalize** their destructive behavior by accusing the people they are destroying of hate. They are using the psychological defense mechanism of **projection**, projecting their own hatred onto other people. This distracts the average citizen from recognizing the true motives of the radical LGBT community.

These paragraphs will be attacked as hate speech, but they are simply an expression of opinion. People behind cancel culture are unable to tolerate opinions differing from their own. The word "behind" is the perfect word to describe those who want to destroy the lives of people who disagree. Deep in their hearts, they are afraid. They hide their fear and distrust "behind" accumulated power to control others. They hate freedom of every kind because they are slaves to sin themselves (Romans 6:16). They want you to be their slaves. They promote the spread of slavery.

They hate freedom of speech and intend to destroy it, a right guaranteed by the First Amendment to our Constitution. Cancel culture is a form of bias and prejudice similar to racism, but the defining characteristic is the color of your thinking rather than the color of your skin.

The Constitution and the rule of law are the primary obstacles to achieving the ultimate power they desire. So, it follows that they ignore the Constitution, plan to change the structure of the Supreme Court, break the law, and desire to defund the police.

When I write my senators and representatives in Congress, I get a form letter back every time with two parts: Part 1, "Thank you for writing," and Part 2, "We are doing a wonderful job and are delighted to tell you about it"...blah, blah, blah, and more blah. Blah is counterproductive. Blah is a form of speech learned by our representatives during their campaigns. It is like a foreign language to the rest of us. Blah is stonewalling. Blah distracts you from whatever you were writing to your representative about. Blah is a form of distraction leading to confusion and deception. Say **no** to blah. Just say **no** to deception!

The next chapter is the last, the epilogue to this book. Congratulations! You have only a little further to go. Thank you for finishing the course (Acts 20:18-24, II Timothy 4:3-8).

Epilogue

If you have read everything to the epilogue, you have consumed approximately 165,000 words. If you diligently read this book, you spent nearly as much or more time answering questions and looking at resources as you did reading the text. It is time for some reflection. As you read this chapter, notice the only bold type in this chapter is the title. It is time for the reader to identify the process issues. There are, however, some very important ones. Make a note of your findings. Are you making better life decisions? Write your answers below:

____

____

____

____

____

What happened in the Garden of Eden is history and cannot be changed, but your story is still being written. You are writing your own book. It is not too late to change the ending. The most important part of your story begins and ends with Jesus. It is the story about your relationship with Him and about following Him. It is the story about becoming more like Him. It is the story of what you have done to build the body of Christ. Everything else will be forgotten. You can take this story with you on the day of judgment and hear these words from Jesus: "Well done, you upright (honorable, admirable) and faithful servant. You have been faithful and trustworthy over a little; I will put you in charge of much. Enter into and share the joy (the delight, the blessedness) which your Master enjoys" (Matthew 25:13-30). You can write an ending to your story inspired by God. You are working on that ending now, during the time you invested reading this book, and how you apply what you have learned in the future.[212]

Do you have any curiosity about what you might oversee while spending

---

212 Experiencing God, by Henry, Richard, Mike Blackaby, and Claude v. King; This is an outstanding resource to promote spiritual growth.

eternity with Jesus? Look around. See the creativity of the Trinity. Consider the miracles of God. What you see in the creation should excite you about what life God will create for you in eternity.

You have been studying and meditating on the process of change. It is the change in your heart, your thought life, your emotions, and your will that are the most important part of your story to God and to you. God examines the heart of each person and blesses them accordingly. Consider carefully the therapies of Ruth and Abigail and how their hearts changed as they spent time with Jesus. They blessed you by sharing their stories. Now, you can bless others by sharing how God is working in your heart. The apostle Paul writes about this in his letter to Philemon. "[And I pray] that the participation in and sharing of your faith may produce and promote full recognition and appreciation and understanding and precise knowledge of every good [thing] that is ours in [our identification with] Christ Jesus [and unto His Glory]" (Philemon 1:6). There is someone who needs to hear your story. God will give you the words to tell it.

The most important part of your story, the most important process issue, is, has your heart softened to Jesus? Are you ready to pray the following?

> Dear God,
> I need You; I am humbly calling out to You. I'm tired of doing things my way.
> Help me to start doing things Your way.
> I invite You into my life to be my Lord and Savior. Fill the emptiness in me with Your Holy Spirit and make me whole.
> Lord, help me to trust You, Help me to love You,
> Help me to live for You.
> Help me to understand Your grace, Your mercy, and Your peace.
> Thank you, Lord! Amen.[213]

This book is only a taste of what you can find in the Holy Bible. It is only an hors d'oeuvre. The meal is set before you. "Taste and see that the Lord [our God] is good" (Psalm 34:8). Blessings!

213 Bing.com/images, Images of Sinners' Prayers

Appendix

The materials provided in this appendix are to assist the reader in understanding various portions of this book, particularly talk therapy. The reader will find some repetition in the tools and process issues discussed in the book. These hand outs are given to clients for homework to reinforce discussion in the office.

Appendix A

Grande Ronde Psychiatric Services Disclosure Statement

Welcome to Grande Ronde Psychiatric Services. You are to be commended for your decision to seek assistance. In the following paragraphs some guidelines will be reviewed that will help you to have an edifying experience and promote achieving your goals.

The next decision you should begin to think about is how you are planning to resolve the issues which concern you. Some symptoms/illnesses are responsive to medical therapy while others are more effectively treated with talk therapy. Have you considered which of these strategies would be best for you?

Many people have experienced hurts in situations where they had little or no choice about what was happening to them. In order to ensure that you do not have a repetition of that process in our relationship you always have the right to not discuss an experience or refuse any homework assignment. However, I reserve the privilege of making an inquiry at a later time if it seems the issue is important to your continuing progress.

It is not unusual in the process of treatment for clients to experience uncomfortable emotions and other difficulties which are difficult for either of us to anticipate. Yet, at the same time, I want you to feel safe from further injury.

Revisiting past traumas is not the goal of therapy. Rather, identifying thinking errors, addressing loss, and promoting forgiveness in a safe environment can be very helpful. It is not intended for you to relive past traumas but rather to reconnect to emotions in a general kind of way.

It is very important that your meetings and the work you do remain confidential. There are two types of confidentiality: the first type pertains to other people having a general awareness that you are pursuing mental health consultation. In small communities such as where I work I cannot guarantee complete anonymity regarding your arriving and leaving appointments. Your privacy in this regard will be greatly enhanced if you would be careful to arrive and leave on time so as not to encounter other clients. The second type of confidentiality relates to content/issues that are discussed pertinent to your presenting problem. Notes are taken to facilitate continuity of care.

In general this information may only be released with your consent. Grande Ronde Psychiatric Services will be compliant with all federal guidelines regarding the handling of your personal health information. You will be provided two separate handouts, one a summary, and the other a five page document which detail the federal guidelines of the Health Insurance Portability and Accountability Act which establishes rules for handling your protected health information.

If a crisis or emergency should occur please contact me at any time by phone. Consider reviewing the crisis with your spouse, pastor, physician, or support person. Call 911 or go to an emergency room if you are not able to reach me. Most people benefit from having emotional and spiritual support therefore I ask you to consider notifying your pastor and primary care physician that you are receiving treatment. Have a support person to help you… ask me about details.

Should either client or doctor perceive a wrong has been committed in our relationship it is agreed to utilize mediation services initially to resolve the disagreement.

Please bring your payment for each meeting that will not be covered by insurance. Your signature below indicates you have reviewed the above material, have been provided an opportunity to discuss any concerns, and agree to the terms of treatment.

Signature______________________________ Date____________

Witness ____

Appendix B

Interpreting Scripture

Scripture is the very word of God, a record of how He relates to us through His thoughts, plans, emotions, and actions. How important is a proper understanding of God's Word? Well, it also provides examples for us to follow in our own thought lives, plans, emotions, and actions. As such, it is obviously important to understand what He desires to say. It is vital to know there can be no contradiction in Scripture, as the Holy Spirit cannot contradict itself because it always speaks truth. There may be apparent contradictions, but these can usually be resolved through a more serious exploration and meditation on pertinent verses. Some questions may go unanswered because God expects us to accept His Word on faith (Romans 11:33-36). They will all be answered eventually (I Corinthians 13:9-12).

The following paragraphs briefly review process issues for interpreting Scripture correctly. There are several processes to consider. I mention the Holy Spirit first because the Bible seems to give it paramount importance (I Corinthians II: 1-16).

I. The Role of the Holy Spirit is described in the verses below:

(John 16:13) "But when He, the Spirit of Truth (the Truth giving Spirit) comes, He will guide you into all the Truth (the whole full Truth). For He will not speak His own message [on His own authority]; but He will tell whatever He hears [from the Father; He will give the message that has been given to Him], and He will announce and declare to you the things that are to come [that will happen in the future]."

Comment: One of the functions of the Holy Spirit is to guide believers into the truth. This is a process of revealing the truth of God's word as it relates to our daily lives and our future life in heaven.

1. (II Timothy 3:16) "Every scripture is God breathed (given by His inspiration) and profitable for instruction, for reproof and conviction

of sin, for correction of error and discipline in obedience, [and] for training in righteousness (in holy living, in conformity to God's will in thought, purpose, and action."

Comment: This Scripture reiterates that the books of the Bible are inspired by God the Father and provide clarification on His purposes for providing them.

2. (II Peter 1:20-21) "[Yet] first [you must] understand this, that no prophecy of Scripture is [a matter] of any personal or private or special interpretation (loosening, solving). For no prophecy ever originated because some man willed it [to do so—it never came by human impulse], but men spoke from God who were borne along (moved and impelled) by the Holy Spirit."

Comment: The Greek word for prophecy, *propheteia,* in this context, primarily refers to the writer of this Scripture having a proper understanding of the divine will rather than foretelling the future. This verse indicates that a proper understanding of the divine will at the time of writing the scriptures was through the guidance of the Holy Spirit. Man, through his own effort and reasoning, cannot discern the divine will and purposes of God (I Corinthians 2:9-15). This suggests proper understanding of the Scripture today also requires the guidance of the Holy Spirit (John 16:13). This is the reason nonbelievers often get very little from reading the Bible, as they do not have the Holy Spirit guiding them in discovering divine revelation.

This begs the question: does a Christian, who has the Holy Spirit, need to ask for divine guidance every time he picks up his Bible to read? It seems asking for the Spirit to guide our interpretations is an excellent idea as it reminds us of our dependence on God and is a lesson in humility…which many of us desperately need (II Corinthians 12:10, Philippians 2:5-9).

Consider the following example of a violation of the above scriptural processes leading people astray. About thirty years ago, I was at a retreat at a church in the Midwest. After the retreat finished, a pastor was giving me a lift to the airport when he asked if I was familiar with the Jesus Seminar. I had never heard of it. He explained it was a group of about 50 scholars and about twice as many lay people who met periodically to study the sayings of Jesus and then to vote on whether they thought the words or actions were authentic to Jesus. They cast a ballot having four colors of beads to indicate their opinions:

1. A red bead indicated Jesus said it.
2. A pink bead indicated Jesus probably said something like the passage.

3. A gray bead indicated Jesus had not spoken the passage, but it contained a Jesus idea.
4. A black bead indicated Jesus did not say it, and the source was not known.

After the pastor explained the above, I asked this question: "How is the Holy Spirit involved in the process?"

His response: "That is a good question."

Nothing more was said about the Jesus seminar the rest of the way to the airport.

Comment: The Jesus Seminar violated each of the above scriptures defining the role of the Holy Spirit.[214] The Jesus Seminar disbanded in 2006.[215] It is a good example of what happens when the Holy Spirit is excluded from the process. A spirit of error takes charge (1 John 4:1-6). The Jesus seminar concluded there was a fifth gospel. Interpretations that exclude the Holy Spirit are often fueled by pride instead of the Holy Spirit. Pride often produces different denominations, splinter groups, or different interpretations that do not represent the Truth of God's Word. The Holy Spirit is a necessary element in determining the divine will and purpose in each of the processes noted below. The Holy Spirit works in all the spiritual disciplines to arrive at the truth.

II. The Role of Context in the Process of Interpretation.

Some theologians and students of the Bible put most of their efforts at interpretation in the basket of context. They say context is king.

Comment: Articles and books on context sometimes omit to mention the context of the reader. The reader's context is his worldview. Worldview is often skewed and closed to the leading of the Holy Spirit in the process of interpretation. Or, Christians simply forget to ask for guidance from the Holy Spirit while discerning truth. This is one reason commentaries and opinions on interpretation do not agree. There is only one Holy Spirit. If everyone was relying on the Spirit, there should be no disagreement on understanding Scripture.

What is context? Context is defined as "That which surrounds something." The word *context* is a combination of two Latin parts: *con* (together) and *textus*

---

214 There are many criticisms of the Jesus Seminar found by an Internet search

215 en.wikipedia.org, The Jesus Seminar

(woven). The idea is that a thread (or idea) is part of a greater weaving and that, together, they all weave into a larger fabric.[216]

Briefly, it answers questions similar to these:

1. Who wrote it?
2. When was it written?
3. To whom was it written?
4. What was going on in their lives?
5. What was the purpose of the verse, chapter, or book?
6. How do the verses before and after the verse you are studying shed light on what you are reading?
7. Does it make sense with the rest of Scripture?

There are other contexts not mentioned above, such as historical context, cultural context, linguistic/grammatical context, literary context, and visual context.[217] These can all be important. Here is a slightly different set of questions addressing context.[218]

1. What did the original author say? (textual criticism)
2. What did the original author mean? (exegesis)
3. What did the original author say elsewhere on the same subject? (parallel passages)
4. What do other Biblical authors say on the same subject? (parallel passages)
5. How did the original hearers of the message understand and respond to it? (historical application)
6. How does this truth apply to my day? (modern application)
7. How does this truth apply to my life? (personal application)

Do not be dismayed by all these questions. Fortunately, most modern Bibles have an introduction to each book of the Bible which answers many of these questions. Some Bibles, called study Bibles, have cross references or study notes which address context and help clarify the meaning of passages.

III. The Role of Other Believers

---

216 biblestudymethods.org, Interpretation Principle: Context

217 deeperchristian.com, 7 Important Contexts You Need to Know for Bible Study

218 bible.org, The contextual Method of Biblical Interpretation

Pastors and elders have spent many years studying the Word of God. They are honored when you bring a question to them about a Bible passage. Do not allow embarrassment, fear, or any other emotion to prevent you from seeking counsel from mature Christians. The Holy Spirit will guide you in recognizing truth from error in the counsel given.

IV. The Role of Meditation

Meditation is a process that seems little utilized in today's fast-paced world. The world is competing with God for our attention. There are different reasons for meditating, including understanding Scripture better. You can easily think about the meaning of a passage during a break in your daily routine, or during lunch. This helps keep your focus on Jesus as the world brings one distracting problem after another. The Holy Spirit will often surprise you with an insight that could only come from God. This process brings you into the presence of God, and His gift of understanding is escorted by love, joy, and peace. Strengthening your faith is the result (Joshua 1:7-8).

Another strategy is to set aside a block of time, 15-30 minutes or more, to meditate on a specific passage. This is a deeper experience, allowing Jesus an opportunity to conform you to His likeness through the Word. An excellent review of this process is found on the Internet in the article, *How to Meditate on Scripture, a Beginner's Guide* by Barb Raveling.

The Role of Conscience

Scripture tells us God has written His Law in our hearts. This is a reference to the general laws of God, which provide guidance on how we should relate to each other, i.e., with agape love, patience, kindness, etc. (I Corinthians 13:1-8). It means you should treat others the way you would like to be treated. Therefore, you have no excuse for being a fool in relationships with others. You have no excuse for your evil desires (Romans 1:19-22).

Your conscience may speak to you when you behave poorly. This does not mean the Bible in its entirety or the Gospel of Christ has been written in our hearts. The Holy Bible is a complete exposition of the story God has written for each of us. It speaks the same to each reader on divine revelation about the person of Christ while giving specific instruction to each person who is uniquely gifted for the path God has prepared beforehand for him to follow (Ephesians 2:10, 4:11-16).

Summary

Martin Luther wrote, "We cannot attain to an understanding of Scripture either by study or the intellect. Your first duty is to begin by prayer. Entreat the Lord, of His great mercy, to grant you the true understanding of His word. There is no other interpreter of the Word of God than the author of this Word, as He himself has said, 'They shall be all taught of God' (John 6:45). Hope for nothing from your own labors, from your own understanding, trust solely in God and the influence of His Spirit. Believe this on the word of a man who has experience."

So... when you are seeking to understand the Word of God and are utilizing commentaries, study Bibles, books such as this, or seeking wisdom from church elders, prayer and the Holy Spirit should always be part of the process of discernment. The Holy Spirit should always be involved in determining the truth of your source.[219] This is also true, of course, in discerning the teachings of Martin Luther. Process always determines outcome.

219 cslewisinstitute.org, How to Understand the Bible

Appendix C

Therapeutic Metaphors, The C-J 5 Story

Historically speaking, sharing information from a therapist's life with a client was frowned upon. My experience suggests if the story demonstrates the humanity of the therapist, does not glorify the therapist, and provides achievable solutions to the client, it can be helpful. Many times, the story will glorify Jesus. Sometimes the therapist may choose to let the client determine what the process point is and try out a new behavior suggested by the story. Below is a story I sometimes used in recovery work.

In 1974, Charney and I decided to get a jeep for exploring the miles and miles of logging roads in Sanders County around Plains, Montana, where I was in family practice. Three years later, we were living in an old country house on a couple of acres a few miles west of Scappoose, Oregon. Logging country in the Pacific Northwest is very different from Northwestern Montana. The big difference is moisture. Plains received about 19 inches per year, while Scappoose got a little over twice that. There were a lot of logging roads around Scappoose which we're definitely on the side of soggy most of the year.

One spring day, Charney and I both had the weekend off. It was a beautiful sunny day. We decided to go exploring with our Jeep. We took the canvas top off and removed the doors. The forests of the Pacific Northwest are magnificent. We were tooling along, enjoying the ambiance, when we came to an extended, watery, muddy mess that was about 50 feet long. I got the binoculars out and could see vehicle tracks coming out on the other side. Or were they tracks entering the mud? I assured Charney we could get through. After all, what is a four-wheel-drive Jeep for, except for situations like this? I backed up so we could get a running start. We got about halfway through. A lot of the mud outside the Jeep had migrated inside the Jeep. There was mud everywhere. Charney was covered with specs of mud. I thought she looked cute with little specks of mud everywhere, kind of like chicken pox.

She assessed the situation somewhat differently. I had a **sinking** feeling deep inside as I looked ahead and behind and could only see mud. After about a minute, our five-year-old daughter in the backseat awakened, unbuckled her seatbelt, stood up in the backseat, and looked around. Then she looked at me and said, "Daddy, we're stuck!" That actually was a very accurate appraisal for a five-year-old. Our 18-month-old boy continued sleeping. Have you ever heard the phrase, "You got us into this mess so you can get us out"? Those words did not break the silence of the forest. There was nonverbal communication from Charney to that effect.

Then I did the unthinkable. I took off my shoes and got out of the Jeep. I could feel the mud oozing between my toes. I hoped there was no broken glass in the mud. I felt under each tire with my hand. There was about three to four inches of mud under each tire before I could feel solid ground. Apparently, the problem was lack of traction, not being high centered. I looked around to see what was available. Someone had gone through the area two or three days earlier and cut a bunch of small alder on both sides of the road. I jacked up the Jeep and started jamming these alder branches under the wheels. I removed the jack. Then I made a path of alder branches from the front of the Jeep all the way to solid ground. These efforts took about an hour. My wife said it was longer! Getting back in the Jeep, everybody buckled up and prepared for an adventure. I don't remember if we prayed. We should have! I pressed hard on the accelerator, giving it plenty of gas. The Jeep leaped forward and continued until we got on hard ground. Charney and I were both laughing in disbelief. She was rewarded with another dose of mud. She looked cuter. She was no longer upset. We were both grateful to get out of the mud hole. I don't remember if we thanked God. We should have!

After telling this story, I would ask the client how the story related to therapy.

There are several process issues in this story. What do you think is the primary process issue prompting the use of this story? Write your answer below.

____

____

____

____

____

The usual purpose for my telling this story is to bring up the issue of a client stuck in therapy… not making progress. The most common cause of therapy failing to progress is a client's unwillingness to address the muddy waters of his past life secondary to fear or shame. You have to get out of the Jeep to find a solution. You have to get out of the safe environment you have created and let go of your defenses to process past traumas. Telling this story provides an opportunity to broach this issue.

Appendix D

Processing New Memories (Handout)

Memories of traumatic events sometimes return unexpectedly in the course of recovery. They can be disturbing. Below are some guidelines to facilitate processing these memories.

1. It is important to remember that having the memory today is not the same as when you went through the experience originally.
2. Always remind yourself, "I am an adult now."
3. Write it down for now; later, share it with someone you trust to maintain confidentiality. You are in a safe place now; there are people who want to help. If you are not in a safe place, work toward being in a safe place as soon as possible.
4. You may experience physical sensations or changes, which are the body's way of bringing to your attention something else is waiting to be processed.
5. Memories will come to you when you are ready; you do not need to do anything to force the process.
6. The fact that you know more about yourself now is a sign you are making progress.
7. These new memories are an opportunity for you to disconnect from the power these experiences have had on your life.
8. If you have a relationship with Jesus, take each of these experiences to Jesus in prayer or meditation by doing the following. Tell Him your thoughts about the experience and feelings of sadness associated with losses. Ask Him to reveal to you the truth about what happened. Keep your focus on Jesus rather than the experience. Do not relive the experience.

Remember, Jesus is in your heart, waiting for you to open your heart to His healing touch. He is always willing to help. Never forget to take Him with you through the memories. He will guide your remembering and help you find peace. Examine the next tool on meditation for details about this.

Appendix E

Meditating with Jesus

Meditating with Jesus is a unique and powerful process. I was first introduced to this strategy about 30 years ago when a client gave me a book, "You Can Be Emotionally Free" by Rita Bennett. In her book, she writes about inner healing of prior trauma… using your imagination to bring Jesus into the process of healing. Using a person's imagination in therapy is an ancient strategy. It can be traced at least to the spiritual exercises of Saint Ignatius, which were made available around 1548 AD.

Very early in my family practice, about 45 years ago, I used guided imagery to help people relax and to create a safe place for them to go. It is surprising how effective this can be. There were two women in my practice at the same time who were pregnant and wanted to deliver without anesthesia. Each of these ladies learned to use their imagination to go to a place of their own choosing, which they associated with a relaxed and peaceful state of mind. They practiced this process for 5 to 6 months prior to their expected delivery dates. When they went into labor, they went to their safe places associated with relaxation and peace. When they came to the hospital for delivery, each of them delivered in about 30 minutes without any medicine for "labor pains." Oops! That was too close to delivering in their car for my comfort level. After those experiences, I asked women to come to the hospital earlier in their labor.

Meditating with Jesus is a type of guided imagery, but the **big difference is that Jesus is largely guiding the process** rather than the client or therapist. Every Christian knows Jesus and the Holy Spirit indwell the heart of believers. Why do Jesus and the Holy Spirit live in the heart of a Christian? One reason Jesus lives there is His desire to be in a constant relationship with each believer. The Holy Spirit resides in your heart to prompt you to listen to the word Jesus gives, to assist in your understanding His Word (the **Key of Doctrine**), to enable you to accomplish what you cannot do on your own (the **Key of Power**), and lastly, to submit your will to Jesus (the **Key of Authority**).

How long does it take Jesus to go from your heart to the imagination of your mind? The answer to that question is different for every believer. It depends on the nature of the relationship the believer already has with Jesus. For someone who has great trust and reliance on Christ, it can be very rapid…a few seconds. Others may have to work at practicing concentrating on Jesus while leaving the cost of groceries at home with the shopping list. Do not be discouraged if you find yourself distracted. Meditation, like most skills, takes practice to develop the skill. I have observed the people who seem to establish meditating with Jesus quickly are often people who are desperate for spiritual help.

A few things I learned from supervising several hundred of these meditations:

1. Being with Jesus is the ultimate place of safety (Psalm 91:1-16).
2. Nearly everyone who meditates with Jesus spontaneously reports experiencing a profound sense of peace during meditation.
3. People who have anxiety disorders rarely feel anxious when they are with Jesus.
4. People who are depressed secondary to trauma do not experience depression when they are in the presence of Jesus…however, they may experience sadness and tears during grief work.
5. The therapist cannot predict what Jesus will do in the meditation… He is extremely creative. He knows precisely what is needed to help the client.
6. When Jesus walked the earth during His three years of ministry, He spoke with authority; He speaks with the same authority during meditations.
7. The client can do this at home, which greatly facilitates progress. This creates less dependency on the therapist and promotes an internal reliance on Jesus rather than self. This is perfectly congruent with Christian theology, "I can do all things through Christ who strengthens me" (Philippians 4:13).

These observations stimulate a question. Why do we not hear more about meditating with Jesus in the church? Here are **six process issues that relate to this question**: The first: pastors sometimes express **concern regarding**

a false Jesus appearing and taking over the mind of the person meditating. This is highly unlikely unless a Christian is already seeking or using demonic power in some aspect of his life. A door point has to be opened in order for a demon to gain entry to a Christian. A demon impersonating Jesus has happened on only a single occasion in the meditations under my supervision. There is a very simple solution if this should happen, which is to ask the false Jesus this question: "Are you the Jesus Christ who has come in the flesh from God and was raised from the dead?" (I John 4:1-3). No demonic spirit can confess that Jesus Christ has come in the flesh from God. When that question is asked, the false Jesus disappears instantly because all demonic activity is subject to the authority of Jesus.

There are many **other kinds of meditation** or visualization that **are** under demonic influence: for example, fantasizing pornography and calling up spirits of the dead. Meditating with Jesus has nothing to do with visualization associated with New Age religion or other pursuits of mysticism. In New Age religion, the purpose of visualization "is to program the mind to discover inner power and guidance." "It is used to develop psychic abilities or make contact with spirits."[220] Using your imagination in that way is a pursuit of evil desire. **Don't do it!!!** In meditating with Jesus, the purpose is to rely on His power to discover the treasures of wisdom, spiritual knowledge, and enlightenment which are stored and hidden in Christ (Colossians 2:2-3). **There is no valid objection to spending time with Jesus! None!** Any objection to spending time with Jesus lacks discernment. It is a deception.

A second issue is alluded to above. **Everyone meditates on something**: music, sports, cars, gardening, money, porn, power, past trauma, what a bad person I am, the possibility of ending my life, etc. When you are meditating with Jesus or meditating on His word, it prevents distraction, which is the first step to deception. The mind of man abhors a vacuum. The question for each person is what he will put into his mind to think about. The sequence for deception is noted again below:

Distraction>confusion>deception>evil desire>sin/ disobedience>consequences

A third issue: nothing irritates Satan more than someone **wanting to spend time in the presence of Christ and relying on Jesus for healing.** Clients do not usually experience anxiety or depression while meditating with

220 www.equip.org/Articles/Visualization-Part-One

Jesus because all their attention is devoted to Him. When meditating with Jesus, the process of deception is interrupted at the first stage. There is no distraction. The focus is on Jesus…where it should be whether meditating or coping with a crisis in real time.

A fourth issue: God desires Christians to rely on Jesus, The Holy Spirit, and the Word when we go through difficult experiences (Deuteronomy 31:6, Proverbs 3:5-6, John 14:26-27, II Timothy 3:16-17). Because we are often **distracted** by the turmoil of painful experiences, we fail to rely on Jesus in the midst of stress. Jesus is patient. He will offer healing from the experience when we are ready. Meditation with Jesus is an excellent strategy to accomplish this. Review the therapies of Ruth and Abigail for examples of this.

A fifth consideration for meditating with Jesus relates to man being made in the image of God (Genesis 1:26-27). It is apparent from God's creation that the imagination of God has no limit. God thought it wise to give men and women imagination. What would please God more than using our imagination to spend time with Jesus?

A sixth issue: the failure of the church to realize all the implications of redemption. Redemption is a term used in the New Testament referring to deliverance from the penalty of sin through the shed blood of Christ on the cross.[221] It implies a restoration of the relationship that existed between God and humanity prior to the sin of Adam in the Garden of Eden. You will recall that God walked with Adam and Eve in the garden and talked with them. The precise nature of their experience with God is uncertain. Scripture indicates they heard the sound of His walking in the garden and heard His voice (Genesis 3:8-13). It seems unlikely they saw His face (Exodus 33:18-23, I Timothy 6:16). In Exodus 33:18, Moses asked God to "show me your Glory." God responded, "I will make all my goodness pass before you, and I will proclaim My name, The Lord, before you; for I will be gracious to whom I will be gracious, and will show mercy and lovingkindness on whom I will show mercy and lovingkindness." Meditating with Jesus recreates the experience described in Genesis chapter 3 and Exodus 33. The person meditating invites Jesus into his mind (Revelation 3:20). Jesus manifests Himself (John 14: 21), and Jesus reveals His love, mercy, healing, and divine wisdom (Colossians 2:2-3) to the person meditating. Wow! What a privilege!

The church does not emphasize the process issues noted above because it is distracted, confused, and deceived, just as you and I are distracted,

221 The Spirit Filled Life Bible, Word Wealth

confused, and deceived. The church is being attacked... accused of being racist, unloving, and irrelevant. The Church is distracted by these accusations and becomes hesitant to speak the truth that comes from the word of God.

Keep in mind the Genesis Principle, which is this: Every good and perfect gift comes from God... and Satan is usually there very quickly to steal, kill, and destroy (Genesis 3:1-6, James 1:17, John 10:10). So... of course, Satan wants to distort, pervert, and steal the opportunity Christians have to meditate with Jesus. Satan's desire is for us to spend time meditating on some aspect of his kingdom. Our responsibility as Christians is to know the Word of God and to use it to counter Satan's deceptions as Jesus did (Matthew 4:1-11). Do not allow fear to create a snare that prevents you from spending time with Christ. In Proverbs 29:25, it is written, "The fear of man brings a snare, but whoever leans on, trusts in, and puts his confidence in the Lord is safe and set on high." When a person meditates with Jesus, he is putting his confidence in the Lord. He will be "safe and set on high" in the context of his meditation.

Would a nonbeliever pursue meditating with Jesus? I have had a small number of nonbelievers who meditated with Christ. Nonbelievers are sometimes curious about Christian spirituality. Scripture suggests a nonbeliever would have to accept the notion that if you want to draw close to God, you have to believe that He exists and rewards the person who earnestly and diligently seeks Him (Hebrews 11:6).

Wisdom suggests most people **would benefit from having their first meditation supervised** by a Christian counselor, pastor, or elder instead of starting out on a solo effort. Some clients have confided their meditations are more successful in my office than at home. The reason for this is unclear. It might relate to there being fewer distractions in an office setting. Perhaps some clients feel reassured, when starting a new strategy, to have someone supporting them emotionally and spiritually.

Distraction wants to insert itself in every attempt to follow Jesus. Think about what happened to the apostles during the passion and crucifixion of Jesus. They abandoned Jesus. They were overcome with fear and sorrow. Peter denied knowing Jesus. They were discouraged. They did not know what to do...all of which sounds a lot like distraction producing confusion. They forgot what Jesus had told them...that He would be crucified and raised from the dead after three days. They didn't get it.

Contrast the apostles with King David. He had written poems and songs to God for years while tending his father's sheep. He practiced keeping his focus on God. When he encountered the Philistine warrior, Goliath, he continued to focus on God. He certainly was not discouraged. He went to fight Goliath with a sling and five smooth stones. He knocked Goliath out with the first stone and then beheaded him with Goliath's own sword. That sequence was more than a little embarrassing for Goliath. Was David anxious? Answer: Little to none! By the time he was a teen, he had already killed a lion and bear while guarding sheep. There was no snare for David facing Goliath, suggesting there was no fear (Proverbs 29:25).

Contrast this experience with David's encounter with Bathsheba. He failed to guard his eyes. He saw her bathing. His mind was distracted from the presence of God. His mind was overwhelmed with her beauty and lust for a sexual relationship producing confusion, deception, and evil desire. In the midst of his deception, he used the power of his office, King of Israel, to bring her to his bedroom and rape her, an egregious abuse of power, an example of evil desire producing disobedience. Then, after she alerted him of her pregnancy, he ordered the murder of her husband on the front lines of battle (more disobedience). God punished David by allowing the newborn child to be taken by illness (consequences).

Distraction>confusion>deception>evil desire>disobedience>consequences

Process issues always determine outcome. Always! It is not easy to continue to focus on Jesus in the middle of a crisis, abuse, or temptation. The degree of difficulty does not diminish the value of working at it. The trauma becomes less important while meditating than what is happening with Jesus. The Divine presence consumes the client's attention. This leaves little room for anxiety or depression.

Appendix F

Overcoming Anxiety and Depression (handout)

The cause of most depression and anxiety falls into two categories: 1) depression biological in origin, 2) depression which has its origin in trauma/intimacy with evil. Biological depression may be associated with vitamin deficiency, endocrine dysfunction, infection, tumors, exposure to toxins, and a relatively small number of psychiatric disorders such as schizophrenia, unipolar and bipolar depression. Although there are several different psychiatric disorders causing biological depression, altogether, they likely do not account for more than 5% of all depression. Contrariwise, there are as many different experiences of trauma as there are people walking on the face of the earth.

Biological depression is best treated by discovering the underlying medical problem and correcting it. Prescribing antidepressants or other psychotropic medications are primarily of help for psychiatric illness of biological origin, such as schizophrenia, unipolar, and bipolar depression. Similarly, prescribing antidepressants for life trauma is often ineffective because there is no medication that completely reverses the impact trauma has on the spirit/mind/body. Trauma, such as abuse of a physical, emotional, or spiritual nature, can impact the whole person in several different ways listed below.

1. False perceptions/thinking errors: children especially, and also adults, take what they learn from the specific circumstances of the trauma to a broader range of situations. This process is referred to as generalization. It results in distorted perceptions or what are sometimes referred to as thinking errors. For example, a fifth-grade girl sexually abused by an uncle may determine in her mind that men are unsafe to be around and that sexual expression is sick and anxiety-producing. This may discourage dating as she moves into adolescence and young adulthood and/or failure to experience pleasure during marital intimacy.

2. Disconnection from emotions: traumatic experiences are emotionally painful. The feelings of confusion, guilt, shame, fear, hurt, sadness, and disappointment are so strong that it seems one cannot bear it… so people disconnect from the emotions associated with the experience. These feelings do not disappear into the atmosphere. They are parked somewhere in the brain, and when enough of them are stored instead of expressed, the person starts to experience symptoms of depression, anxiety, or both. There are many different manifestations of depression and anxiety.
3. Dysfunctional behaviors: our thought life and emotions are two of the primary factors that influence our will and determine behavior, so it should not be surprising that faulty thinking and emotions outside our awareness would generate behaviors that do not work well. An example is extreme social isolation often seen in survivors of sexual abuse or war trauma.
4. Physiological changes: traumas reset various aspects of our nervous system function and the organs those nerves control. This results in anxiety, depression, nightmares, flashbacks, exaggerated startle response, and physiological changes such as heart beating strong or fast, high blood pressure, excessive sweating and rapid breathing in response to stressors, susceptibility to colds and flu (diminished immune response), etc.
5. Spiritual issues: it is nearly a universal phenomenon for people who experience trauma to question God. Why did God allow this to happen? Does God care? Why didn't God protect me? Many people do not diligently search for the answers to these questions and instead become angry with God and stop relating to God. **Cessation of communication usually leads to failed relationships. That includes your relationship with God.**

Everything a human being does falls into one of these five categories, the **five domains of humanity: cognition, emotion, behavior, physiology, and spirituality.** Thinking about trauma in this way helps us to understand that traumatic experiences impact every aspect of our being, yet there is no medicine that corrects our faulty thinking or reconnects us to our feelings. We do have medicines that raise or lower levels of various neurotransmitters in the brain. Sometimes these medications can elevate mood, promote sleep, and reduce anxiety. However, this is symptomatic treatment. Medicines do not effectively treat the **five domains of humanity** which have been damaged. This is the principal reason why many people do not experience a complete cure for their depression while taking antidepressant medication.

If you had a brain tumor causing unbearable headaches, you would ask your physician to remove the tumor if possible because you know you would not feel well until the source of your headache was treated. In fact, if the doctor refused to treat your tumor, you would look for another doctor to get a second opinion and do something about what was causing headaches.

Every patient, in consultation with their physician, should determine the primary cause of their depression and anxiety. Is it primarily biological or primarily related to traumatic life events? If the cause is primarily biological, the treatment will focus on biological therapies, with talk therapy playing only a supportive role. If the depression or anxiety is primarily related to life events, medicine may be helpful but not expected to completely resolve the symptoms. It will be necessary to work on the five domains noted above. What do you think you will need to work on to resolve your anxiety or depression? Write your answers in the space provided below.

____

____

____

____

____

Appendix G

Responding to a Spirit of Fear (Handout)

We often allow ourselves to come under the influence of fear when life brings a threatening experience that we are helpless to stop. We do not know what to do to prevent injury. We do not know how to cope. There may be nothing we can do to stop what is happening. When we are helpless to alter the circumstances that hurt us, the response of the natural man is fear/worry/expression of anger/or withdrawal.

The natural man is a person without the word of God, the authority of God, and the Holy Spirit. The result of not responding to the call of God (the wisdom of God) is described in Proverbs 1:20–33. This proverb appears to be addressed to three groups of people: 1) the simple, 2) scorners, and 3) fools. The simple are those who refuse to work at understanding the word of God and how it might apply to their life. They refuse to consider the possibility of being deceived. They are unwilling to work at changing their present condition despite the discomfort they are experiencing. Scorners are proud individuals whose pride prevents receiving the help they desperately need. They can be spiritually and emotionally aggressive. Fools hate knowledge and instruction.

Twentieth-century evangelist Vince Havner described worry as follows: "Worry is like sitting in a rocking chair. It will give you something to do, but it won't get you anywhere." What distinguishes worry from being in a rocking chair is the person who worries sometimes thinks he is making progress. That sounds like deception. **Worrying is a distraction** that prevents a person from doing something that will improve their situation. **Distraction leads to confusion and confusion to deception.** Other worriers realize worrying is useless but are unable to stop. That sounds like restriction. The restriction occurs in one or more of the Five Domains of Humanity: cognitive, emotional, behavioral, physiological, or spiritual realms. **Where there is a restriction, look for demonic oppression.**

It would seem that a believer would have nothing in common with the simple, scorners, and fools. Scripture instructs that light overcomes darkness and encourages us to be children of light (Luke 1: 78-79, Ephesians 5:1-17). Yet in the parable of the unjust steward (Luke 16:1-8), Jesus notes that "sons of light" lack understanding in the management of their affairs compared to the "sons of this world" (Ephesians 5:14-16). This happens as a result of believers refusing to allow the light of God's word, the authority of God's kingdom, and the power of the Holy Spirit to work in every aspect of their lives. Sometimes we are like a church building which may have electricity/ the power of the Holy Spirit turned on in the sanctuary where worship is taking place, yet other rooms in the church building are in complete darkness. Common examples of darkened rooms in our minds are stewardship, finances, sexual purity, use of time, parenting strategies, anger, unforgiveness, etc.

The **process** that ensues when believers ignore the **plea of wisdom** is detailed in the following quotation from Proverbs 1:20-33.

"Wisdom cries aloud in the street, she raises her voice in the markets; she cries at the head of the noisy intersections [in the chief gathering places]; at the entrance of the city gates she speaks: How long, O simple ones [open to evil] will you love being simple? And the scoffers delight in scoffing and [self-confident] fools hate knowledge? If you will turn (repent) and give heed to my reproof, behold I [wisdom] will pour out my Spirit upon you, I will make my words known to you. Because I have called and you have refused [to answer], have stretched out my hand and no man has heeded it, and you treated as nothing all my counsel and will accept none of my reproof, I also will laugh at your calamity; I will mock when the thing comes that shall cause you terror and panic—When your panic comes as a storm and desolation and your calamity comes on as a whirlwind, when distress and anguish come upon you. Then will they call upon me [Wisdom] but I will not answer; they will seek me early and diligently but they will not find me. Because they hated knowledge and did not choose the reverent and worshipful fear of the Lord, would accept none of my counsel, and despised all my reproof. Therefore shall they eat of the fruit of their own way and be satiated with their own devices. For the backsliding of the simple shall slay them, and the careless ease of [self-confident] fools shall destroy them. But whoso hearkens to me [wisdom] shall dwell securely and in confident trust and shall be quiet, without fear or dread of evil."

The description above is very similar to what behavioral science currently refers to as anxiety or panic disorder. Anxiety is defined in Webster's Dictionary as "painful or apprehensive, fearful, uneasiness of the mind usually over an impending or anticipated ill." Panic disorder is a clinical syndrome characterized by rapid onset of anxiety reaching a peak over 10 to 15 minutes and then subsiding over a similar period of time. Both anxiety and panic are often associated with thoughts about dying, having a heart attack, or some other sort of impending doom. There are concomitant physiological signs, including sweating, rapid heart rate, strong heartbeat, shortness of breath, and tingling or numbness, that reinforce the thought that the person is experiencing some type of health catastrophe.

A sense of **helplessness** associated with trauma often creates a door point in which we agree with Satan's kingdom that we should go through life subject to fear instead of being subject to God. After the door point is opened, Satan's demons remind us of our original fear, accuse us of being pathetic Christians, and suggest we should restrict activities. The source of these accusations often goes unrecognized. We must learn to cope with anxiety-producing experiences, or it becomes pervasive, affecting many areas of our lives. Occasionally the anxiety becomes so intense, people refuse to leave their homes. This condition is known as agoraphobia, which literally means a fear of open places.

Since anxiety manifests through several physical signs, **it is wise to be examined by a physician to exclude a diagnosis** of heart disease or some other physical problem. **Work with your medical doctor to determine the cause of anxiety.** Always consult with your physician before discontinuing any medical treatment.

Appendix H

The Doorbell Exercise (Handout)

Jesus encourages all people to follow him (Matthew 16:24). **In order to follow Jesus, it is necessary to keep our eyes on Him.** This is difficult because the world has any number of different strategies to tempt us to take our focus off Jesus. The struggle to stay connected to Jesus is one of several characteristics that separates the follower of Jesus from the nonbeliever. In all things, the focus of the believer should be on Jesus. This is inclusive of the things that a Christian does to recover from an injury to the soul. Injury to the soul occurs when one person misuses power in a relationship with another person in order to gratify himself without considering how the second person is hurt by what is happening. In the field of behavioral science, this type of injury is known as abuse. You may not have considered yourself as having experienced abuse, but if people in your life have misused power, you have experienced some degree of injury to your soul. All abuse is a sin of the misuse of power.

Psychological and spiritual injuries to the soul are usually associated with some combination of painful emotions: confusion, guilt, shame, fear, hurt, sadness, and disappointment. It is a natural response for both children and adults to disconnect from these painful emotional states by parking these uncomfortable feelings somewhere in their minds where the feelings are out of awareness. This results in less awareness of the painful experience, but these emotions unconsciously and constantly influence choices. This results in behavior patterns that are frustrating, unproductive, and may result in further injury to self or others.

Injury to a person's soul often results in losses of some sort. These losses need to be grieved. What to do? Scripture counsels to take our emotional pain to Jesus (Psalm 30:5,11, Isaiah 53:4, II Corinthians 7:8-10). This is referred to as spending time in the house of mourning (Ecclesiastes 7:2-4). As we surrender our pain to Christ, He will use it to develop new behaviors which are consistent with the plan God has for each of us (Romans 8:28, II Corinthians 7:10, Ephesians 2:10). Jesus is knocking on the door of your heart (ringing your doorbell) even as you read this to allow Him to spend time with you (Revelation 3:20). He desires to pour His love on your wounds, to relieve you of your pain, and to guide you into the truth about the nature of your hurtful experiences. The process is described as follows:

1. Select one experience from your day involving another person which was difficult for you in some way. Write one sentence describing what happened and another sentence on your thoughts about what happened.
2. Identify the main feeling (from the list in paragraph two above) associated with your experience. Notice where you experienced that feeling in your body, the physical sensations associated with it, and stay with those feelings/physical sensations long enough to describe them to Jesus. Tell Him everything that comes into your mind. You will discover as you describe your feelings, you can leave them with Jesus.
3. Pray re: what God's purpose is for you in the above experience (Romans 8:28). Listen until you know in your heart what that purpose is.
4. Pray for grace, wisdom, and strength to be obedient to what God is calling you to do.
5. Do it!
6. Be patient with yourself! Jesus took three years to accomplish the ministry given to Him by the Father. It may take some time for you to develop this skill and to use it in your recovery process.

You might be asking, "What is the difference between the doorbell exercise and meditating with Jesus?" The principal difference is the doorbell exercise focuses on coping in the present while meditating with Jesus often has its focus on coping with impact of past abuse experiences. With some clients, it is easier to begin by dealing with smaller interpersonal stressors that are occurring in the present. This would include dealing with stressors that occur between the therapist and client. Examples would include a client being late for an appointment, continually refusing to work on homework assignments, attempting to prolong the meeting, calling the therapist after hours, failure to make co-pays, etc. The doorbell exercise also provides more structure, which some clients like.

Of course, prayer and meditation can also be used for dealing with present circumstances.

Appendix I

The Mirror Exercise (Handout)

As with many other aspects of recovery, this homework can be difficult for many clients. My use of this exercise has been mostly with women, as I've had very few male clients in my practice. Many men seem afraid of therapy. The first part of this exercise is usually conducted during a meeting at my office reading the Father's Love Letter. It is very effective if read while the client is meditating with Jesus or listening with eyes closed. The Father's Love Letter may be found online at www.fathersloveletter.com and may be downloaded at no charge. The Father's Love Letter is a compilation of scriptures from the Old and New Testaments which describe the relationship between God and his children. Each statement is followed by a scriptural reference that supports what is said. I do not mention the references when reading the letter to a client, and they are omitted here. The client can review the references at home at their leisure.

The Father's Love Letter

My child,

You may not know me, but I know everything about you. I know when you sit down and when you rise up. I am familiar with all your ways. Even the very hairs on your head are numbered. For you were made in my image. In me you live and move and have your being. For you are my offspring. I knew you even before you were conceived. I chose you when I planned creation. You were not a mistake, for all your days are written in my book. I determined the exact time of your birth and where you would live. You are fearfully and wonderfully made. I knit you together in your mother's womb. And brought you forth on the day you were born. I have been misrepresented by those who don't know me. I am not distant and angry but I am the complete expression of love. And it is my desire to lavish my love on you. Simply because you are my child and I am your Father. I offer you more than your earthly father ever could. For I am the perfect father. Every good gift that you receive comes from my hand. For I am your provider and I meet all your needs. My plan for your future has always been filled with hope. Because I love you with an everlasting love. My thoughts toward you are countless as the sand on the seashore. And I rejoice over you with singing. I will never stop doing good to you. For you are my treasured possession. I desire to establish you with all my heart and all my soul. And I want to show you great and marvelous things. If you seek me with all your heart, you will find me. Delight in me and I will give you the desires of your heart. For it is I who gave you those desires. I am able to do more for you than you could possibly imagine. For I am your greatest encourager. I am also the Father who comforts you in all your troubles. When you are brokenhearted, I am close to you. As a shepherd carries a lamb, I have carried you close to my heart. One day I will wipe away every tear from your eyes. And I'll take away all the pain you have suffered on this earth. I am your Father, and I love you even as I love my son, Jesus. For in Jesus my love for you is revealed. He is the exact representation of my being. He came to demonstrate that I am for you, not against you. And to tell you that I am not counting your sins. Jesus died so that you and I could be reconciled. His death was the ultimate expression of my love for you. I gave up everything I loved that I might gain your love. If you receive the gift of my son Jesus, you receive me. And nothing will ever separate you from my love again. Come home and I'll throw the biggest party Heaven has ever seen. I have always been Father, and will always be Father. My question is… Will you be my child? I am waiting for you.

Love, Your Dad. Almighty God[222]

The above letter is a beautiful expression of God's love and truth working together. The letter is read slowly, with pauses at various points to allow the client to consider what has just been read. It is read in the office the first time, usually while the client is meditating. The therapist should seek the

---

222 Father's Love Letter used by permission Father Heart Communications ©1999 FathersLoveLetter.com

leading of the Holy Spirit about points in the letter where the client may be directed to meditate. It might be different for different clients. For example, after the statement "You are fearfully and wonderfully made," the client may be asked to meditate on what that says about God's love. I always pause after the statement "You are my treasured possession" and say, "Ask Jesus to show you what that means… that you are his treasured possession."

In the office, after this is read, the instructions for homework are given as follows. *Please read this every morning, after you are fully awake… wide-eyed and bushy-tailed, in front of a mirror, alternately reading a sentence or two, and then looking at yourself in the mirror. After finishing reading, say the following prayer: "Lord, help me to see myself the way You see me. Help me to love myself the way You love me… in a way that builds me up and encourages me to follow You." Do this every morning until you love yourself the way God loves you and see yourself the way God sees you. It may take weeks to months in order to accomplish the goals of the exercise.*

In the office, many clients will agree to this homework. However, at home, the first time they look in the mirror, it may stimulate all the negative attributions they have been holding for years about who they are as a person. Some will stop doing the exercise after their first attempt. For this reason, it is necessary at the time of the next appointment to make an inquiry about what it was like to do this. The inquiry should include their thoughts about the exercise, thoughts about themselves, and any feelings that were generated during the exercise. It is not uncommon for clients to say, "I couldn't look in the mirror," "I wanted to break the mirror," or "I just couldn't do this." This is where the therapeutic relationship is paramount. The therapist needs to encourage the patient to work at accomplishing this, recognizing that the client may not get through the whole exercise initially. Every client is different. Nearly everyone can read a few sentences of the letter. After a period of time, they will get through the whole letter. Then they can start using the mirror and the prayer. The therapist will need to continue to explore the nature of their experience and encourage progress…perhaps pointing to other areas of progress since the beginning of therapy as evidence the person can change. This is not an assignment usually given in the first few weeks of therapy…but there may always be an exception to the rule. This homework finishes when the client has replaced his negative thoughts about self with the love and truth of the Father. There is nothing wrong with continuing the practice indefinitely.

In Ephesians 5:29, Paul writes the following: "For no man ever hated his own flesh, but nourishes and carefully protects and cherishes it, as Christ does the church...." How does it happen that so many people have difficulty looking in a mirror while listening to themselves read positive statements about their personhood? Two thoughts come to mind: the first is they have had many adverse experiences in life with associated abuse lessons about themselves which are negative. The accuser, Satan, then magnifies these abuse lessons, which are usually associated with the emotions of guilt and shame. Guilt and shame prevent discovering how God perceives them. They hide from God as Adam and Eve hid in the Garden of Eden.

The second reason relates to their strategies for coping with abuse, which often do not work well. These strategies usually rely on the self and the defenses of the mind. People unconsciously think they are protecting and caring for the self, but because of deception, the opposite is occurring. Because they remain anxious or depressed, they believe there is something intrinsically wrong with who they are as a person. They forget anxiety and depression are natural responses to abuse. Satan begins the process of accusing all over again. Satan is crafty, subtle...and relentless. This homework assignment interrupts these patterns of thinking. The goal is to love yourself as God loves you and see yourself as God sees you.

Appendix J

Suicidal Thoughts and Behaviors

The following information is provided to increase your knowledge base about the issues of suicidal ideation, attempts, and successful suicide. It is not to have lay people play the role of the evaluator of suicide risk. **If you think someone is suicidal, refer them to a professional for evaluation.**

An important issue in therapy is that of responsibility. A client is responsible for all of his own thoughts, emotions, and behavior. This includes any thoughts or behaviors which are suicidal in nature. This principle precludes a therapist from being responsible for a client's suicide. The only exception to this is a therapist who is actually counseling a client to take his own life. There are some therapists who would counsel a client to suicide because that is their own plan if life gets difficult.

Similarly, a therapist is responsible for all of his own thoughts, emotions, and behavior. Most therapists who work with severely depressed or psychotic clients will have one or more suicides in the course of a long career. Taking responsibility for a client's suicide leads to therapist burnout. A therapist may be negligent in the counsel he gives for managing a suicidal client, but he cannot be responsible for that client's suicide. Negligence on the part of a therapist may lead to a lawsuit for damages. It should also lead to changed behavior on the part of the therapist…or leaving the profession.

The following discussion about suicide is not intended to make you professional in assessing suicide risk. Many people have contact with friends or relatives who are depressed and may be suicidal. This discussion is provided to increase knowledge about the issue of suicide…which might prevent loss of life. If you have a **concern about a personal acquaintance being suicidal, the person should be referred for a professional evaluation**.

A majority of people making suicide attempts have one thing in common:

a sense of **hopelessness**.[223, 224] The cause of hopelessness is highly variable. People can be hopeless about their financial status, loss of employment, loss of professional status, prison time, death of a spouse, family dysfunction, or a myriad of other issues. These stressors may lead to discouragement or clinical depression…and the belief that nothing will change. The belief that nothing can change is another deception. It contradicts the reality that something changed to create the current dilemma. Certainly, something else for the better can change in the future.

The stressors are content related… **hopelessness is a process issue** that leads to a decision of suicide (II Corinthians 7:10). The thinking process in the client is something like, "This is horrible; there is no possibility of change for the better; I can't tolerate this any longer." This is another thinking error. There is a simple solution for hopelessness, no matter what the content issue: **change your focus! Change your thinking!** This is one of those things that is extremely easy to say and incredibly difficult to accomplish. When you find yourself in a **mindset of hopelessness,** it seems impossible to think of anything else but the elements of the crisis. But, if you are able to focus on Jesus or the Scriptures, the Holy Spirit will enable you to change your focus.

This is the process we discussed in the chapters on the D Words: distraction (resulting from the crisis) > confusion > deception/hopelessness > evil desire (suicidal thoughts) > disobedience (suicide attempt) > consequences (death). Suicidal thoughts are a manifestation of evil desire. The person experiencing hopelessness is being influenced by demonic oppression. Hopelessness is a state of mind resulting from confusion, deception, and evil desire, from not knowing what to do to change the circumstances. It may not be possible to change the circumstances immediately. **It is possible to learn to change your focus.** Then change the circumstances as quickly as possible.

Both Christians and nonbelievers may decide this is the time to discover what the Bible says about hope. Using a good concordance, do a word study on hope. This strategy meets the person in his current state of mind while offering an opportunity to change his focus. For a nonbeliever, it could produce an interest in learning about Jesus.

The process of deception raises an interesting question: What are you being distracted from? The answer for a Christian is that you are being distracted from your relationship with Christ. You are being distracted from all the blessings

---

223 www.ajc.com, Hopelessness and the Increasing Rate of Suicide in America

224 www.suicide.org, Hopelessness, a Dangerous Suicide Warning Sign

you have in life. There is always hope in your relationship with Christ because of what Paul writes in his letter to the Philippians, "I can do all things through Christ who strengthens me" (Philippians 4:13). There are many Scriptures that address discouragement and the antidote, which is hope (Psalm 9:9, 34:17, 42, Proverbs 23:18, Isaiah 40:31, Jeremiah 29:11, Matthew 11:28, I Corinthians 10:13, Philippians 4:6-9). Start by focusing on these and other Scriptures. Read them over and over. Memorize them. Repeat them when Satan puts thoughts in your mind about how bad things are. Sing spiritual songs. Scripture instructs us "to come into the presence of God with singing" (Psalm 100:1-2), "in His presence is fullness of joy" (Psalm 16:11), and "the joy of the Lord is my strength" (Nehemiah 8:10). King David did these three things beginning when he was a boy, and God gifted him with extraordinary physical strength. By the time he was a young man, David had killed a lion and bear in protecting the sheep he was herding. When you sing to the Lord, He will strengthen you. And… ask for strength and you will receive it (Matthew 7:7-11). Pray for God to show you the way through your circumstances. Be patient! This is not easy, but following Jesus is not easy…yet that is what we are asked to do (Matthew 16:24-27). We can learn to do hard things!

The answer for a non-Christian is the same. You must change your focus from the circumstances generating the hopelessness to positive things. Changing your focus is simply changing your thinking. Think about the positive things in your life. Do a life survey looking for the positive: vocation, financial status, relationships, hobbies, the beautiful things around you, and the activities that bring pleasure. If the client says there is nothing positive in his life, ask him to do something that generates a positive experience, then build on that. Focus on these things. Examine your expectations… are they realistic? Discuss them with a person you trust. Being in therapy is positive. When people lose hope, they withdraw, stop working, stop eating, and become inactive. When depressed, reach out to people who love you, eat healthy meals when you have a poor appetite, go to work, exercise, go to beautiful places and write down what you see…then meditate on the beauty, take pictures and look at them at home. Obtain resources about cognitive therapy for depression and **use** them. Consider meeting with a therapist for two reasons: 1) for help implementing these interventions, 2) for an assessment of the need for medical treatment or hospitalization. Some depressions are biological in nature and will benefit from medical therapy.

Several things must be considered in assessing current suicide risk: past suicide attempts, current plans for an attempt, the context of the current attempt, including assessment of lethality and intent for carrying out a plan, support systems outside the hospital, and current substance use. Many people contemplating a suicide attempt are coping with depressive thoughts and feelings by using pot/alcohol/street drugs or prescription anti-anxiety agents/narcotic/sedative-hypnotic agents. These chemicals may contribute to altered states of mind and suicidal thoughts.

In taking a history of past suicide attempts, sometimes it is learned that a past attempt was associated with very high lethality. For example, a client put a .357 magnum to his chest and pulled the trigger but survived. He thought he was aiming at his heart, but the bullet missed the heart, missed the major blood vessels, and damaged a very small part of one lung. In a case of that nature, a careful exploration must be conducted to determine what is providing hope in his present life that will diminish suicide risk.

These risk data need to be added up to develop a plan to decrease the probability of another attempt in the near future. There are no guarantees. Something can happen in a client's life that will stimulate a profound depressive mood and hopelessness in a few seconds. A factor increasing concern is the absence of a spouse or a close friend to support the client in his natural environment.

There are screening tools available on the Internet to evaluate suicide risk. The ASQ brief screening test is one of those; it has four questions:

1. In the past few weeks, have you wished you were dead?
2. In the past few weeks, have you felt that you or your family would be better off if you were dead?
3. In the past week, have you been having thoughts about killing yourself?
4. Have you ever tried to kill yourself?

A positive answer to any of those four questions indicates a need for further evaluation by a professional. **This should not be used** for a person with a recent attempt history. They need a more thorough evaluation. It is only a **brief screening tool**. Most clients who are depressed appreciate an inquiry of this nature and are not put off by it.

It is important for you to remember you are not responsible for other persons' thoughts, emotions, or behavior. No matter how long you meet with clients or your degree of expertise, it is always difficult to predict their future behavior, especially suicidal behavior.

Has this book been helpful to you?

If so, we'd like to hear your own personal stories about how this book has helped you. Go to the book's web page at:

https://www.dovechristianpublishers.com/catalog/non-fiction/Lessons-Life-Kindergarten

or point your smartphone camera at this QR code:

On that page, you'll find a link to send your personal stories to Dr. Trudel, as well as additional information about issues covered in the book.

www.ingramcontent.com/pod-product-compliance
Lightning Source LLC
Chambersburg PA
CBHW071753050426
42335CB00065B/1800

* 9 7 8 1 9 5 7 4 9 7 2 6 6 *